Reference Points
A Guide to Language, Literature, and Media

Authors
Robert Dawe
Paul Malott

Contributing Author
Wendy Mathieu

Series Consultants
John Borovilos
Barbara Fullerton
Margaret Iveson
Wendy Mathieu
Dirk Verhulst

Publishing Consultant
Anthony Luengo

Assessment Consultant
Sharon Jeroski

Prentice
Hall

Toronto

Prentice Hall Senior English
Viewpoints/Reference Points Advisory Group

National Library of Canada Cataloguing in Publication Data

Dawe, Robert T. (Robert Thomas), 1948–
  Reference points

Includes index.
ISBN 0-13-019871-4

1. English language – Rhetoric. 2. Readers (Secondary). I. Malott, Paul. II. Title.

PE1408.D395 2001   808'.042   C2001-930052-2

Publisher: Mark Cobham
Product Manager: Anita Borovilos
Managing Editor: Elynor Kagan
Project Manager: Anthony Luengo
Developmental Editor: Vivien Young
Production Editor: Angelie Kim
Copy Editor: Lynne Hussey
Supplementary Editorial Staff: Monika Croydon, Laura Edlund, Kathy Evans, Kathleen ffolliott, David MacDonald
Cover Design: Jennifer Federico, Zena Denchik

Cover Image: Corel Photos
Art Director: Alex Li
Interior Design: David Cheung Design Inc, Monica Kompter
Page Layout: David Cheung Design Inc.
Production Coordinator: Zane Kaneps, Sandra Magill
Photo Research/Permissions: Maria DeCambra, Michaele Sinko
Literary Permissions: Maria DeCambra, Michaele Sinko

1 2 3 4 5 G 05 04 03 02 01
Printed and bound in Canada

The publisher has taken every care to meet or exceed industry specifications for the manufacturing of textbooks. The spine and the endpapers of this sewn book have been reinforced with special fabric for extra binding strength. The cover is a premium, polymer-reinforced material designed to provide long life and withstand rugged use. Mylar gloss lamination has been applied for further durability.

Contents in Brief

Contents

Preface

Learning to communicate is at the heart of our learning, our work, and our social lives. *Reference Points* is intended to provide some basic *maps and supplies* to assist you as you navigate through these spheres of activity. It includes the essential communication skills you will need as a lifelong learner and as a private citizen.

Each chapter presents opportunities for you to become a more

- *precise*, *sophisticated writer*, who writes often for various purposes, who writes clearly and coherently with precision and an engaging style, and who correctly applies the conventions of grammar and usage.
- *fluent*, *critical reader*, who reads widely and with enjoyment, who reads independently and with increased comprehension.
- *confident speaker*, who has thoughtful conversations, who debates issues, and who interviews and questions, not just to gain a response, but to develop the capacity to probe more deeply.
- *attentive listener*, who stays focused and listens objectively, and who takes notes to clarify understanding.
- *discerning viewer*, who thinks in visual terms, who understands how images, words, and sounds are integrated to convey meaning, and who uses visual text to represent ideas and insights in an artistic way.
- *literate citizen*, who is equipped to *learn a living*, who can embrace contradictions and complexities, who can apply current technology, and who can contemplate solutions and design products for better businesses and better communities.

This text will ask you to respond to works of fiction and non-fiction from published and student writers, and to news and current affairs coverage in newspapers and magazines. You will also be asked to listen to radio shows and to songs, and to view television programs, films, and other artistic productions.

Reference Points stresses the importance of providing elaboration and support in *all* your communications. You are encouraged to communicate fully both *what* you feel and think about a particular topic and *why* you feel and think that way. You will be asked to provide a range of responses in the activities throughout each chapter.

- In Chapter 1, you will receive an overview of various forms of communication. You will engage in discussions, apply reading and writing strategies, and create graphic organizers and other visual representations.

- In Chapter 2, you will summarize and gather information as you write personal and critical responses in the form of reviews, reports, and essays.

- In Chapter 3, you will respond creatively in journal entries, descriptive paragraphs, and short narratives.

- In Chapter 4, you are asked to visualize, hear, and create your own poetry, and to try your hand at script writing.

- In Chapter 5, you will focus on some of the complexities of the media through debates, articles, letters to the editor, posters, and cartoons. This chapter will ask you to become both a discriminating interpreter and a producer of media.

- In Chapter 6, your communication assignments will prepare you for the workplace in terms of resumé writing, interviews, business letters, reports, and presentations.

In short, you will be asked in *Reference Points* to observe the world around you in its various forms and to represent events and characters (both real and imagined) in your own compositions, speeches, and visuals in a detailed, accurate, and interesting manner.

Finally, this text fosters collaborative group work. Through activities you will carry out in small-group and whole-group settings, this text promotes a co-operative attitude. We want you to realize through experience that the primary aim of effective discussion and debate is not to win an argument, but to clarify and refine the way you think about a subject. Whether that subject is a Shakespearean sonnet or a business plan you've developed to create your own summer job, our goal in *Reference Points* is that you will learn to expand your thinking.

Acknowledgements

We would like to thank all the members of our advisory group who reviewed the manuscript and offered suggestions for improvement. We would also like to thank the following students for their contributions.

Roxanne Button
Christi Davis
Penny Dawe
Peter Dawe
Chris Howell

Krista Hynes
David Skinner
Jeff Stafford
Jordan Stead
Gokul Vidyaskar

Adam Warren
Christy Wingrove
Stephen Young

Communicating for Many Reasons

Communicating with Results

This text will help you to strengthen your communication skills of reading, writing, speaking, listening, viewing, and representing. It will make you a more perceptive, skilful, and confident communicator in preparation for post-secondary education and the world of work.

Throughout *Reference Points*, you will receive direction and guidance to help you

- improve the content of your writing, presentations, and talks.

- establish a clear purpose for your writing, select and integrate information, and illustrate and develop your central idea.

- enhance the organization of your work by establishing and maintaining unity and focus, and by arranging ideas in coherent, flowing paragraphs.

- read and view a variety of texts, including media communication, with a more critical eye for deeper understanding and response.

- build competence in oral and written style, and in the use of appropriate grammar and sentence structure.

- speak clearly, and in a sincere and compelling manner.

- choose words and expressions for precision and variety.

- facilitate effective group discussions, role play, public speaking, and debate.

- become an active listener, attending to a speaker's intonations, pitch, and delivery, as these affect the interpretation of, and response to, the message given.

The various chapter topics and practice exercises in this text are designed to develop in you, the learner, the capacity to enjoy and understand a variety of written, oral, and visual texts.

Communicating in All Facets of Life

LEARNING FOCUS

- identify examples of effective communication in daily life
- think about what communication reveals about yourself and others
- communicate clearly and effectively

As a student, you will be asked to communicate for a variety of reasons. The need for effective communication does not end, however, when you leave school: it is ongoing throughout your life. We communicate both at the workplace and as private citizens. We communicate for functional purposes, just to get things done. We communicate creatively and critically to share our vision and viewpoint with a wider audience.

Whether we are connecting with others formally or informally, the way we organize our thoughts and the words we use will influence how they regard us. Our speaking and writing reveal our attitudes. As *channels* through which we make ourselves understood, they are crucial to how we function in and explore the world around us.

Whether we find ourselves involved in the world of business, the arts, science and technology or recreational adventure, we need to use language to make sense of your experiences. For all of us, communicating our experiences allows us to learn even more from them. In this way, too, we can share what we have learned with others. Consider the following examples:

Jim Hayhurst, Sr., former chairperson of Outward Bound Canada, was part of a Canadian expedition that in 1988 attempted to climb Mount Everest. His book *The Right Mountain—Lessons from Everest on the Real Meaning of Success* is the story of that climb. On the cover jacket of the book he states:

> Success. It's one of the most alluring words in our vocabulary. We dream about it. Plan for it. Chase after it. But just what is it we're after? What defines success?
>
> In the eighties, it was simple. Success meant "climbing higher, going farther" and everyone was out to claw their way to the top. Today, success is far more personal. It comes from a sense of what we believe as individuals rather than what society tells us to believe.

Moshe Safdie designed the National Art Gallery in Ottawa, and Habitat, the innovative housing project that became one of the star attractions of the world's fair known as Expo '67, in Montreal. In thinking about the complex technological era that we inhabit, Safdie reflects:

> I think one concern—not in terms of practice but in terms of a larger world—is being overwhelmed by excessive information. One needs to develop the skills and disciplines to edit that information.

In the case of Canadian astronaut Roberta Bondar, we see how experience has heightened her sense of civic and planetary responsibility:

> My space flight made me realize that the environment is not negotiable. As human beings on the surface we have a very short-term conception of survival—we need to think about the survival of the planet as a whole. We're so small we think the horizon goes on forever. When you're in space, you realize it doesn't.

Activities

Making Sense of Language

1. Search your favourite newspapers, magazines, **Web sites**, or videos for memorable, insightful, or inspirational comments by people from various walks of life. Be prepared to explain to others in the class what you find particularly appealing about the quotations you have collected.

2. Is there an "unclimbed Everest" in your life? Write a paragraph or give a brief talk to discuss some goal you would like to achieve. Think about this goal in terms of your definition of personal success.

3. Imagine that your friend's grandmother wants to buy a computer. She visits a few stores, but finds herself besieged with unfamiliar terms such as *megabytes*, *RAM*, *bandwidth*, and *modem*. List the most important words and concepts you feel she will encounter and will need to know in order to make a well-informed purchase. If yourself do not know much about computers, what sources might you use to find information? How do you gauge the sources' reliability? What would be the best strategies to use in organizing your findings for your friend's grandmother? What criteria might be used to decide how much you will tell her? How much information is enough?

4. Find the lyrics from a song you like, and see if there are any you do not understand. Ask if any of your classmates or friends have suggestions on how to interpret them. Check other songs by the same songwriters, music magazines, or music Web sites to see if you can find clues to their meaning.

Learning Through Careful Speaking and Listening

SPEAKING One of the most powerful ways of communicating is through the spoken word.

The following factors determine the impact of an oral message:

- **tone** (pleasant, angry, apologetic, humorous, sympathetic)
- **pitch** (rising and falling, or high and low)
- **volume** (loud or soft)
- **tempo** (slow-paced or rapid)

We speak for a wide range of reasons: to stimulate creative thought, to ask questions, to share information and ideas, to give instructions or directions, to provide opinions, to engage in debate or discussion. We speak individually to friends and acquaintances, and we present information to groups in both formal and informal settings. As you can see from looking at the chart below, we use language differently depending on the situation.

SPEECH						
RANGE OF APPROACHES						
Small Talk	Private Conversations	Discussions and Informal Debates	Interviews	Business Meetings	Formal Debates	Formal Presentations
Informal ←						→ **Formal**

No matter what your purpose for speaking, you will have greater success in delivering your message if you pay attention to some basic tips:

✓ CHECKLIST | EFFECTIVE SPEAKING

- ✓ Identify your purpose before you begin.
- ✓ Choose language appropriate to the purpose.
- ✓ Organize your thoughts carefully.
- ✓ Speak directly to your listener(s). Make them feel important.
- ✓ Be thorough. Complete every sentence or idea.
- ✓ Enunciate clearly. You want your message to be heard.

LISTENING When you are engaged in listening—to a friend sharing a story, to an audio tape or interactive CD, to an oral presentation—your goal is to be a careful and courteous listener. Good listening involves both our ears *and* our minds.

✓ CHECKLIST | EFFECTIVE LISTENING

- ✓ Come alert and prepared to pay attention.
- ✓ Maintain an open mind. Do not automatically reject certain information.
- ✓ Concentrate on what is being said at that moment; avoid thinking too far ahead.
- ✓ Listen actively. Take careful notes on the information you hear.

NON-VERBAL COMMUNICATION The **body language** that accompanies speaking or listening is sometimes more important than the oral communication itself. Eye contact, gestures, posture, facial expressions, and body movements all contribute to, or detract from, the message.

✓ CHECKLIST | EFFECTIVE USE OF BODY LANGUAGE

✓ Maintain an upright but relaxed stance. This shows you are interested.

✓ Make sure your gestures and facial expressions complement your message, and do not overwhelm it.

✓ Use a confident handshake.

✓ Maintain direct eye contact. Do not let your gaze wander.

✓ Be aware of others' personal space.

Learning by Creative Brainstorming

LEARNING FOCUS
- stimulate your creative thinking
- work with others to generate ideas
- share your new ideas

Language is a powerful instrument not only for communicating, but for thinking and learning. We need frequent opportunities to think things through for ourselves, to argue with ourselves, and to build our own ideas through communication with others.

Brainstorming, like **freewriting**, is a technique used at the start of the creative process to generate ideas. It can be done on an individual basis where you write down your thoughts in isolation, or it can be a group effort where you talk with others. By writing down these ideas and recording all your thoughts, no matter how disjointed, you work toward uncovering meaning.

CHECKLIST | GROUP BRAINSTORMING

✓ Encourage each group member to say whatever he or she knows about the subject.

✓ Accept all contributions without judgment, prejudice, or comment.

✓ Appoint a group recorder to write down the ideas on a chalkboard or flip chart.

✓ At the end of the session, evaluate the ideas and decide which ones to keep.

✓ Classify and arrange the ideas for future use.

Brainstorming is successful when all group members participate. The following questions will help you monitor the success of your brainstorming sessions:

- Did you contribute ideas?
- Did each group member contribute?
- Did any one person take a leadership role in the discussion?
- How did the group work together?

Read the poem entitled "Serene Words" by the Chilean poet Gabriela Mistral found in the "Learning by Note Making" section on page 22. Below is a list of comments that might be generated from a collective brainstorming session about this poem.

STUDENT SAMPLE: BRAINSTORMING

Group Notes on "Serene Words" by Gabriela Mistral

- The speaker is middle-aged.
- The title makes no sense. We need to get a definition of "serene."
- The speaker seems to contradict herself in the poem.
- The speaker has a positive attitude about life.
- The natural world is a place of beauty.
- Life is really a mixture of joy and pain.
- Love is immense and it can help us cope with many setbacks.
- "Putting me to sleep." Does this mean death?

Activities

Brainstorming in Action

1. Find a poem, song, or short story that is interesting to you personally. Make four copies and bring it to class. Form groups and brainstorm each group member's selection in turn. Determine the main ideas of each selection.

2. Read the poem "Betrayals" by Maria Mazziotti Gillan found on page 27. In a group, brainstorm ideas regarding the central insights the poet is trying to convey in her poem.

Learning by Presenting Your Thoughts

LEARNING FOCUS
- learn to think on your feet
- practise expressing your thoughts formally and informally
- present your ideas in a group

From time to time, you will be called upon to present your thoughts to the class in the form of a speech. A speech gives you a chance to share your ideas with others.

Sometimes this will be *off-the-cuff*—an **impromptu speech** where there is little time for preparation. Think of your responses to questions in class as short impromptu speeches. Impromptu speaking will help you develop the ability to organize information quickly into a clear message, and to speak in a confident manner without the benefit of much preparation.

When giving a **planned speech**, you need time to prepare. Some speakers write out the complete text of their speech and read it to the audience, while others memorize it all. It sounds more conversational and natural to plan the speech in advance, but you should not read directly from notes. With practice you can learn how to combine written notes, the memorization of some key points, and some on-the-spot improvisation to give an effective speech.

Activities

Giving a Speech to the Class

Using one of the following quotations as a prompt, or selecting one of your own, prepare and deliver either an impromptu or a planned speech to your class. Be aware of your body language as you present.

- *Failures are made only by those who fail to dare, not by those who dare to fail.* —Lester B. Pearson

- *We can do not great things: only small things with great love.* —Mother Teresa

- *The destiny of any nation, at any given time, depends on the opinions of its young men and women.* —Johann Wolfgang Goethe

- *Doubt yourself and you doubt everything you see. Judge yourself and you see judges everywhere. But if you listen to the sound of your own voice, you can rise above doubt and judgment. And you can see forever.* —Nancy Kerrigan

- *The illiterate of the twenty-first century will not be those who cannot read and write, but those who cannot learn, unlearn, and relearn.* —Alvin Toffler

- *What schools are today, the nations will be tomorrow.* —Agnes Macphail

Learning by Asking Probing Questions

Whether the questions you ask are spontaneous or part of a formal questionnaire, it is important to develop the ability in high school to question effectively. Asking probing questions requires you to discriminate, and to bring a healthy skepticism to what you read, view, and hear. Do not merely accept information as is.

Effective questioning involves asking yourself questions, asking questions of others, and providing precise answers to those who question you. Novels, poetry, articles in magazines and newspapers, or stories on the radio or television news may raise questions not fully answered in the text itself. It is important to know what it is you do *not* understand so that you can raise your queries in class or at a student–teacher conference.

It is good practice to ask questions that are interpretive in nature, **open-ended questions** that require more than a right or wrong answer, and those that call for a response supported by specific references and evidence. For example, if a student reading William Golding's novel *Lord of the Flies* asks, "Why were all the boys so mean to Piggy?" the answer will not be a predictable one. The response requires thoughtful reflection. Brainstorming and freewriting will help you concentrate on formulating more precise answers to interpretive questions.

 CHECKLIST | ASKING PROBING QUESTIONS

- ✓ Ask questions that are compelling, clear, and easy to understand.
- ✓ Determine exactly what it is you want to find out.
- ✓ Seek answers from a variety of sources.
- ✓ Ensure that personal biases do not interfere with your ability to think clearly and objectively about a subject.

Activities

Asking Probing Questions

1. Request a university or college calendar, or a booklet for a course or career program you plan to attend after high school. Read the general admission requirements or view them on the institution's Web site. Complete a list of ten critical points of information regarding admission you were able to garner from your search. Develop three to

five questions you need to have clarified. Send an e-mail message or make a phone call to get answers to your queries.

2. Choose an article or short story you have read recently. Formulate at least three questions not fully answered in the selection. Write out possible answers, and exchange and discuss with a partner.

Learning by Interviewing

LEARNING FOCUS
- recognize the characteristics of an effective interview
- use an interview for various purposes
- evaluate an interview

The process of interviewing, or formally questioning experts to gather data from different perspectives, is another oral learning technique. An interview may help you confirm or clarify what you already think. It can help you examine an issue, consider opposing viewpoints, and develop a new perspective.

Journalists use interviews to elicit answers to questions of concern to them and their audience. Interviews introduce a human element to news articles and television features and bring the reader or viewer closer to the source of the information. Effective interviewing requires solid preparation, careful listening, and thorough note taking to get the essence of what is being said. The interviewer needs to take care to change neither the words nor the **context** of what has been said.

✓ CHECKLIST EFFECTIVE INTERVIEWING

- ✓ Gather background information on a topic in preparation for the interview.
- ✓ Make a list of questions from your research to stimulate discussion.
- ✓ Arrange in advance a time and place for the interview.
- ✓ Establish rapport by providing a proper introduction and putting the interviewee at ease.
- ✓ Keep a balance between questions that probe for factual data and those meant to elicit opinions and commentary.
- ✓ Ask open-ended questions to draw out interesting details.
- ✓ Ask follow-up and supplementary questions that delve more deeply into the details of an issue.
- ✓ Listen carefully to responses, giving the interviewee time to complete answers to questions.
- ✓ Show appreciation to the interviewee by acknowledging the quality and precision of the responses.
- ✓ Bring the interview to a logical conclusion, ending on a strong note.

The following excerpt is from the transcript of a face-to-face interview a student conducted with Robertson Davies, a distinguished Canadian writer of essays, plays, and novels, before his death in 1995. The interview probes Davies' views on literacy.

MODEL: INTERVIEW

A Chat About Literacy

Often an interview begins with a clarification of terms, concepts, or issues to be discussed. Note the use of an open-ended question at the start.

Davies: So we're going to talk about literacy, are we? So what do you think the word means?

Student: Being able to read and write; isn't that it?

Davies: That's it, certainly. But literacy is one of those words that means different things to different people. For instance, if I say that somebody is illiterate, what do you think I mean?

Student: That they can't read and write. Or not very much.

A good interview has a definite purpose or goal. In this case, the interviewer is seeking a clearer definition of literacy.

An effective interviewer listens carefully to what is said and tailors the next question to that response.

Davies: There, you see? Already you have made a qualification when you say, "not very much." There are hundreds of thousands of people who would be very cross if you called them illiterate, but it is true that they can't read and write very much. People who can't read and write at all are not numerous in a country like Canada. Most people can write their names, and they know what signs that say STOP and GO mean, and perhaps even DANGER. But they can't read the directions on a bottle of medicine, for instance, or the handbook that comes with the car they are driving. Often they are clever at concealing the fact that the world of print is closed to them. That is a very dangerous kind of illiteracy.

The interviewer asks questions designed to gather facts, opinions, and specific details.

Student: How many kinds of literacy do you suppose there are?

Davies: Suppose we say three. There is the kind we have just been talking about—being shut off from everything that requires understanding of even quite simple things that are written down. Of course that really only applies in a country like ours, where the written word is so important. There were millions of people in the past, and there are millions now, who do not live in what we might call the Verbal World. A hundred and fifty years ago you could be an efficient farmer or blacksmith without being able to read or write. You were a valuable person and you knew your job thoroughly. You could get somebody else to do any reading or writing you needed. But now we live in a world where that is impossible. Though there are other parts of the world—Central Africa, for instance—where reading and writing count for very little—it would be wrong to say that people who do not belong to our Verbal World are stupid. Millions of those people want to join the Verbal World, and CODE* helps them. But we are talking about our world right here, which is very much part of the Verbal World.

Student: But you said there were three kinds of literacy. What is Number Two?

Supplementary questions help put the interviewee back on topic and draw out additional information.

Davies: Number Two takes in all the people who can read and write, have no trouble with medicine bottles or books of directions, and may be skilled in technical work of some complexity. They read the newspapers; sometimes they read magazines. They don't pay much attention to books, unless the books are concerned with their work. Some of them are professional people who read and understand complicated books about law, and medicine, and insurance, and all kinds of business. They have fair-sized vocabularies and their grammar is pretty good, but not precise. No doubt about it, they are literate, in the Number Two sense of the word.

Student: What's Number Three, then? It seems to me you have been talking about everybody that matters.

The interview becomes more natural and conversational if the interviewer does more than just ask questions. Note the personal observations made here.

Davies: The whole idea of literacy is filled with shady areas that overlap. The Number Two people can read anything that concerns them. But consider yourself, as an example. Do you want to join the adult world knowing your job and the daily news, and nothing else?

Student: I'm not sure I understand. What else is there?

The interviewer should not hesitate to ask for clarification or additional information.

Davies: I am sure you know what else there is that is involved in literacy. There are the people who wish to clarify their thinking. To a tremendous extent thinking is a matter of language.

*CODE (Canadian Organization for Development through Education) was founded in 1959. It is a Canadian charitable organization dedicated to supporting literacy and education in Africa and the Caribbean.

Always maintain a polite tone. Remember that an interview is not a debate.

Student: Yes, but everybody has language. Even the Number One people you talked about have language.

Davies: Not to the same degree that the Number Two people have language. And the Number Three people have language in a degree that the Number Ones and the Number Twos do not have it, because they can use it to extend their personal knowledge in a way that goes far beyond the others. They can use language to ask hard questions, and explore kinds of thinking that the Number Ones and the Number Twos never bother their heads about. They can define things accurately and they can discuss things intelligently about which strict accuracy is impossible. They are the people who enlarge human knowledge—perhaps only their own knowledge, or perhaps the knowledge of the whole world....

Asking for examples can help focus the interview.

Student: Give me an example.

Davies: Well—here's an example. Suppose you become a doctor, a healer. Are you going to be content with what you have learned in medical school, and never venture beyond it? I hope not. I hope you would be one of those who perpetually question what you have learned and look for new approaches to medicine. If nobody had ever done that we would still be treating tuberculosis by hanging bags of herbs around the necks of sick people, because that was what our teacher had told us.

If the questions are genuine, as they seem to be here, there is an increased chance of the interviewer learning something new.

Student: But that's thinking. What has that got to do with literacy? When I think of literacy I think about having to read books I am told to read in school—books that tell stories, or poems that don't even do that. I don't see how that teaches you to think.

Davies: Yes you do. Those books have taught you to think: What good is all this stuff? What does it tell me? That's thinking.

Activities

Interview Techniques

1. To gauge your understanding of the interview above, write a paragraph in which you describe and distinguish among the three different literacy levels (Numbers One, Two, and Three) mentioned above. Give specific examples of each type of literacy to support and clarify your answer.

2. Listen to an interview on radio or view a talk show or television news documentary where an interview is taking place. Critique the quality of the interview in terms of
   - the effectiveness of the interviewer and interviewee.
   - the information and entertainment value of the discussion.

3. As a class project, organize a series of presentations on the theme "Some Interesting People Live in this Neighbourhood." Conduct an interview, either on your own or with the help of a partner, of a unique person from your community. Prepare questions and refer to the checklist in this section beforehand. Seek permission to video- or audiotape the interview for the class, and also record a brief introduction to the interview and a thank-you at the end.

Learning by Discussion and Informal Debate

There is a definite continuum from the easy discussions you engage in with your friends, through the spontaneous debates that occur in class or out, to polished presentations with rules and procedures. Discussion and debate are introduced here not as formal presentations (see Chapter 5) but as informal learning exercises to generate thinking on important issues and ideas.

Effective discussion involves careful listening to all opinions, and then selecting from these the perspective that comes most naturally to you. In the process you defend your own position, but you also keep an open mind and acknowledge the arguments of the other side. Discussion and debate develop the skills of critical thinking, logical and sound reasoning, open-mindedness, and broader understanding of issues.

Ask yourself these questions before you next engage in discussion or informal debate:

- Do I value discussion and debate as a forum for intellectual teamwork?
- Do I conduct research (read, view, listen) to help me contribute significantly to discussions?
- Do I concentrate on the fundamental issues of the topic at hand?
- Do I try to define the problem clearly and analyze it thoroughly before trying to persuade others of my point of view?
- Do I raise questions and seek answers to issues surrounding the topic?
- Do I examine all sides of an argument?
- Do I argue convincingly and sincerely, without excessive emotion?
- Do I counter an argument with ideas rather than attacking the person?

Activities

Exploring Discussion and Informal Debate

1. Conduct small group discussions on a subject that seems controversial to you. Appoint a chairperson for each discussion group to be responsible for keeping the participants within the limits of the topic. The chairperson should try to involve all group members in the discussion and should be prepared to ask some pertinent questions. Another task for the chairperson (or another group member if preferred) is to keep notes of the discussion for use in giving a summary statement at the end. An audio- or videotape recorder may be used. Use one of the following topics (or choose your own):
   - downloading music and MP3 through the Internet, and the impact of this on music sales
   - censorship in today's society
   - standardized testing as a means of student assessment
   - halfway houses in residential neighbourhoods and NIMBY (not in my backyard)

2. Check in newspapers and magazines, listen to the radio (e.g., CBC's *Cross Country Checkup*), or view some television documentaries to find local, provincial, or national issues that lend themselves to discussion and debate. Bring your list of issues to class for discussion.

Learning Through Careful Reading and Writing

I read in order to gain entry into the deeper, more thoughtful regions of other people's minds. I write in order to gain entry into those same regions of my own mind. —Barbara Gowdy

READING We read for a wide range of reasons—to satisfy our curiosity, to be entertained, to learn more about a given subject, to understand the world around us. Reading books, newspapers, magazines, reference materials, media advertising, and electronic messages keeps us in the know.

School and business environments, although becoming increasingly visual, are print-based. Even subjects like mathematics and science, whose textbooks were once so filled with numbers, equations, and diagrams, now have more printed text. Word problems probe into *how* and *why* a certain kind of data and its mathematical or scientific model is important. Good reading strategies are important across the curriculum.

PEANUTS reprinted by permission of United Feature Syndicate, Inc.

WRITING We write to explore and clarify our ideas and experiences. In broad terms, writing can be a **personal response**, where we make connections between our own experiences, beliefs, and values, and those found in text. Writing can also be a **critical response**, where we analyze and evaluate the material in terms of its purpose, perspective, language, and context.

Here are three general ways that one can categorize kinds of writing:

- **Transactional writing**, such as instructions, essays, business letters, and reports, uses a somewhat impersonal and functional approach with a prescribed format and a specific style. (See "Learning by Doing" on page 20 and Chapters 2 and 6.)

- **Expressive writing** explores and records personal experiences and thoughts. The journal format is an obvious example of this. (See this chapter for a discussion of subject journals, and Chapters 2 and 3 for more on journal writing.)

- **Creative writing** combines perceptions, feelings, and ideas, using artistic forms with distinctive features. Short stories, poems, and songs are common examples. (See Chapters 3 and 4.)

Learning by Using Reading Strategies

Various reading strategies can help you to gain the most from your reading. One effective technique is known as **SQ3R**. This method has five steps in the reading and study process: **s**urvey, **q**uestion, **r**ead, **r**ecite, **r**eview.

LEARNING FOCUS
- identify and practise various purposes for reading and writing
- respond to a text before, during, and after reading
- respond personally and critically to texts

THE SQ3R METHOD

Step 1: Survey

- Survey the entire page, passage, or chapter to get an overall picture of what it is about.
- Pay attention to the headings, chapter and section titles, illustrations, margin notes, and boldfaced type.
- Scan the introduction and conclusion, as these provide preview and summary information of the content.

Step 2: Question

- As you survey the material, ask yourself questions on what you read.
- Turn the headings and subheadings into questions. Your reading then focuses on answering that question.

Step 3: Read

- Read material carefully.
- Look for **thesis statements** and **topic sentences**.
- Make notes as you read, and pause periodically to rephrase, in your own words, what you have read.
- Reread difficult sections. If you cannot determine the meaning of a word from its context, check its meaning in a dictionary or glossary of terms.

Step 4: Recite

- Repeat what you have learned, out loud or to yourself, to help you discover the meaning of a passage.
- Test yourself on how thoroughly you understand what you have read by reciting it to yourself. You will then be able to determine whether you need to reread parts of the material.

Step 5: Review

- Review immediately after the initial reading if you have to answer any assignment questions.
- Review immediately after the initial reading to make notes, and to construct an outline, illustrated diagram, or summary of the chapter on note cards for future reference.
- Review before any quizzes, tests, or examinations to refresh your memory on the important definitions, concepts, time lines, and so on.

Another strategy is to examine what you are reading in terms of the three stages of the reading process: **prereading**, **in-process reading**, and **post-reading**. Consider, for example, Timothy Findley's novel *The Wars*, which tells the story of a nineteen-year-old Canadian officer, Robert Ross, during World War I. The novel describes in detail the nightmare world of trench warfare: mud, fire storms, and chlorine gas. Examine the excerpt on page 19 in terms of the three stages of the reading process.

PREREADING STAGE These are some useful techniques to employ *before* you begin to read:

- Establish your purpose for reading.
- Consider the author's possible purposes for writing (e.g., to inform, to persuade, to entertain, to instruct).
- Consider the topic of the passage and why it was chosen.
- Use a **KWL** organizer to determine what you do *Know* about the subject, what you *Want* to know, and what additional information you will *Learn* from this text. Complete this information in three columns in your notebook.
- Activate your prior knowledge:
  - Have you read or heard other novels, stories, poems, historical accounts of World War I?
  - Have you seen films, photographs, or paintings of this period that might help you place this passage in context?
- Ask yourself how the novel's title relates to the context of the selection.
- Determine whether there are clues about the context in the cover or in-text illustrations.
- Make preliminary predictions about the book, based on previewing the selected passage on the following page.

IN-PROCESS READING STAGE Use the following techniques *while* you read the excerpt on page 19 and other selections.

- Stop occasionally to see if you understand what you are reading.
- Adjust, confirm, and revise your predictions made during pre-reading.
- Read to find answers to some of your questions, and develop more questions as you read and reread the passage.
- Reread to understand unfamiliar words.
- Pause to summarize the passage in your own words.
- Make inferences to draw conclusions from your new understanding about characters, issues, and ideas.
- Create mental pictures of the scene in an effort to visualize what is happening.
- Describe the **mood** and **tone** that is conveyed in the passage.

The Wars

by Timothy Findley

The mud. There are no good similes. Mud must be a Flemish word. Mud was invented here. Mudland might have been its name. The ground is the colour of steel. Over most of the plain there isn't a trace of topsoil: only sand and clay. The Belgians call them 'clyttes,' these fields, and the further you go towards the sea, the worse the clyttes become. In them, the water is reached by the plough at an average depth of eighteen inches. When it rains (which is almost constantly from early September through to March, except when it snows) the water rises at you out of the ground. It rises from your footprints—and an army marching over a field can cause a flood. In 1916, it was said that you 'waded to the front.' Men and horses sank from sight. They drowned in mud. Their graves, it seemed, just dug themselves and pulled them down.

All this mud and water was contaminated. Dung and debris and decaying bodies lay beneath its surface. When the rivers and canals could no longer be contained—over they spilled into clyttes already awash with rain.

Houses, trees, and fields of flax once flourished here. Summers had been blue with flowers. Now it was a shallow sea of stinking grey from end to end. And this is where you fought the war.

POST-READING STAGE The post-reading period provides an opportunity to reflect on what you have read. Such questions as the following may be asked:

- What was your first reaction to the text?
- What emotions did you feel as you read the passage?
- What words, phrases, sentences, or images stood out?
- What did you like or dislike about the author's language?
- What is the main idea or dominant impression in the passage?
- What did you learn from reading it?
- Did the text remind you of any other works (e.g., plays, movies, articles, stories, novels)? What is the connection between the two?
- What questions did you have after reading this passage? Were there any parts that were confusing to you?

Activities

Reflecting on Reading Through Writing

1. In a journal entry, describe your reaction to the Timothy Findley selection. What emotions did you feel as you read it?

2. Read a selection of poetry by Siegfried Sassoon, Wilfred Owen, Robert Graves, or Isaac Rosenberg. Alternatively, read extracts from Erich Maria Remarque's classic war novel, *All Quiet on the Western Front*, Kevin Major's novel *No Man's Land*, or Barbara Tuchman's non-fiction book *The Guns of August*. In paragraph form, compare the ideas and impressions of one or two of these writers with those of Timothy Findley.

3. Examine your school textbooks in mathematics, science, and technology. Find sample pages that illustrate the need for critical, careful reading to fully comprehend the word problems, detailed definitions, and technical descriptions in the text. Share your findings with the class.

Learning by Doing

LEARNING FOCUS
- analyze the characteristics of written documents
- read and understand a document
- complete an application form

Document literacy is the ability to interpret and use information from a range of text formats, such as forms and brochures, or more visually-based graphs, maps, and displays. A common example of the need for document literacy is found in application forms, surveys, or questionnaires. In filling out such a document, it is important to read the form thoroughly, to follow all directions carefully, and to understand the significance of any definitions and *fine print* before starting. If you do not provide complete and accurate written information, your application might be rejected.

Activities

Reading and Writing for a Practical Purpose

Write, phone, or e-mail Human Resources Development Canada (HRDC) to ask for an application form for a Social Insurance Number. (For the HRDC URL, see the Pearson Canada Web site, at <www.pearsoned.ca/referencepoints/links>.)

When you receive the form, read the instruction page carefully. Ask yourself these questions:

- Why does this form ask for the information it requests?

- For whom is the text constructed?

- What does this text tell you that you didn't already know?

ABOUT THE AUTHOR

Richard B. Primack is Professor of Plant Ecology at Boston University. He received his B.A. from Harvard University and his Ph.D. from Duke University. His main research deals with the conservation biology of rare plants in Massachusetts and the ecology of tree communities in Malaysia. He also is involved in conservation and policy issues relating to the use of tropical forests in Malaysia, India, and Central America, and is currently editing a book with Tom Lovejoy on the ecology, conservation, and management of Asian rain forests. Dr. Primack is the book review editor for the journal *Conservation Biology*. He is also active in the Tropical Forest Foundation and the Tropical Ecosystems Directorate of the U.S. Man and the Biosphere Program.

ABOUT THE BOOK

Editor: Andrew D. Sinauer

Project Editor: Carol J. Wigg

Copy Editor: Norma Roche

Book Design and Production: Joseph J. Vesely

Cover Design: Christopher Small

Cover Photograph: Art Wolfe

Composition: DEKR Corporation, Woburn, MA

Cover Manufacture: New England Book Components, Inc., Hingham, MA

Book Manufacture: R. R. Donnelley & Sons, Harrisonburg, VA

- What document(s) would have to accompany your application for a Social Insurance Number (SIN)?

  Now complete the application form. Exchange application forms for peer revising and editing to ensure that your form is completed accurately before sending it in.

Learning by Keeping Subject Journals

LEARNING FOCUS
- use personal thoughts to generate ideas
- use journals to develop ideas
- clarify understanding through reflection

Some students choose to keep their school notes in a **subject journal** or learning log. This is a place to gather your ideas and notes from various school subjects to use later in more formal responses. Your subject journal is where you can freely explore the essential ideas raised in class, to prepare for future discussions. You can also write questions about what you are studying, and jot down notes for class projects and assignments.

A subject journal may be divided into two columns: one side (left) can be used for note making during reading and studying time, while the other side (right) can be reserved for note taking on the same topic during lectures, discussion groups, field trips, or lab experiments. The note taking column may also be used for comments, questions, and further reactions to preliminary readings or notes.

Learning by Note Making

LEARNING FOCUS
- make notes to collect and record information
- organize information into meaningful units
- use notes to analyze information

It is difficult to remember *all* the detailed information you encounter daily in various school subjects. Making careful notes can help trigger new ideas later. The process of **note making** allows you to stretch your mind and write down, as you read and study, everything that occurs to you about a particular topic.

Note making refers to all the references and facts you write down and summarize to help you remember information without referring back to the complete original source. During a *first* reading of the material, read to get a general overview or first impression of the content. Make short notes in your subject journal or notebook and jot down major themes and concepts. During a *second* reading, expand on notes on the writer's **thesis**, and on important concepts, facts, and ideas you may wish to revisit. In some subjects, outlines, diagrams, charts, and concept maps will help you remember the important steps in a particular process. Plan to use these as part of your note making strategy.

The checklist below is particularly helpful when making notes from handouts or from texts you own. (The first three suggestions do not apply to texts from the school or public library.)

 CHECKLIST | **EFFECTIVE NOTE MAKING**

- ✓ Underline key words and phrases.
- ✓ Highlight important information.

On one side of the poem "Serene Words" below, you will find a sample note making response. The other side provides a sample note taking response (see page 23).

MODEL: NOTE MAKING AND NOTE TAKING RESPONSE

Note Making
(Student's own reflections on the poem)

- *Check a dictionary and thesaurus for the meaning of the word "serene."*
- *The speaker compares the realization of a truth to the freshness of a flower.*
- *She compares the sweetness and richness of life to golden wheat.*

- *I'm not sure what is being said here. I do see that the wind is personified and that the breath of the wind is sweet as honey.*

- *The beauty of a tiny lily can capture us and catch our gaze and make a long, difficult walk more pleasant. Is there contrast in this stanza?*

- *The beauty of a bird can bring us happiness, so can the heavenly sound of a skylark.*

- *Does the last line suggest that the speaker is dying?*

Serene Words
by Gabriela Mistral

Now in the middle of my days I glean
this truth that has a flower's freshness:
life is the gold and sweetness of wheat,
hate is brief and love immense.

Let us exchange for a smiling verse
that verse scored with blood and gall.
Heavenly violets open, and through the v[
the wind blows a honeyed breath.

Now I understand not only the man who [
now I understand the man who breaks int
Thirst is long-lasting and the hillside twis[
but a lily can ensnare our gaze.

Our eyes grow heavy with weeping,
yet a brook can make us smile.
A skylark's song bursting heavenward
makes us forget it is hard to die.

There is nothing now that can pierce my [
With love, all turmoil ceased.
The gaze of my mother still brings me pea[
I feel that God is putting me to sleep.

✓ Make annotations in the margins of the text.

✓ Find specific details.

✓ Write longer notes in your subject journals.

✓ Jot down questions to find answers to on your own or to discuss with your teacher or a peer.

✓ Elaborate on points using any new information from supplementary reading or a teacher lecture.

✓ Study your notes periodically to help you assimilate the material for tests and assignments.

Note Taking
(Notes from teacher's lectures)

• Gabriela Mistral (1889-1957) was the winner of the 1945 Nobel Prize for Literature.

• Is "Serene Words" an effective title?

• This is a lyric poem conveying the personal feelings of the speaker about the beauty of nature and the power of love.

• Juxtaposition: notice how the speaker contrasts the "immensity" of love to the puniness of hate.

• There is a tone of comfort and joy in this poem. The speaker conveys an attitude that no matter the "hate," the "blood and gall," "weeping," "turmoil," there is a sense of beauty and "freshness" and "peace." A sense that beauty and love can compensate for all the pain and suffering around us. This seems to be the poem's central insight or theme.

• Connotation is used:
   – "a flower's freshness"
   – "a smiling verse"
   – "heavenly violets"
   – "the man who breaks into song"
   – "skylark's song..."
   All these phrases suggest a unified impression of the beauty of nature, happiness, and a sense of comfort.

• Notice how the speaker connects the phrase "love immense" in stanza one with the line "with love, all turmoil ceased" in the last stanza. Is the speaker saying that love, a mother's care, faith in a greater being, can soften even the tragic sting of death itself?

Learning by Note Taking

The process of **note taking** differs from note making in that it relies primarily on the skill of *listening* as opposed to that of *reading*. Effective note taking during class lectures, field trips, group presentations, or demonstrations requires that you listen carefully.

Good listening involves concentration: you must attend not only to *what* is said but also to *how* it is said. Listen for *key words* or *key phrases* (e.g., *first of all, secondly, to summarize*) and repetition used by the speaker to emphasize a particular point. Effective note taking requires that you discriminate between important information and less relevant anecdotes and digressions. Observe the speaker's facial expressions and gestures, as well as accompanying chalkboard or overhead notes. Taking in-depth notes enables you to make the subject matter part of your own thinking. You will then be able to see what it is you understand and what is still confusing you.

LEARNING FOCUS

- understand the difference between note making and note taking
- take notes to collect ideas and information for communicating
- take notes to analyze and evaluate information and ideas

✔ CHECKLIST | EFFECTIVE NOTE TAKING

- ✓ Be clear about the purpose of any lectures, presentations, or field trips *before* participating in them. This will prepare you to take effective notes.
- ✓ Write the date, subject, and the specific topic of your note taking at the top of your page.
- ✓ Leave space between your notes so that you can add relevant information later.
- ✓ Take as many notes as you can: it will help you to remember all the details.
- ✓ Use your own shorthand system for abbreviations, and sketch simple illustrations to represent concepts and processes.
- ✓ Restate in your own words what you hear so that you can understand it later when you review your notes.
- ✓ Listen for key phrases indicating the speaker's priorities in what is being said.
- ✓ Ask yourself questions about the speaker's main and supporting points.

Activities

Note Making and Note Taking

1. For your next out-of-class reading assignment, open your notebook to a fresh page. On the left-hand side write down your responses to your reading. You may wish to read the whole piece first, or you may jot down ideas or questions about it as you progress from paragraph to paragraph. Note any unfamiliar terms or concepts. Comment on the relevance of the piece to the subject area (e.g., does it follow from previous topics? If it's a new topic, is it sufficiently introduced and explained?). Be sure that somewhere in this initial response you try to summarize what you feel are the key points.

   Next, when you are discussing the piece in class, arrange your lecture, discussion, or lab notes on the right-hand page. After you've completed the topic, ask yourself the following questions: How did my left-hand-side notes (note making) affect what I wrote on the right-hand side (note taking)? Did all the questions from the left-hand side get answered? Are there any concepts or terms that I still don't understand? Did anyone else in class ask questions that were similar to mine?

2. Begin to keep a subject journal or learning log for your various school subjects. At the end of a two-week period, get together with some of your peers who are studying several subjects with you. Compare your journals and textbook-annotated notes using the following criteria:
   - quantity and quality of note making
   - quantity and quality of note taking
   - questions cited
   - thoughts and feelings expressed on a topic
   - references to assignments and projects

   Repeat these reflective sessions throughout the year and observe how the quality of your note making, note taking, and understanding of the subject topics improve.

Learning by Paraphrasing Texts

Explaining a piece of writing in your own words is referred to as paraphrasing. A **paraphrase** gives the meaning of the piece, sometimes with more detail than the original, and demonstrates that you understand the text you have read.

There is no set length—with long chapters of prose, your paraphrase may be shorter than the original. With

LEARNING FOCUS
- use paraphrasing to further your understanding of a text
- express a writer's ideas in your own words
- compare your ideas with those expressed in an original work

short lyric poems, the paraphrase is usually longer. When paraphrasing poetry, you lose the precise description of the original.

Paraphrasing can help to identify a writer's conflicting emotions and attitudes. Poets and writers of fiction sometimes cluster ideas in seemingly illogical or abrupt sequences to create a mood of confusion or turmoil. During an initial reading or even a second reading of Gabriela Mistral's poem "Serene Words," we may be puzzled. By paraphrasing, translating it into related or expanded phrases, we discover the subtleties of meaning in the original. For example, we might paraphrase stanza two of Mistral's poem as follows:

> Let us trade the painful and spiteful words we've written for those words that will make us smile. In such poetry, we witness the blossoming of flowers, and in such a world the wind is soothing and fragrant.

When we paraphrase, we substitute words and sometimes also rearrange the **syntax** (word order) to clarify the meaning of the original. Sometimes we lose the vividness, beauty, and suggestiveness of the original imagery when we turn to plainer or less specific language (e.g., "heavenly violets" to "blossoming of flowers"). Remember that paraphrasing is a technique to help us understand a piece of writing, *not* a *replacement* for the original.

Stanza three might be paraphrased as follows:

> Now that I am older I understand not only the person who hopes or pleads for the good in life; I also understand the person who is so full of joy that he celebrates it by singing aloud. And even though our desires and yearnings last into old age, and even though our life is like an uphill struggle, if we keep an alert mind and heart, a single flower can capture our full attention with its beauty.

It is important to retain a sense of objectivity when paraphrasing. Although by the very words you choose you are providing a personal perspective, try in your rewording to be as true to the original meaning as possible.

Activities

Paraphrasing a Poem

1. In small groups, decide on a poem, short story, or piece of non-fiction you would like to paraphrase. Provide each member of your group with a copy of the selection. Individually, write a paraphrase

of the selection without consulting the other members of the group. When you are finished, compare your paraphrases. Compose a new paraphrase based on your collective interpretations.

2. Read the poem "Betrayals," by Maria Mazziotti Gillan, which follows. Write a paraphrase of the poem, using suggestions in this section to help you. When you are finished, exchange your paraphrase with a partner. Prepare a final version, based on your shared interpretations.

READING SELECTION: POEM

Betrayals
by Maria Mazziotti Gillan

At thirteen, I screamed,
"You're disgusting,"
drinking your coffee from a saucer.
Your startled eyes darkened with shame.

You, one dead leg dragging,
counting your night-shift hours,
You, smiling past yellowed, gaping teeth,
You, mixing the egg nog for me yourself
In a fat dime store cup,

How I betrayed you,
over and over, ashamed of your broken tongue,
how I laughed, savage and innocent,
at your mutilations.

Today, my son shouts,
"Don't tell anyone you're my mother,"
hunching down in the car
so the other boys won't see us together.

Daddy, are you laughing?
Oh, how things turn full circle,
My own words coming back
to slap my face.

I was sixteen when you called one night from your work.
I called you dear,
Loving you in that moment
past all barriers of the heart.
You called again every night for a week.
I never said it again.
I wish I could say it now.

Dear, my Dear
with your twisted tongue
I did not understand you
dragging your burden of love.

Learning by Writing a Précis

LEARNING FOCUS
- prepare a summary of a piece of writing
- express a writer's ideas in your own words
- interpret ideas expressed in a prose passage

To **précis** is to summarize concisely (not just paraphrase), in your own words, the content of something you have read. The summary is typically about *one third* the length of the original and it contains *only* what was in the original. Being able to précis effectively will greatly increase your ability to understand and remember what you have read.

Before writing reports and research essays, it will be necessary for you to read and condense articles from various sources for your report or essay. Sometimes, you will need to provide clear, well-written, and succinct summaries of reports you have written for those who lack time to read the originals. Précis writing is definitely a useful skill to learn.

Steps in Writing a Précis

1. Skim the material to get the overall meaning in terms of subject and content.

2. Read the information thoroughly, two or three times, paying particular attention to key phrases and major points.

3. Look up in a dictionary or thesaurus any words or terms you don't understand.

4. Find or compose a key sentence that reflects the central idea of the entire piece of writing. This sentence should become the **thesis statement** of your summary.

5. Look for evidence of a plan of development or outline in the original, and note main topics and subtopics.

6. Select or compose a series of topic sentences that express the central idea of each paragraph or section.

7. Omit all unnecessary words and phrases, and use adjectives and adverbs sparingly.

8. Omit or condense examples and descriptive passages, and reduce long explanations to bare facts. Direct quotations should, as a rule, be changed into reported speech; any conversations should be concisely summarized.

9. Compose an effective concluding sentence for your summary that ties all its parts together.

10. Ensure that the précis is a coherent, smooth-flowing composition with adequate transition between ideas. The ideas should follow the same order as the original.

The following excerpt is from the April/May 1998 issue of *Equinox*.

READING SELECTION: MAGAZINE ARTICLE

Endpoint
by Laurel Aziz

When Rachel Carson wrote *Silent Spring* in the 1960s, the world was introduced to the potentially devastating effects DDT could have on wildlife. Carson changed commonly held attitudes about chemicals recklessly used in the environment, but her warning focused largely on direct contact with large lethal doses and dangers of excess. Since her time, however, many other scientists have believed that the trace elements of contaminants accumulating in nature have the same potential to damage fragile ecosystems and to make wildlife and people sick. Until now, what was missing was a comprehensive hypothesis to explain the mechanism at work.

Today, a growing body of wildlife observation, laboratory tests on animals and cultured cells, and human epidemiological data show that residues of many chemicals that are used in industry and commonly found in the home behave like hormones. The synthetic impostors infiltrate the tissues of living things, where—at doses far below those necessary for fatal poisoning—they act on the endocrine system. "From the beginning, I've been concerned about the implications for wildlife and humans alike," [scientist Glen] Fox says. "There is a great similarity in vertebrates." If you consider what he saw on Scotch Bonnet Island, Ontario in 1975—loss of breeding and parental instinct, sterility, disease and congenital sickness in offspring—and apply that model to any higher-order animal on earth, you have the potentially chilling scope of endocrine disruption, or what scientists call the endpoints.

Though the threat from hormone mimics is invisible, it pervades our lives. Chemical manufacturers have ingeniously fulfilled their post-World War II promise of "a better life through chemicals," and in doing so, they have filled our world with chemical-based products, ranging from pesticides and paints to detergents, plastics, and batteries, that are now under suspicion. An estimated 100,000 chemicals are used in manufacturing worldwide. To meet society's acquired taste for bigger, brighter, shinier stuff at rock-bottom prices, more than one tonne of chemicals is produced each year for every person on earth. According to the World Wildlife Fund (WWF), 50 million kilograms of herbicides, insecticides and fungicides alone are used annually in Canada; more than 850 of these products are registered for use around the house. If the absence of "hard" science has postponed the establishment of the strictest-possible preventive standards, the day of reckoning has finally arrived. Scientific and environmental groups are demanding long-overdue answers to questions such as: How far-reaching is this threat? Are both the science and the policy in place to protect wildlife and public health? How will a future global economy affect Canada's health and environmental standards? Is there policy to change the way we manage these chemicals in the future? (456 Words)

Below you will find a précis of Laurel Aziz's article. Notice how it manages to summarize the contents of the selection in approximately *one third* of the original length.

MODEL: PRÉCIS

The opening sentence combines the chief ideas from the original first paragraph. To tighten the wording, the concept of the "comprehensive hypothesis" is omitted.

Certain details and technical references have been deleted for ease of comprehension.

A few specific examples of the types of illness remain to ensure clarity.

The closing question format of the original has been reworded as an emphatic final sentence.

Since Rachel Carson's work in the 1960s on the negative effects of DDT, scientists have progressed from studying the dangers of direct contact with lethal doses of chemicals to the less visible dangers caused by trace elements of contaminants. Current research reveals that chemical residues of industrial and household products mimic the behaviour of hormones. The consequences of this hormone simulation may include sterility, disease, and congenital sickness. Since more than one tonne of chemicals per person is produced yearly to meet consumer demands for better and cheaper products, scientists and environmental groups are now concerned about the absence of strict preventive standards. Determining the scope of this threat will help Canadians to see what kinds of improved restrictions on chemical use are needed for the future. (127 Words)

Activities

Précis Writing

1. Look at magazines, newspapers, or the Internet for an article that interests you. Following the "Steps in Writing a Précis" from page 28, write a précis reducing the article to one-third of its original length. Bring both the original and your précis to class, exchange with a partner, and give each other feedback on your summaries.

2. Read the article below, from *Maclean's* magazine, and summarize it in your own words. Be sure to relay the essential message of the piece in your précis.

READING SELECTION: MAGAZINE ARTICLE

Why I Stay...For Now
by James Cherry

I never imagined I'd become a poster child for anything. But lately I've become one—because I resisted the "brain drain." My brush with media notoriety started with a profile in my local newspaper, the *Ottawa Citizen*, after I won the Governor General's Medal at Carleton University for my Ph.D. work. In recent weeks, I've appeared both on national TV and, now, in nationally circulated print.

Why the fuss? Because I recently turned down an offer of $105,000 (U.S.) a year to live in a terrific city, Boston, to work for one of the world's best-known corporations, IBM Corp. I chose to *stay* in a terrific city, Ottawa, for a much lower salary, working for a small start-up company, Philsar Semiconductor Inc. Not everyone understands why.

When I started my Ph.D. in 1992, I didn't anticipate that cellular phones (my thesis topic) would become so hot. Thanks to that, and because my thesis supervisor was well-respected and connected, I was in high demand when I finished in 1998, at age 28. Alongside the IBM offer, my best competing offer in Canada was with Philsar.

I opted for Philsar—and to remain in Canada—for three reasons. First, my partner is in a university program here. If we went to the United States, her tuition fees would be much higher, thus reducing my salary advantage. And while Philsar's offer was smaller up front, it offered stock options that could prove lucrative if things go well. And having had a large portion of my post-secondary education paid for by government scholarships, could I really stiff Canadian taxpayers by immediately running south?

Many of Canada's best and brightest apparently have little problem going south—if the brain drain is as real as some reports suggest. I don't have a survey to back me up, but I personally know significantly more people who stayed than left. At Philsar, we've managed to convince some Americans to move to frigid Ottawa! Things can go both ways.

Why do some Canadians choose to work in the United States? The money is usually better: is it unreasonable to go where you're compensated best? Much of the States has nicer weather (San Diego is gorgeous all year round). Depending on what state you move to (Texas certainly, California perhaps not), you pay less tax than in Canada. On the downside, the San Francisco Bay area (the heart of high-tech) has some of the worst traffic and most exorbitant house prices in North America. The States lacks socialized medicine, and you must contend with the citizens' dreaded "right to bear arms." And in my unscientific opinion, U.S. society feels less tolerant and more self-centred than that of Canada. Several people who have raised children there have warned me against doing so myself.

I did a Ph.D. because, ultimately, I want to teach at university. Will Finance Minister Paul Martin's recent tax cuts, and my love of Canada, be enough to keep me here? Ask me today, and I lean toward saying yes: high-tech opportunities in industry and university are improving. But my partner might have a harder time. Perhaps when she graduates, she'll find the big, bad U.S. of A. much better for jobs. And circumstances and priorities change. Maybe the tax advantage of the States will be too great. Maybe I'll have had enough of cold winters. Maybe we'll find a city where raising a family doesn't seem so bad. I don't imagine the choice being easy. We'll see what the future brings.

3. Find some posters, comic strips, editorial cartoons, or additional articles that address the issue of *brain drain*. In a group, compare the viewpoints presented with those in the article above.

Learning Through Careful Viewing and Representing

Viewing requires us to take meaning from visual information. We must derive an understanding of *content* and *purpose* from the image we see. We must analyze and evaluate the visual message and place it in context.

Visual communication can take various forms. It can be a **still image** such as a picture, photograph, cartoon, or symbolic display, or a **moving image** such as those seen on television and in films or plays. It can also be **visual media** such as posters, billboards, **storyboards**, advertisements, and Web pages. (See Chapter 5 for more on visual communication and the media.)

Representing combines images, with or without the spoken or written word, to convey a visual message. It is an effective complement (or alternative) to writing or speaking as a means to communicate knowledge, thoughts, and experiences.

At a basic level, representation can entail simplifying information in visual or graphic form. Various kinds of **graphic organizers** as well as standard tables and graphs are examples of this. Representing can also involve great creativity, as well as a complex emotional relationship with the viewing audience. Dramatic presentations and media representations in various forms are examples of this.

Learning by Constructing Graphic Organizers

LEARNING FOCUS
- explore relationships among ideas
- present information visually
- make sense of new information

Sometimes in a school situation you will collect so many facts and ideas on a subject that the amount of information will seem overwhelming. Learning to arrange and organize this material into smaller, manageable chunks will provide a focus and sense of order to your material. Constructing graphic organizers such as **thought webs, cluster charts, flowcharts, time lines, problem–solution charts, cause and effect charts, pro–con charts, comparison and contrast charts,** or **Venn diagrams** as methods of structuring the ideas will help you make more sense of the information.

If you are completing an assignment on the principal stakeholders in the Canadian Business Enterprise System, you might create a cluster chart such as the one below to help develop ideas on the main topic:

A CLUSTER CHART ILLUSTRATING THE BUSINESS ENTERPRISE AND ITS RELATIONSHIPS

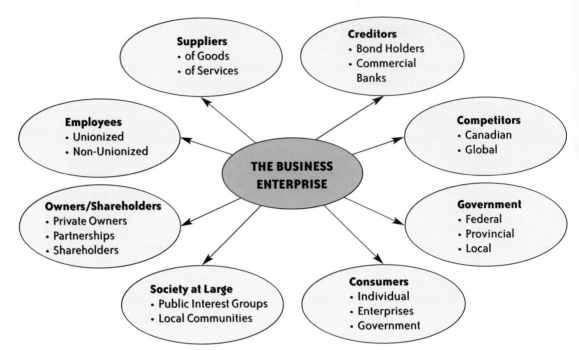

You might create a Venn diagram such as the following as a pre-drafting tool to compare and contrast work done in the old versus the new economy. The similarities between the two economies are listed in the space where the circles overlap; the differences are placed in the non-overlapping sections.

A VENN DIAGRAM COMPARING THE OLD AND NEW ECONOMY

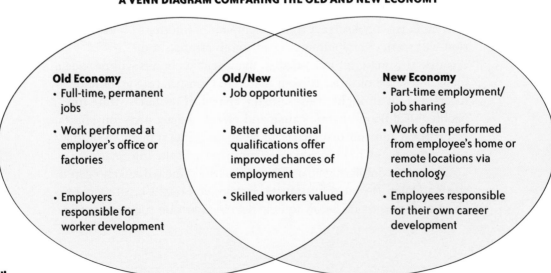

The following flowchart would be helpful for you in identifying the stages in the recycling process:

FLOWCHART IDENTIFING THE STAGES OF THE RECYCLING PROCESS

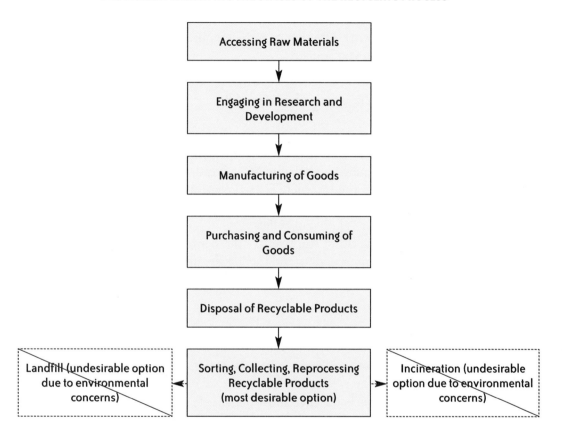

Activities

Working with Graphic Organizers

1. Examine some of your school texts or magazines to find examples of how graphic organizers are used to clarify a topic or concept. (Definitions of each of these organizers can be found in the glossary.) Look for some of the following:
   - cause and effect chart
   - cluster chart
   - comparison and contrast chart
   - flowchart
   - problem–solution chart

- pro–con chart
- time line
- Venn diagram

2. Find some information on one of the following topics: health care in Canada, employment trends, environmental concerns (or select a topic of your own). Use one or more graphic organizers to convey the information you collect.

Learning by Viewing the World Around You

LEARNING FOCUS

- interpret visual messages
- become a more critical viewer
- use visuals to convey meaning

In our daily lives, we see visual images all the time—in books, magazines, newspapers, in media advertising, on television, and over the Internet. These images affect us in various ways. They may evoke strong emotions, shape our thoughts, and help define our values and beliefs.

In the visual world of the twenty-first century it has become increasingly important to understand the images around us. The checklist below provides some basic suggestions on how to get the most out of a visual message.

✓ CHECKLIST | EFFECTIVE VIEWING

✓ Establish the primary purpose for the image (e.g., to inform, to entertain, to persuade).

✓ Draw on your own knowledge and experience to understand the image.

✓ Take stock of your own reaction and emotional response.

✓ Be an active, critical viewer: question and evaluate what you see.

✓ Reflect on your impression of the image either orally or in writing.

We are typically drawn to visuals since they provide a more immediate method of communication than the printed word. When people buy newspapers and magazines, often the first section they turn to is the comics. **Comic strips** and **cartoons** reveal what is going on in the world around us. They show a *slice of life*, where an insight is provided in each episode.

Look at the Calvin and Hobbes comic strip on page 37. Consider how the cartoonist, Bill Watterson, skilfully combines the verbal and the visual to get his message across. Note, too, how the facial expressions and gestures of the characters help generate the humour expressed in the words.

Now examine the following award-winning Canadian advertisements. Note the minimal use of verbal information. The message, however, is made entirely clear through these effective images.

PICK ME

MUD ANGEL

Proud to send Team Sunlight to the Borneo 2000 Eco-Challenge.
Go ahead. Get dirty.

ALL PURPOSE Q-TIPS

Activities

Exploring the Visual World

1. Review the Calvin and Hobbes comic strip on page 37. Is it more than just entertainment? What is the message or idea behind it? Does it help you reflect on life in a different way? Write a one-paragraph journal entry to convey your response to the storyline presented. Create your own follow-up episode with words and visuals.

2. Make an overhead transparency of a favourite comic strip. Give an oral presentation to your class in which you discuss its message. Explain why you feel it is popular. What might the fact that you chose this particular comic strip show about you as a person?

3. Consider a topic of interest to you (sports or fitness, technology "toys," popular music, fashion trends). Throughout a term or semester, compile a collection of images that illustrate the topic, from as many sources as possible (pictures, photos, comic strips, cartoons, advertisements). Mount your collection in a scrapbook or digitize it for a multimedia presentation.

Learning by Role-Playing

LEARNING FOCUS

- use your imagination to express yourself
- express the thoughts and feelings of other people
- evaluate role-playing presentations

Role-playing (acting out situations) can be a useful learning tool. It allows you to respond to course content by using your imagination and by projecting the feelings, attitudes, and behaviour of someone else. Through watching an effective role play or engaging in one yourself, you can focus on a particular point of view, investigate the background behind certain events, and clarify issues. It can also be helpful for examining situations of conflict. You can role-play, for example, a situation in which a farmer, miner, or concerned family member stands up for a particular economic, environmental, or occupational safety concern. Through exploring and presenting a particular scene, you become more involved than through simply reading about an issue. You come to understand the motivations behind a particular behaviour.

Activities

Role-Playing a Scene

Consider the role play suggestions for activities below. Immediately after each role play, hold a group discussion in which participants and observers reflect on and react to the session using these criteria:

- evidence of good preparation and planning
- interest level (was the issue worth exploring?)
- effectiveness of overall presentation
- sense of time, place, character
- intended audience and purpose
- authenticity
- seriousness of commitment to the roles
- aspects of human behaviour displayed (motives, conflict, tensions, point of view)
- evidence of logical thinking

1. Choose a short story or novel you have read recently. Select from it a situation in which a character is experiencing conflict or must make a difficult decision. With a partner, role-play a scenario with another character in which this conflict is explored, clarified, and potentially resolved.

2. You may be familiar with *Heritage Minutes*, a series of sixty-second snapshots of significant events and personalities in Canadian history. View several *Heritage Minutes* snapshots on video, or log on to the Pearson Canada Web site at <www.pearsoned.ca/reference-points/links> for the current *Heritage Minutes* URL. With a partner, discuss the effectiveness of each Heritage snapshot using the criteria outlined above.

3. Research an important Canadian or provincial event of your choice (political, economic, social) and perform it as a role play, portraying the behaviour, thoughts, and feelings of the people at that time.

Learning and Computer Technology

The computer has the capability to integrate all of the communication-skill areas. It enables us to bring together on one screen a wide range of elements: text, pictures, photographs, video and music clips, and animation. It is a tool for creative thinking, facilitates the writing process, and is an aid in collecting and classifying information.

Using the Computer as a Resource

The computer is invaluable for a wide range of school applications, as seen below:

LEARNING FOCUS
- consider ways in which you use the computer as a resource
- make meaningful selections from electronic sources
- organize your research and writing in files

- Word processing software permits you to edit, cut, paste, and reformat documents with great speed and efficiency. You may also import graphics, tables, and charts from other sources with ease.

- Desktop publishing and graphics software enable you to produce attractive and professional looking reports, brochures, newsletters, and personal creative writing at your own desk.

- **CD-ROM** discs, which store written, visual, and auditory information on a wide range of topics, are inexpensive and easily accessible.

- **The Internet**, a massive network of information, allows you to access up-to-the-minute data using your computer, a **modem**, and appropriate **browser** software. (Although mainstream publishers check to ensure their authors and their information are reliable, anyone can publish material on the Internet. See Evaluating Web Sites, page 46.)

- **E-mail** (electronic mail) provides fast, efficient sharing of ideas and observations. A **listserv** enables you to send e-mails and read the correspondence of other subscribers, to explore a common interest or profession. A **newsgroup** is another type of discussion group, in which subscribers share opinions. Web site **chat rooms** provide more immediate communications, in which messages are typed and received in **real time**. An **instant messaging** application such as ICQ, which you can download from the Internet, runs in the background and informs you when others are on-line, enabling you to chat, and send messages and files. This is as close as you can get to the immediacy of a telephone conversation.

TIPS ON WORKING WITH FILES On the typical personal computer today, you will generate numerous documents and file folders. Whether you are using a Windows- or Mac-based operating system, structuring your file folders properly will allow you to take charge of your computer.

The following suggestions can help you to manage your files effectively:

- If the information on your file is important, be sure that you save it to your hard disk and either take a printed copy, back it up on a floppy disk, or transfer it to a remote location (another computer).

- Give your files *meaningful titles* rather than generic names like "research" or "April 2000." Otherwise you may waste time looking for poorly titled information.

- Organize your files into as many reasonable categories and folders as you can. You might want to create separate folders for schoolwork and personal files or even subdivide your schoolwork files into subjects, homework tasks, and general research sections.

- When working on a project over a longer stretch of time (perhaps several weeks), be sure to label the versions of your drafts with different file names by the date or version number. Otherwise, it is difficult and time-consuming to tell which version is the most recent.

- When sending a number of file attachments by e-mail, make sure that you write a brief explanatory note, letting the person know *what* you're sending and, in some cases, *why* you're sending it. You might also ask for confirmation of receipt of the message, if your software does not automatically provide this.

- Check with your receiver before you e-mail to ensure that they have the proper software and compatible version to open the file documents you are sending.

Regardless of your level of interest or involvement with computers, by imposing order on your personal archives of information, you will be able to make better use of the technology.

Activities

Working with Application Programs

1. Form groups of three and conduct interviews with computer users from different walks of life. For instance, one person might interview an experienced office worker to discuss how computers have changed her workplace; another might ask a librarian how they

have affected his job; and the third person might ask an insurance broker how computers have affected how she does collision repair estimates. Remember that you may conduct interviews face to face, over the phone, or even via e-mail. Compare your results and compile a brief report outlining the positive, negative, and most interesting highlights of your investigations.

2. Research current and developing aspects of computer use in education and the workplace. Form small groups to
   - interview staff members from the Distance Education department of one or more community colleges or universities to discover trends in computer-based home study programs.
   - question a telecommuter (someone who works from home) about current and future use of computer technology in her work.
   - find an office worker who can inform you about increasing workplace use of communication tools such as video conferencing.

   Make an oral presentation to share your findings with the class.

3. Find a partner and assume that you are members of a fundraising committee for a local charity. You have organized an upcoming dance for pre-teens, a bike-a-thon for teens, and a curling tournament for seniors. Now you need to draft and design flyers to advertise your events. Using desktop publishing software, create *three* different layouts for *each* event. When you finish, ask other pairs in the class to choose which one they feel is most effective for each target audience. Ask for specific reasons to support the choices made.

© Lynn Johnston Productions, Inc. / Distributed by United Feature Syndicate, Inc.

Learning to Use Electronic Mail and the Internet

Whether you use e-mail and the Internet at school or at home, it is useful to learn how the systems work. Even a basic understanding will help you become faster and more efficient in using these computer tools.

INSTALLING AND USING E-MAIL When installing e-mail you will need either a **dial-up** account with a telephone line and a modem, or a high-speed system from a telephone or cable company. High-speed systems have made the Internet more accessible, as they can download and transmit information rapidly. Your **ISP** (Internet service provider) will assign you a login name, a password, and an e-mail address.

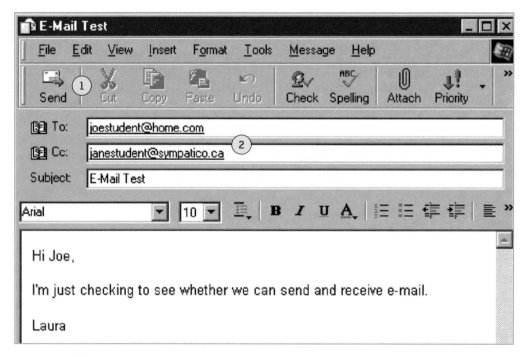

① The toolbar, located below the pulldown menus (File, Edit, View, and so on), provides frequently used shortcut features identified by specific icons. It allows the user to revise, edit, and customize an e-mail message and to attach and send a file along with it.

② This screen tells to whom the e-mail is sent, and to whom cc (courtesy or carbon copies) and bcc (blind carbon copies, where the name of the recipient is invisible to other recipients) are sent. The subject of the e-mail should be specific enough so that the receiver knows the content even before opening the message.

Remember the following when sending and receiving e-mail:

- E-mail messages do not protect your privacy—they are not *secure*.
- You should typically not respond to unsolicited e-mail messages.
- An attached file you did not ask for, even one that appears to have been sent by a friend, may contain a virus that could damage your computer.

USING THE INTERNET The Internet provides a channel for connection to a massive global network of information. It is important to remember that information from the Internet has not been evaluated or censored in any way. It has merely been posted there for ready accessibility.

Steps in an Internet Search

1. Your Internet provider will usually provide Web **browser** software such as Microsoft Internet Explorer or Netscape Navigator.

2. You can now connect to the **World Wide Web**, a huge network of computers storing data. (To distinguish between the Internet and the Web, it is helpful to think of the Internet as a library and the World Wide Web as the actual books inside the library.)

3. Information is stored on the Web on specific **Web sites** (individual books) each consisting of **Web pages** (text pages).

4. Use the underlined or colour-coded **hyperlinks** (hotlinks) to jump to related topics either on a different Web page within the Web site or to go to a new Web site entirely. It is easy to get distracted by hotlinks and **pop-ups** to advertisements.

5. If you are certain of a Web site address or **URL** (Uniform Resource Locator), type it in as soon as your browser comes up on the screen.

6. If you have only a general idea of the information you want to find, simplify your search for pertinent Web sites using a **search engine**, such as Yahoo, AltaVista, or others, which arranges information in subject categories. Familiarize yourself with various search engines, since each may turn up different sites to match your search. Do not rely on just one search engine when conducting research.

7. Narrow your search by using **Boolean operators**. This allows you to impose some logic by using true–false statements and the words *and*, *or*, and *not* to refine and clarify your search. If you don't use such operators, and you simply key in *euthanasia*, for example, you may find thousands of sites that won't pertain specifically to your particular topic of *euthanasia and medical laboratory testing*.

8. Always **bookmark** useful sites. If you haven't copied down the exact Web address in your notes, you may have trouble finding the site again. As well, remember that unlike books, Web sites have to be maintained on servers, so what existed today may be removed or *under construction* tomorrow.

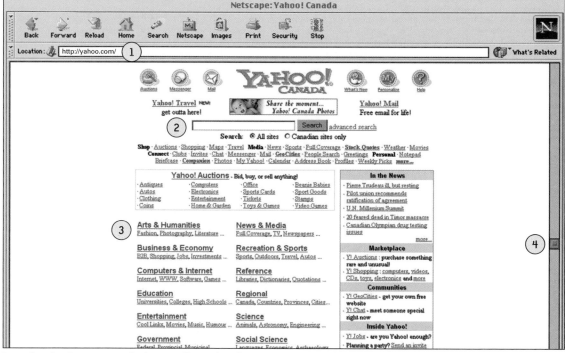

Reproduced with permission of Yahoo! Inc. © 2000 by Yahoo! Inc. YAHOO! and the YAHOO! logo are trademarks of YAHOO! Inc.

(1) The ending *.com* in the Web site address line tells the viewer that this is a commercial site. A site may denote its country of origin. For instance a Canadian site might be designated *.ca*. A government site would be indicated by *.gov*; a non-profit organization site by *.org*; and a college or university site by *.edu*.

(2) If you know the exact topic you want to research, you can type the specific search words in the search window.

(3) This Web site is organized by pre-selected topics. Selecting a topic will allow you to link with pertinent data.

(4) Moving the scroll bar up and down will allow you to see the full range of pre-selected topics available.

EVALUATING WEB SITES Ensure that you can identify the source for the Web site when conducting research on the Internet. For instance, a site prepared by a reputable government organization or a major college or university is likely to be more reliable than one that does not identify its author(s) or point of origin. Remember also that commercially-sponsored sites may choose to publish only information that is approved by the sponsor. Always be on the alert for potential bias in your sources and for those which may contain more fiction than fact.

Educators, librarians, and organizations such as the Center for Media Education (CME) and Media Awareness Network Canada (see its current URL at the Pearson Canada Web site, at <www.pearsoned.ca/referencepoints/links>) promote the tremendous educational and cultural potential of the Internet. They also reinforce Web awareness issues, concerns, and risks associated with its use. The Internet has sites that may be inappropriate or offensive as well as those which violate the privacy or safety of individuals. Caution and common sense should be exercised during each Internet search.

Ask yourself the following questions when evaluating Web sites:

- Is the name, telephone number, and address of the individual or company responsible for the Web site provided?
- Is the source of the information clearly identifiable? If not, why do you think it is missing?
- Is there someone to whom you can direct your questions and comments?
- What do you know about the Web page or Web site sponsor? Does the group or individual have known biases?
- Is the style of writing sound and believable or misleading and full of unsubstantiated claims?
- Is the viewpoint objective or does it appear biased in a specific direction?
- Are links listed to other sources with different viewpoints?
- Can you determine the relationship between the information and these other sources?
- Is the information thorough, easy to understand, and current?
- When was the site created? When was the site last updated?

Activities

Using Electronic Mail and the Internet

1. Conduct a series of class discussions using the following questions:
   - Have any commercial sites for children and teens you have found on the Internet stated their privacy policy and explained how information collected will be used?

- Why do Internet advertisers focus so much on the child and teenage market?
- Do you feel that Internet advertising aimed at children should be regulated? Who should regulate this advertising?

2. Complete some research to determine what guidelines organizations such as the Better Business Bureau (BBB), Canadian Marketing Association (CMA), Canadian Association of Internet Providers (CAIP), or any other agencies have in place to regulate Internet advertising for children and teens.

3. Find a Web page or site of interest on the Internet or a site that is appropriate to a project you are working on. Cite the source and write a paragraph or two evaluating the site you have chosen. Include a print copy of the first page of the Web site. Present a log of the search strategy you used to locate the site.

4. The Nigerian poet Ken Saro-Wiwa mobilized the Ogoni people to protest against the devastation of their environment by the major oil companies. He also protested his people's denigration by Nigerian military dictators. An initial search of the Internet yielded his heroic prison letter, published in the *Mail and Guardian* newspaper in May, 1995. Saro-Wiwa concluded his letter as follows:

> Whether I live or die is immaterial. It is enough to know that there are people who commit time, money, and energy to fight this one evil among so many others predominating worldwide. If they do not succeed today, they will succeed tomorrow. We must keep on striving to make the world a better place for all of mankind—each one contributing his bit, in his or her own way.
>
> *I salute you all*—Ken Saro-Wiwa
> Military Hospital, Port Harcourt, Nigeria.

Conduct a further search on the Internet to find some additional writings on the life and works of Ken Saro-Wiwa. Run the search on two different search engines and compare the results from the two searches. Was one better than the other? Why? How? Share what you find with the class.

5. The Web has not replaced print resources: it is a complement to books. Examine Naomi Klein's book *No Logo: Taking Aim at Brand Bullies* (Knopf Canada), and her section devoted to Ken Saro-Wiwa. Compare the quality of her printed information to the material you found on Saro-Wiwa on various Web sites.

Communicating Through Responding to Text

Looking at Texts

Texts come in a wide range of styles. There are **literary texts** such as novels, poems, and plays. There are purely **informational texts** such as news reports, textbooks, and research reports. Increasingly, texts are presented in visual form, such as cartoons, photographs, and graphics on **Web sites**.

Literary texts can be classified in terms of **genre** and **form**. Each literary genre (short story, poetry, drama, etc.) has unique forms, patterns, and structures. For example, within the genre of poetry there are standard forms (ballads, sonnets, odes, etc.) that may follow conventions of line and stanza length, rhythm, and rhyme.

Some anthologies of literature are organized by genre. Others centre around particular **themes** or central insights. Yet others are organized by **mode** or *kind* of writing (e.g., tragedy, comedy, romance). Mode also refers to the *manner* of writing (e.g., narrative, descriptive, expository).

At their best, texts raise questions that have always intrigued human beings. Who are we? How do we live together? What do we want as individuals and as a society? Literary text allows us to visit places, meet characters, and explore situations we might never have known about or imagined. In order for us to understand the world we live in now, we need frequent opportunities to speculate about the past (historical fiction), the present (contemporary fiction), and the future (fantasy and science fiction). The more we read, the more we will learn from examining meaning and form.

Text, Author, and Reader

LEARNING FOCUS
- understand your relationship with a text and its author
- consider various levels of meaning in a text
- understand various interpretations of a text

Professional literary authors present ideas, plots, settings, fictional characters, and real people using carefully chosen words. They assume that you, the reader, know the dictionary meaning (**denotation**) of the majority of words they have chosen to include. The words used may also *imply* meaning (**connotation**) arising from association or frequent use in a certain **context**. Take the two words *balloon seller* for example. They suggest more than the denotative meaning of someone carrying balloons around a street for sale. The reader may associate the balloon seller with circuses, fairs, birthday parties or with the joys and magical sense a child experiences as summer arrives. The more carefully a literary work is examined, the more connotations can be recognized and the richer the literary experience becomes.

Authors' words take on life when you read (or view or listen to) what they have created. For instance, you and your friends might read the same short story, but your individual responses will vary depending on your different backgrounds, personality traits, and memories. Knowledge of text is not something that is simply *found*. It is *created* by the interplay between you and the text and by your own careful reading and rereading, or viewing and re-viewing, of the text. It evolves as you engage in discussions with teachers and classmates and write down your thoughts and feelings about a variety of literary works.

Activities

Reacting to Text

1. Read the short poem below. Then answer the following questions:
   - What is the denotative meaning of the word "rust"?
   - What connotations does the verb "rust" acquire in the poem?

Rust

by Mary Carolyn Davies

Iron, left in the rain
   And fog and dew,
With rust is covered. Pain
   Rusts into beauty too.

I know full well that this is so:
I had a heartbreak long ago.

2. Write a brief **personal response** to this poem. During the course of a class discussion, compare your response to those of your peers to show how different backgrounds, personality traits, and memories affect readers' responses.

A First Reading and the Response Journal

LEARNING FOCUS

- make personal connections with what you read
- ask questions and make predictions while you read
- compare your own ideas with those of an author

A *first reading* of a literary work usually results in a rough general sense of the work. At this stage, your imagination and intellect begin working with the author's words to recreate the characters, setting, and ideas included in the work. The details come more or less into focus depending on your knowledge and experiences.

As you saw in Chapter 1, a **journal** is a place where you can write down your personal reflections. A **response journal** relates specifically to your reactions on reading (or viewing) a text. Such writing helps you to explore and clarify your initial ideas about a literary work.

 CHECKLIST WRITING A RESPONSE JOURNAL

✓ Make lists of interesting words and ideas.

✓ Make observations about setting, plot, and character.

✓ Describe connections from your own life to specific events, characters, and points of interest in the text.

✓ Draw images and scenes that illustrate the text.

✓ Collect interesting quotations from the text.

✓ Raise questions to ask yourself, your teachers, and your classmates.

Read the following poem, "Family Group," by Kay Smith. Then read the student response journal that follows it.

READING SELECTION: POEM

Family Group

by Kay Smith

I look out the bus window at the grey rain,
at houses flush with the pavement in a shabby street,
at trees unstirred by the calendar fact of April;
in our city spring has a hard birth.

The bus stops for a boy in faded jeans,
who looks seventeen not a day older,
and a girl a year younger perhaps, wearing
too thin a coat for the still wintry weather.
With one hand the boy grips a carton,
and with the other a paper bag of groceries;
the girl carries in her arms a crying infant,
the blanket worn from many washings.

The face of the young mother is grave but serene
as she cradles in her arms the child whose crying
is the smallest sound of grief as sad as the rain;
the young father sighs as he balances his parcels.

There seems nothing to remember about this little group
Unless it is the pathos of their youth and poverty,
yet I think I'll remember them against falling rain
and unbudded trees in a shabby street.

To such as these life opens once her secret heart,
and what weeps now was once a breath of ecstasy.

STUDENT SAMPLE: PERSONAL JOURNAL RESPONSE

*Is the poet the speaker? More often it is some **persona** the poet creates.*

The poem "Family Group" by Kay Smith reveals a poet's experience of seeing a young couple at a bus stop with their baby. It is a grey dreary day in April as the narrator looks out a bus window through the rain.

The reponse focuses first on literal meaning: who, what, when, where, why.

She sees a young boy and girl in faded thin clothes carrying a young baby. Both teenagers seem weighed down by the burden of parenthood as the girl tries to comfort the crying infant. The poet says that there is nothing to remember about the group but the image of their poverty and youth against the rain and shabby street.

The writer states a personal preference and gives reasons for liking the poem.

I enjoyed reading this poem because it deals with a relevant topic for teenagers. It leads readers to think either about their own life or the life of someone else they know whose life has been changed by actions taken without the thought of consequences. The teenagers here are forced to become adults before their time.

After I finish reading this poem, I ask myself:

These questions are an attempt to connect with the young girl's experiences.

- Where is the couple going?
- What does their home look like?

Thinking about myself or my friends in the same situation, I wondered:

- Does the girl long for new clothes?
- Does she long to be back in school?
- What was her relationship with her parent(s)?
- Has all that changed?

The response here touches on mood and theme.

This poem is not pretty. It gives the reader a sense of poverty and of jumping into adulthood and parenthood too quickly.

Activities

Response to First Reading

1. Write another verse for the poem "Family Group" in which you describe what happens next in the lives of the characters.

2. Complete a first reading of a short story, novel, or poem, and write a response journal entry giving a personal reaction to the text. You

may use the following questions and incomplete statements to get you started:

- What was the selection about?
- Did I like it? Why? Why not?
- How am I like any of the characters?
- Did any of the characters remind me of other people?
- This text reminds me of…
- This text made me realize that…
- This text made me wish that…

3. Find one person in the class who has read the same text as you. (It can be a novel, poem, or non-fiction.) Write partner journals. First, write your own journal about a section of the text. Then switch your response with a partner. He or she will read your journal entry and write a response or comment about it in journal format.

Group Discussion About Texts

LEARNING FOCUS

- increase your understanding of a text through group discussion
- compare your personal responses with those of others
- reconsider or revise your own responses through discussion

After you have had an opportunity to react personally to a first reading of a literary text, it is helpful to share your reaction with others and compare your response with theirs. Your classmates, with their individual personalities and life experiences, will have their own interpretations of the text. For example, comments by some group members might encourage you to notice words, phrases, ideas, or images you have overlooked, or to reread parts of the text that you may have misunderstood.

When a group of students read the poem "Family Group" they wrote down reactions to their first reading (see below). Notice how new questions and layers of meaning emerge as the discussion progresses.

STUDENT SAMPLE: GROUP DISCUSSION

COMMENTS FROM A COLLABORATIVE DISCUSSION
ON "FAMILY GROUP"

- Some of us think that the poet is the speaker. The poet and speaker are not necessarily the same person, are they?
- Who and how old is the speaker? Is she another mother? Another teenager?
- How can spring have "a hard birth"? Is there another "hard birth" in this poem?

- Do the phrases "not a day older" and "a year younger" just indicate the characters' ages? Why are the phrases contrasted? Does the wording add another dimension to the poem?
- What is the meaning of the word pathos?
- I noticed an example of personification in the second last line. Life is personified.
- I'm not sure that the title really captures what this poem is about.
- This poem is about loss of innocence, you know, like Ralph's weeping at the end of <u>Lord of the Flies</u>. Remember that? Anyone agree or disagree with me?

Activities

Working in Groups

1. After you and a classmate have had an opportunity to write journal responses to a selection of writing, read and discuss each other's journal entries. Try to work with a classmate who is likely to have different views on the text so that each of you can practise listening attentively and responding tactfully to opposing viewpoints.

2. Choose a literary work you have recently read. Bring copies of the selection to class and be prepared to lead a group discussion about what you think is the most important or interesting episode in this work.

3. Participate in a bulletin board/Web conference in which you post personal responses to a literary work. Respond at least three times to posts from others on the Web.

The Second Reading and Second Journal Response

LEARNING FOCUS
- read closely to support your interpretations and responses
- gain a deeper understanding of the text
- move from a personal to a critical response

A *second reading* is a closer, more precise reading than the first, and involves additional questioning and more careful **note making** or **note taking** (see Chapter 1). This is especially true for poetry. Since poetry tends to compress a great deal of meaning into comparatively few words, it often requires more concentration, discussion, and rereading than other genres.

Sometimes a second reading will confirm exactly what you thought originally. At other times, it will make you re-think all or parts of the text.

During a first reading of a literary work, your interpretation is influenced by having read only *part* of the text. But in a second reading, your interpretation is influenced by the *whole* text, because you are now aware of what is to come.

A *second journal response* synthesizes insights gained from first and second readings and follow-up group discussions. You move toward a more **critical response**, as opposed to the **personal response** found in your first journal entry. For literature responses, there is also a more detailed interpretation of theme, character, setting, and of the elements of style and genre.

Read the second journal entry that follows the poem "Family Group." It was written after the student had completed her first journal entry (see page 52), and had participated in a group discussion on the poem. In this excerpt from the second journal entry, the student is discussing the theme of the poem. Note how it presents a more analytical interpretation of the work than was shown in her first journal response.

STUDENT SAMPLE: CRITICAL JOURNAL RESPONSE

Here the student is providing a detailed interpretation of the poem's theme.

The theme of a literary work is its central idea or insight. It is the unifying generalization about life, either stated or implied. Kay Smith in "Family Group" presents a theme that speaks to the reader's emotions and intellect.

The reader feels sympathy for this young couple as they try to cope with the burden of a new baby. In her word choice, the poet emphasizes how little they have: "faded jeans," "too thin a coat for the still winter weather," "a paper bag of groceries." The reader instinctively wishes that the couple had not gotten themselves into this situation and that there was a way to offer some support. This description of the family group at the bus stop jolts the reader to reflect on life and the consequences of one's actions.

Note the in-depth references to specific lines of the poem.

The student provides unique insight into the title's significance.

Caring for and supporting a family is challenging even in the best of times; however, supporting a family when a couple is very young and very poor can be daunting. The poem has a mood of despair but there is a glimmer of hope in the title: "Family Group" speaks of togetherness, it speaks of unity. This couple is stronger together than they would be as individuals in this situation. Their support for each other now may be their only chance....

More precise questions should be answered in a second journal entry. Use the chart below as a guide for your journal writing. Although these questions relate primarily to fictional works, they can be used when writing about non-fiction as well.

WRITING A SECOND JOURNAL ENTRY

Questions on Main Idea and Theme
- Does the title summarize or even hint at the meaning of the work?
- What universal questions does the selection raise?
- Are there recurring images that add to the reader's understanding of the theme?
- Is there a line in the text that best summarizes the author's central insight?

Questions on Plot
- What are the main conflicts evident in this selection?
- What methods does the writer use to arouse the reader's curiosity or to build suspense?
- Is there a solution to the problem?

Questions on Setting
- Is the work set in a specific time and place?
- Is there a predominant atmosphere?
- Is the setting appropriate and does it help reinforce the theme?

Questions on Character
- Does the main character change at any point?
- Are the characters realistic or are they stereotyped?
- To what extent do we learn about the inner life or psychology of the characters?

- What role does the main character(s) or minor character(s) play?

Questions on Genre and Form
- What can you say about the genre the writer has chosen?
- If the selection is a poem, does the poet use a conventional form or is the poem written in free verse?
- Does the form and organization of the poem help the poet convey the theme?

Questions on Style
- Does the writer use imagery (sight, sound, touch, taste, smell) effectively?
- How effective is the writer's use of figurative language?
- Is there variety in sentence structure and length?
- In a prose selection, how do the length of the sentences and paragraphs affect the pace of the text?
- In poetry, how do the length of the lines and use of rhythm and rhyme affect the meaning of the text?
- To what extent and to what effect is dialogue used?
- How does the writer use effective word choice and punctuation to convey the theme?

Activities

Second Journal Response

1. Read the prose selection "Anne Frank's Fear" (see page 58). This piece was found in a notebook of Anne's writing along with her famous diary. Although it is in diary form, it is actually a short story.
   - Write a first journal entry giving a personal reaction to the text.
   - Share your initial journal entry with a partner or a small group to compare first reactions to the selection.

- After the group discussion, write a second journal entry. Analyze the selection in more detail in terms of the questions posed in the chart on page 57.

READING SELECTION: DIARY ENTRY

Anne Frank's Fear
by Anne Frank (from Tales of the Secret Annex*)*

March 25, 1944

It was a terrible time through which I was living. The war raged about us, and nobody knew whether or not he would be alive the next hour. My parents, brothers, sisters, and I made our home in the city, but we expected that we either would be evacuated or have to escape in some other way. By day the sound of cannon and rifle shots was almost continuous, and the nights were mysteriously filled with sparks and sudden explosions that seemed to come from some unknown depths.

I cannot describe it; I don't remember that tumult quite clearly, but I do know that all day long I was in the grip of fear. My parents tried everything to calm me, but it didn't help. I felt nothing, nothing but fear; I could neither eat nor sleep—fear clawed at my mind and body and shook me. That lasted for about a week; then came an evening and a night which I recall as though it had been yesterday.

At half past eight, when the shooting had somewhat died down, I lay in a sort of half doze on a sofa. Suddenly, all of us were startled by two violent explosions. As though stuck with knives, we all jumped up and ran into the hall. Even Mother, usually so calm, looked pale. The explosions repeated themselves at pretty regular intervals. Then, a tremendous crash, the noise of much breaking glass, and an ear-splitting chorus of yelling and screaming. I put on what heavy clothes I could find in a hurry, threw some things into a rucksack, and ran. I ran as fast as I could, ran on and on to get away from the fiercely burning mass about me. Everywhere shouting people darted to and fro; the street was alight with a fearsome red glow.

I didn't think of my parents or of my brothers and sisters. I had thoughts only for myself and knew that I must rush, rush, rush! I didn't feel any fatigue; my fear was too strong. I didn't know that I had lost my rucksack. All I felt and knew was that I had to run.

I couldn't possibly say how long I ran on with the image of the burning houses, the desperate people, and their distorted faces before me. Then I sensed that it had got more quiet. I looked around and, as if waking up from a nightmare, I saw that there was nothing or no one behind me. No fire, no bombs, no people. I looked a little more closely and found that I stood in a meadow. Above me the stars glistened and the moon shone; it was brilliant weather, crisp but not cold. I didn't hear a sound. Exhausted, I sat down on the grass, then spread the blanket I had been carrying on my arm, and stretched out on it.

I looked up into the sky and realized that I was no longer afraid; on the contrary, I felt very peaceful inside. The funny thing was that I didn't think of my family, nor yearn for them; I yearned only for rest, and it wasn't long before I fell asleep there in the grass, under the sky.

When I woke up the sun was just rising. I immediately knew where I was; in the daylight I recognized the houses at the outskirts of our city. I rubbed my eyes and had a good look around. There was no one to be seen; the dandelions and the clover-leaves in the grass were my only company. Lying back on the blanket for a while, I mused about what to do next. But my thoughts wandered off from the subject and returned to the wonderful feeling of the night before, when I sat in the grass and was no longer afraid.

Later I found my parents, and together we moved to another town. Now that the war is over, I know why my fear disappeared under the wide, wide heavens. When I was alone with nature, I realized—realized without actually knowing it—that fear is a sickness for which there is only one remedy. Anyone who is as afraid as I was then, should look at nature and see that God is much closer than most people think.

Since that time I have never been afraid again, no matter how many bombs fell near me.

2. As part of a **jigsaw** assignment, form small home groups of four to five students to discuss a literary work. One individual from each home group will form expert groups to focus on a different character from a novel or a play:
   - Choose a character from the beginning of a novel or play you have read and follow him or her throughout the text.
   - Note essential details about this character (actions, beliefs, motivations, changes, relationships, etc.).

When each expert group has completed the analysis of its chosen character, group members should return to their home groups to share what they have learned with each other.

3. As a group, construct a **phrase collage** (a group of words, quotations, and visuals) from a literary text. After rereading the text, select fifteen to twenty quotations that seem memorable to members of the group. These quotes can be typed in a large font and arranged on a class bulletin board, accompanied by appropriate graphics. Make an oral presentation to the class explaining why group members felt that these quotations and visuals were especially memorable.

The Writing Process

When writing a response journal (a form of **expressive writing**), particularly a first journal entry, you are concerned primarily with exploring and recording personal observations and reactions to the selection. Revising and editing are usually not a priority at this stage.

The second journal entry, however, involves analysis and interpretation. Here the writer has to develop a first draft, work in ideas and details from the selection, and ensure that the opening paragraph identifies the focus of the analysis. Careful review of this first draft will be necessary, especially if it is to be shared with an audience. For any writer, moving beyond a first draft requires systematic attention to the writing process.

Stages in the Writing Process

The process of writing varies for each individual who sets pen to paper or faces a blank computer screen. Although there is no set recipe, there are standard stages that writers go through to produce a successful result. As a high school student, you should proceed carefully through the various stages of the writing process. As you gain experience and confidence as a writer, you may find that you use a less sequential approach. You may go through only the stages relevant to your particular writing assignment, you may combine stages, you may even temporarily skip a stage and return to it later. For now, though, follow the stages of the writing process in the order presented below.

LEARNING FOCUS
- review the stages in the writing process
- review and practise various strategies appropriate to each stage
- write to analyze ideas and information

PREWRITING At this thinking and planning stage, do the following:

- Decide on a subject.
- Take into consideration the interests of your audience.

- Limit the focus of your subject so that it is not too broad.
- Formulate a tentative thesis statement.
- Generate ideas for a subject.

You can engage in prewriting in a number of ways: brainstorming; reading books, magazines, and newspapers; searching the Internet; talking with peers; recording first-hand observations and experiences.

It may be useful to structure the ideas arising from your prewriting activities by using a **graphic organizer**. A student planning an assignment on Margaret Laurence's novel *The Stone Angel*, for example, might use a **cluster chart** such as the one below to group together words and ideas related to the main topic of *tragedy*.

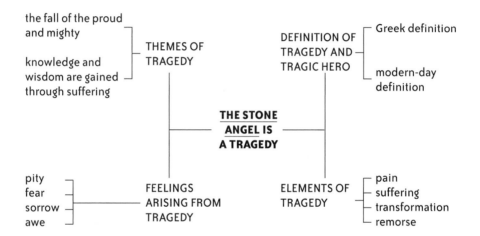

DRAFTING/COMPOSING Use the ideas generated in the prewriting stage to compose a first draft. Drafting involves selecting words, composing sentences, developing paragraphs, exploring questions, connecting ideas, and experimenting with meaning. It also involves discovering your own personal **style** and **voice**. The process of composing the first draft usually helps you clarify and expand on your preliminary ideas.

Your introductory paragraph *sets the scene* for what comes later. Get the reader's attention from the start through a thought-provoking question, a personal **anecdote**, or anything else that is consistent with the point of view or personality you wish to project in your writing. This is where you need to state your thesis and establish an organizational pattern for what comes later.

REVISING Now you must bring focus and clarity to your first draft by rethinking what you have written. Add concrete details and examples to your draft and eliminate anything that is unnecessary.

Successful paragraphs have three main characteristics: **unity, co-herence**, and **emphasis**. *Unity* means that the paragraph contains only what is relevant to the topic. Everything else should be omitted. As you write and revise, ask yourself, "Is this fact, idea, or statement pertinent to my topic?" *Coherence* refers to the logical arrangement and progression of ideas within a paragraph. Writers achieve coherence by presenting their ideas in a proper sequence and by using transition or connective words to show clearly how ideas follow from one another. *Emphasis* means that specific elements and key ideas stand out in some way, perhaps through **parallelism** in grammatical structure.

 CHECKLIST REVISING

✓ Provide a forceful topic sentence and a strong conclusion.
✓ Substitute more effective words and appropriate diction as needed.
✓ Rearrange sentences in a logical sequence.
✓ Add supporting details and examples relevant to the topic (unity).
✓ Remove redundant, unrelated, and unnecessary details.
✓ Replace clichéd, vague, or monotonous passages.
✓ Provide smooth connections within and between paragraphs (coherence).
✓ Use purposeful repetition of words, synonyms, grammatical structure (emphasis).

EDITING/PROOFREADING Editing requires a positive mindset. You have to *want* to find errors in style and structure. It involves clarifying your written draft and cutting words and whole sentences where necessary. It requires a thorough checking of spelling, grammar, **usage**, and formatting. It also involves proofreading to ensure that you have a final draft suitable for publication.

 CHECKLIST EFFECTIVE EDITING

✓ Use a dictionary, a spell checker, a thesaurus, and a style guide.
✓ Read your writing aloud or silently to check for proper grammar, punctuation, and fluency.
✓ Exchange your writing with a classmate to review each other's work for errors.
✓ Know when to say, "I've done my best—this is enough."

The paragraphs below are part of a student essay on the topic "Reducing Stress." Note the editing changes made by the student on the sample itself. Additional suggestions for revision, made by the teacher, will help the student to create a final draft.

STUDENT SAMPLE: EDITING

to overcome stress

One of the most important ways would have to be exercise. The trick is to do a complete body workout at least once a day. This may include push-ups, different types of crunchs, weight lifting, jogging, etc. This is an excellant way to relieve tension and the best way to take out agression when angry. Without tension and anger it's difficult to be stressed out.

Staying organized and focused is

Another method that helps me reduce stress is staying organized and focused. I always stay on top of my assignments, never miss my math homework, and am always prepared for tests. There's nothing worst then when you completely forget about an assignment until the night before. You end up either staying up all night, and it usually ends up being garbage, or just getting zero. Also, when you go to a class and realize you have a test when you didn't study, you sometimes feel like panicing! The trick is to never let this happen. Stay focused and organized with your school work. Its really not that hard.

attend to

e *than*

completely forgetting

completing a poor assignment

k

Avoid use of *etc.* except in parentheses. The final (clincher) sentence of this paragraph should focus on the word "exercise" to help with paragraph unity.

Try reversing the wording at the start of this paragraph (e.g., "Staying organized and focused is another method that helps reduce stress."). It sounds less mechanical.

Re-emphasize in the closing sentence that this technique is effective in reducing stress.

PUBLISHING Publishing means *making public*. This takes place when you:

- Share your writing with your teacher and peers during a writer's conference to help you decide which selections to put before a larger audience.
- Produce writing products such as essays, school newspapers, and magazines.
- Organize a **reading circle** that meets periodically to share writings.
- Submit your work to local newspapers or literary magazines.
- Enter your work in writing competitions.

- **E-mail** your work to friends and acquaintances or to *writers-in-residence* on the Internet.
- Post your writing on creative-writing Web sites and in **e-zines**.

   (See Appendix A for additional information on the writing process and assessment criteria.)

Activities

Following the Stages of the Writing Process

Complete a short writing assignment, using the following statement to get you started: "The twenty-first century is an era of opportunity." Incorporate the stages of the writing process discussed in this section. When you submit your assignment, attach the following:

- a cluster chart you used to record brainstorming ideas during prewriting.
- your first draft with handwritten notes showing evidence of revising and editing.

The Writing Product (The Essay)

An **essay** (from the French *essayer*, meaning *to try*) is a composition discussing a topic in either an informal or formal style. This is the prose form in which you will be asked to write most frequently.

   A well-written essay

- has a purpose (to entertain, to inform, to analyze, to problem-solve, to convince).
- considers a defined audience (in terms of age, education level, etc.).
- has a specific structure and organization.
- requires unity and coherence of ideas.
- has a definite **style** (personal and informal, or objective and more formal).
- employs words appropriate to the audience and purpose.
- provides a strong introduction to catch the reader's attention.
- develops ideas in an orderly sequence with well-supported evidence.
- leads the reader to a logical conclusion that summarizes the main ideas.

   An essay may involve **expository writing**, where the writer explains a subject using logical reasoning and examples to develop ideas. It may use **persuasive writing**, with sound evidence and appeals to the emotions to convince the reader to adopt a particular point of view or take specific action. Or it may entail **descriptive** or **narrative writing**, as you will see in Chapter 3.

Methods of Essay Development

LEARNING FOCUS
- review various methods of essay development
- select appropriate organizing structures
- organize information to clarify thinking and improve communication

Effective essay development requires sufficient elaboration and enough concrete evidence, detail, and explanation of facts to support your thesis statement. The way you develop your information and ideas will depend on your subject and how well you know it. It will also depend on your audience and purpose for writing the essay. Common strategies of development are presented below:

DEFINITION This method of development answers the question "What is it?" Writers develop paragraphs and essays by definition to explain an important word or term. When using this form of development, make sure you select a concept that is complex enough to *justify* thorough analysis. You will need to do some creative exploration as you consider how to define the topic for your reader.

Textbooks for science and the social sciences frequently provide precise definitions of terms such as *biomass, psychometry,* or *photosynthesis.* English reference texts may define literary devices like *paradox, pun,* and *hyperbole.*

EXAMPLE AND ILLUSTRATION This method answers the question "For example?" to clarify an idea. Writers (see David Suzuki's essay on pages 70–72) use examples to support a thesis or to make the subject more interesting. A carefully chosen example makes the idea real and relevant to the reader.

STUDENT SAMPLE: EXAMPLE

(as seen in *The Stone Angel* by Margaret Laurence)

Hagar, for the most part, thinks highly of herself. In addition, she is by no means prepared to bare all, or to risk the possibility of looking weak or merely "average" in the eyes of others. The following example illustrates this proud arrogance. Hagar realizes that she has no actual savings of her own, only what has been scraped together throughout her marriage. In the pursuit of a means of employment, she stumbles upon her step-daughter, Jessie, who suggests selling eggs door-to-door. The proud Hagar gives the appearance of being revolted by such a prospect. "I sniffed and gave her to believe it was beneath me, for she was a slovenly creature, that Jessie" (126).

CLASSIFICATION AND DIVISION This method of development uses precise definitions and explanations to show the relationships between concepts or ideas. It answers the question "What kind is it?" or "What parts make up the whole?" In an essay on literary genres, for example, a student may structure information by category, such as the short story, the novel, poetry, drama and so on. By classifying and dividing, writers are able to break down and explain complex ideas.

COMPARISON OR CONTRAST Here the reader's attention is directed to similarities and differences. This method answers the question "How are two or more things alike or not alike?" In *comparison*, similarities are carefully established and developed. In *contrast*, the differences between the two things are emphasized. If a writer wanted to discuss the elements of fiction (plot, setting, character, theme) in two novels, he or she could discuss separately the elements in one novel, then move to a discussion of the second text. This would require the reader to draw conclusions about comparison and contrast in the novels. A more integrated method of comparison or contrast could be achieved if the plot, for example, were thoroughly analyzed before moving to a discussion of setting, character, and theme in both texts.

CAUSE AND EFFECT Here the interdependence of events is analyzed. This method answers the questions, "Why did it happen?" (causes) and "What were the results of this occurrence?" (effects). It may include such *cause* words as *because* or *since* as well as *effect* words like *therefore* or *consequently*. As curious human beings, we want to know why something turned out successfully or why things went wrong.

STUDENT SAMPLE: CAUSE AND EFFECT

Communities today take pride in having clean streets and walking trails that are free from litter. Every spring there are organized cleanups of local lakes and rivers, as well as of the city itself. Some cities promote "clean and beautiful" campaigns that encourage community groups to clean up their local neighbourhoods each spring. As well, there are many sponsored cleanups of local schools and community parks. Because of this increased interest in our surroundings, many people are beginning to give the environment the respect it deserves.

Cause-and-effect reasoning is a major way of thinking and organizing essays. When you are determining causes for particular situations it is important to research all possible causes and consider all conceivable effects. You need to select the most significant causes and arrange them in a logical order, remembering that a particular event might have multiple causes and, in turn, result in multiple effects.

PROCESS ANALYSIS This method of development involves sequential (often chronological) ordering of information. It answers the question "How does it work?" (for example, instructions or directions) or "How did it happen?" or both. A process follows a logical sequence of steps (e.g., the writing process). Analysis involves taking a subject apart and explaining its components in order to understand the relationship between the whole and its parts. There are many examples of process analysis in science textbooks and how-to manuals (e.g., how to build a birdhouse, the use and care of a microscope, how to create a safe laboratory environment). Later in this chapter you will be taken through the process of preparing a research essay.

NARRATION AND DESCRIPTION *Narration* involves telling a story, while *description*, closely linked, involves creating a mental picture of a subject. The author provides sensory details that enable readers to see, hear, touch, smell, and taste an experience in their imagination. Writers of narration and description, like reporters, must be good observers who can recreate scenes of people, places, action, and dialogue in vivid detail. Writers of exposition, argumentation, and persuasion often use narration in the form of short anecdotes as well as descriptions to illustrate a particular thesis.

Activities

Methods of Development

1. As you read newspapers, magazines, and textbooks, find paragraphs or essays that show writers using various methods of development to support their thesis statement and ideas. Bring these examples to class to share with your teachers and peers.

2. Write a 300–500 word expository essay on any of the following topics, using the method of development suggested for each.
   - The number of students dropping out of high school is a major concern for young people, educators, parents, and society at large. In an essay, examine what you consider to be the main causes and the main effects of the dropout problem. (Cause and Effect)
   - There are many types (genres) of movies available both at cinemas and on videocassette: romance, action, and comedy are examples. Classify the different types and discuss the characteristics of each. You may want to conclude by focusing on your favourite type of movie. (Classification and Division)
   - There are both similarities and differences in the experiences of attending school in your land of birth, and of being a student in a country you have immigrated to. Compare the two experiences; then contrast them. (Comparison and Contrast)
   - Most schools like to boast about their high level of school spirit. Such school spirit develops as a result of many different factors: quality of academic programs, student–teacher relationships, the co-curricular program, and so on. In an essay, explain the process a student council might follow to develop good school spirit. (Process Analysis)
   - Life in Canada during the winter can be difficult, but many people seem to really enjoy it. Using examples and illustrations, show that many Canadians get pleasure from such a harsh climate. (Example and Illustration)

The Personal Essay

The **personal essay** tends to be informal in style, written in the first person, and subjective in tone. Newspapers and magazines, in their regularly featured **columns**, provide a forum for this kind of essay. A personal essay often contains background information, examples, and anecdotes to make the treatment of subject matter unique,

LEARNING FOCUS

- understand the characteristics of a personal essay
- create an effective introduction, body, and conclusion for your essay
- use the characteristics of an effective personal essay in your writing

interesting, and clear. The writer of the personal essay is a lot like a letter writer, communicating ideas, interests, and personality to an acquaintance. However, the essay is an open letter, not just to one person, but to the world at large.

Most personal essays have a traditional essay structure with an introduction, body, and conclusion, as you can see in the student and professional models below.

STUDENT SAMPLE: PERSONAL ESSAY

This is an effective, thought-provoking title.

Does the phrase "remember to forget" work in this sentence? Would "choose to forget" be more appropriate wording here?

This introduction gives the thesis statement and expands on it by giving reasons for the lack of respect.

The writer uses personal experience narrative and actual dialogue to make a point.

In the body of the essay, examples are provided to develop the thesis statement more fully.

Lest we forget what we are to remember...

...those who gave their souls, both in life and death.

When we look at those who remain from this noble generation, it seems that we no longer remember to honour, but rather remember to forget.

With veterans dying off at a rapidly increasing rate and the last two generations having been saved from the experiences of war, it has evidently become easier for young people to turn a blind eye on the occasion of Remembrance Day. We lack knowledge, and this leads to a loss of respect. Nobody seems to realize exactly what we are remembering anymore!

I walk down the halls of my school on the eve of Remembrance Day, preparing for a special ceremony to honour all veterans of war. Around me are the sounds of apathetic teens. There are those who ask, "What difference does it make if I go to a Remembrance Day ceremony in my school gym or not?" I reply by saying that it's respectful to go and honour those who died in war. What is their response? "What does it matter to us? They're dead!" There are those who enjoy Remembrance Day simply because they get the day off school, but they don't care why. Again, I have to ask myself, why is it that everyone chooses to forget?

It shouldn't take having another war for our generation to realize just how lucky we are not to know the horrors it brings. So long as we have the privilege of living with the freedom we so readily take for granted, we should be willing to take a meagre two minutes out of our day to reflect on the past. It doesn't take much more than that to pay respect to those who died so that we could live our lives without fear. We should also take the time to really look at those veterans in uniform standing at war memorials on Remembrance Day, and actually think hard about what it was they did for us. We need to try and understand what they saw and lived through, and realize that even though they survived where others did not, this doesn't mean they are any less injured. Now they live with memories of having watched good friends die or of narrowly escaping death themselves. Our minds cannot even begin to conceive what that must be like but that does not mean we should deny that it's there. Our veterans live with those tormenting memories so that we will never have to. They voluntarily helped countries in need, in the name of Canada, making us recognized around the world. Those few who remain—they continue to remember, while we begin to forget.

Though I have no family connection with anyone who fought in the wars, I will continue to pay homage to those who did. For it doesn't take much to see just how important a difference they made, if only you stop and take the time to think.

So as we take this day off, relaxing in the comforts we take for granted, I can only pray that the wars we are beginning to forget have managed to teach us something. Let us not let those who paid for our freedom with their lives die in vain.

Could the last two paragraphs be combined as a concluding paragraph and linked more closely to the opening statements of the essay?

MODEL: PERSONAL ESSAY

The title gives the topic to be discussed and draws the interest of the reader.

The introduction provides the thesis statement.

Reconnecting with the Earth
by David Suzuki

Like the electronic "information" we consume, the sphere of our activity and of the connections that make up the little world we live in have become a collection of disconnected fragments. We consume or use with little sense of the repercussions beyond our immediate surroundings.

Life in industrialized societies has become so complex that we need specialists of all kinds—plumbers, electronic experts, muffler and brake specialists, nurses, TV repairers. Although I use a computer and drive a car, for example, I don't understand the intricacies of how they work or how to fix them when they don't.

Connective phrases such as "and so" are used to join paragraphs and give the essay coherence.

And so we tend to see the world as a mosaic of disconnected bits and pieces rather than as an integrated whole in which we understand the relationship between cause and effect. We lose sight of the fact that we are biological beings who live in a finite world where matter is endlessly recycled through biological action in air, water, and soil. And not knowing where our consumer goods come from or where they end up, it's hard to relate how we live with the environmental consequences.

In cities we place our garbage at the curb in plastic bags, cans, or boxes, and like magic, it conveniently disappears from our view and our minds. I once spent a day at a waste disposal site near Toronto, looking at what was being discarded. There were all kinds of material that didn't have to be there: grass clippings (and leaves in the fall), wood that could be chipped, paper of every conceivable type, plastic containers, metal objects. Even with Toronto's vaunted blue box program, the output of unnecessary garbage is enormous.

The personal anecdotes help to give Suzuki's writing a strong voice. The tone is consistently serious. The reader realizes Suzuki is genuinely concerned about the environmental consequences of our actions.

I thought of that dump while flying in a tiny commuter plane from Montreal to Val d'Or. During the short flight, a continental breakfast was served in a plastic case. Inside were a plastic cup of yogurt, a plastic cup of orange juice, a plastic bag containing a stirring rod, spoon and fork as well as individually wrapped sugar, cream and hand towel. Coffee was served in a foam cup. By the end of the meal, each passenger had a mound of packaging that was then swept into a plastic bag and deposited at the airport. This is repeated thousands of times daily all over the country. A visit to a dump makes you realize that we have to replace this unnecessary waste with reusable things.

A few years ago while filming an introduction to a report on the biological functions of different kinds of muscle, I used the light and dark meat of a chicken to illustrate. The lighting man exclaimed with surprise, "Is chicken meat a *muscle?*" When our food comes neatly packaged in plastic containers, the link between a piece of meat and a once-living animal becomes tenuous. But as animals ourselves, we are totally dependent on other living organisms for every bit of our nutrition. A visit to a slaughterhouse and a factory farm would be a powerful reminder of our biological roots and our need for other life-forms.

Suzuki's paragraphs provide concise, specific examples that illustrate his succinct style.

It's the same with plants. Few of us have spent any time on a farm or understand the factors that propel farmers to rely on chemicals to ensure high yields while struggling against weather, pests, and disease or the compromises that are made to enhance food's shelf life, transportability, and appearance. As soil and water accumulate pesticides, fungicides and preservatives, fruits and vegetables are bound to incorporate them. If young people spent time working on a farm, they would have a far different appreciation of the food they eat, not to mention the economic plight of farmers.

In cities and towns, we take our water and sewers for granted—just turn on the tap and out it flows. Flush the toilet or pour waste down the sink and we send it on its way without a thought about where it ends up. Yet often the water we consume is drawn downstream from someone else's effluent or from wells into which leachate from dumps is draining. Beaches that are no longer swimmable are directly related to the flushing of our toilets. Every responsible citizen should make an extensive tour of our sewer outlets and water treatment facilities to see how our activities are interconnected.

It's the same with energy. We turn our lights and machines on and off with little thought of where the energy comes from and its environmental cost. Only when there's a power failure are we aware of how dependent we are on electricity. Canadian folklore says that our great rivers and fossil fuels deposits provide a near limitless source of energy. But we are far less informed about the ecological destruction that accompanies huge hydroelectric dams or potential greenhouse warming from coal- and oil-fired plants. All we want is to be sure to have electricity at the flick of a switch.

We have to acquire a deeper understanding of the total costs of modern life in the context of a finite planet. Every benefit and convenience has hidden effects that we inflict on the environment. Children need to learn their lessons from first-hand experience at slaughterhouses, farms, factories, water sources, hydroelectric and nuclear power plants, sewage treatment facilities, garbage dumps, pulp mills, logging and reforestation areas, mining sites, et cetera. Even in the largest urban centres, we are still interconnected and dependent on our surroundings far beyond city limits.

Note how the cause-and-effect relationship is emphasized through concrete language: "flush" and "pour waste."

Suzuki begins this paragraph in almost the same way as another one. Which one? Is this purposeful or random repetition?

This persuasive essay ends on a strong note. It urges us to understand our dependence on our environment.

Activities

Focus on the Personal Essay

1. Find examples of personal essays in the writing of classmates, or in newspapers and magazines. Compose a brief summary of what you learned from the essay about the subject matter and about the personality of the essayist. Along with your classmates, list the topic and writer of the essay on the class bulletin board under the heading: "Personal Essays: A Range of Topics."

2. Listen to radio and television commentaries in which journalists or private citizens comment on topics that interest them. Identify one that strikes you as having the form of a personal essay. Request a transcript of this commentary from the radio or television station to bring to class for discussion.

3. Write a personal, informal essay communicating facts, thoughts, and feelings on a topic that is important to you. Your essay should clearly reveal your stance on the subject and something of your personality. As you write, consider your audience and purpose, your tone (humorous, serious, satiric), and specific methods of development.

Critical Writing

Many of the essays you write in school are more formal and objective than the informal style of the personal essay. They involve critical writing and often require informative, detailed treatment of the subject. For example, when preparing a report of a field trip or a visit to a community theatre production, you might use a formal essay style. When writing an analysis of a Shakespeare play or an essay for Chemistry on the topic "The Development of Artificial Rubber," you would be asked to use formal essay style.

Critical Writing for Tests and Exams

Writing on demand in response to test and examination questions is a frequent requirement in many subject areas in high school. Some of these test questions involve a response in the form of a short **critical**, or **analytical**, **essay**, with evidence of analysis, argument, or persuasion.

LEARNING FOCUS

- evaluate the effectiveness of essay answers for tests or exams
- show understanding of the characteristics of an effective essay answer

© Lynn Johnston Productions, Inc. / Distributed by United Feature Syndicate, Inc.

Examine the student response below to a question on imagery in the poem "Family Group." (See page 52.) Note how the reply shows evidence of critical thinking and analysis.

STUDENT SAMPLE: DEMAND RESPONSE

Test Question: Imagery is an important literary device in most poetry. Select two images from the poem "Family Group" and discuss the effectiveness of each.

This student identifies the imagery and shows how it is used effectively to appeal to the senses.

Test Response:
Imagery is quite predominant in the poem "Family Group." An image is when words or phrases are used to create a mental picture in the reader that appeals to one or more of the senses. One example of an image is "…in her arms a crying infant, the blanket worn from many washings." This phrase creates a mental picture: a small weak baby with disheveled hair, crying pitifully from within the confines of a small, ragged blanket, worn thin and faded with

The analysis is detailed and illustrated by carefully chosen examples.

age. This powerful image appeals to our sense of sight as we see this group in our mind. As well, it appeals to our sense of hearing, for we can hear the child's forlorn cries. These images contribute to the mood, creating a portrait of a sad, struggling family. The imagery also contributes to the theme, or main idea, showing how the impatience and rush of growing up and having a family before one is ready only leads to unhappiness and suffering for everyone.

Each image is discussed in a separate paragraph. The student explains how imagery is used in the poem to create mood and convey theme.

Another example of an image is "wearing too thin a coat for the wintry weather." This image creates a picture of a young woman, still in her teens, grasping a thin, worn coat tightly to her body. You can almost feel the chill of this young woman as she desperately tries to find warmth on a cold spring day. This image also effectively conveys the mood of the poem, because we can feel the sadness of the situation. The images support the main idea of the poem because they accentuate the fact that there is a time to grow up, and rushing into adulthood before we are ready leads to hopeless consequences.

Critical Writing and Literary Analysis

A critical essay can take the form of **literary analysis** when it provides a thorough interpretation of a literary work. This kind of critical response requires specific (quoted) references to plot, character, and setting to support and develop a thesis statement. Value judgments and generalizations about the literary work cannot be convincing without adequate evidence.

Sometimes you will be given a few class periods (rather than the **demand writing** of a timed test) to respond to a piece of literature. Review the chart below before writing your next literary analysis.

LEARNING FOCUS

- understand the characteristics of an effective literary analysis
- select and use evidence from a text to support a literary analysis
- write an effective literary analysis

WRITING A LITERARY ANALYSIS	
Key Questions	**How to Address the Key Questions**
• What is the poem or prose selection about?	• Provide the name of the selection. • Include a brief summary to acquaint the reader with the text. • Give a personal reaction from a first reading. • Search your memory for experiences in your own life that have some parallel to what you have read. • Identify the theme if it is clear.
• What can be said about the poet's or author's style?	• Identify the denotative and connotative meaning of selected words. • Determine whether there is a distinctive voice. • Note the punctuation used in the piece. • Explain how figurative language (e.g., **simile**, **metaphor**, **personification**) is used to convey the sights, sounds, smells, and tastes the writer experiences.

WRITING A LITERARY ANALYSIS (CONTINUED)	
Key Questions	**How to Address the Key Questions**
• What can be said about the poet's or author's style?	• Show awareness of the writer's use of **irony**, symbols, or **allusions**, if these exist. • For poetry, examine the contribution of **rhythm** and **rhyme**.
• What form does the text take?	• Identify the genre used. • For poetry, consider the organizational pattern (form) of the poem. • For prose, examine specific writing structure (expository, narrative, descriptive) of the paragraphs. • Discuss the form in terms of its unity of thought, expression, coherence, and emphasis.

Read the poem "Ulysses" below, written in the form of a **dramatic monologue** in which the central character, Ulysses, is addressing silent listeners (his fellow seafarers). Then read the literary analysis that follows, and note how the student has addressed the key questions from the chart above.

READING SELECTION: POEM

Ulysses
by Alfred, Lord Tennyson

It little profits that an idle king,
By this still hearth, among these barren crags,
Match'd with an aged wife, I mete and dole
Unequal laws unto a savage race,
That hoard, and sleep, and feed, and know not me.
I cannot rest from travel: I will drink
Life to the lees; all times I have enjoy'd
Greatly, have suffer'd greatly, both with those
That loved me, and alone; on shore, and when
Thro' scudding drifts the rainy Hyades
Vext the dim sea: I am become a name;
For always roaming with a hungry heart
Much have I seen and known; cities of men
And manners, climates, councils, governments,

Myself not least, but honour'd of them all;
And drunk delight of battle with my peers,
Far on the ringing plains of windy Troy.
I am a part of all that I have met;
Yet all experience is an arch wherethro'
Gleams that untravell'd world, whose margin fades
For ever and for ever when I move.
How dull it is to pause, to make an end,
To rust unburnish'd, not to shine in use!
As tho' to breathe were life. Life piled on life
Were all too little, and of one to me
Little remains: but every hour is saved
From that eternal silence, something more,
A bringer of new things; and vile it were
For some three suns to store and hoard myself,
And this grey spirit yearning in desire
To follow knowledge, like a sinking star
Beyond the utmost bound of human thought.

     This is my son, mine own Telemachus,
To whom I leave the sceptre and the isle—
Well-loved of me, discerning to fulfill
This labour, by slow prudence to make mild
A rugged people, and thro' soft degrees
Subdue them to the useful and the good.
Most blameless is he, centred in the sphere
Of common duties, decent not to fail
In offices of tenderness, and pay
Meet adoration to my household gods,
When I am gone. He works his work, I mine.

     There lies the port: the vessel puffs her sail:
There gloom the dark broad seas. My mariners,
Souls that have toil'd and wrought and thought with
     me—
That ever with a frolic welcome took
The thunder and the sunshine, and opposed
Free hearts, free foreheads—you and I are old;
Old age hath yet his honour and his toil;
Death closes all; but something ere the end,
Some work of noble note, may yet be done,
Not unbecoming men that strove with Gods.

The lights begin to twinkle from the rocks:
The long day wanes: the slow moon climbs: the deep
Moans round with many voices. Come, my friends,
'Tis not too late to seek a newer world.
Push off, and, sitting well in order smite
The sounding furrows; for my purpose holds
To sail beyond the sunset, and the baths
Of all the western stars, until I die.
It may be that the gulfs will wash us down:
It may be we shall touch the Happy Isles,
And see the great Achilles whom we knew.
Tho' much is taken, much abides; and tho'
We are not now that strength which in old days
Moved earth and heaven; that which we are, we are;
One equal temper of heroic hearts,
Made weak by time and fate, but strong in will
To strive, to seek, to find, and not to yield.

STUDENT SAMPLE: LITERARY ANALYSIS

The student begins by answering the key question of what is happening in the poem (literal meaning).

The poem "Ulysses" by Alfred, Lord Tennyson tells the story of Ulysses (his Greek name was Odysseus), who had been away from his home kingdom for many years fighting "far on the ringing plains of windy Troy" (line 17). When Ulysses comes back home to his wife and son Telemachus, he is not content to pass laws and rule a people that "know not me" (line 5). This poem is told from Ulysses' point of view. It is like a **soliloquy** because we seem to get his inner thoughts as he talks to his fellow seafarers about their adventures in the past.

> Much have I seen and known; cities of men
> And manners, climates, councils, governments…
>
> (lines 13–14)

Two quotes are used to illustrate the student's understanding of point of view and of the thoughts expressed in the poem.

Ulysses tells of his desire to travel even more:

> I cannot rest from travel: I will drink
> Life to the lees
>
> (lines 6–7)

The focus is on the theme of the poem. This is effectively supported by specific examples.

This line suggests that Ulysses intends to get every drop of substance and experience from life before it is too late. This in part is the theme of this poem—the human desire to go where no one has gone before, to experience the "frolic" of adventure before we are too old. The mood of this poem is one of optimism and hope. Ulysses is an adventurer who has a wanderlust and a yearning for the excitement of faraway places. He is courageous, as well, willing to challenge the unknown, "the dark broad seas" (line 45). Ulysses wants to be on the move. He says:

> How dull it is to pause, to make an end,
> To rust unburnish'd, not to shine in use!
>
> (lines 22–23)

In the above **metaphor**, Ulysses is saying that we are not made to vegetate, "to rust," like an old knife or sword. He says to his friends, "Come… / 'Tis not too late to seek a newer world."

> (lines 57–58)

Ulysses is contrasted with his son Telemachus, who seems a more practical person, more of a realist, than his father. Telemachus is content to stay at home and do those day-to-day, mundane, "common duties" of ruling his "rugged" subjects. Ulysses says of his son, "He works his work, I mine."

> (line 43)

A discussion is provided on the poet's style, his use of metaphor, simile, and contrast. The student both identifies the figurative language and interprets its use for the reader.

This poem contains many figures of speech, metaphors and **similes**, comparisons that help us to understand the character of Ulysses. For example, he says, "I will drink / Life to the lees" (lines 6–7). This metaphor compares life to a drink that must be completely consumed to the last drop.

Later in the poem Ulysses says his purpose is "to follow knowledge, like a sinking star" (line 31). This simile shows Ulysses' desire to see all things, know all things, before he dies. There is a sense of urgency expressed in this simile.

The student concludes by noting the device of repetition. This observation reveals his insight into the character of Ulysses.

Finally, the repetition of verbs in the last line of the poem is effective. It emphasizes Ulysses' desire never "to yield," never "to rust," never to give up.

Activities

Literary Analysis

1. In small groups reread both the poem "Ulysses" and the literary analysis that follows it. Using the "Writing a Literary Analysis" chart on pages 75–76 to help you, evaluate the student analysis. Discuss the points you might add or change in your own analysis of the same poem.

2. Read the poem below. Write a literary analysis to provide a thorough interpretation of the work. Use the questions in the chart to guide your analysis of the poem.

READING SELECTION: POEM

Where There's a Wall
by Joy Kogawa

Where there's a wall
there's a way through a
gate or door. There's even
a ladder perhaps and a
sentinel who sometimes sleeps.
There are secret passwords you
can overhear. There are methods
of torture for extracting clues
to maps of underground passages.
There are zeppelins, helicopters,
rockets, bombs, battering rams,
armies with trumpets whose
all at once blast shatters
the foundations.

Where there's a wall there are
words to whisper by loose bricks,
wailing prayers to utter, birds
to carry messages taped to their feet.
There are letters to be written—
poems even.

Faint as in a dream
is the voice that calls
from the belly
of the wall.

3. Joy Kogawa was born in Vancouver. After the Japanese bombed Pearl Harbor in 1941, she and her family, along with other Japanese Canadians, were separated from their homes and possessions and sent to internment camps in British Columbia and Alberta. Complete some research, using the library and the Internet, on the experience of Japanese Canadians during World War II. Present your findings to the class.

Critical Writing as Short Reports and Reviews

LEARNING FOCUS
- understand the characteristics of an effective report or review
- respond personally and critically to a play or film
- write a play or film review

A **report** is a short critical essay. It is a means of informing other people, either orally or in writing, about something you have experienced directly, through reading, viewing, or listening. The report could be based, for example, on an account of a field trip, a science experiment, or a movie.

✔ CHECKLIST | WRITING A SHORT REPORT

✓ Do any required reading or research in advance so that you are familiar with the subject.
✓ Make detailed in-process notes to aid with report writing.
✓ Organize material into a unified and coherent form.
✓ Ensure content is factually accurate.
✓ Ensure content is grammatically correct.

WRITING A THEATRE REVIEW A common kind of report you will be asked to write in high school is the **review**. The purpose of a review is to provide an opinion about the quality of a piece of work. You may, for example, attend a theatre performance put on by your local high school or a community group. In your review you should provide a brief **synopsis** of the plot (the theatre program or promotional poster can help) and classify the play (tragedy, comedy, etc.). The program will also provide the name of the actors and perhaps a brief biography of the playwright. In addition, it might contain photographs from the play that you can include in your review.

✓ CHECKLIST | WRITING A THEATRE REVIEW

- ✓ Read the script of the play before seeing the production.
- ✓ Consider how the production compares with the original script.
- ✓ Mention where and when the play was performed.
- ✓ Examine the presentation of characters, conflict, and theme.
- ✓ Comment on the quality of the acting, set design, lighting, and directing.
- ✓ Analyze audience response to the production.
- ✓ Write out your notes as soon as possible, while the details are still fresh in your mind.
- ✓ Shape your review to suit your audience.
- ✓ Consider any space and time limitations (e.g., set by school, community newspaper, or local radio or television station).

Below is a student review of a high school production of *An Enemy of the People* by Henrik Ibsen.

STUDENT SAMPLE: THEATRE REVIEW

The headline for the review indicates that the production pleased the audience.

The introduction informs readers of the reviewer's positive response to the production.

A detailed description of the set design situates the readers, giving them a sense of what it would be like if they had attended the theatre themselves.

An Enemy of the People not an Enemy of the Audience

You file into a St. John's high school auditorium waiting for the curtain to rise, and classical music fills the air. It is opening night for *An Enemy of the People*, written by Henrik Ibsen. The audience is in for a treat. Behind the calm exterior of the stage, nervousness pervades the performers from the advanced theatre arts class who are waiting anxiously behind the scenes. Director Gordon Ralph takes the nineteenth-century context of the play and gives it a contemporary twist, providing a message that is truly ageless.

The first thing you note as you enter the auditorium is the extensive blue-and-yellow-walled set, decorated for that time period with antique pictures, chandeliers, and even an old-fashioned printing press, thanks to Sarah Bannister, Debbie Jackman, and Delyth Thomas. The impressive set, the school's biggest yet, is complete right down to the last detail. As the characters open doors on the set, the audience has a clear view of other rooms behind the actual wall. This is a beautiful touch and is a pleasant treat from the usual one-dimensional set. This arrangement gives a realistic feel to the house. As the show is about to start, the real brass chandelier lights up and then quickly plunges into blackness, as does the stage. The show begins.

A clear synopsis of the play, outlining the central conflict, is provided.

The two lead actors, Patrick Cook (Dr. Stockmann) and Chris Martin (Mayor), pull off the serious nature of this play beautifully. The two duel flawlessly and present the audience with the main conflict of the drama—a little town in Norway that is saved from economic depression with the discovery of mineral baths. However, Dr. Stockmann discovers that the baths are polluted and should be closed. He is the good citizen, placing honesty over politics, while the Mayor opposes him in the role of the power-greedy figure that wants money for the town despite the threat to the citizens' health.

The reviewer should offer an explanation when she uses theatre jargon, i.e., "blocking." The term refers to how the director places the actors on stage.

The blocking was skilfully executed, and throughout the explosive scenes, the characters sustain their roles skilfully. The high calibre of this production should also be credited to the people behind the scenes. Karen Lawlor, stage manager, and Kristy Clarke, producer, held the play together and made sure it was successfully staged on every level.

The reviewer deals with a change to the original script and the audience's reaction to this.

The climax of this five-act play—much to everyone's surprise—comes with the audience's participation. The play gets taken out of its historical context and contemporary issues are dealt with through a *verbal attack* from a couple of rowdy "observers" watching the play. The entire cast, as well as the director, gather on the stage and decide on a new, modern ending that leaves the audience dumbfounded.

The conclusion encourages readers to attend the production.

An Enemy of the People is a spectacle that should not be missed. Show time is at 8 p.m., but be sure to arrive early. This play takes off right from the beginning. Within minutes, you will be whisked back to a troubled nineteenth-century Norwegian town. As you leave, keep in mind that your next glass of water may not be what it seems—and NEVER drink the bath water in Norway.

Activities

Writing Short Reports and Reviews

1. Write a short report to describe a recent field trip you attended for school. Check your report for factual and stylistic accuracy before you submit it.

2. Attend a live performance of a play and write a review of the production. Make reference to the plot, characters, acting, setting, and directing. Present your review to the class.

Critical Writing and Book Reviews

Book reviews are also considered short reports. They express an opinion about the value of a particular book. Both fiction and non-fiction reviews can be found in magazines, newspapers, and on the Internet (see the Pearson Canada Web site, at <www.pearsoned.ca/referencepoints/links>). Such reviews are meant to inform the public about new books, to offer a short critical analysis, and to evaluate these books so readers can make informed choices.

You can assess the quality of a book review by asking the following questions:

- What elements of the book does the reviewer discuss?
- What details does the reviewer supply to illustrate or support his or her point of view?
- What is the reviewer's opinion of the book?
- Was the review interesting to read? Why or why not?
- Did the reviewer provide enough information for you to decide whether or not to read the book? Why or why not?

Consider the following review by Mike Ross, which appeared both in the *Edmonton Sun* and on the Internet. It discusses the novel *The Englishman's Boy*, by Guy Vanderhaeghe.

LEARNING FOCUS

- understand and analyze the characteristics of an effective book review
- inform others about a book you have read
- write a fiction or non-fiction book review

MODEL: BOOK REVIEW

The title and subtitle hint that Mike Ross has written a positive review.

Destiny Beckons

Vanderhaeghe is headed in some very big directions

by Mike Ross — Edmonton Sun

The Englishman's Boy

Guy Vanderhaeghe (McClelland and Stewart)

If I told you that the next big force in frontier fiction and western movie scriptwriting is a kid who grew up in Esterhazy, Sask., you probably wouldn't believe me.

The reviewer begins by emphasizing the novel's strong points—its dialogue and vivid language.

If I told you that he can write dialogue every bit as convincing as Larry McMurtry of *Lonesome Dove* fame, a few of you might stand up and take notice.

Well he can, and what's more he can describe the early days of the Canadian and American West in language that is as indelible as that of the greatest Prairie-culture writer of all time—Wallace (Wolf Willow) Stegner, an American who grew up in southern Saskatchewan.

Strong praise for Guy Vanderhaeghe, who will be reading from his ground-breaking novel *The Englishman's Boy* at Greenwoods' Bookshoppe tomorrow night at 7 p.m.

In my unhumble opinion, this author is the only Canadian writing today who can match the seemingly effortless literary grit and whimsy of Alice Munro and Michael Ondaatje.

Vanderhaeghe, forty-five, now works as a visiting English professor at S.T.M. College in Saskatoon—that is, when he's not quietly asserting himself with a collection of short stories, a couple of plays, and a trio of novels.

> **The reviewer adds to his praise by referring to other works of Vanderhaeghe, giving a list of his literary awards and prizes.**

His short story collection, *Man Descending*, won him a Governor General's Award in 1982. His novel *My Present Age* was shortlisted for the Booker Prize two years later. And *The Englishman's Boy* is a major contender for another Governor General's prize this year.

Not too shabby, eh?

What Vanderhaeghe has accomplished with his new novel is nothing short of mesmerizing.

The story, actually two stories, run toward each other like a Hollywood stunt stallion tracking a wild horse.

> **The reviewer notes that the author's unique accomplishment is his flawless combination of two narratives—one taking place on the western frontier, the other on a Hollywood movie set.**
>
> **The reader is given a quick overview of the plot and the main characters.**

The book's chapters alternate between the way things were on the western frontier, culminating in the Cypress Hills Massacre, and what movie moguls did to alter that history as they tried to leave their mark in cinema-crazy Hollywood.

Back and forth the action sways as one of the novel's central characters, Shorty McAdoo, now old and decrepit, living on the fringe of the California desert, begrudgingly tells his story to a Canadian gumshoe.

At the same time we follow the life of a boy who was won in a bet by an Englishman, as the lad struggles for survival with a wolfer party out to avenge the theft of their horses by a handful of Aboriginals a half-century earlier.

The chapters literally leap off the pages at the reader, gathering a deadly and earnest momentum as they march inexorably toward their tragic conclusions. Where there lies truth, betrayal can not be far behind.

Vanderhaeghe's attention to detail is noted.

A writer who never loses sight of his stories, Vanderhaeghe makes us feel that we are right there in the middle of every scene, every little detail branded on our consciousness. Our senses are stirred as if we are actually experiencing the stories first-hand, no mean feat for a writer.

There is a prediction that *The Englishman's Boy* has movie potential and that Vanderhaeghe will be asked to write the script. The review is so positive that readers will want to read this book and other works by Vanderhaeghe.

As surely as this book will be talked about for years to come, and its author lauded throughout the world for his storytelling, there is the promise of much, much more to come from Vanderhaeghe.

The Englishman's Boy is the very kind of novel that Hollywood filmmakers and independent moviemakers long to bring to the big and small screens.

Somewhere out there a Clint (*Unforgiven*) Eastwood or Arthur (*Missouri Breaks*) Penn will see the possibilities.

It's inevitable that *The Englishman's Boy* is destined to get there. When that happens it should surprise no one that Vanderhaeghe, a natural dialogue writer, is the logical candidate for scripting his own work.

✔ CHECKLIST | WRITING A FICTION REVIEW

- ✓ Include a short section on the elements of fiction (e.g., setting, characters, plot, theme) found in the work.
- ✓ Provide key details and a brief analysis.
- ✓ Give reasons for recommending or not recommending it.
- ✓ Compare it to other similar pieces of fiction.
- ✓ Use a style that is informative and easy to read.

✔ CHECKLIST | WRITING A NON-FICTION REVIEW

- ✓ Consider the purpose of the book.
- ✓ Discuss the significance of its subject.
- ✓ Evaluate the accuracy of the information provided.
- ✓ Explain the use of evidence (documents, statistics, anecdotes).
- ✓ Examine the sources of the material included.
- ✓ Discuss the style of the book.
- ✓ Assess the use of visual and graphics, such as photographs, diagrams, and maps.

Activities

Writing Book Reviews

1. In a newspaper, magazine, or on the Internet, find a review of a book you have read. From your perspective, is the reviewer's view of the book accurate? Have any important points been left out? What, if anything, would you like to see added to the review?

2. Write a review of a fiction book you have recently read. Refer to the elements of fiction (plot, character, setting, theme). Tell just enough of the story to create interest. Use quotations and events from the book to support your points, and state clearly what you like or dislike in the book, and why.

3. Write your own review of a work of non-fiction you have read. (Use the checklist on the previous page to help you.) Present your review to the class.

Writing Research Essays

Short critical essays can be based on information from your own reading, discussions with peers, and notes made while listening to your teacher or on a field trip. However, you will also be assigned critical essays that require more extensive research. For these you will need to collect resource information, analyze it from a particular perspective, and present your findings in written form.

The products of such carefully planned assignments (typically five to ten pages in length) are often called **research essays**. They frequently involve persuasive (and sometimes argumentative) writing, intended to convince your audience to accept your point of view. A research essay is more than a random compilation of facts—it involves careful selection and organization of ideas and information to support the **thesis statement**. The final product of your research should lead to the expression of an informed point of view.

Stages in the Development of a Research Essay

Writing an effective research essay requires you to go through several stages:

LEARNING FOCUS

- understand the characteristics of an effective research essay
- use specific stages in developing an essay
- use selected strategies at each phase of the essay-writing process

STAGE ONE: CHOOSING AND LIMITING YOUR TOPIC Determine early in the research process the aspect(s) of the topic you wish to investigate or analyze. You should also decide on your *purpose* and *audience*. To make the topic manageable, consider the following:

- Can this topic be researched in the time allotted?
- Am I interested in the topic?
- Can I make it interesting to my audience?
- Is there sufficient information available to complete some thought-provoking research?

At this stage, you should begin to formulate some specific research questions you want to address in the essay. You need to answer the following questions, as well:

- What do I know about this topic?
- What else do I need to know?
- What do I want my audience to learn from this research?

Imagine, for example, that you are preparing to write an essay on the novels of J.R.R. Tolkien. You might make effective use of a **thought web** (see below) to help you brainstorm and then limit your subject.

STAGE TWO: MAKING A TENTATIVE THESIS STATEMENT An effective thesis statement should take a *position*, one that you believe your research will prove. This will be a single sentence that formulates both the central idea of your research and your point of view on the topic. In a sense, the thesis statement is your answer to the central question or problem you have raised. To continue the earlier example, if you chose the novels of J.R.R. Tolkien as your topic, you could narrow it down to investigate the reason for the popularity of Tolkien's trilogy, *The Lord of the Rings*.

Your tentative thesis statement might read as follows:

> It is the combined effect of the use of language, the presence of a wide variety of poetry and song, the elements of heroism, and even aspects of Tolkien's own character that contribute to the legendary status of <u>The Lord of the Rings</u>.

As you complete the research for your report, you may find that your tentative thesis statement is no longer valid. Sometimes in research, as you read, collect, and evaluate more information on your topic, new evidence might cause you to revise the original statement. Like a scientist who makes a hypothesis and then tests it in the lab, you generate a **thesis** and test it during your research and rough drafts.

STAGE THREE: RETRIEVING SOURCES OF INFORMATION Although it is important that the primary voice in a research paper be your own (i.e., your personal opinion and writing style), it is essential to substantiate this with information from a number of sources. You can draw from a wealth of information—in print and electronic form—to strengthen and refine your initial thesis.

The origin of first-hand information (e.g., discussion or observation, interviews, questionnaires) is known as a **primary source**. The place where you find information one step removed from the origin is referred to as a **secondary source**. This information has been gathered, reported, and analyzed by someone else (in books, newspapers, magazines, computer Web sites, etc.). Focus on the specific resources you need, locate these resources, and evaluate whether the information is reliable and supports your topic and your point of view.

As you conduct your research, use note making and note taking strategies (see Chapter 1) to reconstruct the information. The subject area of your research may also require a sophisticated level of visual literacy as you explore the use of photographs, diagrams, Web pages, videos.

MAJOR RESEARCH SOURCES

PRIMARY SOURCES
First-hand Observations Personal reactions from field trips and laboratory work are good sources of information, particularly for papers in science and social sciences.

MAJOR RESEARCH SOURCES (CONTINUED)

Interviews and Conversations These can involve either direct personal contact, or telephone, e-mail or video-conferencing discussions with experts in the field you are writing about. Remember to make thorough notes and observe the rules of good interviewing (see Chapter 1).

Questionnaires and Surveys These require sufficient time to construct the proper instruments and an understanding of how to analyze the data you receive (see Chapter 6 for survey creation tips).

SECONDARY SOURCES

Library Catalogues and Computer Files School and local libraries are invaluable resources for many subject areas. Library catalogues (print or electronic) provide information by subject, title, and author, along with call numbers to help you locate books on the library shelves. In most libraries, card catalogues have been replaced by computer databases.

Periodical Indexes These are listings of current articles on various topics available in newspapers and magazines. Articles in periodical indexes are listed by subject, title, and author. The *Canadian Index* provides a list of relevant newspaper articles. Indexes like the *Canadian Periodical Index* and the *Reader's Guide to Periodical Literature* will guide you to magazine articles on your research topic. Many indexes are available on CD-ROM.

Non-Print Resources These include audio- and videotapes, photographs, and filmstrips. Catalogues for these sources are kept by most libraries.

Government Departments and Agencies Numerous articles and reports are published through government offices. They contain important, current information and statistics on topics such as fisheries, forestry, careers, unemployment, and medical research. Again, these are available either in print form or electronically on government databases and Web sites.

The Internet This global network (see Chapter 1) provides access to print, audio, and visual resources on numerous topics. Most libraries have Internet access.

Electronic Libraries On-line encyclopedias and electronic libraries are valuable sources for research, containing vast databases of print and visual information. The home page of one such source can be found on page 91.

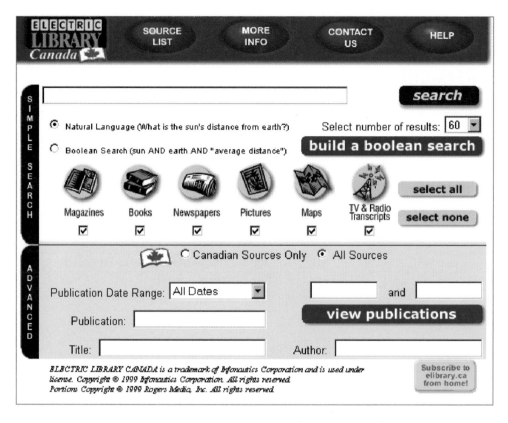

STAGE FOUR: MAKING A TENTATIVE OUTLINE At this stage, you begin to place the information you have found in order by creating a preliminary topic or subject outline. As your research progresses, you will obviously have to revise it as your growing knowledge of your subject brings new ideas to your attention. A well-written outline gives your essay necessary form and direction. It also prevents you from straying into irrelevant topics.

Review below the topic outline for a research essay. Notice how it uses broad topical divisions.

STUDENT SAMPLE: OUTLINE

Outline for a Research Essay

Subject: Reasons for Success and Popularity of J.R.R. Tolkien's trilogy, <u>The Lord of the Rings</u>.

The thesis statement provides both the topic of the essay and the position that will be supported.

Thesis Statement: It is the combined effect of the use of language, the presence of a wide variety of poetry and song, the elements of heroism, and even aspects of Tolkien's own character that contributes to the legendary status of <u>The Lord of the Rings</u>.

The outline indicates the major divisions of the research.

I.   Introduction
  A. The success and popularity of the trilogy <u>The Lord of the Rings</u>
  B. Combined reasons for J.R.R. Tolkien's greatness

There may be a need to revise the outline as new information is found.

II. Tolkien's effective use of descriptive language
  A. Vivid imagery to set the story's scenes
  B. Vivid imagery to describe characters
  C. Vivid imagery to establish mood

III. Tolkien's scheme of languages (speech)
  A. The Hobbits' speech
  B. The Orcs' speech
  C. The Elvish speech

IV. Tolkien's use of poetry and song
  A. Heightening atmosphere and mood
  B. Revealing aspects of a character's personality
  C. Supplying background information

Each topic is divided into several subtopics that include examples from the text.

V.   Tolkien's heroic, courageous characters
  A. The ranger, Aragorn
  B. Éomer, Marshall of the Mark
  C. Gil-galad

VI. Personal aspects of Tolkien's own character
  A. His family tragedies
  B. His perseverance

The conclusion reviews important points and returns to the thesis statement.

VII. Conclusion - Through careful analysis, however, one can see that it was not only one of these factors, but rather a combination of all of them, that has helped ensure the success and popularity of <u>The Lord of the Rings</u>.

STAGE FIVE: READING AND ORGANIZING NOTES As you read or view the various materials to support your thesis statement, evaluate the information in terms of its accuracy, currency, and usefulness. You will also need to create jot notes to help you gather information to support the headings and subheadings in your tentative outline. Some students keep track on their computers, while others use index cards for their notes. On the front of the index card, record the **bibliographical information** so you know the exact source of your notes. Write the jot notes you obtain from that source on the back of the card(s).

Author: Grotta-Kurska, Daniel   *Index Number:* 1

Title: J.R.R. Tolkien: Architect of Middle Earth

Publisher: Running Press Books

Place and Date of Publication: New York, 1976

Each time you take additional notes from the same source, place the index number in the upper right-hand corner of the card(s). You won't have to repeat the publication information—you'll know that #1 is from Grotta-Kurska.

Topic or Subtopic from Tentative Outline:
Personal aspects of Tolkien's own character

In 1896, when he was four years old, his father "died of acute peritonitis... from a minor case of the flu that went unchecked" (Grotta-Kurska 16). Death would strike his family again when he was twelve, this time taking his mother. These two tragedies would have overshadowed the joys of young life for most, but Tolkien managed to persevere (25).

The topic or subtopic headings and relevant notes will help you later as you arrange the information in your rough draft. All cards under the heading "Personal aspects of Tolkien's own character" will be grouped together. Notes on "Tolkien's effective use of descriptive language" would be found on another set of cards. The page references should be recorded on the cards in case you need to check the source again, and to help you acknowledge your sources of information.

The index number in the top right corner tells you at a glance the source of your notes. The notes themselves will be either

- a **précis** of a paragraph, a page, or a longer section. Be careful to summarize accurately (see Chapter 1).

- a **paraphrase** (see Chapter 1). You must acknowledge the source of the original idea.

- a **direct quotation**, which is a direct copy from the text placed in quotation marks with the page number cited. When information or ideas have been stated particularly well or concisely, it is fine to use a direct quotation. Try to use direct quotes only for information essential to the report; otherwise, write the information in your own words.

STAGE SIX: WRITING THE FIRST DRAFT As you read and take notes, you will undoubtedly find information that you hadn't considered in your preliminary thoughts on the subject. As you find new material, you need to revise your rough outline.

With the new outline as a guide, you are ready to compose the draft paragraphs of your research paper. First, scan your note cards and arrange them in order according to your headings and subheadings. You now have notes on headings that you have added. There are also notes that you won't need to use in this paper. The first draft, like the final one, should have a distinctive introduction, body, and conclusion. The questions asked around the various headings and subheadings can become the basis of the topic sentences for your paragraphs. Try to use your own words as much as possible, without too many direct quotes.

You have two goals: to arrange your ideas in the order presented in your outline and to develop each main idea that you introduce. If you're writing by hand, and even if you're typing directly into a computer, double-space your first draft to leave room for insertions and corrections.

As you copy details and evidence from your cards to support the various headings, be careful to acknowledge the sources of the information. Many teachers favour the use of **parenthetical references** (in-text notes) when documenting sources. The student writer whose research essay on J.R.R. Tolkien is found at the end of this chapter has used the **MLA style** (name–page method) of in-text source citation. This style acknowledges, in the body of the paper, facts or others' ideas by placing the author's name in parentheses along with the page number (not separated by a comma) at the end of the last sentence taken from each specific source.

Tolkien's love for his own work is another reason for his popularity. It motivated him to create a world with such meticulous depth and detail that one is in awe at the sight of it. Unlike others of his time, Tolkien was a romantic, one who would abandon the realistic and analytical views of many of his peers. He would "come to the aid of dragons, show them as real as truth," for they were to him as "everyday and real as the weather" (Ready 20).

If you refer to the author by name in the sentence containing the paraphrase or direct quotation, just indicate the page number in parentheses. The author's full name and the title of the source is then documented in a Works Cited or Bibliography section of the essay (see Stage 9 below).

Some teachers may require the **APA style** of parenthetical referencing (name–date method) or a system of **footnotes** or **endnotes**.

STAGE SEVEN: REVISING AND EDITING Use the following questions as a guide when doing the final check of your research essay:

- Are my purpose and main idea clear?
- Is my thesis statement fully developed?
- Is the content of the report complete?
- Does it follow the order presented in my outline?
- Is each topic sentence supported by detailed facts?
- Do my language and content suit my audience?
- Are my title and introductory paragraph(s) interesting?
- Is there a strong ending?
- Have I defined all important terms?
- Have I adequately answered my research questions?
- Is my paper free of errors in punctuation, grammar, and usage?
- How can I improve in my next research project?

STAGE EIGHT: PUBLISHING OR PRESENTING THE FINAL DRAFT You should make every effort to type your assignments. Ensure that your research essay is in the correct format, with proper spacing. Always give your manuscript a final reading before you submit it to your teacher.

Research papers (or **abstracts**) may be shared with an audience as part of an oral presentation (see Chapter 6). Various kinds of presentation software are available for creating graphs, Web pages, slides, and other visual effects in an oral presentation and debate.

STAGE NINE: PREPARING REFERENCES Prepare a detailed record of exactly where you found sources for your references. The print and non-print references for a research paper can be presented in one of two forms:

- A **works cited** section (references section in APA format) lists works actually cited in your paper, either quoted directly, or paraphrased.
- A **bibliography** lists *all* works from which you obtained any information for your paper, even if some are not cited in your paper.

The Works Cited Section allows an interested reader to consult the original sources used. It also serves as a springboard for expanded research.

Sample Works Cited or Bibliography Entry

Tolkien, John Ronald Reuel. <u>The Fellowship of the Ring</u>. London: HarperCollins, 1999.

Part of the research process involves knowing what constitutes **plagiarism** and what the consequences are of presenting others' ideas without standard documentation. To guard against plagiarism:

- Acknowledge the source of the information at the end of each paraphrase, summary, or direct quotation by enclosing in parentheses the last name of the author and the relevant page numbers.
- Put the writer's words into your own language. Do not use the diction, syntax, and style of the original *unless* you use direct quotations.
- If something is not *common knowledge* to you, it is better to over-document than to under-document and commit plagiarism. Acknowledging your sources of information lends weight to your arguments and investigation.

(See Appendix A for further information on proper documentation of sources.)

Examine the excerpt from a student research essay that follows. Consider the stages of the essay development process outlined earlier as you read it.

The Success and Popularity of J.R.R. Tolkien's Trilogy The Lord of the Rings

The introduction to a research essay is usually longer than for an ordinary essay. It may contain background historical or biographical information to lead into the topic.

Perhaps one of the most famous authors of modern fantastic literature, John Ronald Reuel Tolkien has captivated whole generations with his magnificent works, the most noteworthy being his trio in the classic The Lord of the Rings series. These three works in particular have earned him legendary status among a countless variety of readers, ranging from the most astute and critical literary scholar to the common "leisure reader," who may indulge in these tales simply for the sheer fun of it. Rarely do twentieth-century authors achieve such a level of recognition and acclaim, joining the ranks of such revered figures as William Shakespeare and Edgar Allan Poe. It is the uncommon nature of this praise that prompts many to question its validity, to inquire as to whether or not it is well-founded. Indeed, in the case of J.R.R. Tolkien, it is certainly well-deserved, of that there is no doubt. What is often in doubt, however, has been the specific source behind the author's success and worldwide popularity. The simple answer to the question "What makes Tolkien great?" has been hotly debated by many critics, each pointing to different aspects of the man's writing style and character as the ultimate source of his creativity. Even the renowned author himself had no idea why he was so adored by his fans: "The fame and success that The Lord of the Rings brought Tolkien…both surprised and perplexed him" (Grotta-Kurska 8).

In the introductory paragraphs the writer makes the thesis statement and provides a preview of how this research essay will be developed.

Note the use of the MLA style of source citation. Because the quote is under four lines, it appears in the body of the essay.

However, despite arguments to the contrary, no one factor led to the immense popularity of this series. Indeed, to attribute the success of Tolkien to one quality alone would show a disregard for all the various other mechanisms at work within the novels, and would therefore be simplistic. It is the combined effect of the use of language, the presence of a wide variety of poetry and song, the story's elements of heroism, and even aspects of Tolkien's own character that contribute to the legendary success of The Lord of the Rings. These various factors, when carefully woven together, form the building blocks for one of the greatest masterpieces in literature.

The writer takes one aspect of his outline, Tolkien's use of descriptive language, and develops it into a topic sentence for this paragraph.

The most noteworthy aspect of Tolkien's trilogy, and one of its claims to fame, is his use of language, both as a means of description and in the vocal sense, as a means of communication. Examples of the former seem to be sprawled across every page of the three novels, supplying the reader with enough detail to paint a clear, realistic picture of Middle Earth's people and places. Indeed, Tolkien supplies the reader with enough vivid imagery to fully create and set the story's scenes, and to adequately describe his many wondrous characters. One such point, where setting is the focus of the description, is during a chapter entitled "The Old Forest" within the first novel. Here, the hobbits travel through a treacherous, but nonetheless wondrous, old wood, where a heavy fog often obscures their path. During one incident, the fog clears, and Tolkien provides this picture:

> As if through a gate they saw the sunlight before them. Coming to the opening they found they had made their way down through a cleft in a high steep bank, almost a cliff. At its feet was a wide space of grass and reeds; and in the distance could be glimpsed another bank almost as steep. A golden afternoon of late sunshine lay warm and drowsy upon the hidden land between. In the midst of it there wound lazily a dark river of brown water, bordered with ancient willows, arched over with willows, blocked with fallen willows, and flecked with thousands of faded willow leaves. The air was thick with them, fluttering yellow from the branches; for there was a warm and gentle breeze blowing softly in the valley, and the reeds were rustling, and the willow-boughs were creaking. (Fellowship 152)

Through the use of visual and auditory imagery, Tolkien takes the reader into the depths of the Old Forest, right alongside the four hobbits on the shore of the River Withywindle.

Tolkien's description of his characters is just as in-depth as that of the story's setting, providing readers with clear images of what many of these "people" look like. This is especially vital for situations where a fictional being (which is usually a Tolkien-creation) is involved, for it may be difficult for the reader to picture this product of the author's imagination. After all, the average individual would not be able to describe an *ent*, for such a thing is not real. Therefore, it is essential for these fictional character de-

---

Side notes:

Tolkien, the author of this quotation, is identified in the same sentence, just before the quote. Therefore, the reference needs only the book's title and page number of the quote.

When a quotation is indented, the reference, in parentheses, comes after the period. A shortened version of the title may be used.

This topic sentence connects description of characters to the previous paragraph, which discussed the setting. It serves as an effective transition sentence, providing coherence.

scriptions to be accurate and complete. Staying with the example of an ent, here is a description of one such creature when it is discovered by (or rather, it discovers) the hobbits Pippin and Merry in the forest of Fangorn:

> They found they were looking at a most extraordinary face. It belonged to a large Man-like, almost Troll-like, figure, at least fourteen foot high, very sturdy, with a tall head, and hardly any neck. Whether it was clad in stuff like green and grey bark or whether that was its hide was difficult to say. At any rate the arms, at a short distance from the trunk, were not wrinkled, but covered with a brown smooth skin. The large feet had seven toes each. The lower part of the long face was covered with a sweeping grey beard, bushy, almost twiggy at the roots, thin and mossy at the ends. But at the moment the hobbits noted little but the eyes. These deep eyes were now surveying them, slow and solemn, but very penetrating. They were brown, shot with a green light. (Two Towers 66)

Thus the reader is given a picture of Treebeard, the ent, one of the more unusual characters in Tolkien's fantasy. Were it not for the author's thorough description of this particular man of wood, the readers would find themselves in an awkward situation.

The frequent use of poetry and song throughout The Lord of the Rings has also been a contributing factor to the popularity of Tolkien. Throughout all three novels, the author supplies a multitude of rhymes, poems, and songs that serve to intensify the atmosphere by evoking feelings in the reader, to reveal aspects of a certain character's personality, and to supply the reader with background information or facts that are relevant to the continuity and understanding of the story.

The presence of heroism within a story is often a factor in its achieving popularity. Whether it is part of human nature, or simply some mass preference, audiences seem to take pleasure in reading about heroic, courageous characters and their actions. This may be partly due to the feelings that such actions evoke in the reader, such as delight, excitement, and admiration. These are all positive emotions, feelings that people prefer to have coursing

---

Note the inclusion of a long quotation so that readers may discern for themselves the strength of Tolkien's descriptive writing. This illustrates the development of one of the outline subtopics.

Some teachers may prefer you to use italics instead of underlining for book titles.

A new topic sentence provides more reasons to keep the thesis statement in the forefront.

This topic sentence introduces more evidence to explain Tolkien's popularity.

through them as they read. They make an author's story seem more entertaining, more exciting, motivating a reader to delve further into it. Tolkien takes advantage of such an element, using it to keep his audience interested in his trilogy.

Indeed, even critics believe that Tolkien creates an attractive aspect of the story in his heroic characters, particularly because:

The writer quotes directly rather than paraphrasing because the quotation from Ready is clear and well written.

> Tolkien heroes never despair; they know that although the night will be a smothering blanket of dark and the floods of Evil will lap against the very brim of their protection, even break through here and there and devastate, the dawn will come, has come so far already, the dark is getting paler all the time, the walls will hold, the waters will ebb. (Ready 39)

Supporting the thesis statement, this paragraph provides an example of heroism (Aragorn's).

This eternal vigilance against evil is an attribute possessed by several of Tolkien's characters, particularly the ranger, Aragorn. This is a character who repeatedly demonstrates that he is worthy of the status of a true hero. He seems to be constantly putting forth examples of his courage fighting against evil whenever he is needed. One of his more noteworthy acts of heroism is at the titanic battle for Helm's Deep. Here, he helps the Riders of Rohan, men who he had had little affiliation with until a few hours before. Yet, despite this, he comes to their aid when the minions of Saruman besiege them. In this particular instance, he and the Marshal of the Mark, Éomer, fight off Saruman's horde, charging against them despite grievous odds:

The use of a number of direct quotes from Tolkien's works demonstrates thorough investigation and analysis. These are necessary to produce an effective research essay.

> Together Éomer and Aragorn sprang through the door, their men close behind.... Charging from the side, they hurled themselves upon the wild men. Andúril [Aragorn's sword] rose and fell, gleaming with white fire....

> Dismayed the rammers let fall the trees and turned to fight; but the wall of their shields was broken as by a lightning-stroke, and they were swept away, hewn down, or cast over the Rock into the stony stream below. (<u>Two Towers</u> 139)

The battle is long and hard; there is little time for Aragorn to pause. Fatigue would come quickly, and soon the brave warrior "leant wearily on [his] sword" (141) and "stumbled in his weariness" (143). Yet despite this, he fights on, battling the army of wild men and orcs that continues to surge forward against the walls of Helm's Deep. Such bravery and unwavering loyalty to the men of Rohan, who are strangers to him, make Aragorn a character to be admired.

Another topic sentence with another reason supporting the thesis of Tolkien's popularity. The repetition of the word "popularity" emphasizes the writer's position.

Some have pointed to more personal aspects of Tolkien's character as being the source of his popularity. These claimants point to factors in the author's personal life, maintaining that they were the primary guiding forces behind all the latter sources mentioned. The element of heroism previously discussed, for example, is often seen as being a reflection of Tolkien's own brave and "heroic" qualities. He is said to "never blink in the heroes theme for it is a theme that he has lived with all of his life" (Ready 10). Daniel Grotta-Kurska tells us that from the time Tolkien was a young boy, he had dealt with hardships. In 1896, when he was four years old, his father "died of acute peritonitis…from a minor case of the flu that went unchecked" (16). Then, when he was five, he was shipped off to boarding school, away from his mother and home in Sarehole. Death would strike his family again when he was twelve, this time taking his mother. These two tragedies would have overshadowed the joys of young life for most, but Tolkien managed to persevere. Showing a kind of heroism of his own, he endeavoured to live his life to the fullest, despite the poor hand that fate had dealt him. This inner courage would inspire him to create such brave figures as Gil-galad and Aragorn, to act as an outlet for his writings of their long quests and noble deeds (32).

When the secondary source author's name (Daniel Grotta-Kurska) is included in the text, the reference will be the shorter simpler page reference only (16) or (32).

The Lord of the Rings is one of the most famous works of modern fantastic literature, having achieved a level of popularity that surpasses that of its peers. Rarely does a modern work, especially one of fantasy, achieve such recognition among readers across the globe, so rare that one cannot help but question why it has become a classic. The source of this popularity and recognition has been a topic that has been hotly debated by literary scholars and critics, who point to a multitude of different factors.

These last paragraphs bring the essay to a close. The student writer restates his thesis statement to emphasize the central argument of his research.

Among the many cited reasons, people have pointed to Tolkien's use of literary device and description, the presence and creativity of his poetry and song, his use of languages, the inclusion of heroic elements, and even aspects of his own personality. Through careful analysis, however, one can see that it was not just one of these factors, but rather a combination of factors that had helped to ensure the success of <u>The Lord of the Rings</u>. Indeed, to limit Tolkien's worldwide popularity to any one reason would be an insult to the great author's memory, a total disregard for all of the other qualities that are present in his writing.

Works Cited

Works Cited entries are listed alphabetically. When an entry exceeds one line, the second and subsequent lines are indented five spaces.

Grotta-Kurska, Daniel. <u>J.R.R. Tolkien: Architect of Middle Earth</u>. New York: Running Press Books, 1976.

Ready, William. <u>The Tolkien Relation</u>. Vancouver: Copp Clark, 1968.

Tolkien, John Ronald Reuel. <u>The Fellowship of the Ring</u>. London: HarperCollins, 1999.

Tolkien, John Ronald Reuel. <u>The Two Towers</u>. London: George Allen and Unwin, 1966.

Activities

Writing a Research Essay

1. With the help of one of your subject teachers, select a literary, social sciences, or scientific subject about which you would like to write a research essay. Follow the nine steps above to select a topic, and collect and organize your information. Submit your outline and note cards along with the final copy of your research essay. Include a separate title page for your essay.

2. Write a précis (also known as an abstract) of your research paper, and give a brief presentation to the class on your research. Your abstract should include
   • your thesis statement.
   • the scope of your research.
   • the main findings of your research.

Communicating Creatively in Prose

An Invitation to Think, Talk, and Write Creatively

Creative communication comes in various forms. This chapter focuses on communicating creatively in **prose**, the most common form of written or spoken communication. However, people can also communicate creatively through paintings, song lyrics, video sound and graphics, and in many other ways.

Whatever the form, creative work is difficult, often frustrating, but ultimately rewarding. Communicating creatively requires that you, as an artist, think imaginatively and critically about what you want to say, stick to a work routine, and above all, persevere.

Many people face blocks to their creativity at times. Whether you are a novelist, cartoonist, songwriter, or visual artist, the germ of an idea grows slowly and good ideas may be hard to come by. However, persistence pays off, as writer Natalie Goldberg notes in the excerpt below.

READING SELECTION: PERSUASIVE PROSE

Write Anyplace
by Natalie Goldberg

Okay…. You have $1.25 left in your chequing account…. You know you have lived a life of unfulfilled dreams…. It is twenty degrees below zero outside, your nose itches, and you don't have even three plates that match to serve dinner on. Your feet are swollen, you need to make a dentist appointment, the dog needs to be let out, you have to defrost the chicken and make a phone call to your cousin in Boston. You're worried about your mother's glaucoma, you forgot to put film in the camera, Safeway has a sale on solid white tuna, you are waiting for a job offer, you just bought a computer and you have to unpack it. You have to start eating sprouts and stop eating doughnuts, you lost your favourite pen, and the cat peed on your current notebook.

Take out another notebook, pick up another pen, and just write, just write, just write. In the middle of the world, make one positive step. In the centre of chaos, make one definitive act. Just write. Say yes, stay alive, be awake. Just write. Just write. Just write.

Finally, there is no perfection. If you want to write, you have to cut through and write. There is no perfect atmosphere, notebook, pen, or desk, so train yourself to be flexible. Try writing under different circumstances and in different places. Try trains, buses, at kitchen tables, alone in the woods leaning against a tree, by a stream with your feet in the water…. If you want to write, finally you'll find a way no matter what.

Keeping a Personal Journal

Creative artists hone their perceptive skills by shrewdly observing the world around them. They examine daily life, listen to conversations, read books, magazines, and newspapers, and collect scraps of information. In this way they accumulate a storehouse of ideas for future reference.

LEARNING FOCUS
- generate and gather ideas for writing
- assess the suitability of ideas for various forms of creative writing
- work with others to revise and edit your writing

The ideal place to gather all these ideas together is in a **personal journal**. A journal is a forum for personal writing about experiences and issues. It is a place to make your start at stringing words, ideas, and images together. Your personal journal may take the form of a notebook, a tape recorder, or an ideas file on your computer. Whatever the format, it is a place to collect clippings, cartoons, pictures, first writing attempts, and detailed notes to kick-start the creative process.

For the most part, you write or sketch in your journal for *yourself*, so revising a journal's contents is not crucial. However, as you convert a personal journal entry into a specific genre such as a story or poem, reworking becomes vital. To help you revise and edit your work, share your journal entries with teachers and peers. They can ask questions about your entries and make constructive suggestions regarding your next efforts.

Activities

Creativity and Journal Writing

1. In small groups, discuss an occasion when your creativity was blocked, either when writing or doing another creative activity. How did you solve the problem?

2. Collect favourite quotations, pictures, cartoons, and newspaper clippings to post in a personal journal. Decide how you will organize your journal and give it a thought-provoking title. Then reflect on some of the words and images you've gathered.

Creating Detailed Journal Entries

LEARNING FOCUS
- identify, use, and evaluate sources of ideas for creative writing
- select and use vivid words and images
- use memory and experience as a basis for writing

In our daily lives, we witness many success stories and tragedies. It's hard to miss the obvious, dramatic events that happen around us in our communities and that we see in the **media**. However, the mundane aspects of life can be equally useful sources for personal journals. A serious artist will pick up details the less observant among us miss, and will make ordinary things seem wonderful and new. He or she might find the seeds of stories, poems, or paintings in T-shirt slogans, the smells of a shopping mall's food court, or the sights and sounds at a bird feeder.

Whatever the source of ideas, it is the *detailed notes* in a journal that will give life and crispness to future creations. The quality of your journal depends on how you tune in to the world around you. A writer might see, for example, a particular painting or photograph that stimulates the imagination. The painting "An April Storm" by Robert Duncan (see below) shows a young woman taking feed to animals in the barnyard during a storm. After viewing it, one writer was prompted to create the journal entry that follows.

An April Storm
by Robert Duncan

MODEL: JOURNAL ENTRY

JOURNAL NOTES: MAY 22

- Who is the girl in the painting?
- What is her name?
- Why is she there alone tending to the animals?
- Where is her family?
- What is the time and place? Is this a Canadian scene?

The girl looks cold; her coat and dress look damp from the snow. The sheep, the cow, the pony, the ducks, hens, and the small border collie seem to long for food and shelter. The scene is rather rustic. The barn is not painted; just rough boards with iron stains from the door hinges and hardware. The mood is one of desolation. There are stains of animal tracks and urine on the snow.

Now note how the journal entry has been expanded by this writer into a short story also titled "An April Storm."

MODEL: SHORT STORY

An April Storm
by Robert Dawe

Phyllis Bussey had a head full of pictures, clear images of her past. The sounds, the scents, the vivid sketches of a lifetime tumbled around in her brain like the shadows from a burning oil lamp flickering on a kitchen ceiling.

Background information is provided about the young woman in the painting, a character the writer names Phyllis.

Sometimes those images were pleasurable and cheering—the fragrance of honeysuckle outside the window on August mornings after a night of warm rains; the welcome first sound of a baby son; the reds of strawberries amid white fresh cream that Phyllis remembered from that long ago Sunday when Peter had taken her to the Island to have supper with his parents, Jacob and Rachel Bussey.

However, one image continually flashed and flickered over all the others, shrouding all the glow and sparkle, all the radiance and lustre of her life with shade and shadow and cloud.

Added descriptive details convert the journal entry into a short story.

On that April evening, Phyllis stood in the barnyard outside their rustic stable with the winds tugging at her dress and wet snow soaking her auburn hair and clinging like cement to her short jacket, scarf, and stockings. All the animals moved toward the bucket she gripped in her crimson hands. The procession included three sheep, a milk cow, a pony, four ducks, some hens, a lone rooster, and a small border collie that seemed to be curled out of shape by the wind. The animals seemed torn between the temptation of the food and the inviting rough plank door of the shelter.

The word "drung" refers to a narrow lane or passage between houses, or fenced gardens.

Phyllis was surprised to see the three figures walking up the drung, along the three-rail fence that separated the approaching men from the farmyard where she was standing. She recognized by his limp Uncle Tom Pawn, an acquaintance of her father's. Uncle Tom had lived near her mother and father since she was a baby. Everyone called him Uncle Tom, although she didn't really know if there was any blood relation. Uncle Tom was respected along the Shore from Topsail Beach to Crowin's Head in Seal Cove. "Strong as a bull" they said of him. There was a legend about his fight with the railway engineers and track crews in July 1882 when the railway right-of-way sliced through his meadow and gardens. She remembered her father's version of the "Battle of Foxtrap" and his explanation that Uncle Tom's limp was actually the consequence of some altercation with a horse or bull or piece of farm machinery. Whatever the truth, Phyllis remembered how much younger men gave Uncle Tom a wide berth. He had always been kind and gentle to Phyllis. When her mother died he brought fresh meat and barley soup to her and her father. He had squeezed her arm tightly at the grave-side, and it was Uncle Tom who spoke to Johnnie Ryan and got her that first job at Ryan's General Store and Premises.

She had opened the stable door and ushered the animals inside by the time the three men neared the gap and entered the yard across a tiny bridge of unhewn stones that straddled the stream. The stream ran the length of Kelly's Island and flowed swiftly along the drung, cascading down the big hill, plunging like a falcon into Conception Bay.

As the men moved off the bridge, Phyllis recognized the other men. Reverend Elliot from the parish of Foxtrap followed Uncle Tom, and there was Henry Searle, who had carried them across the bay to Kelly's Island in his motorboat. Henry's was the unofficial ferry to the Island, carrying livestock, lumber, vegetables, and fish to and from the fourteen families who inhabited the tiny island. Almost a year ago now, Henry had carried Rachel Bussey across the bay for the last time to the church in Foxtrap and her burial place on the coastal hills, three miles across the water from the island.

This explains why Phyllis stood alone in the cold.

Phyllis' husband, Peter Bussey, had gone "to the ice" some weeks earlier to hunt seals. There would be cash from the voyage, especially if the seals were plentiful. They'd need such cash for provisions for spring seeds and more livestock. But primarily, Peter wanted cash to pay the St. John's lawyer who was straightening up the deed on Jacob Bussey's land. Peter had gone to see the lawyer after the baby was born in December. Phyllis had been handling chores both inside and out since Peter had procured a berth on the S.S. *Southern* on March 12, 1914.

Phyllis thought at first that the three men had come to see her aging father-in-law, Jacob Bussey. Uncle Tom had come often before to buy a sheep or some hens or just to sit and talk and smoke his pipe in the Bussey's kitchen. He had come during Christmas, just after the baby was born, "to have a drink," he said. But Phyllis knew he had come with coins and the handcrafted cradle and the tiny wheelbarrow for her baby son. Since her own father had died, Uncle Tom was Phyllis' last connection with home. She had cooked a good supper for him. He had stayed the night, played cards with Peter and Jacob, and held her infant son. On that night Phyllis' world had felt solid and whole.

She was about to greet the three visitors now and tell them to go on into the warm kitchen for tea, when Uncle Tom's huge hands gripped her damp shoulders. Reverend Elliot moved closer with "I'm sorry, Phyllis; there's some bad news; the *Southern* is lost; went down, we're told, with a full load of seal pelts; all hands lost."

Strong nouns and vivid verbs are used to create a gripping scene.

Phyllis looked past the visitors across the whitened meadow, gazed beyond the three-railed fence, back to the rock bridge and surveyed with sobbing eyes the entire yard. There were spots of urine and sheep manure; there were pools of water and muck where the horse and cows had stood just minutes before. Snow was now cemented to the rough boards of the stable, and those patches of rust stains from the iron nails and hardware made the scene more desolate and cold.

A thesaurus has been used to revise and edit the writing to create a polished final product.

She didn't remember moving to the house. There were sounds of animals inside the barn bleating and neighing; questioning why their evening meal had not been served. There was an amber light from the kitchen window but, as she looked across at the house, the snow and the water and the tears blurred her vision. The whole yard was cold; her feet were cold; her shoulders sagged under the weight of the wet coat; she was colder than she had ever been before. There was a burning in her eyes and in her brain. The image of the scene, the feel of Uncle Tom's fingers against her shoulders, the thought of Peter somewhere in the frigid Atlantic—all this tumbled and tossed into her thirty-year-old brain; it etched, it scorched, an image on the cerebral canvas, an image of fright and pain and loss and sorrow, overpowering all other sensations that had ever shared that space.

Activities

Visualizing Words

1. As you travel to and from school, make notes (a paragraph or two) in your personal journal. As an alternative, observe and record events that happen to you or other people over a twenty-four-hour period. Remember that observing means activating *all* the senses—sight, smell, hearing, touch, and taste.

2. In your journal, recall a memorable experience. This can be something enjoyable or painful, or simply humorous. Before you write, visualize the experience as clearly as you can. Then describe specific details, including the people, the setting, and your feelings at the time.

3. Work with a partner to create a story from memory, through word associations. One partner should pick a word (e.g., *vacations*). The other partner then gives all the associations he or she has with that word, while the other records them. Switch roles. After each partner has a list of word associations, use them to recount a story from the past. The word list will help you remember events and their specific details.

4. Think of someone you like or know well (e.g., a good friend or relative). Visualize how your subject talks, acts, gestures, interacts with others. Then, in a brief talk to your classmates, describe your subject in detail.

Creative Writing that Works

LEARNING FOCUS
- choose appropriate forms and topics for writing
- make effective word choices
- use sensory detail and imagery

Communicating creatively involves crafting your work to get the message you intend across to your audience. Here are some tried-and-true techniques to help you do so.

WRITE CLEAR, SPECIFIC SENTENCES Readers can get lost in rambling, wordy, or awkward sentences. Avoid them. To bring a scene to life, provide your readers with precise, true-to-life details.

WRITE ABOUT WHAT YOU KNOW BEST Use the familiar as your inspiration. Describe situations or events you are confident you understand. Think of people you know; observe how they get along; look at why they agree or disagree, and how they resolve conflict.

TELL THE TRUTH Serious artists try to reveal the truth, honestly confronting real problems that children, teens, and adults face. For example, writers like Paul Zindel (*The Pigman*), Barbara Smucker (*Underground to Canada*), and Kevin Major (*Hold Fast*) show how teens and adults live, rather than how they *should* live. Even in the fantasy genre or in myths, the underlying truths about life expressed in a work are what give it conviction. Such works of art may be controversial; nevertheless, they reflect reality and are therefore powerful.

SEE CHARACTERS AS REAL PEOPLE Carefully describe the physical appearance and body language of the characters you create. Delve into their minds to investigate their thoughts, feelings, and motivations. Examine their interactions with others and listen to what others say about them.

In the passage below, the reader is given a clear understanding of the character—a young baby with definite opinions—through humorous and creative description.

STUDENT SAMPLE: CHARACTER DESCRIPTION

You know, being a baby isn't all that it's cracked up to be. You'd think that my day would be filled with non-stop enjoyment and merriment and that being waited on hand and foot would be a blessing. The fact of the matter is, we have to go through a heck of a lot in the run of a day. It's not all a walk in the park, you know. That simple pleasure is reserved for sunny afternoons and weekends. Every day is an absolute adventure for us. We have obstacles in our everyday lives that are inconceivable to a person beyond the age of five. Let's face it, once you get past toilet training, the rest is smooth sailing.

Take last week, for example. I awoke in the wee hours of the morning with an incredible gut-wrenching hunger that made my stomach ache with emptiness. Being unable to communicate with words, as I had not yet acquired the skills necessary for everyday human speech, I was forced to use my very well-developed throat muscles to propel a deafening shriek to the ears of my mother. This, of course, worked exceptionally well in conveying my need for nourishment.

CHOOSE WORDS FOR MAXIMUM EFFECT Use *specific* nouns rather than *general* ones (e.g., *bread, cheese, and barley soup*, not just *lunch*). Provide vivid verbs: a steamer's paddle wheel *toiling* rather than merely *turning*. Use familiar words in a fresh way; have fun playing with words.

GIVE YOUR READER SENSORY DETAILS
Use language that appeals to the senses of sight, sound, touch, smell, and taste. This enables your reader to experience the content of your writing fully.

MAKE APT AND STRIKING COMPARISONS
Effective writers use **figurative language** for conciseness, clarity, and impact. Comparing one object with another can help your readers imagine the scene more clearly. Think carefully about word choice—make each word count.

Note the effective word choice in the story "An April Storm" on pages 107–109:

> On that April evening, Phyllis stood in the barnyard outside their rustic [adjective] stable with the winds tugging [personification] at her dress and wet snow soaking her auburn hair and clinging like cement [simile] to her short jacket, scarf, and stockings.

CONSIDER GENRE AND FORM Communication can be crafted in various written formats. Literary texts, for example, are classified in broad terms according to **genre** (e.g., short story, novel, folk tale, drama). You may be directed to use a particular genre or you might choose one out of interest or habit. Within each genre there are unique **forms**. For example, within the genre of the **folk tale**, there are such forms as the **legend, fairy tale,** and **fable**. Read a wide variety of genres and forms, analyze them, and experiment with them in your writing. Evaluate your purpose and audience and choose the genre and form of your writing accordingly.

Activities

Writing Creatively

1. As a class, brainstorm to develop a list of subjects for a piece of writing. On your own, choose *two* of the topics and write a paragraph on each one.
   - The first topic should be something from the list that you have personal experience with or know *a lot* about.
   - The second topic should be one about which you know *very little*.

   Is it any easier to write about the topic you are familiar with?

2. Write a paragraph describing either a character or setting that could be used within a short story.

3. Find *two* examples of literary selections you consider to be strong writing, from different genres and forms. Bring your selections to class and explain their strengths, showing why you have chosen them as models. Analyze your samples in terms of
   - genre
   - form
   - use of sensory details
   - use of figurative language
   - use of effective word choice

Descriptive Writing

Descriptive writing depends on careful word choice to create images of people, places, and objects. This kind of writing varies widely in its characteristics and purposes. One way to consider it is to think in terms of two extremes: scientific and impressionistic writing.

OBJECTIVE SCIENTIFIC DESCRIPTION This kind of description is like an accurate snapshot or diagram. It is found in **transactional writing**, such as science textbooks, technical manuals, and police records. It provides a concise, factual account, rendering exactly *what* was observed. The observer is detached—the final work tells little, if anything, about the writer. The key to objective description is precise detail.

The following excerpt about sharks, from a high school biology text, illustrates objective, scientific description.

MODEL: OBJECTIVE DESCRIPTION

Modern Biology
by Albert Towle

The voracious predatory habits of some shark species have given them a reputation as killers. Yet fewer than 10 per cent of shark species are known to attack humans unprovoked. Whale sharks, for example, are gentle 18-m giants that graze on plankton.

The writer describes the shark's fins, giving their correct scientific name and function. Note the concise, factual style of writing.

Sharks swim with a side-to-side motion of their asymmetric tail fins. Just behind their heads are paired pectoral (PECK-*tuhrul*) fins, which jut out from their bodies like the wings of a plane. These fins compensate for the downward thrust of the tail fin.

Information is provided on the structure of the shark's teeth and on how the teeth have been adapted to the shark's feeding habits.

The shark's mouth has 6 to 20 rows of backward-pointing teeth. When a tooth breaks or wears down, a replacement moves forward. One shark may eventually use more than 20,000 teeth. The structure of each species' teeth is adapted to its feeding habits. Sharks that catch primarily large fish have big, triangular teeth with sawlike edges that hook and tear prey. Bottom-feeding species that eat mollusks and crustaceans have flattened teeth that can crush shells. Sharks that eat small fish have long, thin teeth that grasp slippery prey.

Scientific style is evident in the formal word choice: "specialized nerve cells that connect with the olfactory lobes of the brain."

The ability of sharks to detect chemicals—that is, their sense of smell—is particularly acute. Paired nostrils on the snout have specialized nerve cells that connect with the olfactory lobes of the brain. Water entering the nostrils is continually monitored for chemicals. Sharks can detect blood from an injured animal as far as 500 m away. Sharks also have a well-developed lateral line system. In most species the sense of sight is less developed than the sense of smell.

SUBJECTIVE IMPRESSIONISTIC DESCRIPTION This type of description is found in creative writing such as poetry and prose. Here the writer's observations are *selective* (e.g., describing the magnificence of a scene or the offensiveness of a certain character) and *responsive* (i.e., demonstrating the writer's feelings in response). Subjective writing tells at least as much about the writer as it does about the person, place, or object being described. The focus of this writing is the writer's attitude toward the subject.

Compare the scientific description above of a shark with Hemingway's more subjective description that follows, of the Mako shark that comes to attack the old man's marlin in *The Old Man and the Sea*.

MODEL: SUBJECTIVE DESCRIPTION

The Old Man and the Sea
by Ernest Hemingway

Words like "beautiful" and "handsome" convey a sense of admiration for the shark. These words emphasize the responsive nature of the writing.

The sense of the shark's speed is conveyed by the words "knifing" through the water "without wavering."

Hemingway writes in a poetic style, with the conciseness and precision of a poet. Note his use of simile to describe the shark's teeth: "shaped like a man's fingers when they are crisped like claws."

He was a very big Mako shark built to swim as fast as the fastest fish in the sea and everything about him was beautiful except his jaws. His back was as blue as a sword fish's and his belly was silver and his hide was smooth and handsome. He was built as a sword fish except for his huge jaws which were tight shut now as he swam fast, just under the surface with his high dorsal fin knifing through the water without wavering. Inside the closed double lip of his jaws all of his eight rows of teeth were slanted inwards. They were not the ordinary pyramid-shaped teeth of most sharks. They were shaped like a man's fingers when they are crisped like claws. They were nearly as long as the fingers of the old man and they had razor-sharp cutting edges on both sides. This was a fish built to feed on all the fishes in the sea, that were so fast and strong and well armed that they had no other enemy. Now he speeded up as he smelled the fresher scent and his blue dorsal fin cut the water.

Most descriptive writing falls somewhere between the two styles, combining objective details and subjective responses to the subject. A writer must keep in mind the purpose of the writing and the intended audience when selecting an appropriate descriptive style.

Characteristics of Descriptive Writing

LEARNING FOCUS
- analyze the role of purpose and audience in descriptive writing
- create and assess vivid descriptions
- analyze and use point of view in descriptive writing

Regardless of where a piece of descriptive writing falls on the spectrum, it must offer a multitude of details to create a strong overall image. How the writer describes a person, place, or object depends on the writer's *physical* and *psychological* **point of view**. For example, a writer can physically observe a street scene from a balcony above or from within the street crowd; a harbour can be viewed from the beach or from a cliff. A writer must also choose a psychological point of view. For example, a banker or an actor will probably have a different perspective on a lobster trap than someone who works with one daily.

As well, the writer must organize observations in a particular manner:

- from general observation of the whole scene to more specific observation of its parts
- spatially—left to right, top to bottom, end to end
- chronologically—from beginning to end, dawn to dusk
- sensorily—according to the senses appealed to

✔ CHECKLIST | EFFECTIVE DESCRIPTIVE WRITING

- ✓ Create images of people, places, and objects using careful word choice.
- ✓ Provide details organized in a systematic fashion.
- ✓ Select details depending on physical or psychological points of view.
- ✓ For objective description, stick to exact detail and specific facts.
- ✓ For subjective description, be selective and responsive when describing your thoughts and feelings.

Take a look at the following excerpt, which combines many of the characteristics of descriptive writing.

MODEL: DESCRIPTIVE ESSAY

Holiday Memory
by Dylan Thomas

The setting is established, with details appealing to sound, sight, and touch.

August Bank Holiday. A tune on an ice-cream cornet. A slap of sea and a tickle of sand. A fanfare of sunshades opening. A wince and whinny of bathers dancing into deceptive water. A tuck of dresses. A rolling of trousers. A compromise of paddlers. A sunburn of girls and a lark of boys. A silent hullabaloo of balloons.

The author indicates his physical and psychological points of view.

I remember the sea telling lies in a shell held to my ear for a whole harmonious, hollow minute by a small, wet girl in an enormous bathing-suit....

And mothers loudly warned their proud pink daughters or sons to put that jellyfish down; and fathers spread newspapers over their faces; and sand-fleas hopped on the picnic lettuce; and someone had forgotten the salt....

Note how Thomas personifies the sun and the butter to create a playful image.

This was the morning when father, mending one hole in the thermos-flask, made three; when the sun declared war on the butter, and the butter ran; when dogs, with all the sweet-binned backyards to wag and sniff and bicker in, chased their tails in the jostling kitchen, worried sandshoes, snapped at flies, writhed between legs, scratched among towels, sat smiling on hampers....

I remember the princely pastime of pouring sand, from cupped hands or buckets, down collars and tops of dresses; the shriek, the shake, the slap.

I can remember the boy by himself, the beachcombing lone-wolf, hungrily waiting at the edge of family cricket; the friendless fielder, the boy uninvited to bat or to tea.

I remember the smell of sea and seaweed, wet flesh, wet hair, wet bathing-dresses, the warm smell as of a rabbity field after rain, the smell of pop and splashed sunshades and toffee, the stable-and-straw smell of hot, tossed, tumbled, dug, and trodden sand, the swill-and-gaslamp smell of Saturday night, though the sun shone strong, from the bellying beer-tents, the smell of the vinegar on shelled cockles, wrinkle-smell, shrimp-smell, the dripping-oily backstreet winter-smell of chips in newspapers, the smell of ships from the sun-dazed docks round the corner of the sand-hills, the smell of the known and paddled-in sea moving, full of the drowned and herrings....

And the noise of pummelling Punch, and Judy falling, and a clock tolling or telling no time in the tenantless town; now and again a bell from a lost tower or a train on the lines behind us clearing its throat, and always the hopeless, ravenous swearing and pleading of the gulls, donkey-bray and hawker-cry, harmonicas and toy trumpets, shouting and laughing and singing, hooting of tugs and tramps, the clip of the chair-attendant's puncher, the motor-boat coughing in the bay, and the same hymn and washing of the sea that was heard in the Bible....

And two small boys fought fiercely and silently in the sand, rolling together in a ball of legs and bottoms....

But over all the beautiful beach I remember most the children playing, boys and girls tumbling, moving jewels, who might never be happy again. And "happy as a sandboy" is true as the heat of the sun.

Dusk came down; or grew up out of the sands and the sea; or curled around us from the calling docks and the bloodily smoking sun. The day was done, and the sands brushed and ruffled suddenly with a seabroom of cold wind.

The repetition of "I remember" and its variations provide a personal perspective; sensory details evoke the feeling of the sand.

Thomas uses metaphor in referring to the boy as a "lone-wolf."

Note the focus on smells.

There is repetition of words and sentence structure (**parallelism**) and repetition of past participles such as "tossed" and "dug."

Details build in layer upon layer. The focus is on sounds; the dominant impression is of a day filled with shouting and laughing.

In this paragraph Thomas again uses parallelism (e.g., "children playing, boys and girls tumbling").

The words "but" and "dusk came down" in the final paragraphs cue the reader to the organization of the piece.

And we gathered together all the spades and buckets and towels, empty hampers and bottles, umbrellas and fish-frails, bats and balls and knitting, and went—oh, listen, Dad!—to the fair in the dusk on the bald seaside field.

Activities

Looking at Descriptive Writing

1. Subjective writing reveals far more about a writer's personality, thoughts, and feelings about a topic than does objective writing.

   Reread the two paragraphs about sharks in this section and the descriptive essay "Holiday Memory" by Dylan Thomas.

   By using specific examples from the three selections, demonstrate (orally or in writing) that we learn more about the personalities of Hemingway and Dylan Thomas by reading their writings than we learn about the scientist from his article on sharks.

2. Examine the texture and shape of an object—for example, a garden tool, the inner components of a computer, a piece of artwork. Describe exactly what you observe without expressing any of your feelings toward the object. Then describe it again, this time implying by your choice of words a clear sense of the impression you want your reader to receive.

3. Choose *one* of the topics below. Write three paragraphs using a combination of objective and subjective description (one paragraph from each of the points of view listed for your topic). Carefully organize your description and use an effective topic sentence in each paragraph.

TOPIC	POINTS OF VIEW
• a high-school dance	• new student, principal, graduate
• professional hockey in Canada	• team owner, player, fan
• life in the twenty-first century	• senior citizen, parent, teenager
• a local teen hangout	• owner, local teen, neighbour

4. Search books and magazines for an example of a descriptive essay. Bring a copy of it to class to share with your peers. Using an overhead transparency or a handout of selected quotations, demonstrate to the class the specific characteristics of descriptive writing evident in your selection.

Narrative Writing

Narrative writing tells *what* and *where* something happened, *who* was involved, and *how* and *why* it took place. It recounts an event and it tells a story. News reporters, historians, and biographers all recreate stories from others' experiences.

Narrative essays are sometimes indistinguishable from the short story in terms of technique. However, a narrative essayist recreates *actual experience* by rendering real events (**non-fiction**) into words; the writer carefully selects details relevant to the essay's purpose and audience. In contrast, short-story writers and novelists create *from their imaginations* a world of characters that act out experiences and ideas for the reader. The experiences in these stories might resemble actual events, but the work is **fiction**.

 CHECKLIST │ EFFECTIVE NARRATIVE WRITING

✓ Organize events into a beginning, middle, and end.

✓ Use **temporal reference points** (on Sunday, before the war) and **transitional words** (first, then, next) to create a sense of the flow of events over time.

✓ Use vivid verbs and concise sentences to create an impression of action.

✓ Use adjectives to create images that accurately describe people and settings.

✓ Allow the reader to figure out the meaning of the story: imply rather than state it directly.

Narrative Essay

Read the narrative essay "Swan Song" by Chilean author Pablo Neruda, winner of the 1971 Nobel Prize. Note how the essay includes many of the characteristics of effective narrative writing.

LEARNING FOCUS
- analyze the elements of narrative writing
- identify purpose and structure in narrative writing
- analyze and use narrative techniques

MODEL: NARRATIVE ESSAY

Swan Song
by Pablo Neruda

The narrator introduces the *what* of his story (the killing of swans), the *where* (Lake Budi), and his *purpose*—to render the event into words.

Temporal reference points such as "on Lake Budi some years ago" help structure the essay.

Note the use of metaphor in creating an effective image (the neck of the swan is compared to a tight stocking of black silk).

We see the caring nature of the writer here ("cradling" the grieving swan in his arms on the way to the river in an effort to get the swan "to fish for itself").

I'll tell you a story about birds. On Lake Budi some years ago, they were hunting down the swans without mercy. The procedure was to approach them stealthily in little boats and then rapidly—very rapidly—row into their midst. Swans like albatrosses have difficulty in flying; they must skim the surface of the water at a run. In the first phase of their flight they raise their big wings with great effort. It is then that they can be seized; a few blows with a bludgeon finish them off.

Someone made me a present of a swan: more dead than alive. It was of a marvelous species I have never seen since anywhere else in the world: a black-throated swan—a snow boat with a neck packed, as it were, into a tight stocking of black silk. Orange-beaked, red-eyed.

This happened near the sea, in Puerto Saavedra, Imperial del Sur.

They brought it to me half-dead. I bathed its wounds and pressed little pellets of bread and fish into its throat; but nothing stayed down. Nevertheless, the wounds slowly healed and the swan came to regard me as a friend. At the same time, it was apparent to me that the bird was wasting away with nostalgia. So, cradling the heavy burden in my arms through the streets, I carried it down to the river. It paddled a few strokes, very close to me. I had hoped it might learn how to fish for itself, and pointed to some pebbles far below, where they flashed in the sand like the silvery fish of the South. The swan looked at them remotely, sad-eyed.

Adverbs and adjectives like "remotely, sad-eyed" evoke an emotional response from the reader.

The word "toiled" shows the sacrifices the narrator is making to save the swan.

For the next twenty days or more, day after day, I carried the bird to the river and toiled back with it to my house. It was almost as large as I was. One afternoon it seemed more abstracted than usual, swimming very close and ignoring the lure of the insects with which I tried vainly to tempt it to fish again. It became very quiet; so I lifted it into my arms to carry it home again. It was breast high, when I suddenly felt a great ribbon unfurl, like a black arm encircling my face: it was the big coil of the neck, dropping down. It was then that I learned swans do not sing at their death, if they die of grief.

Activities

Working with the Narrative Essay

1. What are the values expressed in the narrative essay above? Find evidence of the writer's purpose in relating this story. Did the writer achieve his purpose? Explain your answer in a well-written paragraph.

2. Identify the structure of the essay (i.e., the beginning, middle, and end). How effective are the individual parts of the essay? Explain.

3. Comment orally or in writing on the effectiveness of the writer's
   - mixture of long and short sentences.
   - use of compound (two-word) modifiers.
   - use of figurative language.
   - choice of verbs.

4. Write a 500-word narrative essay in which you recreate an experience that either disturbed or impressed you in some way. Choose details carefully. Be clear about the meaning you wish your story to convey to your audience, but do not state the meaning directly.

Biography

A special kind of narrative non-fiction focuses on individuals. A **biography** is the story of a person's life written by someone else. Sometimes, particularly in journalistic writing, the term **profile** is used to refer to a short biography.

The purpose of a biography is to give a clear picture of its subject's personality and significance. However, it is more than a string of events and facts about a person arranged in chronological order. Writing a biography involves researching facts about a person. The biographer must be concerned with getting at the truth of a person and, because of this, needs to enter into the research with an open mind. Biographies allow us as readers (or viewers) to move beyond our narrow personal perspective to gain a broadened understanding of other human beings.

LEARNING FOCUS
- analyze the elements of biographical writing
- respond personally and critically to biographies
- apply techniques of biography to your own writing

✓ CHECKLIST WRITING A BIOGRAPHY

- ✓ Include observations of the person's physical appearance, actions, conversations, and surroundings.
- ✓ Include evidence from birth and school records, newspaper clippings, and any other sources.
- ✓ Provide reactions of other people to the subject.

✓ Show evidence of interaction with others (e.g., excerpts from letters, pictures from family albums).

✓ Provide carefully selected and arranged details.

✓ Present a definite point of view, though an accurate and impartial one based on examination of the facts.

✓ Offer a central insight or dominant impression of the person.

MODEL: PROFILE

This paragraph sets the context of the subject's work and achievements.

Concrete detail is used to describe Donlon's physical appearance and her enthusiasm for music.

The Power of Much
by Robert Sheppard

Denise Donlon
Age: 44
Occupation: vice-president and general manager of MuchMusic
Defining characteristics: bustle, social conscience, pop-music caregiver

Even in its quieter moments, the open-floor nerve centre of MuchMusic's video empire is not for the faint of heart. Located in a funkified rococo building on Toronto's trendy Queen Street, MuchMusic is what the world of interactivity is all about. Rock videos blast from every conceivable corner and, of course, across the country on specialty channels. Pop stars troop through its glittered chambers. Teenagers are constantly smushing their faces against its storefront windows. Doctors, educators, rights activists are regular supplicants, trying to channel the power of Much for every good cause. "We had David Bowie here once, and, of course, we were all gaga," says Denise Donlon, the resident den mother. "I heard him call his manager and say, 'This is really great. But, you know, it all seems to be run by *children.*'"

Donlon laughs at the recollection, a throaty, barrel-chested laugh that seems to reverberate from every part of her six-foot, one-inch frame. But this is no joke. She truly believes in the punch line. MuchMusic grew out of television visionary Moses Znaimer's eclectic empire and his passion for innovation. But it is innovation with a point of view: to have a TV enterprise run by enthusiasts, people who are more keen on the content than the technology. And Donlon, the woman credited with helping launch dozens of Canadian acts—Blue Rodeo, Barenaked Ladies among them— just because she believed in them, is chief enthusiast.

Note the use of understatement—Donlon "just happened to fall into" this work. The details following it show her hard work over the years, which prepared her for the job at MuchMusic.

The writer sometimes lets the subject *speak for herself*. He might have interviewed others to include their reactions. This would have added depth and plausibility to the profile.

This paragraph includes more facts on her personal life (her husband, son, mother). It also provides details about her active business life. We are given a dominant impression of Donlon's enthusiasm and energy.

Donlon says she just happened to fall into this line of work. It was probably more of a lurch. While booking bands at the University of Waterloo in the mid-1970s, she discovered—when award-winning acts had to sleep on her dorm floor to make ends meet—that there was something seriously wrong with the business of music in Canada. So she set out to correct it. She organized a national conference of campus coordinators to hear directly from bands and booking agents (it's now an annual event). She jettisoned her own Joni Mitchell ambitions ("reality set in") and became a publicist, then a roadie, hauling out equipment and organizing events for a series of Vancouver-based acts. Then, when opportunity came and Znaimer offered her the reporting job on his New Music program, she balked. Fear of flying? "Yeah, I saw myself as a big, ugly kid with a speech impediment." She lisps, and she recalls the situation with such disarming sincerity that it is easy to see why Znaimer persevered and eventually gave her the keys to the playground.

Married to folksinger Murray McLauchlan (they have an eight-year-old son, Duncan), Donlon lives the boom-box life of the busy pop-music executive: frequent business trips to New York City or Buenos Aires to check on affiliates; reporting outings to Sierre Leone with camera crew and rap group in tow to package the horrors of western Africa for the clicker generation. One part Peter Pan, one part pragmatic Wendy, Donlon says she gets her energy from her mother who overcame a life of hardship in England— abandoned by her family to a girl's home for eight years—to start over in Canada and infuse her new family with dreams of the future. MuchMusic—popular music—is about dreams, too, of course. But it is also a way for the generations to interact, to share some of the same big-life ideas. MuchMusic's goal, says Donlon, is to add context to the energy. "And sometimes," she notes, almost wistfully, "out of naïveté can come purity."

Activities

Understanding the Biography

1. In journal form, write a **personal response** to the ideas, values, and perspectives expressed or implied in the biographical essay about Denise Donlon. Compare these with your own beliefs.

2. Now write a **critical response** to the profile of Donlon. Consider the following in your response:
   - the details included and how the writer arranged them
   - the central impression the profile has created
   - whether the writer got at the truth of the personality
   - ways this profile could have been expanded to improve the story

   Think of two questions *you* might like to ask Denise Donlon in an interview.

3. Read, or view on television, a biography of a well-known person. Complete an oral report for the class focusing on how the material for the profile was selected and arranged. Did the biography provide a central insight or dominant impression of the subject? Did you think the biography was fair and balanced, or was it prejudiced in any way?

4. Create a brief biographical sketch of a person you admire. Gather and organize sufficient details so that your subject comes alive for the reader. Exchange profiles with a partner and orally critique each other's work.

Autobiography, Memoir, and Oral History

LEARNING FOCUS
- analyze the elements of autobiographical writing
- respond personally and critically to autobiographies
- apply the techniques of autobiography to your own writing

An **autobiography** (sometimes called a **memoir)** is an account of someone's life written by that person—in other words, narrative writing about personal experience (e.g., Helen Keller's *Story of My Life*, or Jean Little's *Little by Little*). It offers the writer an opportunity to stare destiny in the face objectively and honestly. A memoir can also be the writer's recollections of a particular time period, events, or people.

A special kind of autobiography is **oral history**, where an interviewer records the spoken recollections of people who are members of a particular community, or who shared an era or certain events. Where traditional history and biography have focused on accounts of powerful, well-known, or extraordinary figures, oral history highlights the stories of "ordinary" people, where the voices of the community become the text. Combined, these accounts form a composite social history. Contemporary Canadian writer Barry Broadfoot, for example, has documented the oral histories of men and women of the Depression of the 1930s in his book *Ten Lost Years*.

As biographies do, autobiographies, memoirs, and oral history enable us to see how events shape people's lives. They help us gain a better understanding of the human experience in general.

✓ CHECKLIST | STARTING AN AUTOBIOGRAPHY

✓ Reflect on the chronology of events in your life.

✓ Interview family members and friends.

✓ Look through family scrapbooks, photo albums, letters, journals, and other records.

✓ Select a significant episode or episodes from your life that you remember vividly.

✓ Describe the episode or episodes in detail.

Read the following chapter from the autobiography *The Story of My Experiments with Truth* by Mohandas (Mahatma) K. Gandhi.

MODEL: AUTOBIOGRAPHY

Faith on Its Trial
by Mohandas K. Gandhi

Though I had hired chambers in the Fort and a house in Girgaum, God would not let me settle down. Scarcely had I moved into my new house when my second son, Manilal, who had already been through an acute attack of smallpox some years back, had a severe attack of typhoid, combined with pneumonia and signs of delirium at night.

The doctor was called in. He said medicine would have little effect, but eggs and chicken broth might be given with profit.

Manilal was only ten years old. To consult his wishes was out of the question. Being his guardian I had to decide. The doctor was a very good Parsi. I told him that we were all vegetarians and that I could not possibly give either of the two things to my son. Would he therefore recommend something else?

"Your son's life is in danger," said the good doctor. "We could give him milk diluted with water but that will not give him enough nourishment. As you know, I am called in by many Hindu families, and they do not object to anything I prescribe. I think you will be well advised not to be so hard on your son."

"What you say is quite right," said I. "As a doctor you could not do otherwise. But my responsibility is very great. If the boy had been grown up, I should certainly have tried to ascertain his wishes and respected them. But here I have to think and decide for him. To my mind it is only on such occasions, that a man's faith is

The context for the episode is established. Note the chronological sequence of events.

The reader is introduced to Gandhi's main conflict (i.e., the struggle between his religious convictions and the doctor's insistence that his sick son should eat eggs and chicken broth to fight the sickness).

truly tested. Rightly or wrongly it is part of my religious conviction that man may not eat meat, eggs, and the like. There should be a limit even to the means of keeping ourselves alive. Even for life itself we may not do certain things. Religion, as I understand it, does not permit me to use meat or eggs for me or mine even on occasions like this, and I must therefore take the risk you say is likely. But I beg of you one thing. As I cannot avail myself of your treatment, I propose to try some hydropathic remedies which I happen to know. But I shall not know how to examine the boy's pulse, chest, lungs, etc. If you will kindly look in from time to time to examine him and keep me informed of his condition, I shall be grateful to you."

The good doctor appreciated my difficulty and agreed to my request. Though Manilal could not have made his choice, I told him what had passed between the doctor and myself and asked his opinion.

"Do try your hydropathic treatment," he said. "I will not have eggs or chicken broth."

This made me glad, though I realized that, if I had given him either of these, he would have taken it.

I knew Kuhne's [hydropathic] treatment and had tried it too. I knew as well that fasting also could be tried with profit. So I began to give Manilal hip baths according to Kuhne, never keeping him in the tub for more than three minutes and kept him on orange juice mixed with water for three days.

But the temperature persisted, going up to 104°. At night he would be delirious. I began to get anxious. What would people think of me? What would my elder brother think of me? Could we not call in another doctor? Why not have an Ayurvedic physician? What right had the parents to inflict their fads on their children?

I was haunted by thoughts like these. Then a contrary current would start. God would surely be pleased to see that I was giving the same treatment to my son as I would give myself. I had faith in hydropathy, and little faith in allopathy. The doctors could not guarantee recovery. At best they could experiment. The thread of life was in the hands of God. Why not trust it to Him and in His name go on with what I thought was the right treatment?

My mind was torn between these conflicting thoughts. It was night. I was in Manilal's bed lying by his side. I decided to give him a wet sheet pack. I got up, wetted a sheet; wrung the water out

---

The term *hydropathy* (hydropathic treatment) refers to the use of water as a therapeutic treatment for disease.

The questions here show Gandhi's internal conflicts and how he is affected by his decision. Details in this paragraph add to the candidness of the account.

The term *allopathy* refers to conventional medicine.

Gandhi's character is revealed by his actions: we witness his strong religious faith and his unselfish care of a sick son.

of it and wrapped it about Manilal, keeping only his head out and then covered him with two blankets. To the head I applied a wet towel. The whole body was burning like hot iron, and quite parched. There was absolutely no perspiration.

I was sorely tired. I left Manilal in the charge of his mother, and went out for a walk on Chaupati to refresh myself. It was about ten o'clock. Very few pedestrians were out. Plunged in deep thought, I scarcely looked at them, "My honour is in Thy keeping oh Lord, in this hour of trial," I repeated to myself. *Ramanama* was on my lips. After a short time I returned, my heart beating within my breast.

No sooner had I entered the room than Manilal said, "You have returned, Bapu?"

"Yes, darling."

"Do please pull me out. I am burning."

"Are you perspiring, my boy?"

"I am simply soaked. Do please take me out."

I felt his forehead. It was covered with beads of perspiration. The temperature was going down. I thanked God.

"Manilal, your fever is sure to go now. A little more perspiration and then I will take you out."

"Pray, no. Do deliver me from this furnace. Wrap me some other time if you like."

I just managed to keep him under the pack for a few minutes more by diverting him. The perspiration streamed down his forehead. I undid the pack and dried his body. Father and son fell asleep in the same bed.

And each slept like a log. Next morning Manilal had much less fever. He went on thus for forty days on diluted milk and fruit juices. I had no fear now. It was an obstinate type of fever, but it had been got under control.

Today Manilal is the healthiest of my boys. Who can say whether his recovery was due to God's grace, or to hydropathy, or to careful dietary and nursing? Let everyone decide according to his own faith. For my part I was sure that God had saved my honour, and the belief remains unaltered to this day.

Details of the conversation between father and son help the reader to imagine the episode.

How do you feel about Gandhi's not giving his son what the doctor prescribed? What would you have done in a similiar situation?

Activities

Understanding the Autobiography

1. Respond in a journal to Gandhi's "Faith on Its Trial." Note any questions or concerns you have after reading it. Consider in your response what influence your own knowledge, values, and perspective had on your reading. Also consider whether you felt Gandhi dealt with his situation in an objective, truthful manner.

2. As a whole class or for a small group assignment view the award-winning film *Gandhi*. Share with the class what you found to be the most revealing episode in the movie.

3. Conduct an interview with a person (e.g., an elderly person, a refugee) or group to examine an important experience. Transcribe the information to compose an oral history.

4. Research movie releases based on true stories that are biographical in nature (e.g., *The Hurricane*, about former boxer Rubin Carter, *The Messenger*, about French martyr Joan of Arc, or *Man on the Moon*, about comedian Andy Kaufman). Choose one example for comparison. Compare any written information you can find from biographies and autobiographies with the movie version. Make a presentation to the class to illustrate the similarities and differences between the two formats and indicate your personal preference.

5. Write a narrative essay (500 words) about an important incident in your life—an essay that might later be expanded into an autobiography.

   To research your essay, you might

   - ask questions of your parents and other family members about your past.
   - recount something important about your parents or other family members.
   - describe the place(s) where you grew up.
   - gather information about events in your life before the age of six.
   - consider a particular year of your life, a special vacation, a special gift.
   - describe an influential friend.
   - recall some involvement in sports, drama, or a particular hobby.
   - reflect on the funniest or saddest thing that has happened to you.
   - discuss your dreams or your ambitions.

Traditional Narrative

Reading a variety of narrative forms is the foundation for a thorough literary training. From our earliest years on, we encounter many, many stories—narratives of different lengths and types. All the stories we hear or read and all the movies we see, become part of one great interlocking family of stories. As we mature as readers, listeners, and viewers, we begin to notice these recurring elements of stories:

- characters who embark on a quest to discover who they are and where they belong
- the use of **symbolic language** (a lamb representing innocence, yellow leaves signifying old age) to convey meaning
- an old narrative being given a different twist by the writer

Traditional narratives come in various forms, including those described below.

MYTHS A **myth** is a story involving gods and heroes. Myths, in every culture, date back to an age of oral tradition in which stories were passed on by word of mouth. They explain some aspect of nature or human existence, such as how Earth was created, or the cycle of the seasons. Although myths might appear primitive to our modern scientific minds, they reflect a people's attempt to understand the world according to the knowledge available to them at the time.

Myths embody feelings, concepts, and widely held beliefs. For example, in the myth described below, Prometheus defies the god Zeus in order to bring fire to humanity. He shows leadership and courage in rebelling against an unjust authority. Romantic writers of the nineteenth century were fascinated by Greek and Roman myths such as this one, and borrowed from these classics for their own writing.

MODEL: MYTH

Prometheus Brings Fire to Man

retold by Barbara Drake

The great flood that ended the Silver Age not only destroyed the men of the time, it also shook loose all the ice and snow which had been stuck up in the northern part of the world. The climate

In Greek mythology Zeus is the supreme god and ruler of humankind. Athena is the goddess of wisdom.

of the earth was no longer mild, and the new men Prometheus had made suffered greatly from the cold. They spent a lot of time complaining about the bad weather and said that it was a cruel joke for someone to create them just to lead such miserable lives.

"These men are more disagreeable than the others," said Zeus.

When Prometheus heard this, he knew that Zeus would soon decide to drown these men, too, unless something was done. The best thing Prometheus could think of to make men's lives better was the gift of fire. With fire, man could warm himself, cook his food, and forge metal for tools and weapons. He could make lights at night, so that the world would not seem such a dark, dreary place. Prometheus also knew that Zeus would never agree to this, so he made his plans secretly.

Olympus, identified with Mount Olympus in northern Greece, is the mythical home of the Greek gods.

He gave a last look at Olympus, for he knew he could never return, and he told Athena goodbye. She had been his best friend there. Without another backward glance, Prometheus set out for the fiery home of the sun. He broke from the sun a fragment of glowing coal and, hiding it in the hollow of a giant fennel-stalk, he carried it down to earth. There he lit a central fire and showed men how to use it. Then he taught them how to make it for themselves by rubbing sticks together.

This is a myth of explication (i.e., it explains the phenomenon of fire). It embodies beliefs about power, human vulnerability, and progress.

Sitting around their evening fires, eating roast ox or lamb, men said to each other that they didn't know how they had survived before, without this fine thing, fire.

WHAT ARE FOLK TALES?

- A **folk tale** is a traditional prose story handed down from generation to generation, orally or in writing.
- Folktales include **legends**, **fables**, **fairy tales** (e.g., "Rumpelstiltskin" from Germany, "The Boy who Drew Cats" from Japan), **trickster tales** (featuring Anansi, for instance, from Africa), tall tales (about Paul Bunyan, for example), **jests**, and humorous narratives.
- They reflect universal emotions, conflicts, and dilemmas; thus, many of the same tales, with variations, can be found around the world. Cinderella, for example, has many versions, including a Canadian Aboriginal Cinderella.
- Their origin is often anonymous—produced by a people collectively, rather than by one storyteller.
- They portray heroes who set out on a quest, surmounting obstacles and adversaries along the way.

WHAT ARE FOLK TALES? (CONTINUED)

- They may involve
  - natural or supernatural forces (the wolf, a fairy godmother, dragons).
  - vulnerable children (Little Red Riding Hood).
  - threatening adults (a wicked stepmother).
  - contrast (good/evil; beauty/beast; wise/foolish; selfish/selfless).
  - reversals of fortune (Cinderella's transformation from rags to riches).
- They use repetition of words and phrases to help the teller memorize and retell the tale.
- For plot resolution, they depend ultimately on the hero's strength, cleverness, or courage.
- Although they were often created for children, the original versions contained gory details that were later *sanitized* in the children's versions.

LEGENDS A **legend** tells, or is popularly believed to tell, a true story about an actual person or event in history. These tales often change over time, so the facts become fictionalized. The stories of Robin Hood and King Arthur are considered legends. Folk **epics** such as Homer's *Odyssey*, *Kalevala* from Finland, and *Beowulf*, in Old English, are extended legends, written as narrative poetry. Like myths, legends are often about heroes and the supernatural. Their central characters, though, are humans instead of gods and goddesses. Like myths, legends were told and retold orally, and passed down from generation to generation.

Many modern-day novels of heroic fantasy follow the tradition of legends. *A Wizard of Earthsea,* by Ursula Le Guin, and J.R.R. Tolkien's trilogy, *The Lord of the Rings*, tell stories of heroes who must face dangerous opponents. Movies and television likewise abound with tales of characters like Luke Skywalker and Xena, Warrior Princess, who fight to uphold good against the forces of evil. In modern times, legends have evolved around individuals who perform feats of superhuman proportions, or those who have become icons in their field. (Think of Mother Teresa's renown and the status of Madonna and Wayne Gretzky as legends.) There is also a type of modern legend rooted in everyday reality. These present-day **urban legends** are bizarre, often scary, **tall tales**. They change in the retelling with real names and real place names inserted; essentially they are rumours that develop into an extended narrative.

The legend of King Arthur is reputedly based on a British chieftain of the sixth century. Arthur's knights of the Round Table participated in great adventures and performed heroic deeds for their king. The stories of King Arthur were transmitted orally for centuries until Sir Thomas Malory gathered and organized them in written form in the fifteenth century. Modern writers like Mary Macleod have adapted some of Malory's narratives. In the selection below, Macleod retells the story of how Arthur became king.

How Arthur Was Crowned King

adapted by Mary Macleod

"To joust" refers to knights on horseback engaging in combat. "To tourney" meant to engage in a tournament with teams of knights on each side. The aim was to win a prize, awarded by a beautiful lady.

Notice how Macleod retains the style of Sir Thomas Malory (e.g., "That will I, gladly" for "I will gladly do that"). This archaic (no longer used) style gives us a flavour of bygone days. Look for other phrases and words like "sticketh" and "lo," which are examples of an *uncommon* style for modern readers.

Sir Kay is at first dishonest, attempting to take credit for removing the sword from the stone.

On New Year's Day, after church, the barons rode to the field, some to joust, and some to tourney, and so it happened that Sir Ector, who had large estates near London, came also to the tournament; and with him rode Sir Kay, his son, with young Arthur, his foster brother.

As they rode, Sir Kay found he had lost his sword, for he had left it at his father's lodging, so he begged young Arthur to go and fetch it for him.

"That will I, gladly," said Arthur, and he rode fast away.

But when he came to the house, he found no one at home to give him the sword, for everyone had gone to see the jousting. Then Arthur was angry and said to himself:

"I will ride to the churchyard and take the sword with me that sticketh in the stone, for my brother, Sir Kay, shall not be without a sword this day."

When he came to the churchyard he alighted, and tied his horse to the stile, and went to the tent. But he found there no knights, who should have been guarding the sword, for they were all away at the joust. Seizing the sword by the handle he lightly and fiercely pulled it out of the stone, then took his horse and rode his way, till he came to Sir Kay his brother, to whom he delivered the sword.

As soon as Sir Kay saw it, he knew well it was the sword of the Stone, so he rode to his father Sir Ector, and said:

"Sir, lo, here is the sword of the Stone, wherefore I must be king of this land."

When Sir Ector saw the sword he turned back, and came to the church, and there they all three alighted and went into the church, and he made his son swear truly how he got the sword.

"By my brother Arthur," said Sir Kay, "for he brought it to me."

"How did you get this sword?" said Sir Ector to Arthur.

And the boy told him.

"Now," said Sir Ector, "I understand you must be king of this land."

"Wherefore I?" said Arthur, "and for what cause?"

Legends, like myths, have elements found in short stories (point of view, plot, conflict, suspense, description of character and setting, etc.).

"Sir," said Ector, "because God will have it so; for never man could draw out this sword but he that shall rightly be king. Now let me see whether you can put the sword there as it was and pull it out again."

"There is no difficulty," said Arthur, and he put it back into the stone.

Then Sir Ector tried to pull out the sword, and failed; and Sir Kay also pulled with all his might, but it would not move.

"Now you shall try," said Sir Ector to Arthur.

"I will, well," said Arthur, and pulled the sword out easily.

At this Sir Ector and Sir Kay knelt down on the ground before him.

"Alas," said Arthur, "mine own dear father and brother, why do you kneel to me?"

"Nay, nay, my lord Arthur, it is not so; I was never your father, nor of your blood; but I know well you are of higher blood than I thought you were."

Merlin was a mighty magician who had convinced Arthur's real father, King Uther Pendragon, to let Sir Ector bring up the child for Arthur's own advantage and protection. Many legends contain some supernatural magical element (e.g., Merlin and the mystery of the sword in the stone).

Then Sir Ector told him all, how he had taken him to bring up, and by whose command; and how he had received him from Merlin. And when he understood that Ector was not his father, Arthur was deeply grieved.

"Will you be my good gracious lord, when you are king?" asked the knight.

"If not, I should be to blame," said Arthur, "for you are the man in the world to whom I am the most beholden, and my good lady and mother your wife, who has fostered and kept me as well as her own children. And if ever it be God's will that I be king, as you say, you shall desire of me what I shall do, and I shall not fail you; God forbid I should fail you."

The seneschal is manager of the king's estate.

"Sir," said Sir Ector, "I will ask no more of you but that you will make my son, your foster brother Sir Kay, seneschal of all your lands."

"That shall be done," said Arthur, "and by my faith, never man but he shall have that office while he and I live."

Then they went to the archbishop and told him how the sword was achieved, and by whom.

On Twelfth Day all the barons came to the Stone in the churchyard, so that any who wished might try to win the sword. But not one of them all could take it out, except Arthur.

Many of them therefore were very angry, and said it was a great shame to them and to the country to be governed by a boy not of high blood, for as yet none of them knew that he was the son of King Uther Pendragon. So they agreed to delay the decision till Candlemas, which is the second day of February.

But when Candlemas came, and Arthur once more was the only one who could pull out the sword, they put it off till Easter; and when Easter came, and Arthur again prevailed in presence of them all, they put it off till the Feast of Pentecost.

Then by Merlin's advice the archbishop summoned some of the best knights that were to be got—such knights as in his own day King Uther Pendragon had best loved, and trusted most—and these were appointed to attend young Arthur, and never to leave him night or day till the Feast of Pentecost.

When the great day came, all manner of men once more made the attempt, and once more not one of them all could prevail but Arthur. Before all the lords and commons there assembled he pulled out the sword, whereupon all the commons cried out at once:

"We will have Arthur for our king! We will put him no more in delay, for we all see that it is God's will that he shall be our king, and he who holdeth against it, we will slay him."

And therewith they knelt down all at once, both rich and poor, and besought pardon of Arthur, because they had delayed him so long.

And Arthur forgave them, and took the sword in both his hands, and offered it on the altar where the archbishop was, and so he was made knight by the best man there.

After that, he was crowned at once, and there he swore to his lords and commons to be a true king, and to govern with true justice from thenceforth all the days of his life.

> Candlemas is a religious feast day on which candles used on church altars are blessed.

> Pentecost comes seven Sundays after Easter.

> It was the common people who demanded that Arthur be anointed their king.

> Legends tell of heroic deeds, often superhuman in scope.

PARABLES A **parable** is a brief story that illustrates a lesson or moral. In a parable the moral is *implicit* (implied, suggested) rather than *explicit* (directly stated for the reader). In parables the reader must extract the meaning for themselves.

A traditional parable is the biblical story of the Good Samaritan, who helped a man lying hurt in the road, who others had passed by. John Steinbeck's novel *The Pearl* has also been referred to as a parable.

Its **protagonist**, Kino, dreams of finding a great pearl, longing for the riches it will bring his young family. After he finds it, however, he learns through great suffering and loss (the death of his son) that the pearl does not bring happiness. Finally, he throws it back into the sea. As readers we learn that we often lose the object of our desires.

Some cartoons, like the one below from Calvin and Hobbes, illustrate a moral lesson; they can be considered a form of parable. Note the comment by cartoonist Bill Watterson at the end of this cartoon strip.

Some of my strips end up being little sermons, and this can be annoying and sappy if it's not handled lightly. One of the ongoing jokes in the strip is that Calvin usually learns the wrong lesson from his experiences, if he learns anything at all. Calvin's expression in the last panel suggests that he is resisting the moral here too.

FABLES Another type of folk tale is the **fable**. A brief story whose characters are usually animals, it also teaches a useful truth or **moral**. The Greek slave Aesop (620–560 BCE) was a storyteller whose name became identified with the widely known Greek animal fables. These were stories that had been handed down through generations of oral tradition. As seen in the following example, a fable's moral is *explicitly* stated (as opposed to *implied*) at the end of the tale.

The Eagle and the Arrow
by Aesop

An eagle was soaring through the air when suddenly it heard the whiz of an arrow, and felt itself wounded to death. Slowly it fluttered down to the earth, with its lifeblood pouring out of it. Looking down upon the arrow with which it had been pierced, it found that the haft [handle] of the arrow had been feathered with one of its own plumes. "Alas!" it cried as it died.

Moral: We often give our enemies the means for our own destruction.

ANECDOTES An **anecdote** is a brief narrative that recounts a single interesting or humorous incident. Anecdotes are briefer than short stories and are often used in writing and speaking to illustrate a point.

Four high-school boys, afflicted with spring fever, skipped morning classes. After lunch, they reported to the teacher that their car had gotten a flat tire. Much to their relief, she smiled and said: "Well, you missed a test this morning, so take seats apart from one another and get out your notebooks."

Still smiling, she waited for them to settle down. Then she said, "First question: which tire was flat?"

ALLUSIONS AND TRADITIONAL TALES Some traditional tales express so many widely held beliefs about human nature so effectively that writers often make allusions to them. An **allusion** is a reference, indirect or direct, to another work. For example, a writer might quote the moral of a fable, such as, "A bird in the hand is worth two in the bush." The writer may not even know the fable, but the moral that concludes it has become a **proverb**, a one-sentence thought that conveys some truth about life concisely. Writers sometimes allude to more recent works, too, from popular fiction to current movies.

It is best to use allusions sparingly. Before using them it is important to consider your audience and purpose carefully.

Benét's Reader's Encyclopedia (HarperCollins), *The Oxford Companion to English Literature* (Oxford), and the *Dictionary of Popular Phrases* (Bloomsbury) are helpful sources on allusions.

Activities

Exploring Traditional Narrative

1. Find examples of myths, legends, fables, parables, or anecdotes. Decide on *one* of these narrative forms. Choose *three* examples of that form and examine them for characteristics of the form. Then, using your examples as models, write your own narrative in the same form. Share your examples and your own writing with the class. If possible, make a tape recording of your story and let the class listen to it.

2. Many modern stories and movies borrow from folk tales—retelling them or using significant portions in new ways. Research to find one example of a borrowed folk tale and report your results to the class.

3. Write an entertaining song about the courage and nobility of a legendary hero. Pretend you are a wandering minstrel and sing your song praising your hero's valiant deeds to the class.

4. Read some legends about Canada's Aboriginal peoples (e.g., "The Loon's Necklace" or "Sedna the Sea Goddess") and recount them to the class.

5. Many myths and folk tales invite illustrations. Select a scene from a myth or folk tale to illustrate, plan your illustration, and explain both your choice of scene and your approach.

6. Read some legends or tales of valiant deeds (for example, parts of Homer's *Iliad* or *Odyssey*, some adventures of the Anglo Saxon hero Beowulf, or tales of the Chinese folk hero Fa Mulan, who defended her country against invaders). Bring excerpts of these tales to class so that your classmates will get a sense of the excitement and adventure, the characters and themes, of these old narratives. You might go a step further and discuss how you would shoot a scene based on a legend if you were a filmmaker.

7. Role-play a scene from a myth or legend you have read and found significant in some way. As an alternative, write your own myth or legend and create an accompanying skit. Present your role play to the class.

A Closer Look at Narrative Fiction

Many fiction writers will tell you they write because they *have* to. However, this urge is just the first step in creating a story. Storytellers, like all other artists, must use the tools and materials of their craft. Just as a painter uses paint, light, and form, or a guitarist uses chords and rhythms, writers skilfully fashion words into narrative fiction.

PEANUTS reprinted by permission of United Feature Syndicate, Inc.

How a story develops will vary from writer to writer, from story to story. Sometimes a piece of dialogue will kick-start the process; another time, a key conflict will get the ball rolling. There is no set pattern to the writing process and no magic formula for success. However, there are identifiable elements that all writers work with.

You will be familiar with many of these elements, not only because you have encountered them before in your reading and writing, but because we all use many tricks of the writer's trade in our everyday conversations. For example, in talking to friends about a concert you attended, you might

- tell them what happened before, during, and after the concert (**plot**).
- describe where and when the concert took place (**setting**).
- describe the ticket scalper who tried to sell you front-row seats (**character**).
- build up your friends' curiosity about the concert's finale (**suspense**).
- fit the experience into the larger pattern of your overall concert-going experience, suggesting what it meant to you (**theme**).

Think of plot, character, and setting as the core of the story—the *what* of the story that the writer must create. The other elements are the *how* of the storytelling.

The **World Wide Web** has numerous sites for writers. Check out the home page for the Canadian Authors Association at the Pearson Canada Web site: <www.pearsoned.ca/referencepoints/links>.

An Overview of the Elements of Fiction

LEARNING FOCUS

- analyze and explain how the elements of fiction influence meaning
- compare your own ideas and values with those in a story
- tell and write a personal or fictional narrative

The major considerations of plot, character, and setting must be addressed by every fiction writer. In addition, a story's theme needs to be established and conveyed. Like the thesis of an essay, the theme is the central idea of the work. However, in contrast to the thesis, a theme is not typically stated, but *implied*.

A writer may also think in terms of the **mood** or atmosphere surrounding the story. **Tone** and narrative **point of view** can have a major impact on mood. In addition, a writer should have a sense of the best **style** to use. Style is the means by which the individuality of the writer finds expression. Word choice, **syntax**, and descriptive language are what largely determine a writer's style.

Although many writers may not create with these concepts *consciously* in mind, they must eventually reread their works to see if these elements have been handled to their satisfaction.

In the short story below, concrete details are used to anchor the story in the reader's imagination. As you read it, look for evidence of the writer's style and mentally identify as many elements of fiction as you can.

MODEL: SHORT STORY

The Wolf

by Hermann Hesse

The desolation of the setting is emphasized. The author tells us the location of the story, in the Jura and Chasseral mountains on the France–Switzerland border. Note the subtle personification of nature in the adjectives "cruelly" and "angry." These simple words help set the mood of the story.

Never had there been so cruelly cold and long a winter in the French mountains. For weeks the air had been clear, crisp, and cold. By day the great slanting snowfields lay dull-white and endless under the glaring blue sky; by night the moon passed over them, a small, clear, angry, frosty moon, and on the snow its yellowish glare turned a dull blue that seemed the very essence of coldness. The roads and trails were deserted, especially the higher ones, and the people sat lazy and grumbling in the village huts. At night the windows glowed smokey red in the blue moonlight, and before long they were dark.

It was a hard time for the animals of the region. Many of the smaller ones, and birds as well, froze to death, and their gaunt corpses fell prey to the hawks and wolves. But they too suffered cruelly from cold and hunger. There were only a few wolf families in the region, and their distress led them to band more closely

We are introduced to the idea of wolves as predators and prey—an aspect of the story's theme. The sparse beauty and the harsh struggle to survive are seen in "narrow shadow gliding" and "dry, tortured howl."

The mixture of fear and sympathy toward the wolves is reinforced by the clustering of adjectives in the phrase "a terrible, menacing, dismal howl."

Even though third-person narration is used, the focus is on the wolves, not the humans or other animals.

Note the details that appeal to the senses: sight—ribs standing out; touch—dry mouths, warm barn, hot, hungry breath of wolves; sound—cows bellowing, bars crashing, hooves thudding; taste—frozen snow.

together. By day they went out singly. Here and there one of them would dart through the snow, lean, hungry, and alert, as soundless and furtive as a ghost, his narrow shadow gliding beside him in the whiteness. He would turn his pointed muzzle into the wind and sniff, and from time to time let out a dry, tortured howl. But at night they would all go out together and the villages would be surrounded by their plaintive howling. Cattle and poultry were carefully shut up, and guns lay in readiness behind sturdy shutters. Only seldom were the wolves able to pounce on a dog or other small prey, and two of the pack had already been shot.

The cold went on and on. Often the wolves huddled together for warmth and lay still and brooding, listening woefully to the dead countryside around them, until one of them, tortured by hunger, suddenly jumped up with a blood-curdling roar. Then all the others turned their muzzles toward him and trembled; and all together burst into a terrible, menacing, dismal howl.

Finally a small part of the pack decided to move. Early in the morning they left their holes, gathered together, and sniffed anxiously and excitedly at the frosty air. Then they started off at a quick, even trot. Those who were staying behind looked after them with wide glassy eyes, trotted a few steps in their wake, stopped, stood still for a moment in indecision, and went slowly back to their empty dens.

At noon the travelling party split in two. Three of the wolves turned eastward toward the Swiss Jura, the others continued southward. The three were fine strong animals, but dreadfully emaciated. Their indrawn light-coloured bellies were as narrow as straps, their ribs stood out pitifully on their chests, their mouths were dry and their eyes distended and desperate. They went deep into the Jura. The second day they killed a sheep, the third a dog and a foal. On all sides the infuriated country people began to hunt them. Fear of the unaccustomed intruders spread through the towns and villages of the region. The mail sleighs went out armed, no one went from one village to another without a gun. After such good pickings, the three wolves felt at once contented and uncertain in the strange surroundings. Becoming more foolhardy than they ever had been at home, they broke into a cow barn in broad daylight. The warm little building was filled with the bellowing of cows, the crashing of wooden bars, the thudding of hooves, and the hot, hungry breath of the wolves. But this time people stepped in. A price had been set on the wolves, and that redoubled the peasants' courage. They killed one with a gunshot through the neck, the second with an ax. The third escaped and ran until he fell half-dead in the snow. He was the youngest and most beautiful of the wolves, a proud beast, strong and graceful. For a long time he lay panting. Blood-red circles whirled before his eyes, and at times a painful, wheezing moan escaped him. A hurled ax had struck him in the back. But he recovered and managed to stand up. Only then did he see how far he had run. Far and wide there were neither people nor houses. Ahead of him lay an enormous, snow-covered mountain, the Chasseral. He decided to go around it. Tortured by thirst, he took a few bites of the frozen hard snow crust.

On the other side of the mountain he spied a village. It was getting on toward nightfall. He waited in a dense clump of fir trees. Then he crept cautiously past the garden fences, following the smell of warm barns. There was no one in the street. Hungrily but fearfully, he peered between the houses. A shot rang out. He threw his head back and was about to run when a second shot came. He was hit. On one side his whitish belly was spotted with blood, which fell steadily in big drops. In spite of his wound he broke into a bounding run and managed to reach the wooded mountain. There he stopped for a moment to listen, and heard voices and steps in the distance. Terror-stricken, he looked up at the mountainside. It was steep, densely wooded, and hard to climb. But he had no choice. Panting, he made his way up the steep wall, while below him a confusion of curses, commands, and lantern lights skirted the mountain. Trembling, the wounded wolf climbed through the woods in the half-light while slowly the brown blood trickled down his flank.

The cold had let up. The sky in the west was hazy, giving promise of snow.

At last the exhausted beast reached the top. He was at the edge of a large, slightly inclined snowfield not far from Mont Crosin, high above the village from which he had escaped. He felt no hunger, but a dull persistent pain from his wound. A low sick bark came from his drooping jaws, his heart beat heavily and painfully; the hand of death weighed on it like a heavy load. A lone fir tree with spreading branches lured him; there he sat down and stared forlornly into the snow-grey night. Half an hour passed.

Our sympathies are now drawn to one particular wolf. The seriousness of the wound is emphasized by Hesse's description of the blood "which fell steadily in big drops." The wolf's pitiful state is reinforced by terms such as "terror-stricken," "panting," and "trembling." Note how the author's tone conveys his attitude toward the subject matter.

The wolf's vulnerability is emphasized in such phrases as "low sick bark" and "faint howl rattled painfully." The wolf's connection to the beauty of his world is shown in how his eyes "clung to the hazy disk."

Then a red, strangely muted light fell on the snow. With a groan the wolf stood up and turned his beautiful head toward the light. It was the moon, which, gigantic and blood-red, had risen, in the southeast and was slowly climbing higher in the misty sky. For many weeks it had not been so big and red. Sadly, the dying wolf's eyes clung to the hazy disk, and again a faint howl rattled painfully through the night.

> The author highlights the brutal, unthinking slaughter of the wolf—"clumsy leggings," "tramping," "they laughed, they boasted, they sang." Note the men's lack of skill in misfiring on an already wounded animal.

Then came lights and steps. Peasants in thick coats, hunters and boys in fur caps and clumsy leggings came tramping through the snow. A triumphant cry went up. They had sighted the dying wolf, two shots were quickly fired. Both missed. Then they saw that he was already dying and fell upon him with sticks and clubs. He felt nothing more.

Having broken his bones, they dragged him down to Saint-Immer. They laughed, they boasted, they sang, they cursed; they were looking forward to brandy and coffee. None of them saw the beauty of the snow-covered forest, or the radiance of the high plateau, or the red moon which hovered over the Chasseral, and whose faint light shimmered on their rifle barrels, on the crystalline snow, and on the blurred eyes of the dead wolf.

> Hesse concludes the story by showing the dignity and beauty of the wolf and his natural surroundings—qualities completely unnoticed by the peasants.

Activities

Thinking About Stories

1. During and after reading "The Wolf," did you identify with the wolves or the people? Why? Where do Hesse's sympathies lie? Write brief paragraphs in answering and quote directly from the story.

2. In a group, brainstorm to discover who the best storytellers are among your family and friends. Why do you like their stories? Are they amusing, gripping, surprising, scary, adventuresome, inspiring? What other words or phrases come to mind when you think of their stories and storytelling styles? Make a list of these people and the qualities you associate with their talent. Present your results for class discussion.

3. What is your favourite story to tell to friends? It may help to dig out old photographs you may have, to see if they revive memories. Imagine how you would tell the story in conversation and try to write it that way. Tell the story to your classmates.

Looking at Plot

LEARNING FOCUS
- respond critically to elements of plot in a story
- assess the effectiveness of a writer's use of plot
- enhance the use of plot in your own stories

The storyline, or series of events in a story, is referred to as the **plot**. Plots can consist of a single string of related events, as often seen in short stories because of their brevity. Sometimes, however, plots are complex, full of complications that keep us looking for clues and patterns. These are the ones for which the saying "the plot thickens" was invented. Within complex storylines, there is often one main plot and a series of sub plots, or secondary plots. Plot may be the *primary concern* for authors. Sometimes it dominates the story structure, as in "The Story of an Hour," by the nineteenth century American writer Kate Chopin (in her collection *A Vocation and a Voice*). This brief story relies on the suspense and shock that results when a woman is informed of her husband's death. She feels grief, followed by a disturbing sense of freedom, only to discover by the end of the story that her husband has actually escaped death.

In contrast, some stories seem so focused on characters, that they are called *character driven*. Contemporary American writer Tillie Olsen's story "I Stand Here Ironing" (in *Tell Me a Riddle*), for instance, consists entirely of a woman's first-person reminiscence of her relationship with her daughter. Even in these stories, though, the writer must put the characters in situations that reveal something about them. In other words, the writer, at some stage of the process, and usually quite early on, must come to grips with shaping a plot. No matter how involved the characterization and setting, plot will focus the reader's attention, helping the reader to make sense of events.

LENGTH AND SCOPE When writing stories, particularly short stories, consider how the length and the scope of your story will fit your overall purpose.

Ask yourself how you can reduce your material to the essence. Then work on enriching that core material. One way writers can do this is to throw the reader directly into the middle of things or **in medias res**. Contemporary Dutch writer Sara Menco (under the **pseudonym** Marga Minco) provides a short story, "The Address," that begins in mid-plot. The story (reprinted in the anthology *ViewPoints*) opens with a young woman returning to her childhood home, where she has a dramatic encounter with an old woman. Later in the story we learn the significance of this face-to-face meeting.

ANECDOTAL WRITING Short stories sometimes offer an anecdotal or slice-of-life style of writing. For instance, rather than give a year-by-year history of a twelve-year-old girl in a small rural township, a writer might just concentrate on one incident. The focus could be the girl's reactions to an afternoon's visit from an older, more sophisticated city cousin. In an effective short story, even the smallest occurrence or gesture may be charged with meaning. So instead of stating "the girl was intimidated by her cousin Andrea," the writer might remark, "She started blinking involuntarily and tried very hard not to stare at Andrea's stylish leather boots."

CONFLICT At the heart of any plot is the **conflict**—the struggle between opposing forces or characters that creates the dynamic tension in a work. One way of viewing conflict is to consider it as of one of three categories:

- human versus the environment
- human versus human
- human versus himself or herself

Hermann Hesse's story "The Wolf," which you read earlier in this chapter, is a classic example of a human-versus-the-environment conflict: the "proud beast, strong and graceful" is finally killed by the "peasants in thick coats." Examples of human-versus-human conflicts may show them as all-consuming, as in Herman Melville's "Bartelby the Scrivener" (in which the narrator has to move his entire office to a new location in an attempt to rid himself of a bizarre employee). On the other hand, they may be lighthearted, as in "A Marriage Interview" by Japanese writer Inoue Yasushi (in *The Mother of Dreams*). In this twentieth-century story, two families set up a meeting between their children in hopes that the two will agree to marry. Conflict arises as the boy and girl express their views, which tend to clash with those of their well-meaning parents. Many stories involve people undergoing internal struggles. One of the most famously poignant of these is James Joyce's "Araby," in which we see the tortured attempts of a young man to confront his infatuation with an unapproachable young woman.

STAGES IN A PLOT SEQUENCE Fiction writers rely on some general conventions for their plots, but it is important to let the chemistry of the characters, setting, and events develop as naturally as possible. Otherwise, the story may appear contrived. The following terms are intended as a jumping-off point for designing a plot.

In the course of action, conflict emerges and **suspense** builds. Suspense does not necessarily mean the heart-gripping anxiety of a thriller. The question, for example, of whether Molly will realize her dream of scaling Mount Everest or whether Rashad will scale the corporate ladder yet maintain his integrity can be equally vital to the readers of those stories. The **climax** is the height of the struggle and usually marks the turning point in the plot. In a short story, the falling action and **resolution** (or **dénouement)** are usually very brief; the tension subsides and conclusion comes quickly. In a novel, these sections are extended and developed in greater detail.

AVOID THE "GOD FROM A MACHINE" One challenge for fiction writers is to resolve a plot in a way that is neither farfetched nor boring. Although our lives may be filled with coincidences, when we encounter too many of them in a story we tend to feel manipulated, or we decide that the story defies credibility. When the author builds up a hopeless situation and then resolves it all with a single "miraculous" turn of events, it is referred to as a *deus ex machina* (god from a machine).

Imagine, for example, the following story. A defence lawyer is struggling to defend a single mother on welfare whom she knows is being falsely accused of armed robbery. Then, just as the closing arguments are being made, one of the witnesses bursts into the courtroom to confess to framing the woman. It's not that the turn of events is impossible, it's just highly *improbable* and may strike readers as corny and contrived.

To avoid painting yourself into a corner when devising your plot, you might want to think about the resolution first and work backwards. This gives you a framework for creating the story.

A c t i v i t i e s

Analyzing Plot

1. Choose two stories that you find exciting and one that seems boring. What is there in the plots of the stories you like that distinguishes them from the dull one? Are there other elements (setting, dialogue, characterization) that make the difference? Write a brief essay explaining how important you feel the plot of each story is to its success or failure in keeping your interest.

2. Imagine you are a script editor. A film company wants you to adapt a particular short story for the screen, but they are unhappy with the story's ending. Find a story with an ending that you find dissatisfying and try composing *two* alternative endings. Include a paragraph explaining how your changes improve the original.

3. Take a story you have completed or are currently writing and rearrange the time sequence. You may wish to use **flashbacks**, rapid **jump-cuts** from scene to scene as in a film, or perhaps two or more narrators to take up the story at different stages.

Looking at Character

With many stories, it is the characters that act as *magnets* for readers. It's not that the reader necessarily likes a given **character**—it's that the character is compellingly portrayed. Consider, for example, the character of the old woman in Eudora Welty's "A Worn Path."

LEARNING FOCUS
- respond critically and personally to characters in a story
- analyze and use techniques of characterization
- draft, revise, and edit a character sketch

MODEL: CHARACTER DEVELOPMENT

A Worn Path
by Eudora Welty

The concise details appeal to sight, sound, and motion.

Note the figurative comparisons— grandfather clock, chirping bird.

The character is presented as fragile (needing a cane) yet resourceful (cane made from umbrella) and determined ("persistent noise").

She was very old and small and she walked slowly in the dark pine shadows, moving a little from side to side in her steps, with the balanced heaviness and lightness of a pendulum in a grandfather clock. She carried a thin, small cane made from an umbrella, and with this she kept tapping the frozen earth in front of her. This made a grave and persistent noise in the still air, that seemed meditative like the chirping of a solitary little bird.

Welty's character may not appeal to everyone, but she does come alive in this passage. The vividness of the portrait invites the reader to wonder about the woman's life. Thus, strong characterization helps a reader develop an interest in, and empathy with, a character.

Writers depict characters to a large degree by letting them act and speak directly for themselves. This requires a range of techniques, including detailed description, dialogue, and shifts in time sequence. Regardless of how these devices are used, the writer instills a distinct tone and point of view.

Many writers envision *all* aspects of a character—appearance, personality, speech, habits, personal history, fears and desires, relationships, and so on. Then they decide how they want the reader to feel about the character, as well as what aspects of character and which techniques will create that feeling.

The Welty excerpt above and the following selection by Alice Munro both illustrate how resourceful authors make details perform *double duty*—they are used to describe the character literally in physical terms, but they also imply a deeper meaning.

MODEL: CHARACTER DEVELOPMENT

Royal Beatings
by Alice Munro

The character's clothes are "a scornful deliberate choice," consciously making herself less appealing.

Flo at this time must have been in her early thirties. A young woman. She wore exactly the same clothes that a woman of fifty, or sixty, or seventy, might wear: print housedresses loose at the neck and sleeves as well as the waist; bib aprons, also of print, which she took off when she came into the store. This was a common costume at the time, for a poor though not absolutely poverty-stricken woman; it was also, in a way, a scornful deliberate choice…. If she thought it worthwhile, and had the resources, she might have had a black-and-pale, fragile, nurtured sort of prettiness…. But she would have to have been a different person altogether; she would have to have learned to resist making faces, at herself and others.

Note how details combine to create unity and coherence.

The phrase "making faces" suggests negativity and contempt.

To achieve depth and realism in a character sketch, it is important to portray a wide range of aspects. Consider the set of questions below:

QUESTIONS TO CONSIDER WHEN WRITING A CHARACTER SKETCH

- What is the approximate age of the character ("X")? Does it matter to the readers if they know X's *exact* age?
- Does X have any obvious physical features (e.g., large green eyes, stocky legs, an egg-shaped birthmark on her shoulder)?
- How does X talk (e.g., slowly, with a high-pitched tone, falteringly)?
- How does X move (e.g., with agility, frailty, gracefulness)?
- What is X wearing? Remember to be *specific*: acid-wash jeans, paisley tie, wrinkled rayon blouse.
- Does X have family? Friends? A spouse? Pets? How does X *act* toward them?
- What is X's profession? If X is a child, what does X enjoy doing?
- Are there important events in X's past? Are these known to X's closest friends, or are they a secret?
- What is X's attitude to life (e.g., enthusiastic, optimistic, relaxed, anxious)?
- How does X manage to get in and out of difficult situations?

Activities

Portraying Character

1. Make a list of your favourite characters from short stories, novels, television shows, and movies. Choose four of them and write a brief essay describing how these characters might interact if they all met at a party.

2. Bring in to class a photograph of a friend or relative whom you think none of your classmates will know. Exchange photos with a partner and, using the questions provided above, create a one-page character sketch based on the picture.

Looking at Setting

Setting, or the *time* and *place* in which a story occurs, is not incidental. The French mountains, dotted with villages and farms but also home to wolves, for example, is critical to the development of Hermann Hesse's "The Wolf." Whether a story takes place in a nameless city in the present, in ancient Egypt, Fredericton in the 1980s, Vancouver in the year 2100, or in a grade twelve classroom three minutes before the school day ends, setting matters.

To anchor their stories and enhance mood, many writers pay special attention to creating the setting. Once again, the best way to create a fictional world is through your five senses. Imagine the sights, smells, sounds, tastes, and feel of the place.

Read the following passage by African American writer Zora Neale Hurston. We view its setting through a third-person narrator, who gives us a glimpse of the yearnings of a young woman in a small community.

LEARNING FOCUS

- respond personally and critically to setting in a story
- explain how setting contributes to a story's effectiveness
- draft, revise, and edit a description of a place

MODEL: SETTING

Their Eyes Were Watching God
by Zora Neale Hurston

The author has chosen to identify the time of year and specific location, firmly establishing a sense of place.

It was a spring afternoon in West Florida. Janie had spent most of the day under a blossoming pear tree in the back-yard. She had been spending every minute that she could steal from her chores under that tree for the last three days. That was to say, ever since the first tiny bloom had opened. It had called her to come and gaze on a mystery. From barren brown stems to glistening leaf-buds...It stirred her tremendously....

Note how the description is animated by the feelings produced in the character by her immediate surroundings.

She was stretched on her back beneath the pear tree soaking in the alto chant of the visiting bees, the gold of the sun and the panting breath of the breeze when the inaudible voice of it all

| We are also shown how this setting, though inspiring, heightens the character's sense of frustration. | came to her...were the singing bees for her? Nothing on the place nor in her grandma's house answered her. She searched as much of the world as she could from the top of the front steps and then went on down to the front gate and leaned over to gaze up and down the road. Looking, waiting, breathing short with impatience. Waiting for the world to be made. |

The description of a setting can also reveal something about the author. Rohinton Mistry, in this excerpt from his novel *A Fine Balance*, creates a setting in which a character's imaginative daydreaming prevails, even as he describes a room disapprovingly:

MODEL: SETTING

A Fine Balance
by Rohinton Mistry

Maneck took in the shabby furnishings around him: the battered sofa, two chairs with fraying seats, a scratched teapoy, a dining table with a cracked and faded rexine tablecloth. She mustn't live here, he decided, this was probably a family business, a boarding house. The walls were badly in need of paint. He played with the discoloured plaster blotches, the way he did with clouds, imagining animals and landscapes. Dogs shaking hands. Hawk diving sharply. Man with walking-stick climbing mountain.

Most short stories have only one or two settings. When you create a setting for a short story, you may find it helpful to think of your setting as a *living entity*. In a sense, your customary surroundings are an extension of yourself, somewhat like a protective shell. We shape and, at the same time, *are* shaped by our environment, so consider how your characters can function in a similar fashion. Have them act and react to the setting.

Activities

Analyzing Setting

1. Choose three stories you have read and write a paragraph on each, explaining how important you feel the setting is to the story's effectiveness. How might the story be different if most of the setting were altered in some way or completely changed?

2. Write a one-page description of the best and worst places you've ever been. Remember to focus on the place itself and the mood it evoked, not on what happened there.

More Elements of Fiction

Together with the major considerations of plot, character, and setting, all writers must consider these additional aspects of fiction:

DIALOGUE Spoken language, as represented in narrative writing, is referred to as **dialogue**. Good dialogue is much trickier to write than most of us imagine. At its best, dialogue is crisp and realistic; it brings characters to life and advances the plot. When writing dialogue, a good fiction writer must have an ear for subtleties of **dialect, cliché,** and **intonation.**

Dialect is a variation of an accepted form of speech—it represents how people talk *in reality*. A dialect may be ungrammatical and riddled with slang, but it is often livelier and more spontaneous than the formal speech we use in a job interview or when talking to strangers. Dialect is the way sisters talk to sisters, fathers talk to their best friends, and how peer groups create private slang, sometimes intended to exclude others. Good writers listen carefully for dialects in conversation, for "mistakes" and unconventional usage, and use these effectively when writing dialogue.

FYI The short story writer J.D. Salinger has been praised for his ear for everyday conversation. A good example is when one of his characters wants to know if the other has had supper and inquires, "Jeat jet?"—a compressed version of the sentence "Did you eat yet?"

Clichés may be used in writing dialogue, because that's how some of us speak. Examples of clichés would be time-worn phrases such as "The bottom line is…" or "What goes around, comes around."

Intonation has to do with *how* you say something, an important factor in writing effective dialogue. Try repeating the following phrase with the different emphases as indicated and note what the changes in intonation imply.

- *I'm* so glad to see you (suggesting someone else may not be).

- I'm so *glad* to see you (I might be disappointed to see you, as opposed to merely relieved or mildly pleased).

- I'm so glad to see *you* (implying that one might not be glad to see your friend).

Examine the use of dialogue in Vanderhaeghe's story "Reunion." In the passage below, the husband, Jack Cosgrave teases his wife, Edith, as they drive to her family reunion.

MODEL: DIALOGUE

Reunion
Guy Vanderhaeghe

The author provides no comment after Edith speaks. The reader is left to imagine her tone. There is thus no slowdown in the pace of the scene.

"How long is this holy, blessed event, this gathering of the tribe Stiles, to continue?" he asked with the heavy irony that had become second nature whenever he spoke of his in-laws.

"I don't have the faintest. When you're ready to leave just say so."

"Oh no. I'm not bearing that awful responsibility. I can see them all now, casting that baleful Stiles look, the one your father used to give me, certain that I'm tearing you against your will out of the soft, warm bosom of the family. Poor Edith."

"Jack."

Note the comments after Jack's dialogue. They reveal his attitudes in a humorous way.

The voice of the characters is captured through the use of distinctive words and speech patterns.

"What we need is a secret signal," Cosgrave said, delighted as always by any fanciful notion that happened to strike him. "What if I stamp my foot three times when I want to go home? Like this?" He pounded his left foot down on the floorboards three times, slowly and deliberately, like a carnival horse stamping out the solution to an arithmetic puzzle for the wondering, gaping yokels.

 ✓ CHECKLIST | WRITING GOOD DIALOGUE

✓ Listen to speech in various situations—conversations, class presentations, newscasts.

✓ Listen closely to **colloquial language**—how people around you *really* talk (ungrammatically, in unfinished phrases, using a lot of slang, cutting each other off).

✓ Consider how speech patterns and the style of language used varies from person to person and from situation to situation.

✓ Read your dialogue aloud to check that the diction and style are true to the character and the situation.

✓ As you read, circle anything that sounds *false* and return to it later for revision.

✓ Ask someone else to read your dialogue to see if they catch the tone and speech rhythms you're trying to convey.

SHIFTS IN TIME Moving back and forth in time—in other words, not telling the events of a tale sequentially, from beginning to end—can help a writer develop character and increase the reader's interest.

A **flashback** invites the reader to look at a character's formative experiences and the resulting growth or regression. These glimpses of their histories can increase the reader's sympathy for and understanding of characters. Flashbacks can round out characters and give them depth; they seem less like puppets and more like self-determining beings with memories and dreams of their own.

"The Open Boat" by Stephen Crane tells the story of four men stranded in a dory following a shipwreck off the Florida coast. In this excerpt, the newspaper correspondent in the dory comes to feel more deeply about others in life-and-death situations.

MODEL: FLASHBACK

The Open Boat
by Stephen Crane

In his childhood the correspondent had been made acquainted with the fact that a soldier of the Legion lay dying in Algiers, but he had never regarded it as important. Myriads of his school-fellows had informed him of the soldier's plight, but the dinning had naturally ended by making him perfectly indifferent. He had never considered it his affair that a soldier of the Legion lay dying in Algiers, nor had it appeared to him as a matter for sorrow. It was less to him than the breaking of a pencil's point.

Now, however, it quaintly came to him as a human, living thing...; it was an actuality—stern, mournful and fine.

Writers can also provide a hint of the future with **foreshadowing**. Observe how, in the opening paragraph to Saskatchewan-based writer Dianne Warren's story "The Wednesday Flower Man," we are given hints of the anger and sense of rivalry felt by the narrator, which foreshadows much of her offbeat behaviour throughout the story. The narrator is deeply annoyed that the "delivery boy" gets the manager's job in the flower shop, when she believed she was in line for the promotion. The passage also foreshadows another occurrence: later in the story, the narrator breaks into an apartment to become the recipient of the bouquet mentioned below.

MODEL: FORESHADOWING

The Wednesday Flower Man

by Dianne Warren

This afternoon Dennis will be delivering, for the last time, the usual box of roses to the apartment on Ninety-first Street. I wonder if he'll be doing anything special to commemorate the occasion. Probably not. I wonder who they'll hire to take his place. Who Dennis will hire to take his own place, I should say. It burns me to even think about it.

POINT OF VIEW As self-aware beings, we are forever creating and receiving impressions of people, events, and places. Sometimes we judge them harshly; sometimes we make allowances for them; sometimes we imagine we know them better than they know themselves. When these impressions are converted into story form, the writer chooses a narrative **point of view** or perspective. He or she must decide whether to tell the story from *inside* one of the characters, and if so, which one. When telling the story from *outside* the characters, the writer must decide what range of knowledge the **narrator** has.

A narrator who is all-knowing is referred to as an **omniscient narrator**. This third-person point of view allows the storyteller to reveal more than one specific character could possibly know. This perspective offers something like a bird's-eye view of the scene, with mind reading and eavesdropping included. A third-person narrator who stands outside the story's characters but narrates from the point of view of *one character* (thereby providing a sense of authenticity) is called a **limited omniscient narrator**. Both these styles are objective. In contrast, **first-person narration** is subjective; the storyteller is passionately involved and necessarily biased. The second-person perspective (the *you* point of view) is not often used in fiction writing.

The choice the writer makes has a tremendous impact on our interpretation and enjoyment of a story. Imagine, for example, "The Wolf" told from each of the following perspectives: the wolf's, one of the peasants', and an all-seeing, all-knowing narrator sympathetic to the peasants. Each of the stories could have essentially the same plot, the same setting, and the same cast of characters. However, each telling would be dramatically different.

The third-person perspective allows the narrator to share knowledge of the characters, their pasts, and what is in store for them. Recall in

"The Wolf" how Hesse uses the omniscient perspective to give an overview of that long winter in the mountains, then to move to the sufferings of both humans and animals. From there the viewpoint shifted to the motivations and actions of the wolves, came to focus on the wounded wolf, and finally to the peasants. Ultimately, Hesse's sympathy lies with the wolf, but he focuses his narrative powers on each set of characters in the story in turn.

One advantage of the limited omniscient style is that the author can explore the inner thoughts of characters while at the same time allowing readers to feel differently from the narrator. There is the possibility, though, in third-person narration, of going overboard in analyzing characters; the reader may feel that he or she is not given enough room to assess each character. Try to achieve a balance between what you say directly and what you want readers to deduce for themselves from the characters' dialogue, actions, and appearance. When in doubt, remember the first commandment of writing, "Don't tell me—show me." The passage below provides no narrative commentary on the character Miss Brill; the impression we receive of her comes straight out of the character's own thoughts.

MODEL: LIMITED THIRD-PERSON NARRATION

Miss Brill
by Katherine Mansfield

Note the subtle judgment applied to the character, as we see her need to eavesdrop on those sitting next to her at a concert.

Only two people shared her "special" seat: a fine old man in a velvet coat, his hands clasped over a huge carved walking-stick, and a big old woman, sitting upright, with a roll of knitting on her embroidered apron. They did not speak. This was disappointing, for Miss Brill always looked forward to the conversation. She had become really quite expert, she thought, at listening as though she didn't listen, at sitting in other people's lives just for a minute while they talked round her.

One benefit of using first-person narration is that readers will tend to identify quickly with the narrator, from a sense of getting the story firsthand. Another advantage is that your story has a better chance of producing a coherent emotional response, as you are focusing on one person's reaction to the events.

Take a look at the following piece by a student writer, written in first-person style. By choosing to retell a well-known folk tale from an unusual perspective, the writer lends new life as well as a comic tone to the story.

Jack and the Beanstalk Revisited

Last week I had one of the toughest cases in my seventeen years as a criminal lawyer. My client, Bernard Aristotle Giant, III (known as B.A. Giant to those he does not crush or send running off screaming) accused Jack Beanstalk—yes, the guy with the magic beans—of theft and trespassing.

I'll set the scene for you.

This modernized narrative by a student is comic because of the incongruities in plot and character. Things in this new version are unexpected and exaggerated. Note how the writer has taken creative liberties with the original story.

I had just called to the stand the aforementioned Mr. Beanstalk. I informed him that there had been numerous publications about incidents that had taken place between my client and him, but none from my client's perspective. There had never even been so much as a report involving statements or information from Mr. Giant's point of view.

I asked him to clarify for the court that he, Jack Beanstalk, had indeed climbed up the magical beanstalk leading to my client's private property. I was thinking to myself as I asked this, "Man, if he doesn't admit to that, I'm going to have a problem." Then I went for the tougher question. I asked him if it was true that he had in fact entered my client's home, hidden there, and proceeded to steal several gold coins, a golden-egg-laying goose, and a golden harp. Guess what he said? He stated that Mrs. Giant had forced him to remain in the house and then further claimed that she had insisted he take the coins, goose, and harp. I had already brought Mrs. Giant to the stand earlier in the day. She had admitted that she had invited Jack inside, but had never suggested that Jack Beanstalk remove any of their possessions.

So we had Beanstalk on the major charge of theft, but that was not enough for the "Big Guy" (a.k.a. B.A. Giant). He came forward with important information, never before released in public. He claimed that the beanstalk Jack had climbed was actually his personal property. He had always wanted his own beanstalk, and since that kind of plant cannot be grown on a cloud, such as the

155

one B.A. lived on, he had purchased a small piece of land on the ground. It was just by chance that the plot bordered Jack's backyard. So my client claimed that Jack was trespassing on his property from the instant he began climbing up the beanstalk. He then produced a deed of land supplied by the Royal Giants Real Estate Foundation supporting his claim to the plot of land. He also submitted as evidence a partially used bag of giant bean seeds. At that point, Jack Beanstalk jumped up and pointed out that B.A. Giant could have purchased the seeds at any time and that they were irrelevant to this case.

We broke for the day at that point. The judge ordered a sample of beanstalk to be analyzed to see whether the seeds were indeed authentic. Upon our return to court the next morning, results from the lab were back and supported B.A. Giant's trespassing claim. The stubborn Jack refused to accept this, still claiming that he had bought the beans and planted them himself.

The evidence was now strong enough for the judge to make her decision on the theft. Jack Beanstalk was found guilty and fined $1,000 plus the cost of the stolen coins he had used to buy his cow back. He was also ordered to return the golden harp and golden goose. As for the trespassing charge, the judge said that she needed a few minutes and left the courtroom.

By the time she returned, a fight had broken out between Jack Beanstalk and Bernard Aristotle Giant and it took quite a while for order to resume in the court. The judge's verdict on the trespassing charge was that Jack had indeed been trespassing when he reached B.A. Giant's cloud and he was fined $300 for this. B.A., however, was required to return his plot of land on the ground to the local government as the beanstalk he had grown violated four zoning laws.

So there you have it—my toughest (not to mention weirdest) case ever and the true story of "Jack and the Beanstalk."

First-person narrative also adds a sense of realism to a story. Notice how in the following excerpt from Alberta writer Mark Anthony Jarman's novel *Salvage King, Ya!* we can feel the frustrations of an aging professional hockey player as he struggles to keep up with the demands of the game.

MODEL: FIRST-PERSON NARRATION

Salvage King, Ya!

by Mark Anthony Jarman

The narrator's sense of being a *has-been* is increased by the young player's ignorance of Derek Sanderson, a well-known hockey player from the 1970s.

I can't get off the ice. My partner's been off a minute or two. No whistles. We're flying around bottled up in our end. Finally I lug it out and almost puke by our bench; my throat convulses but I stop it.

I sit down saying, "Now I know how Derek Sanderson felt." He kept puking over the boards in his last days.

The young player asks, "Who's Derek Sanderson?"

The obvious disadvantage of the first-person point of view is that you can reveal the thoughts and feelings of only *one* character directly. In addition, unless you are writing about a character very similar to yourself, you must work especially hard to maintain uniformity of speech throughout the story. You must also be careful not to betray your own values and speech habits, as these may not match your character's profile.

TONE The **tone** of a story might be comic or serious, a mixture of the two, or a whole range of other possibilities. The writer conveys tone, or attitude to the narrative's subject or audience, through word choice and style.

Here are two extremes of tone, the first from the story "A & P" where the author, John Updike, finds humour in a checkout clerk's wry observations about the customers.

MODEL: TONE

A & P

by John Updike

You could see them, when Queenie's white shoulders dawned on them, kind of jerk, or hop, or hiccup, but their eyes snapped back to their own baskets and on they pushed. I bet you could set off dynamite in an A & P and the people would by and large keep reaching and checking oatmeal off their lists and muttering "Let me see, there was a third thing, began with A, asparagus, no, ah, yes, applesauce!" or whatever it is they do mutter.

At the other extreme, note the somber, formal tone used in "The Fall of the House of Usher" by Edgar Allan Poe.

MODEL: TONE

The Fall of the House of Usher
by Edgar Allan Poe

During the whole of a dull, dark, and soundless day in the autumn of the year, when the clouds hung oppressively low in the heavens, I had been passing alone, on horseback, through a singularly dreary tract of country; and at length found myself, as the shades of the evening drew on, within view of the melancholy House of Usher. I know not how it was—but, with the first glimpse of the building, a sense of insufferable gloom pervaded my spirit.

Notice how each author communicates as much about his narrator as he does the topic discussed. In the first example, we have a sense of a young man talking to us in a cocky, conversational style. In the Poe excerpt, the use of formal phrases such as "singularly dreary" and "insufferable gloom," and the inverted **syntax** of "I know not" are clues. They indicate both an earlier period of history and a narrator who is well educated, refined, and rather melancholy.

IRONY Differences between reality and appearance are emphasized through the device of **irony**. Irony may involve contrast between

- what a character says, and what he or she really means (**verbal irony**).
- what a character says or believes, and what the audience actually knows (**dramatic irony**).
- what happens, and what was expected or appropriate (**situational irony**).

A near-relation of tone, the literary device of **irony** can give fictional stories greater depth of meaning. It can help readers see characters, situations, and values in a new light.

Consider the following example from Matt Cohen's story "The Expatriate," about a young man living in Toronto.

MODEL: IRONY

The Expatriate
by Matt Cohen

The writer puts an unexpected twist on the customary notion of someone being *employed* in a variety of ways. Irony exists in the fact that identity typically comes from one's employment, not unemployment.

He was twenty-eight years old and since he had left university a few years ago he had been unemployed in a variety of ways. Currently he was an unemployed writer of films. Before that, he had been an unemployed taxi driver, a status that he preferred.

Two frequent sources of irony are **hyperbole** and its opposite, intentional understatement. Hyperbole is deliberate exaggeration; for example, a character saying the trout he caught was two metres long. An example of intentional understatement might be a hero describing a particular Tuesday when she stumbled into a bank holdup, was taken hostage, and saved the other hostages by disarming the robbers (sustaining five bullet wounds and a severed foot in the process), as merely a "bad day."

Activities

Putting It All Together

1. With a partner, choose a short story that neither of you has read before. After reading the story, each of you on your own will note how the plot, setting, and characterization are established. Also, examine how tone and point of view contribute to the short story. When you've finished rereading, write a two-page essay explaining what you feel to be the most effective aspects of the story and how well you think the author has managed to convey them. Compare essays with your partner.

2. Reframe a well-known tale (a folk tale, myth, fairy tale, etc.) as a short story. Consider using a different point of view or a modern setting. For example, you might retell the myth of Icarus and Daedalus from Icarus' point of view, or the story of Cinderella from the viewpoint of the wicked stepmother; or you could turn the medieval tale of the knights of the Round Table and the quest for the Holy Grail into the saga of a modern-day sports team on a quest for the provincial championship.

3. Write a two-page story about a particularly bad day that you or a friend or family member had recently. After you've completed it, rewrite your story, looking for ways to find humour in the situation. Feel free to rewrite it from another person's point of view, if you think that will help you to gain a fresh perspective on the events.

4. Write a short story that illustrates some central insight about life. (You may wish to look at newspapers for creative inspiration.) Begin by planning the short story's components, using a **flowchart** or **thought web** to get you started.

   As you write your story, remember to include the following:
   - a strong plot (effective conflict, suspense, and a plausible ending)
   - realistic characters
   - natural dialogue
   - a vivid setting
   - a specific point of view
   - strong imagery and figurative language
   - a varied sentence style
   - active (not passive) verbs and concrete nouns
   - an attention-grabbing title

Communicating Creatively in Poetry and Drama

Exploring Poetry

Poetry is distinct from **prose**, the most common form of writing, in being a more condensed form of expression. It carefully threads together words, images, and rhythms for creative effect. Poets must work with all their senses to vividly imagine their subjects and make them come alive for their readers. Note the following comment by a student poet:

STUDENT SAMPLE: DEFINITION OF POETRY

Poetry is not simply verses and lines, rhymes and tales. It is an expression of the soul, coming straight from the heart. Poetry is an attempt to convey something *beyond* words *in* words—it expresses life's experiences. It is a flow of consciousness, realized or not. Poetry is pure, easy, painful, dark, freeing therapy, hidden in a cloth of words.

Before you start writing your own poetry, consider how you *read* poetry. Just as an apprentice carpenter must examine many buildings to know how they are constructed before starting to build a house, it is wise for an aspiring poet to read poetry, and read it *well*—with care, appreciation, and awareness of poetry's elements and poets' techniques. As you familiarize yourself with poetry in general, you will notice that poets may have quite subtle motivations for writing. This can be seen in the poem that follows.

Overland to the Islands

by Denise Levertov

Let's go—much as that dog goes,
intently haphazard. The
Mexican light on a day that
'smells like autumn in Connecticut'
makes iris ripples on his
black gleaming fur—and that too
is as one would desire—a radiance
consorting with the dance.
          Under his feet
rocks and mud, his imagination, sniffing,
engaged in its perceptions—dancing
edgeways, there's nothing
the dog disdains on his way,
nevertheless he
keeps moving, changing
pace and approach but
not direction—'every step an arrival.'

Without mentioning the creative process overtly, this poem cele-brates poetry as a mode of thinking. It also conveys an approach—that of exploring our world with energy and enthusiasm. The phrase "every step an arrival" emphasizes how we can move forward and yet, simulta-neously, embrace the present.

As you read the poems in this chapter, use the questions below to deepen your understanding and appreciation of poetry:

- Who is the speaker in the poem? Are the speaker and the poet one and the same? Is there more than one speaker?

- Is the poet using an identifiable **persona** as the speaker (e.g., the voice of an elderly person, a young child, a historical figure)?

- To whom, if anyone, is the poem addressed? How does the intended audience for the poem affect how we understand it?

- What is the dominant **tone**? Can you identify the poet's attitude towards the subject matter (amused, judgmental, ecstatic) or the audience (respectful, sarcastic, charming)?

- Is there an identifiable plot? Is an event or occasion being described? Is the poem set in any particular time or place?

- Does the poem make sense on a literal level? Are there any parts that don't make sense?

- Does the poet make generalizations? If so, do these seem true only within the **context** of the poem?

- Do any words or phrases stand out? Has the poet used **diction** (word choice) to good effect? What level of diction (formal, informal, slang) is being used?

- After reading the poem through several times, can you identify a specific **mood**? How does the poem make you feel? Do you think this is how the poet intended you to feel?

- Has reading this poem given you any fresh insights or perspectives? What are they and how do they compare with ideas you held felt before?

Words Under Pressure: Making Every Letter Count

LEARNING FOCUS

- respond personally and critically to the use of images and symbols
- analyze diction, imagery, and figures of speech in poetry
- use effective images and symbols in your own writing

Poets know that their words will be scrutinized for meaning. They make the most of every word choice, using sensory detail, **imagery**, and such figures of speech as **metaphor**, **simile**, and **personification** to give the reader the most meaning in the fewest lines. Unlike novelists and short-story writers, who have many pages in which to develop their ideas, most poets are careful to ensure that each **image**, phrase, and even syllable conveys *concisely* the ideas, feelings, and rhythms of their creative work.

IMAGERY IN POETRY Images add visual clarity to a poem. They are intense, jam-packed with meaning, and can evoke so much for a reader in so few words. Observe how the poet in the seven-line poem that follows uses carefully chosen images to evoke the beauty and bittersweet quality of the transition from summer to winter. Note how the contrast between rural and urban life is developed: the author refers to the "red-faced farmer" (tanned from the outdoors) and the "wistful stars with white faces like town children" (pale from staying indoors).

MODEL: IMAGERY

Autumn
by T.E. Hulme

A touch of cold in the Autumn night—
I walked abroad,
And saw the ruddy moon lean over a hedge
Like a red-faced farmer.
I did not stop to speak, but nodded,
And round about were the wistful stars
With white faces like town children.

The speaker personifies the moon as a farmer and stars as children's faces. These images evoke the nostalgic feelings a farmer might have at the end of a harvest.

Sometimes a single comparison does not do justice to the power or subtlety of an impression. A poet may then decide to dream up as many likenesses as possible. Take a look at how Margaret Atwood has characterized the landlady in the poem below.

MODEL: IMAGERY

The Landlady
by Margaret Atwood

This is the lair of the landlady.

She is
a raw voice
loose in the rooms beneath me,

Observe the careful word choice—"lair" evokes the feeling of a wild animal's den.

the continuous henyard
squabble going on below
thought in this house like
the bicker of blood through the head.

Note the dissonant, jarring sound of the phrase "continuous henyard squabble."

She is everywhere, intrusive as the smells
that bulge in under my doorsill;
she presides over my
meagre eating, generates
the light for eyestrain.

From her I rent my time:
she slams

The poet introduces imagery capturing the boarding house's smells. It is illogical to suggest smells can "bulge," yet it is evocative. The image suggests that the landlady, too, bulges.

my days like doors.
Nothing is mine

The poet shows the nightmarish proportions of the landlady's presence.

and when I dream images
of daring escapes through the snow
I find myself walking
always over a vast face
which is the land-
lady's, and wake up shouting.

She is a bulk, a knot
swollen in space. Though I have tried
to find some way around
her, my senses
are cluttered by perception
and can't see through her.

Poetic closure is achieved through imagery that conjures up the smell of the boarding house. This confirms for the reader the speaker's negative impression of the landlady.

She stands there, a raucous fact
blocking my way:
immutable, a slab
of what is real,

solid as bacon.

It is interesting to note that the best image may not always be the most richly detailed one. Plain, simple wording can sometimes be more meaningful, particularly if it is consistent with the point the poet wishes to convey. In the following poem, images are used sparingly, yet to memorable effect:

STUDENT SAMPLE: IMAGERY

The Tuxedo and the Gown

An easily-visualized image—the standard formal attire of a graduation dance—is sketched in abstract terms ("elegant," "perfect").

An elegant dress,
Or the perfect tuxedo,
And we are, for one night,
The men and women
We will become.

It's strange,
How we are so anxious to leave

The visible beauty of the attire could have been illustrated by concrete words like "emerald-green" evening gown or "tailored perfection" of the tuxedo. However, this is less important to the meaning than the prom-goers' desire to look mature.

Those few hours of adulthood
Behind,
For jeans and t-shirts.

To preserve
The last few moments,
Of a childhood faded to memory
To protect ourselves,
From whatever heartache
Might lie ahead.

The poet suggests that once we see ourselves as adults we cannot slip back into childhood ways.

But we cannot hide adulthood
In the back of the closet,
Next to the tuxedo.
We will find no protection
In jeans and t-shirts.

Elegant dresses and tuxedos
Cannot make us something
We already are.

 CHECKLIST | **WRITING EFFECTIVE IMAGERY**

✓ Free your mind to develop associations.

✓ Note specific details in everyday life.

✓ Examine your subject with the full range of your senses, not just the visual.

✓ Use comparisons to clarify descriptions (e.g., hair as soft as silk or trees like statues).

✓ Create images that evoke connotations rather than providing only denotative (literal) meaning.

SYMBOLISM IN POETRY Related to imagery and evolving from it is the concept of symbolism. A **symbol** represents something else, an idea or a quality, in particular. For example, the dog's eager scouting of the shoreline in Levertov's "Overland to the Islands" could be seen to *symbolize* the kind of energetic investigation valued by poets.

Read the excerpt below from a poem by internationally acclaimed Spanish writer Jésus López-Pacheco.

MODEL: SYMBOLISM

The title refers to Canadian doctor Norman Bethune (1890–1939), known worldwide for his work on the front lines in WWI and in China in the 1930s.

Norman Bethune
by Jésus López-Pacheco

The most humane Canadian of our age
went to Spain when Spain was crying to the world
"Come and see the spilled blood!"
"*My eyes are overflowing*," he said, "*and clouded with blood.*"
He could not look
At the bloodshed he was seeing.
But the blood of the dead was already
just dead blood.

. . . .

The image of "just dead blood" becomes a **paradox** (apparent contradiction). Blood is crucial to human life: spilled blood takes away life, yet new blood gives the gift of life.

The most humane Canadian of our age,
without forgetting the bloodshed,
thought of the living blood still fighting.
And being himself a poet of another kind,
when he saw wounds like "*terrible flowers of flesh*"
he rhymed their edges with stitches
so that the spilling of blood would stop.
But sometimes these flowers suddenly
Withered, for they had lost too much blood.
And the blood of the dead was already
just dead blood.

The repetition of the phrase "just dead blood" is an effective image that takes on the quality of a symbol.

. . . .

The most humane Canadian of our age
climbed on a little truck and went to all the front lines
with bottles of blood. Having discovered
that human vein could flow into human veins,
he founded the "Servicio Canadiense de Transfusion de Sangre,"
"Canadian Blood Transfusion Service."

This "just dead blood" is transformed by Bethune, through his courage and imagination, into a source of hope as it becomes life-saving "bottles of blood."

In the poem "Norman Bethune" we see blood as symbolic of human loss—the actual cost of warfare. It symbolizes, as well, the bond between comrades, enemies, doctors, and even nations. To reduce the interpretation of blood as a concept to any *single* meaning would diminish its power. In contrast, a symbol that keeps hinting at more meanings is said to *resonate*, as the blood symbolism strongly resonates in this poem. The best symbols are those that have an almost inexhaustible quality to them: they provide fresh subtleties and associations with every rereading.

In the following poem by British poet Philip Larkin, we can see how what begins as a two-line simile becomes an extended **analogy** throughout the next two stanzas. As we reflect, we understand how the trees can be viewed as a symbol for the wisdom to acknowledge aging, yet begin each day anew.

MODEL: SYMBOLISM

The Trees
by Philip Larkin

The trees are coming into leaf
Like something almost being said;
The recent buds relax and spread,
Their greenness is a kind of grief.

Is it that they are born again
And we grow old? No, they die too.
Their yearly trick of looking new
Is written down in rings of grain.

Yet still the unresting castles thresh
In fullgrown thickness every May.
Last year is dead, they seem to say,
Begin afresh, afresh, afresh.

We need not try, however, to find symbolism in *every* poem we read. Many poems don't use symbolism at all—what is described simply stands for itself and we do not need to probe for other meanings.

Activities

Working with Words and Images

1. Close your eyes and imagine a perfect place, food, person, or day. How might you describe how you feel about this, without using adjectives such as *beautiful*, *delicious*, or *gorgeous*? What sights, sounds, or other sensory experiences could you compare this experience to? Write a short poem based on your comparisons.

2. The poem "The Landlady" shows evidence of very careful word choice. Read it again to find words that you feel are especially evocative in their connotations. How would an alternative, more conventional word have weakened the poem? Try rewriting the poem, using language that is vague. Then show the two versions to people unfamiliar with the poem to see which version they prefer.

3. Examine the **logos** of your favourite sports teams, music groups, clothing brands, cars, or computer products. What kinds of symbols do their logos use (e.g., symbols of power, speed, endurance, playfulness)? Write a poem about one of your favourite logos, which expresses the meaning this image has for you.

4. Research the life of a well-known Canadian who means something to you, and create a poem, using an image that symbolizes what he or she represents for you or your generation.

Stretching the Imagination

LEARNING FOCUS
- analyze how poetic elements are used to explore the imagination
- describe how poets use poetic techniques to enhance meaning
- increase the clarity, precision, and vividness of your writing

Poets often shed new light on their subjects, requiring their audience to look beyond the literal or superficial. They convey an intensity of perception as they probe and question. They present unusual or even paradoxical perspectives. In exchange for their skilful application of creativity, they ask us to stretch our own imaginations as we interpret what they write.

In much of the poetry you read, you will get a sense of **voice**—the personality of the speaker (sometimes, but not always, the poet) coming through in the work. The element of voice reveals attitudes and opinions to the audience and helps to establish both the tone and the mood of the poem. Observe how in the poem below we are given a strong sense of voice even though the poet provides several perspectives before revealing her own viewpoint.

STUDENT SAMPLE: VOICE

The Zoo

"Come see the animals," they said.
"Visit our city zoo!"
So I did.

There were lions and tigers, snakes
and monkeys, parrots
and elephants.

Children were laughing at the
antics of the chimps, and
feeding them popcorn.

Adults admired the cleanliness
of the cages, and the
courage of the
lion-feeder.

Am I the only one who
saw the
bars?

Note how suspense is built from stanza to stanza.

Various viewpoints are included. It is often valuable to consider multiple voices when composing poetry.

The poet avoids being too accusatory by concluding with a direct question.

For an unusual perspective, take a look at how the following poem uses distinctive imagery to bring us into the miniature world of the snail.

MODEL: POEM

Considering the Snail
by Thom Gunn

The grass is seen as "heavy" and is referred to collectively as a "wood." This brings us into the scale of the snail's perception.

Note the paradox in the line "rain / has darkened the earth's dark." Dark may refer literally to the colour of the soil and figuratively to the mystery of the snail's existence.

The snail is described as having "antlers" (rather than antennae), something majestic and more commonly associated with a reindeer.

The poet pays tribute to the snail, whose slow movements are viewed as passionate and having purpose.

The snail pushes through a green
night, for the grass is heavy
with water and meets over
the bright path he makes, where rain
has darkened the earth's dark. He
moves in a wood of desire,

pale antlers barely stirring
as he hunts. I cannot tell
what power is at work, drenched there
with purpose, knowing nothing.
What is a snail's fury? All
I think is that if later

I parted the blades above
the tunnel and saw the thin
trail of broken white across
litter, I would never have
imagined the slow passion
to that deliberate progress.

Poetry can represent in words what we only dimly perceive or choose to ignore. It can capture a fleeting yet intense sensation. Consider the way the following poem by E.E. Cummings expresses great tenderness and love, without actually using either word. Note that although the poet's style is unconventional in using lowercase letters in his poetry, Cummings uses traditional four-line stanzas.

MODEL: POEM

somewhere i have never travelled
by E.E. Cummings

Note the clever blending of imagery that appeals to various senses.

somewhere i have never travelled, gladly beyond
any experience, your eyes have their silence:
in your most frail gesture are things which enclose me,
or which i cannot touch because they are too near

your slightest look easily will unclose me
though i have closed myself as fingers,
you open always petal by petal myself as spring opens
(touching skilfully, mysteriously) her first rose

The poet compares their life to a flower and then attributes a human element ("heart") to the flower.

or if your wish be to close me, i and
my life will shut very beautifully, suddenly,
as when the heart of this flower imagines
the snow carefully everywhere descending;

The coupling of two words ("intense fragility") that are almost opposites is an example of an **oxymoron**.

nothing which we are to perceive in this world equals
the power of your intense fragility: whose texture
compels me with the colour of its countries,
rendering death and forever with each breathing

Note the transfer of one sense's qualities to another—the eyes emit a "voice." This technique is called **synesthesia**.

(i do not know what it is about you that closes
and opens; only something in me understands
the voice of your eyes is deeper than all roses)
nobody, not even the rain, has such small hands

When creating poetry, it is useful to temporarily turn off your "common sense" or "practical" mental filters. You can do this by free-writing and brainstorming in a personal journal. Be playful with thoughts and ideas. There may be more truth and meaning in what initially seems frivolous than in some of your everyday, practical thoughts. In Janet Lewis' "Lines to a Kitten," which follows, a simple, playful image of a kitten is transformed into a topic for deep reflection. We are left with the impression that we gain the most in life from having *serious fun.*

MODEL: POEM

Lines to a Kitten
by Janet Lewis

The poet begins with an unusual phrase, highlighting the tiny elegance of the kitten.

Note how the arrangement of the words "bent / Upon a fly" perfectly matches the kitten's stance and gaze.

Morsel of suavity
Perched on my knee,
Furred silken breast, your golden eye
With its great crystal lens is bent
Upon a fly
Six feet away, and all your tiny life, intent,
Crouches and peers through the dark slitted vent.

The poet moves from a playful image of the kitten to a description of its powers of concentration. "Only the great / And you" emphasizes the paradox that intense focus is a quality of both the most basic and the most highly developed minds.

Only the great
And you, can dedicate
The attention so to one small thing.
Kin of philosophers, and more, indeed,
Kin of the fur and wing
From whose intensity we read
Abstractions, elemental thoughts, of fear or speed—

You, by your narrowed thought, maintain your place,
Pure quality of your great treacherous race.

Observe in this next selection, the innovative joining of two dissimilar things: the poet compares the natural world to the world of airports.

MODEL: POEM

Airport in the Grass
by X.I. Kennedy

Grasshopper copters whir,
Blue blurs
Traverse dry air

Cicadas beam a whine
On which to zero in flights
Of turbojet termites.

173

A red ant carts
From the fusilage of the wren that crashed
Usable parts

And edging the landingstrip
Heavier than air the river
The river
The rustbucket river
Revs up her motors forever

Activities

Extending Your Perspective

1. With one or more classmates, create a list of subjects from everyday life. Then, for each one, brainstorm ideas to
   • consider the subject from an unusual point of view.
   • consider it from the perspective of a much older or younger person.
   • illustrate paradoxes.
   • question assumptions or reveal unspoken truths.

   Choose one of the subjects and write a short poem to reflect your ideas.

2. Choose an advertisement or article from a current magazine. Use the subject matter to kick-start some free-writing. Craft the results into a poem. Display your completed poem and the original ad or article side-by-side in the classroom.

Structure, Word Order, and Rhythm

In poetry, words are carefully arranged for meaning. Most of the poems you have read in this chapter and many you will read elsewhere are written in **free verse**. This poetry format has no regular rhythmic pattern but closely resembles spontaneous daily speech. Consider, for example, the following model:

LEARNING FOCUS

- analyze how elements of poetic structure enhance meaning
- explain how rhythm reinforces meaning and affects the reader
- revise your writing to improve your use of word arrangements and rhythm

MODEL: FREE VERSE

Enlightenment and Muscular Dystrophy
by Eli Coppola

The speaker associates distance covered and how it was covered (e.g., "first miles" and "giant strides") with happier times.

The first miles were easy,
you've heard it before.
I took sixteen years in giant strides,
on impulse, in flight.
Breath-less, care-less
child.
And it was over about that quickly.

Here the poet uses **enjambment** and repetition to striking effect (e.g., "broken / stay broken").

I was left with a string of small water planets,
a charmed circle I wear around my throat.
It's taken me these fourteen years to learn that certain things
broken
stay broken.
And also to notice the space the breaking has made
that lets the whole world in.

Now wherever I go I always go slowly.
Gravity and I have long conversations through my legs.
I cooperate with the smallest pebble
I study imperceptible inclines

The word spacing contributes to meaning; it suggests tremendous physical effort as well as shifts in thought pattern.

I fall and I   get up and I fall and   I get
up and   I fall and   I   get up.
My miles are good long miles.

When I work hard I think better.
But I lose a little more each year,
a few degrees of motor control.

Note the relationship between optimism, "always less than they predict," and reluctant sense of loss, "more than I can surrender."

So far always
less than they predict,
and always more
than I can surrender

The adjective "fierce" hints at both the disease's strength and the speaker's own resistance to despair.

This year, in a photograph, I did not recognize my hands.
It's a fierce thing, this enlightenment.

WORD ARRANGEMENT The poet Robert Frost once remarked that "free verse is like playing tennis without a net." This comment emphasizes the fact that self-set boundaries and forms challenge poets to hone their skills, much as professional athletes work within tighter rules and limits than a group of friends playing a pick-up game in a parking lot. Therefore, before poets break the rules of standard versification, they often study and experiment with patterns used by poets throughout the centuries.

Poems are traditionally arranged into a **stanza** format, a grouping of lines in a poem to form a unit. The most common formats are as follows: couplet (two lines), quatrain (four lines), sestet (six lines), and octave (eight lines). A **refrain** is a repeated phrase, line, or lines in a poem. In song lyrics, a refrain is typically called a **chorus**. In addition to stanzas and refrains, poets can use line breaks, word and line placement, word and line spacing, and indentation to arrange words.

RHYTHM Many poems have regular patterns of line length and rhythms within the lines. Indeed, certain poetic forms *require* particular **rhythm** and line length patterns. To understand rhythm, we look at **metre**, the pattern of *stressed* and *unstressed* syllables. As well, we break lines of poetry into **metrical feet**, *units* of stressed and unstressed syllables. Think of the word *apple*; the stress is on the first syllable—**ap**-ple. In contrast, the stress is on the second syllable in the word *among*—a-**mong**.

Wide variations exist in metred line lengths, denoted by Greek prefixes (e.g., *di* for *dimeter* [two feet] or *tetra* for *tetrameter* [four feet]. The most popular rhythm pattern in English poetry is **iambic pentameter**. Iambic pentameter has five (*pent*) metrical feet, each unit consisting of an unstressed syllable followed by a stressed syllable. Examine the line of poetry below from Wallace Stevens, written in iambic pentameter. Notice the markings used to indicate the five metrical feet marked for the unstressed and stressed syllables. Note also how the divisions between metrical feet sometimes separate a word's syllables.

How **high**/ that **high**/est **cand**/le **lights**/ the **dark**

The more common kinds of metrical feet in poetry are as follows, with stressed syllables in bold:
iamb (iambic)—off-**hand** (◡ ╱)
trochee (trochaic)—**gar**-bage (╱ ◡)
dactyl (dactylic)—**heav**-i-ly (╱ ◡ ◡)
anapest (anapestic)—in-ter-**cede** (◡ ◡ ╱)

These variations are sometimes used as substitutes in regular patterns:
spondee (spondaic)—**big shot** (´´)
pyrrhic (pyrrhic)—the eva-sion (ᵕ ᵕ)

By setting up a pattern, a poet can then emphasize certain words and, by improvising on this basic pattern, can make substitutions, occasionally placing the stressed syllable where we expect an unstressed one, or vice versa. In the following lines from another Wallace Stevens poem, notice, for example, how the substitutions (underlined in the model) give added emphasis to the words "test," "sweet," and "questionings," which are key to the meaning of the passage.

MODEL: RHYTHMIC IMPROVISATION

Sunday Morning
by Wallace Stevens

She **says**,/ "I **am**/ content/ when **wak**/ened **birds**,
Before/ they **fly**,/ <u>test</u> the/ real/ity
Of **mist**/y **fields**,/ by **their**/ <u>sweet quest</u>/ionings…"

You don't need to polish your own poems so they are as refined as this. However, it is helpful when composing poetry to read your lines aloud, perhaps even tapping out the strong beats in the lines to see that you have established a suitable rhythm for your subject matter. To get a sense of the music of poetry, read the two excerpts and full-length poem that follow, paying special attention to their careful modulation of rhythm and sound.

MODEL: RHYTHM

From a Railway Carriage
by Robert Louis Stevenson

The dactylic rhythm gives a feeling of rapid movement.

Faster than **fair**ies, **fast**er than **witch**es,
Bridges and **hous**es, **hedg**es and **ditch**es;
And **charg**ing a**long** like **troops** in a **batt**le,
All through the **mead**ows the **hors**es and **catt**le;
All of the **sights** of the **hill** and the **plain**
Fly as **thick** as **driv**ing **rain**;
And ever **again**, in the **wink** of an **eye,**
Painted **sta**tions **whist**le **by**.

The substitution of anapestic rhythm adds variety to the pace of the stanza.

MODEL: RHYTHM

Dutch Interior
by May Sarton

The iambic pentameter's formal elegance is perfectly suited to the woman's stoic nature. The troachic substitutions such as "**Bent** to" or "**deep** in" and the spondees "**Raw grief**" and "**light flows**" emphasize key ideas.

Bent to her sewing, she looks drenched in calm.
Raw grief is disciplined to the fine thread.
But in her heart this woman is the storm;

Alive, deep in herself, holds wind and rain,
Remaking chaos into intimate order
Where sometimes light flows through a windowpane.

MODEL: RHYTHM

Identi-kit
by Veronica Forrest-Thomson

The poet maintains a steady rhythm by using three strong beats per line. In the second line, either "me" or "with" might be emphasized, depending on personal interpretation.

The rhymes give a sense of structure to the poem, reinforcing the idea of traits "cohering."

This poem follows Shakespearean sonnet logic, using three quatrains and a concluding couplet, but it does not use the precise Shakespearean rhyme, nor does it use iambic pentameter.

Although not a *full* rhyme, ending with the *d* sounds, the poet does use a *half* rhyme to close.

Love is the **old**est **cam**era.
Snap me with your **eyes**.
Wearied with my**self** I **want**
a **pic**ture that **simplifies**.

Likeness is not important
provided the traits cohere.
Dissolve doubts and contradictions
to leave the exposure clear.

Erase shadows and negative
that confuse the tired sight.
Develop as conclusive definition
a pattern of black and white.

For I wish to see me reassembled
In that dark-room of your mind.

Activities

Exploring Word Arrangements and Rhythm

1. Reread the poems "From a Railway Carriage," "Dutch Interior," and "Identi-kit" with particular attention to their rhythm and to the effect of this rhythm.

   For each poem, write a paragraph in which you address the following questions:
   - What message is the poet trying to convey?
   - What mood and tone are used?
   - How does the rhythm suit the poem and the poet's apparent purpose?

2. Choose a paragraph from a newspaper article. Turn the paragraph into a poem by arranging words and phrases, repeating sections, and rewriting as necessary. Use a range of rhythmic patterns. Read aloud and refine your poem until you are satisfied with it. Then consider what effects you have created in arranging words as you have.

3. Take the rhythm of a popular song and substitute your own lyrics, perhaps in the form of a **parody**, or even just a variation on the theme of the original song to make it fit your own experience. (Think, for instance, of how "Weird Al" Yankovic rewrote Michael Jackson's "Beat It" as "Eat It," and Jimmy Webb's "McArthur Park" as "Jurassic Park.")

Rhyme and Other Sound Effects

Sound effects such as **rhyme**, rhythm, repetition, and created or *nonsense* words are universal in their appeal. Poetry has its roots in the basic human love of sound and movement—of shouting, singing, stomping, and dancing. It is also rooted in prehistory—when tales could not be written down and were told from memory. Rhymes often helped the teller remember the tale.

LEARNING FOCUS
- analyze the use of rhyme and sound devices to create special effects
- use sound devices to stimulate your imagination
- use sound devices to enhance your oral expression

There may not be any specific reason why poets are so fond of rhyme, but certainly the most practical result of using rhyme is that it makes their poems easier to commit to memory. Rhyme is pleasing to the ear and can help emphasize key words. Writing in rhyme may also appeal to a poet's desire for a challenge; creating rhymes can be a difficult yet satisfying task. Rhyme tends to contribute, as well, to a sense of closure in a stanza or entire poem.

MODEL: RHYME

There Was an Old Owl

Anonymous

There was an old owl who lived in an oak;
The more he heard, the less he spoke.
The less he spoke, the more he heard.
Why aren't we like that wise old bird!

The first poems many of us hear are nursery rhymes. These rhymes satisfy our affection for soothing, stirring sounds. Have you ever found yourself reading a wonderful chiming rhyme aloud to a young child and being caught up in the infectious enthusiasm it evoked? Read the following excerpt aloud. The rhyme scheme is denoted by letters at the end of the line.

MODEL: RHYME

I Had a Hippopotamus

by Patric Barrington

Note the use of a regular rhyme scheme.	I had a hippopotamus; I kept him in a shed	a
	And fed him upon vitamins and vegetable bread;	a
	I made him my companion on many cheery walks	b
	And had his portrait done by a celebrity in chalks.	b
The poet uses coined nonsense words to complete the rhyme and to provide a pronunciation challenge.	His charming eccentricities were known on every side,	c
	The creature's popularity was wonderfully wide;	c
	He frolicked with the Rector in a dozen friendly tussles,	d
	Who could not but remark upon his hippopotamuscles.	d
	If he should be afflicted by depression or the dumps,	e
	By hippopotameasles or the hippopotamumps,	e
	I never knew a particle of peace till it was plain	f
	He was hippopotamasticating properly again.	f
Another nonsense word, "hippopotamissis" is created to provide the "punchline."	I had a hippopotamus; I loved him as a friend;	g
	But beautiful relationships are bound to have an end.	g
	Time takes, alas! our joys from us and robs us of our blisses;	h
	My hippopotamus turned out a hippopotamissis.	h

180

Rhyme is not just for the line endings. Note the following example of internal rhyme from the Renaissance poet Edmund Spenser:

There is a lady sweet and kind,
Was never a face so pleased my mind.

Here the vowel sounds (underlined) in the second line mirror the first to give a pleasing yet unforced-sounding melodic ring to the couplet.

Rhyme is a great source of pleasure because it challenges our ingenuity and makes us smile when it surprises us, as the well-loved and zany writings of Dr. Seuss show in such children's classics as *Green Eggs and Ham, Horton Hears a Who!*, or *The Cat in the Hat*. Poets and songwriters often take chances by making up new words or using farfetched, unlikely rhymes, such as that used by songwriter John Hiatt in his song "Thing Called Love," where he rhymes "you ain't no Queen of Sheba" with "you know, we ain't no amoebas." Rhyme's power to delight crosses all barriers of age and culture. Perhaps the most obvious proof is the still-growing appeal of rhyming lyrics used in rap and hip-hop.

In addition to rhyme, poets may use any of the following sound devices:

- **alliteration**—repetition of the same sound at the beginning of words close together (e.g., "love's labours lost" or the newspaper headline "Protesters Practise What They Preach")

- **assonance**—repetition of the same vowel sound within words close together (e.g., "she feels the peeking of eyes from the field")

- **onomatopoeia**—words that mimic the sound they convey (e.g., whoosh, zoom, murmur of bees)

✓ **CHECKLIST** | **INCORPORATING RHYME IN POETRY**

✓ Take creative risks with unusual words, even nonsense words.
✓ Use a rhyming dictionary to help with your rhyme scheme.
✓ Where appropriate try to rhyme within lines as well as at line endings.
✓ Do not overuse sound effects as this can create an unintended comic or silly tone.
✓ Read your rhymes aloud and listen to how they sound.
✓ Be careful not to create *tongue twisters*.

In poetry, as in magic shows, don't "use all your tricks at once." To give your thoughts and feelings the respect they deserve, learn to use sound effects sparingly.

Activities

Working with Rhyme and Sound Effects

1. Make a list of some of your favourite-sounding words. This might include strong-sounding words like *glitch*, *snug*, *thwack*, and softer-sounding words such as *whispering*, *reverie*, or *rendezvous*. If you're having trouble thinking of individual words, think of lines of songs or **slogans** you like and see if they contain any words that appeal to you. Write a series of short poems, each highlighting one of your favourite-sounding words.

2. Choose an article or advertisement from a magazine and turn it into a poem with distinct rhyme and rhythm. You might need to change the word order, find synonyms to fit rhyme schemes, and perhaps even leave out small connecting words like *for* or *the* to create a rhythmic pattern. Read your poem aloud to a partner and ask for suggestions. Then refine your poem until you are satisfied with it and consider what effects you have created. Share your poem with the class.

3. Rap lyrics often feature exceptional rhyme, repetition, and rhythm. Write a rap lyric about one of the following topics or choose one of your own: a car breakdown, shopping with your parents, asking someone to go to a movie, the contents of your refrigerator.

Common Poetic Forms

LEARNING FOCUS
- analyze how poetic form enhances meaning, purpose, and expression
- compare perspectives in a variety of traditional poetic forms
- select and use various forms of poetic expression

Just as writers of narrative prose may use specific forms within their genre, so too may poets. The form of expression a poet chooses depends significantly on the purpose for writing. The intent might be to express a feeling, distill a subject to its essence, tell a story, or experiment with visual or sound effects.

A poet may combine purposes and also blend forms: the options for mixing and matching are almost endless. Here is an overview of some of the more common forms of poetry:

FREE VERSE As we have seen, free verse is the least *formal* of poetic forms. Within this form, the poet goes wherever the writing leads. There is no regular line length or rhyme. Many models in this chapter are written in free verse.

CONCRETE POETRY When using this form, a poet will experiment with word arrangements and visual and sound patterns to create a unique effect. Examine the **concrete poem** below in terms of how and why the words are placed where they are.

MODEL: CONCRETE POEM

How Everything Happens
(*Based on a Study of the Wave*)
by May Swenson

                                     happen.
                                to
                             up
                     stacking
                    is
              something
When nothing is happening

When it happens
             something
                 pulls
                    back
                       not
                         to
                           happen.
When   has happened.
     pulling back   stacking up
          happens
      has happened   stack up
When it   something   nothing
         pulls back while
Then nothing is happening.
                        happens.
                  and
               forward
           pushes
         up
      stacks
   something
Then

Sometimes poets use visual effects without actually creating concrete poems. For example, Eli Coppola used word spacing as a visual effect to contribute to the meaning in "Enlightenment and Muscular Dystrophy" (see page 175).

BLANK VERSE This form dates back to the sixteenth century and is still used in modern poetry. The lines are unrhymed (blank) but use iambic pentameter rhythm (with every other syllable stressed in a line starting with the second syllable). **Blank verse** may also be found in dramatic works: Shakespeare used it extensively as both poet and playwright.

HAIKU The **haiku** is a Japanese form that consists of seventeen syllables over three lines:

- five syllables in the first line
- seven syllables in the second line
- five syllables in the third line

A haiku expresses a single idea, image, or feeling, as seen in the following example:

MODEL: HAIKU

The Freshly Cut Grass
by Dorothy Cameron Smith

The freshly cut grass
Comes in on the children's shoes.
The house is laughing.

LYRIC POEMS Traditionally, lyric poems were sung, accompanied by a stringed instrument called a lyre. Now the term has come to mean a subjective, emotional poem, which is often short and frequently shows its musical roots with rhythm or rhyme. As a broad category, **lyric poetry** includes, but is not restricted to, sonnets and odes. Some narrative, or dramatic, poetry may also have lyric qualities.

A **sonnet** is a fourteen-line poem sometimes written in iambic pentameter. Many sonnets focus on the theme of love. There are two main types of sonnets:

- *Italian (Petrarchan) sonnet*—Named for the fourteenth-century Italian poet, Petrarch, it has an **octave** with the rhyme scheme *abbaabba*, and then a **sestet** with the rhyme scheme *cdecde*. Often the octave states a problem, and the sestet presents a resolution.

* *English (Shakespearean) sonnet*—Developed in England in the sixteenth century, it has three quatrains, with the rhyme scheme *abab cdcd efef*, and then a concluding, **rhyming couplet** (*gg*). Typically, the quatrains present a problem and the couplet provides the resolution.

The poem "Identi-kit," found on page 178 of this chapter, is an example of a modern-day sonnet, although it does not conform specifically to either of these rhyme schemes. In the poem, the three quatrains present a problem, and the final couplet provides a form of closure or resolution.

An **ode** is a longer and more formal lyric poem with an elaborate stanza structure. Odes are often delivered at formal public occasions—for example, at funerals or on national holidays. The Romantic poets William Wordsworth, John Keats, and Percy Bysshe Shelley made frequent use of the ode as a poetic form. Modern-day odes tend to celebrate or reflect on intense, personal experiences.

DRAMATIC MONOLOGUE A **dramatic monologue** takes the form of a speaker addressing an unseen, silent audience of one or more people. The speaker reveals his or her innermost thoughts about a dramatic moment or personal ordeal. An example is Robert Browning's "My Last Duchess." In this poem, the central character, a wealthy, dominating duke, addresses his messenger, who has come about arrangements for his second marriage. The Duke shows him a painting of his last wife, and reveals both his own personality and the duchess' tragic end in the statement, "I gave commands; / Then all smiles stopped together. There she stands / As if alive." T.S. Eliot's "Love Song of J. Alfred Prufrock," and "Ulysses" by Alfred Lord Tennyson (discussed in Chapter 2), are also written as dramatic monologues.

BALLADS AND LONGER NARRATIVE POETRY **Narrative poems** tell stories in verse. They date back to an age when stories of historic events and heroic deeds were shared by word-of-mouth and were often made into songs. Today the connection between music and poetry continues, showing up most clearly when the two intersect, as in the work of such artists as singer-poet Leonard Cohen.

A **ballad** is a popular story told about a specific event or person. Ballads typically have four-line stanzas (**quatrains**), each separated by a recurring refrain. Traditional themes of ballads include love, death, or physical courage. The celebrated Canadian balladeer Stan Rogers wrote many songs from the perspective of the ordinary person, and often about historical events. The following song relates the tale of the early explorers who sought a trade route through the remote Canadian North.

MODEL: BALLAD

Northwest Passage
by Stan Rogers

This ballad begins with a refrain, repeated after each verse. The meaning and emotional force grows with each repetition. The refrain also draws in the listeners, who can sing along.

Refrain:
Ah for just one time, I would take the Northwest Passage
To find the hand of Franklin reaching for the Beaufort Sea
Tracing one warm line through a land so wide and savage
And make a Northwest Passage to the sea

Note how Rogers chooses archaic dialect ('tis and 'twas) to flavour the lyrics.

Westward from the Davis Strait, 'tis there 'twas said to lie
The sea-route to the Orient for which so many died
Seeking gold and glory, leaving weathered broken bones
And a long-forgotten lonely cairn of stones

Refrain

In the next three stanzas the speaker compares the heroic deeds of past explorers with his own travels. A sense of wanderlust persists in contemporary times.

Three centuries thereafter, I take passage overland
In the footsteps of brave Kelso, where his "sea of flowers" began
Watching cities rise before me, then behind me sink again
The tardiest explorer, driving hard across the plain

Refrain

And through the night, behind the wheel, the mileage clicking West
I think upon Mackenzie, David Thompson and the rest
Who cracked the mountain ramparts, and did show a path for me
To race the roaring Fraser to the sea

Refrain

The characteristic rhythm and rhyme scheme of the ballad is evident.

How then am I so different from the first men through this way?
Like them I left a settled life, I threw it all away
To seek a Northwest Passage at the call of many men
To find there but the road back home again

Refrain

Longer narrative poems often present a central character caught in a conflict, with a definite outcome. Earle Birney's "David," about two boys on a mountain-climbing expedition in the Rocky Mountains of Alberta, is a powerful narrative poem. "The Forsaken" by Duncan Campbell, and "Michael" by William Wordsworth, are narrative poems that focus on a single incident or character. Such narratives leave the audience with a central insight about life.

Another form of long narrative poetry is the **epic** poem, which focuses on the heroic adventures of legendary or historic characters. Typically, these poems relate to history. The ancient Greek storyteller Homer focuses on the Trojan War in his poem the *Iliad* and on the adventures of Odysseus after the Trojan War in the *Odyssey*; *The Song of Roland*, set in France at the time of King Charlemagne (CE 742–814), tells of an ideal hero, Roland, possibly modelled after the king himself. The epic poem *Ramayana* has been passed down in Indian culture for two thousand years. It relates the story of the heroic prince Rama, who is banished with his wife, Sita, to the forest for fourteen years. Rama eventually returns to his homeland of Ayodhya and governs as a wise and well-respected ruler. The picture below shows Rama's search for Sita, who has been carried off to the kingdom of Lanka by the evil King Ravana.

FYI

Check out the home page for the League of Canadian Poets at the Pearson Canada Web site at <www.pearsoned.ca/referencepoints/links>.

Activities

Working with Poetic Forms

1. Develop a list of topics about which you might write poems. Now try writing *three* poems on just *one* of these topics, each poem using a different form (e.g., haiku, sonnet, dramatic monologue). Present

your results to the class, explaining how each form brought a different perspective to your topic.

2. Listen to a poet give a reading in your community. Then interview the poet to discover why he or she gives readings, the preparation involved, what engages the audience, which poems work and which don't. Write up the interview, summarizing the key insights, and give a brief oral presentation to the class on your findings.

3. Write a song that tells a story in the ballad tradition. Decide if you want it to have a chorus or refrain, and consider the best point of view from which to narrate the events. Perform or have someone else perform your song for the class.

4. Visit a library to find a poem that interests you in some way. Make an audio-visual or multimedia presentation of the poem you have chosen. Convey to the class the poem's central insights, perspectives, mood, and storyline (if it has one) in the visuals and sound effects you select.

Exploring Drama

Drama is more than ornate theatres and weighty works. It includes stage plays, **monologues, readers' theatre,** improvised skits, radio plays, television shows, commercials, films, and much more. Drama provides a variety of forms of artistic expression such as **tragedy, comedy, tragicomedy, farce, melodrama,** and **docudrama.** Drama puts language together with the expressive talents of performers.

This chapter focuses primarily on drama for the stage, as the considerations of radio, television, and film are explored in the next chapter. Whatever the form, the key to drama is that it *mirrors* or *imitates* life and that it requires the audience to suspend its disbelief—to imagine itself, for example, in somebody's home, in a school cafeteria, in ancient Greece, or in Renaissance Europe.

Creating Drama—Taking the Stage

Creative drama frees us to imagine and work cooperatively with fellow actors, directors, stage managers, and audiences. It hones our speaking, listening, and movement skills. Drama, like talk and discussion, helps us to learn through interaction.

Performing drama on stage moves you from the passive role of spectator to an active, creative position where you project yourself into the

LEARNING FOCUS
- respond personally and critically to creative drama
- create and perform drama
- use drama techniques to enhance your communication skills

thoughts and feelings of others. It allows you to translate a written storyline into believable dialogue, with sets, props, and stage directions to help bring it alive for an audience. It helps you to encounter life as it is or was and to understand the complexity of human relationships.

All across Canada, there is vibrant community theatre. It ranges from highly professional festivals (such as the Atlantic Theatre Festival in Wolfville, the Fringe Festival in Vancouver, the Shaw Festival at Niagara-on-the-Lake, and the Stratford Festival) to local amateur or student theatre that re-enacts the history, customs, and culture of a particular region. Most plays have a single playwright; occasionally scripts result from the collaborative efforts of several people.

Activities

Loosening Up

1. Think of an event, and individually or in small groups enact a **tableau** or series of tableaux (images with neither movement nor words). Use costumes and props to help make your visual statement. At the end of your performance, explain to the class why you chose the particular poses, costumes, and props in your tableau.

2. Write an emotion on an index card (e.g., fear, anger, joy) and exchange cards with someone else in the class. In front of the class, take turns expressing the emotion recorded on the card using hand gestures and facial expressions. Your fellow classmates should try to guess the emotion.

3. Create a scene involving conflict between two adversaries with a third person acting as arbitrator. (It could be, for example, two basketball players and a referee; a boy and girl and a teacher; two siblings and their parent.) There should be non-stop dialogue, and the reason for the conflict must become clear to your audience.

Dramatic Literature—Examining the Page

LEARNING FOCUS
- respond personally and critically to drama scripts
- analyze how drama techniques affect the audience
- improvise, prepare, and revise a drama script

You might wonder why we study dramatic literature—the scripts themselves. After all, the word *drama* is a Greek word meaning *to do* or *to act*. Drama is written primarily to be performed and experienced by an audience, and for most playwrights, the work only comes to life when it is actually performed. However, reading dramatic literature offers the same reward that reading other types of literature gives—the opportunity to enjoy, and to grow and learn through the exploration of ideas.

When you read dramatic literature—including your own work and your peers'—consider these questions:

- Does the drama hold your interest?
- Does the conflict seem real or is it contrived?
- Does the plot structure build to a climax?
- Does the dialogue advance the action of the plot?
- Is the dialogue true to the characters?
- Are the motivations behind the characters' actions believable?
- Does the play seem to have a purpose? What is it?
- Who is the intended audience?
- Is the form of the drama suitable to its purpose and audience?
- What theme is developed? How is its message depicted?
- What mood does the drama leave you with? What specifically creates this mood?

To get a taste of what dramatic literature can offer you, consider this **monologue** from *The Red Green Show*. Remember that a monologue is *one* person speaking in front of an audience: there is no interaction with other characters. Try to determine, considering this limitation, how the writers keep the audience interested.

MODEL: MONOLOGUE

Torquin' It Up with Dougie Franklin: Lost Licence
by Steve Smith and Rick Green

We are introduced to a recurring character, Dougie, the owner of a monster truck.

The writers have used understatement to create irony and contribute a comic effect.

The accumulation of details helps develop the personality of this character.

The climax is found in the third paragraph. The use of clichés ("to see with their own eyes," "accidents happen") and the speaker's general tone add to the humour.

Hi ladies, Dougie Franklin here with some very sad news. I had a little accident and my licence was suspended for a while.

I was caught doing sixty on a sidewalk. I ran through a red light, and also through the post that was holding the red light. And I had locked bumpers with a few other cars. Nine cars. Nobody was hurt. The cars were parked. They were parked in a line at a BMW dealership. I ran over nine BMWs. Luckily the only damage to the truck was from a sunroof jammed under the oil pan. I was insured.

Of course they won't insure me now, but they paid for everything. The insurance agent came right down. So did the adjuster. In fact, lots of people dropped by to see with their own eyes. Great publicity for me so I can't complain. Accidents happen. The important thing is that I've learned a lot. Like I've learned that poles don't just hold up traffic lights, they hold up streetlights and power transformers and power cables that can supply half of the downtown core. I've learned that bus shelters make a popping sound as they explode. Stuff like that.

Activities

Studying the Script

1. Divide into groups of four to five students. Each group should collect readings on a particular theme (e.g., love, loneliness, misunderstanding, laughter). Select a series of these related readings (or use selections you have written yourselves) and present them to the class as readers' theatre. Remember that in readers' theatre you can read from the script without having memorized the lines—all the acting is done with the voice. Consider producing a readers' theatre presentation for a school assembly on some theme (e.g., on war or peace for Remembrance Day).

2. Write a critical response to the monologue from *The Red Green Show*. You might consider, for example, how the writers create natural-sounding speech, how the character is developed, and how the tone and purpose of the work are conveyed to the audience. Be prepared to share and support your response with the class.

3. Develop a two- to three-minute monologue for a character from a poem, cartoon, short story, or novel. You might write the script before rehearsing it, or develop the script through a combination of improvisation, scripting, and revising. Present your monologue to the class using simple props. Afterward, hold a class session to discuss the quality of the presentation and the reasons for your choice of character.

An Overview of Dramatic Elements

LEARNING FOCUS
- respond personally and critically to drama texts
- analyze the use of dramatic elements
- plan, create, and perform effective dialogue

The elements of drama are essentially the same as those of narrative prose, with some additional considerations. There is always a plot, as well as characters, setting, and theme. As well, drama has a point of view (or several), a dominant tone, and a style crafted with attention to mood, imagery, or symbolism. The key differences between narrative prose and drama are the central role of **dialogue** and the unique need in a play for stage directions.

PLOT The stages of plot development in drama are similar to those in other literary genres. In many works, there is an introduction or **exposition** that explains the characters and their situation. The rising action or **complication** introduces the conflict to be resolved. The height of the tension is the climax, and the **resolution** comes in the **dénouement** where loose ends in the plot are tied up. Dramas do not always present tidy conclusions, however, as drama imitates life, with its often unresolved problems and unanswered questions. Ultimately, a drama has been successful when the audience is left questioning and contemplating insights from the piece long after it's over.

It is important to remember that plot is more than an unrelated string of incidents: it is connected throughout a play in a series of cause-and-effect relationships. Just as a novel is divided into chapters, all but the shortest dramatic works are divided into smaller parts. **Acts** are the major divisions within dramas, and plays of one, three, or five acts are common. (Shakespearean plays have five acts.) **Scenes** are divisions within acts. Typically, any change in the time or place of the drama requires a scene change. Scenes may be further divided into **episodes** (sometimes referred to as *breaks*); in a single episode, no major character enters or leaves the stage.

SETTING Some shorter dramas have one setting, while in other productions the setting changes many times. The significance of setting to the drama varies. Just as with narrative prose, in some works the time and place is merely part of the background, while in others it is a significant factor, contributing to the plot or echoing the mood. Sometimes the setting is understood, as it would be by the production crew of *The Red Green Show*; at other times, the scriptwriter requires precise, finely detailed settings, and documents these carefully.

In stage plays, scenery painted on screened **backdrops**, furniture and other **props**, sound effects, music, lighting, and the costumes and makeup worn by the actors all help to establish the setting and contribute to the mood.

CHARACTER People are what draws us to a play. The characters are the *core* of most dramatic works. As in narrative prose, interesting, realistic characters with believable motivations engage the audience, fuel the conflict, and propel the plot. However, in drama, while the role of a scriptwriter is similar to that of a fiction author—both craft the dialogue and describe the action—drama has the added element of the performer who must bring the character to life.

Strong actors have the ability to understand character types. They are able to convincingly bring to life the voice, posture, gestures, movement, and attitudes of the character they are portraying. In addition, they are able to reinforce a playwright's theme and purpose for the audience.

In the chart that follows, you will see listed a number of character types you might meet on the stage:

CHARACTER TYPES IN DRAMA

- **round characters**—complex, fully developed, three-dimensional characters. These characters are dynamic, developing as a result of the action and conflicts of a play.
- **flat characters**—characters that are one- or two-dimensional, built upon one characteristic; this broad category includes **stereotypes**, **caricatures**, and **stock characters**. Flat characters are static or unchanged by the action of a play.
- **protagonist**—the main or pivotal character in a play. Protagonists usually experience change through self-knowledge or their interaction with outside forces.
- **antagonist**—the protagonist's main rival or opponent. The climax of a play is that particular moment in a series of actions when antagonist and protagonist finally clash for the last time.

- **foil**—a character who contrasts with the main character (e.g., in behaviour, attitude, or qualities). A foil can illuminate the protagonist's characteristics.
- **hero**—a protagonist who is heroic, i.e., courageous and honest.
- **anti-hero**—a protagonist who is decidedly unheroic, lacking the typical qualities of a hero.
- **tragic hero**—in Greek or Shakespearean tragedy, a hero who falls from, for example, nobility, prosperity, or happiness to misfortune and misery due to some error in circumstance, judgment, or tragic flaw in character.
- **romantic character**—a character who is passionate, idealistic, individualistic, principled, or adventurous.
- **comic character**—a character, either round or flat, who brightens the performance and brings laughter to the audience.

DIALOGUE AND SPOKEN LANGUAGE Dialogue can be considered the *backbone* of drama. It introduces the work, reveals the personalities of the characters, and tells the story. It also captures the tone of the work and plays an important role in creating the mood.

Although it is the performer's role to convey the character, and use voice and body language effectively, he or she needs something solid to work from. Much depends on the dialogue the playwright puts in the characters' mouths. Playwrights study the speech of people they hear around them, listening to conversation in varied situations and noting dialects, speaking styles, and nuances of expression.

✓ CHECKLIST CREATING REALISTIC CHARACTERS AND DIALOGUE

- ✓ Observe people around you and become familiar with standard behaviours in specific situations.
- ✓ Ensure that the language your character uses reveals the background, personality, and ideas you want to convey.
- ✓ Give your characters unique traits (e.g., a nickname, a particular speech pattern, a birthmark) to make them memorable and distinctive.
- ✓ Make each word your character utters typical of that character only. This reinforces the persona for the audience.

When writing spoken language aside from dialogue, playwrights can make use of three devices unique to drama: **soliloquy, aside,** and **chorus.** A soliloquy is a long speech, a kind of monologue. It expresses the thoughts and feelings of a single character alone on stage. Soliloquies can be particularly useful when much of the action is psychological or internal (as opposed to physical or external), where the central conflict is within the character. An aside is a short speech made to the audience. Although the character is not alone on stage, he or she is supposedly not overheard by the other characters. Though not realistic, soliloquies and asides can show a character's state of mind and provide comment on another character or on the action. A chorus (usually several voices speaking in unison) may comment on the action of the drama or speak aloud the conflicting thoughts of the main characters. The chorus might, for example, give a **prologue** to set the scene or an **epilogue** to conclude the play (see Sophocles' *Antigone*). A chorus acts rather like a narrator in narrative prose, allowing the writer to comment directly on the unfolding drama.

The choice of words should never be haphazard. When reading and writing dramatic scripts, consider carefully what devices are or might be used; their appropriateness to the audience, purpose, and form; and their possible effects on meaning, theme, and mood.

THEME Drama is action. Drama is character. Drama is also a portrayal of the deeper meanings of life (theme). The playwright has something important to say and a purpose to achieve. That purpose could be to examine an issue or to state some philosophical truth. Theme is reflected in the speech and actions of the characters involved in the dramatic tensions. The characters' reactions to conflict give the audience insight into their motivations as well as their strengths and weaknesses.

INCORPORATING THE ELEMENTS OF DRAMA For an example of effective dialogue, rising tension between characters, and ways to work with plot, setting, and theme, consider the following excerpts from a one-act play by Sally Clark. This drama explores the relationship between a daughter and her mother, who is suffering from Alzheimer's disease.

In the scenes below, the setting is a familiar one, the family kitchen. Although the characters are polite to each another, the dialogue reveals the undercurrent of the daughter's frustration with her sick mother, her sadness, and the perverse humour of their illogical conversations.

MODEL: ONE-ACT PLAY

Scene 3

The stage directions indicate the general setting and the movement of characters on stage.

OLD WOMAN and DAUGHTER in kitchen. There are three hard-boiled eggs on the counter. OLD WOMAN hands daughter a hard-boiled egg.

The scene's early dialogue establishes the context—the kitchen at meal time. It also brings the audience right into the issues that are the basis of the conflict.

DAUGHTER: No eggs for me, thank you, Mother.

OLD WOMAN: Wouldn't you like a hard-boiled egg?

DAUGHTER: No thanks. I don't like hard-boiled eggs.

OLD WOMAN: But you used to like hard-boiled eggs.

DAUGHTER: Actually, Mother, I've never liked hard-boiled eggs. I ate them five years ago when I went on that grapefruit and hard-boiled egg diet, but I didn't like them then and I don't like them now. I've never liked hard-boiled eggs.

This is realistic dialogue with its short, tense exchanges, and natural, impulsive speech.

OLD WOMAN: Pardon?

DAUGHTER: No. Thank you.

OLD WOMAN: Pardon?

DAUGHTER: Forget it.

OLD WOMAN: Wouldn't you like a hard-boiled egg?

DAUGHTER: NO! I WOULDN'T!!

OLD WOMAN: There's no need to be rude.

DAUGHTER: Sorry, Mother.

OLD WOMAN: I've cooked three.

DAUGHTER: Yes. I know. You always cook three.

OLD WOMAN: What am I going to do with them?

DAUGHTER: Put them in the fridge with the rest of the hard-boiled eggs.

OLD WOMAN: Pardon?

DAUGHTER: Forget it.

Note how the stage direction here is minimal *[OLD WOMAN mashes up egg...]* to describe the actions concisely.

[OLD WOMAN mashes up egg on a plate; sets it on the floor; calls.]

OLD WOMAN: Butchie! Butchie!

[DAUGHTER looks up.]

OLD WOMAN: Butchie! Butchie!

DAUGHTER: The dog's dead, Mother.

OLD WOMAN: Pardon?

The effects of the mother's illness, i.e., her forgetfulness, become clearer.

DAUGHTER: The dog's dead and his name was Fred. Butch died years ago. There hasn't been a Butchie for at least ten years and Fred's dead.

OLD WOMAN: Who's going to eat his egg?

The dialogue shows the turmoil of the daughter's feelings.

DAUGHTER: I don't know, Mother. Someone better eat his egg. I'm sure as hell sick of eating his egg. Maybe we should buy another dog and let him eat his egg. I honestly don't know, Mother.

OLD WOMAN: Pardon?

Scene 7

These stage directions indicate what the actors should be doing.

OLD WOMAN sits quietly at a table, playing solitaire, nodding happily to herself.

DAUGHTER: *[enters]* Mother.

[Old woman pays no attention.]

DAUGHTER: MOTHER?

[Old woman does not respond.]

DAUGHTER: MOTHER!!!

OLD WOMAN: *[raises head slowly.]* Yes.

DAUGHTER: Mother—WHY DON'T YOU PUT YOUR HEARING AID IN!

OLD WOMAN: Oh heh heh heh.

DAUGHTER: WELL, WHY DON'T YOU?

OLD WOMAN: Mmmm heh heh heh.

DAUGHTER: Come on, we'll put it in together. Where is it?

[OLD WOMAN points vaguely; continues playing solitaire.

DAUGHTER puts it in. OLD WOMAN makes agonized faces.]

This stage direction indicates how the line should be delivered.

DAUGHTER: IS IT IN? *[Shouts into ear.]* DOES IT HURT? AM I HURTING YOU?

[OLD WOMAN taps on aid.]

DAUGHTER: Oh sorry, I forgot. I don't have to shout now, do I?

[OLD WOMAN continues playing solitaire.]

DAUGHTER: Isn't that better, Mother?

[OLD WOMAN nods vaguely. DAUGHTER exits. OLD WOMAN, as though she suddenly remembered something, reaches in ear, pulls out hearing aid and places it in box.]

DAUGHTER: *[returns]* I've got so many things to do today. I'm going to have to leave you for a while. You'll be all right alone, won't you, Mother? Now, there's no need to make lunch.

OLD WOMAN: *[continues playing solitaire]*. Heh heh heh heh.

Here the contrast between the old woman's and the daughter's dialogue becomes most extreme. We see them develop as round characters.

DAUGHTER: So, you won't have to boil any eggs. All right? NO EGGS. Can't think of anything else to tell you. Oh, no need to put the dishwasher on. OK? There's no dishes in it so there's no need to put it on. Don't forget to watch the soap opera and be sure to tell me what happens. Well, watch it anyway and try to remember something.

OLD WOMAN: Heh heh heh.

The stage direction *[looks puzzled]* suggests physical indication of the emotion as well as the manner in which the line should be delivered.

DAUGHTER: *[looks puzzled.]* Well, goodbye, dear. *[Kisses her and leaves.]*

OLD WOMAN: *[pads out to kitchen; offstage.]* Butchie! Butchie!

Many beginning writers rush to resolve the conflict and so prevent themselves from exploring it fully. Notice how Scene 12, which follows, carefully circles around a resolution. The scene starts with a line from the daughter that might have ended the conflict, but as the scene progresses, the character explores other possibilities. Just as people in real life may sense a solution but need to consider the other options first, so do the characters in this play.

MODEL: ONE-ACT PLAY

Scene 12

The characters are identified. A new character, George, is part of this scene.

DAUGHTER and GEORGE.

DAUGHTER: She has got to go.

GEORGE: Yes.

Note the indirect description of the old woman's character. This adds detail to the conflict.

DAUGHTER: I mean it, George. It's like living with a zombie. A pleasant well-behaved zombie, but a zombie none the less.

GEORGE: What does she do, exactly?

DAUGHTER: She sits and laughs all day.

GEORGE: She laughs.

DAUGHTER: Yes. She's very jolly.

GEORGE: What about?

DAUGHTER: Who knows?

GEORGE: You need to go out more.

DAUGHTER: I can't go out because God knows what I'll find when I get home. She still does things, you know.

GEORGE: Like what?

DAUGHTER: She boils eggs.

GEORGE: So, what's the harm in that?

DAUGHTER: Someone has to eat all those eggs.

GEORGE: Yes.

DAUGHTER: You still haven't grasped it, have you? She boils eggs and someone has to eat all those eggs. Have you had a hard-boiled egg recently?

GEORGE: Are you all right?

DAUGHTER: Have you?

GEORGE: No.

DAUGHTER: I have. I have three per day. Sometimes, four per day. Every time I leave her alone, she's out there boiling eggs. I hate hard-boiled eggs. I positively loathe hard-boiled eggs.

GEORGE: Why don't you stop buying eggs?

DAUGHTER: Simple as that, eh? Just stop buying eggs.

GEORGE: Well.

DAUGHTER: Well, what am I going to do when I have to cook something? What am I going to do about that? I have to go out and get an egg, right. You can't buy just one egg. You have to buy a whole dozen.

GEORGE: Sometimes, half a dozen.

DAUGHTER: Yes. Yes. Sometimes half a dozen. That's five eggs, though. Five eggs for her to boil.

GEORGE: So, hide the eggs.

DAUGHTER: Hide the eggs. And where do you hide eggs? Can't hide them outside cause they'll go bad. Have to hide them in the fridge. Right?

GEORGE: Yes.

DAUGHTER: First place she'll look.

GEORGE: I see. [Pause.] Well, don't eat them.

DAUGHTER: It won't stop her. Nothing will stop her. She'll just continue boiling eggs. But, it's all right. The problem's solved. I know what to do.

GEORGE: I think you should go have your cholesterol checked.

How does the playwright distinguish George's voice from that of the daughter? Would you know which one was speaking if you took out the names? How?

The bizarre concluding line adds an unexpected twist.

Check out the home page of the Playwrights Union of Canada at the Pearson Canada Web site at <www.pearsoned.ca/referencepoints/ links>. It offers information about Canadian playwrights and scripts.

Activities

Dramatic Elements in Review

1. Choose a play you have read that shows a substantial change in one of the characters. Make a list of the changes the character undergoes from the exposition, through the climax, to the dénouement of the play. Determine the type of character presented, the motivations and conflicts he or she faces, the effects of these conflicts, and the knowledge gained. Consider whether the character has forced the audience to reflect and to question. Present your chosen character to the class, orally documenting his or her transformation.

2. Listen to a somewhat argumentative conversation. It might be between family members, friends at school, or people on a bus. Recall the dialogue as accurately as you can and make notes about it. Present the dialogue in script form. Include in your script a list of characters and a short description of the action.

3. In journal form, write a personal response to the excerpts from Sally Clark's play. Consider how your ideas and values compare with those in the script. Discuss your response with a partner and determine what has influenced your opinion.

4. Write a critical response to the excerpts from this play. Address the question of how aspects of the plot, the mood, and other elements of drama have contributed to conveying the theme. Share your response with the class as a critical talk.

Production Requirements and Conventions

LEARNING FOCUS
- explain how design elements are used to communicate in drama
- analyze the elements of a stage production
- prepare and perform a drama script

Each type of drama has specific production requirements. **Scripts**, which have the dual role of being both literature and a tool for performers, have their own conventions. The placement of props in scripts for stage plays, the need to indicate sound effects in radio play scripts, and camera angles in scripts for filmed dramas each have accepted conventions.

The playwright's suggestions for making the drama and its characters come alive for the audience are referred to as **stage directions**. Although it is important to provide clear, specific suggestions, stage directions should not appear on every line of script, as this can interfere with the director's and actors' personal interpretations of the script. Review the following set of suggestions for effective script writing and production of stage plays:

CHECKLIST | WRITING SCRIPTS AND STAGE DIRECTIONS

✓ Write scripts clearly, with the elements of performance always in mind.

✓ Provide a list of characters with brief descriptions (in order of appearance, alphabetical order, or order of importance).

✓ Describe each setting, including how props are positioned on stage, for longer works.

✓ Set characters' names apart, in capital letters if preferred.

✓ Write dialogue in easy-to-read, roman (non-italic) type.

✓ Show the difference between stage directions and dialogue, placing directions in parentheses or italics.

✓ Indicate in stage directions how, where, and when to act out a line or gesture.

✓ Make stage directions concise, using them only for those elements (e.g., tone of voice, expression, and gestures) that cannot be conveyed through dialogue.

✓ Indicate all scene changes, characters' entrances and exits, sound effects, lighting, and use of props through stage directions.

The physical layout of a stage and how a performance makes use of it is also crucial to dramatic production. Many scripts, especially those with complex physical action or a cast of many characters, indicate where, for example, a duel takes place, a chair sits, or an aside is spoken. **Blocking** refers to the directions for the actors' movements on stage. Blocking is effective when the entire stage is used and all the actors are easily seen and heard by the audience.

There are a variety of stage layouts. The **proscenium stage**, shown on the next page, is what we often think of when we hear the word *stage*. It is the kind of stage most commonly found in high-school auditoriums. The proscenium stage has a large square arch (the proscenium) that frames the front of the acting area. The **arena stage**, sometimes referred to as *theatre in the round* (despite the fact that the acting area may not actually be round) or the Classical or Greek stage, consists of open space at floor level in the centre of a hall or auditorium. The audience sits in bleacher-like seats on all sides of the acting area. The use of scenery and stage furniture is limited. The **thrust stage**, known also as the Elizabethan or Shakespearean stage, has an extended platform (or apron) that juts into the audience area with a deeper section into which the audience looks. Actors may face in any of three directions and still be seen by the audience. Common in festival theatre, this stage combines the set design strengths of the proscenium stage with some of the intimacy provided by the arena stage. An informal **platform stage** may be erected for various kinds of street theatre or wheeled to its audience, as is the case with a pageant wagon in street parades.

DIAGRAM OF PROSCENIUM STAGE

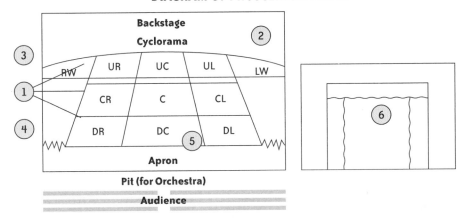

1. Blocking is indicated in terms of nine basic positions: upstage right (UR), upstage centre (UC), upstage left (UL), centre right (CR), centre (C), centre left (CL), downstage right (DR), downstage centre (DC), and downstage left (DL). Right and left on stage is from the point of view of the actor standing on stage. Go *down* toward the audience and *up* away from the audience.

2. The cyclorama is a semi-circular back curtain. When lit, it creates the effect of depth and adds to the mood.

3. Wings (RW and LW) are offstage areas out of audience sight where the prompters sit. They are used for the actors' entrances and exits to and from the stage. Such movements must be carefully timed and orchestrated. The wings also store hand props and set pieces when not in use.

4. The curtains are opened and closed to allow for a change of scenery, indicate the passage of time, or provide act or scene divisions.

5. The apron is the section in front of the curtains where acting may take place.

6. The proscenium arch provides a picture-frame effect to define the stage.

✓ CHECKLIST | STAGE PRODUCTION

- ✓ Lower the curtain or darken the stage whenever a scene changes.
- ✓ Ensure adequate time for costume and set changes between scenes.
- ✓ Create costumes that enhance the setting and characterization.
- ✓ Select props that fit the script's description of character and setting.
- ✓ Provide sound and lighting effects that complement setting, action, and mood.

Activities

Mechanics of Drama

1. Design the set for a scene in a play you have read (or written) in the form of a three-dimensional model or **diorama**. Accompany the diorama with a written description of your set.

2. Interview a lighting director or sound technician in person, over the telephone, or by e-mail to find out about required training and responsibilities of the job. Share your interview with the class.

3. Choose a scene from a story or poem and rewrite it as a scene for a play, including stage directions and suggestions for props and setting. In small groups, prepare and present a performance of your script.

Dramatic Purpose and Form

LEARNING FOCUS

- respond personally and critically to various drama forms
- analyze how dramatic form and structure influence meaning
- create, revise, and perform your own drama script for an audience

As with other forms of literature, dramatic works are written for a variety of purposes—for example, to entertain, to inform, to persuade. In all cases, for a work to be successful, the playwright should be clear about his or her purpose and audience, and choose the form accordingly.

Consider, for example, the **parody**—a humorous, exaggerated imitation of another work, style, or even person. Its purpose is to entertain and, possibly, to inform. An example is *The Red Green Show*, which parodies home-repair shows on television. Part of the show's appeal is its recurring characters, who, like the monster-truck-loving Dougie, are often exaggerated.

A form related to parody is **satire**. Satire uses irony, ridicule, and sarcasm to expose flaws or to make fun of an individual or institution. (The CBC television comedy series *This Hour Has 22 Minutes* and *Royal Canadian Air Farce* both use parody and satire to ridicule our human weaknesses.) Parody and satire overlap, though satire is typically more biting in its humour.

Often drama educates, showing its audience the conflicts and ambiguities people face in their daily lives. The dramatist can develop a theme by presenting characters that have opposing attitudes about a particular issue. As these characters come into conflict with each other, so too do their contrasting value systems.

Sometimes a writer will be tempted to lecture about an issue—especially one that seems significant yet neglected. When this happens, the play becomes a vehicle for the writer's message and the characters are merely mouthpieces. Typically, audiences don't appreciate being *hit over the head* with a dramatist's opinions. However, a writer who develops appealing, believable characters and conflicts can often present a passionate belief through drama without the audience feeling manipulated or cheated.

New Canadian Kid, a play by Dennis Foon, examines the theme of immigration from a point of view not often explored—the immigrant's. It is based on a series of workshops with children from different countries at Lord Roberts Elementary School in Vancouver in 1980. Someone suggested that Foon reverse the language so that the Canadians speak gibberish and the immigrants in the play speak English. Doing so lets an English-speaking audience in on the immigrant's frustrations of a new language, new customs, and feeling unwelcome, as seen in the excerpt below.

MODEL: PLAY

New Canadian Kid
by Dennis Foon

Characters:
MOTHER, a woman from Homeland
NICK, her son
MENCH, a Canadian girl
MUG, a Canadian boy

Nick addresses the audience.

The exposition introduces the protagonist, the situation, and the source of internal conflict.

NICK: My name is Nick. I come from a country called Homeland. But now I live in Canada.

MOTHER: *(off)* Nick!

NICK: Coming ... The day I left Homeland, I said goodbye to my friends. I told them I'd write, that I'd come back soon.

Note the introduction of the lunch bowl. It functions as more than just a prop and acquires symbolic significance in the play.

MOTHER: (*off*) Nick!

NICK: …They gave me this lunch bowl as a going-away present. I like my friends a lot. It was hard to say goodbye.

MOTHER: (*entering*) Come on, Nick, you haven't finished packing.

NICK: I was saying goodbye to my friends. Look what they gave me.

MOTHER: That's beautiful, Nick. We'll have to pack it really carefully. Now come on, Dad's waiting for us.

NICK: Mom, do we have to go?

MOTHER: Nick, we've talked about this already.

NICK: I want to talk about it again.

MOTHER: It's going to be okay. Canada's going to be good for all of us.

NICK: I don't want to leave my friends.

MOTHER: You'll make new ones. Everything's going to be new. Even the language—English.

NICK: English? It'll be like learning to talk all over again.

MOTHER: No, it won't even take a week. You'll love Canada. Let's go.

This monologue furthers the plot and adds to the characterization.

NICK: Canada. So far away. I'd seen airplanes before but I'd never been in one. I was scared at first, everything was shaking. But then we were up in the sky. I missed a half hour of it though—accidentally locked myself in the washroom.

When we landed, we were in Canada. It was winter, really cold. My very first day in Canada, I licked some snow from a frozen fence post and my tongue got stuck. Later, after we found a place to live, I started to go to school…

MENCH: Munch mow-er. [Lunchtime.]

NICK: Munch mow-er?
(*She points to her mouth and exits.*)
Oh, lunchtime, great. (*to audience*) I keep my lunch in this bowl my friends gave me. In Homeland we say that the bowl keeps food and the food keeps life. I like to think of my friends. Hey, wait for me!

NICK *runs off.* MENCH *and* MUG *enter with their lunches and sit.*

MUG: *(pulling out a sandwich, he grimaces.)*

Gahh. Sardeenos mik wheezechiz. [Sardines with cheezwhiz.]

MENCH: *(revealing a Big Mac)* Fridgo grosta mac. [Cold Big Mac.]

(They put their sandwiches back into their lunchboxes in disgust.)

(MUG finds something in his.)

Because so much of the play is written in gibberish, the actors must convey a major portion of the script's meaning through their mannerisms and gestures.

MUG: Wo Yoyo! May Moom-eye pack ein grosta Hershee. Whacko! [Wicked! My mom packed me a giant Hershey. Excellent!]

(He's in seventh heaven. He takes a bite of the chocolate and groans ecstatically.)

(MENCH watches him hungrily.)

(MUG notices.)

MUG: ...Sue vanchen chunken, Mencha? [You want a piece, Mench?]

MENCH: Yoyo! [Yes!] *(she takes a bit)* Taka. [Thank you.]

(MUG opens the wrapper and sees a gigantic bite in his chocolate.)

MUG: Porko! [Pig!]

(MENCH smiles at him sheepishly).

(NICK enters. They watch him. He sits.)

MUG: Sue tinker chay vanchen chunken?
[Do you think he wants a piece?]

MENCH: Ver shure. Gibba Nicknick chunken da hershee.
[For sure. Give Nick a piece of chocolate.]

What do you learn about the individual personalities of the characters through their dialogue?

MUG: Nicknick? Nax vay. [Nick? No way.]

MENCH: Oh, moose. [Oh, come on.] *(to NICK)* Nicknick, sue vantcha chunken da hershee. [Do you want a piece of chocolate?]

NICK: I don't understand.

MUG: Ee bay hershee. Sue nax condo kwit hershee set?
[This is chocolate. Don't you know what chocolate is?]

MENCH: Gibba Nicknick bo chunken. [Give Nick a piece.]

MUG: Nax. [No.]

MENCH: Sue gibba mo encora chunken? [Will you give me another piece?]

MUG: Sue-she. [Okay.] Itsee bit. [Just a bit.]

MENCH: *(taking it)* Ver shure. [For sure.]
(MENCH *runs over to* NICK *with the chocolate.*)

MUG: Oy! [Hey!]

MENCH: *(to NICK)* Tastay. [Taste it.]

(NICK *takes it cautiously.*)

NICK: This looks like chocolate.

MENCH: Tastay. [Taste it.]
(NICK *tentatively nibbles on it.*)

NICK: It is chocolate! I've never seen chocolate wrapped like this! Thanks a lot.

MENCH: Sue bettersket. [You're welcome.]

NICK: *(to MUG)* Thank you very much, Mug.

(MUG *smiles back at* NICK, *then taking the candy back from* MENCH, *wipes off the chocolate where* NICK *bit it.*)

(NICK *does not see this because he has taken the lid off his bowl and begun eating from it.*)

(MUG *puts his candy away then sniffs the air.*)

MUG: Kwesta fumo? [What stinks?]

MENCH: Kumquat fumo? [What stink?]

MUG: Sue nax sniffo da fumo? [You don't smell that stink?]

(MENCH *sniffs, then grimaces.*)

An effective performance requires that actors analyze both the text and subtext (the underlying meaning) of the script. Unless actors understand the personalities and motivations of the characters, they will be unable to communicate the true meaning of the play to others.

Most plots are made up of a series of complications. Their purpose is to intensify the emotions, create suspense, provide the building blocks of the play's structure, and illustrate and determine what happens to the characters.

MENCH: Yo, yo. [Oh, Yeah.]

MUG: Ee bee huey. [I'm sick.]

MENCH: Ee bee spewy. [I'm really sick.]

MUG: Oy, Homelander—sue sniffo da fumo? [Hey, Homelander, you smell the stink?]

NICK: I don't understand.

MENCH: *(indicating that he should sniff)* Snaffa whifto—ee bee grosta kaka. [Take a whiff—it's really gross.]

NICK: You want me to smell something? *(sniffs)* I don't smell anything.

MUG: Lowd ñee bee growdee. [Lord—it's horrible.] ...

(He sniffs, all around, attempting to trace the smell. Finally, he leans over NICK'S bowl, sniffs, and jerks away.)

MUG: Oy, oy! Ee bee chay gorda! Ee bee muncha da Nicknick.

[Hey, hey! It's his bowl. It's Nick's lunch.]

MENCH: Sue jesto. [You're kidding.]

MUG: Yo, ver shure. Sniffo. [Yes, for sure. Smell it.]

NICK: Hey, what's bugging you guys? I'm trying to eat my lunch. *(MENCH sniffs NICK'S bowl and gasps.)*

MENCH: Kay bee shtat, Nicknick? [What is that, Nick?]

NICK: Does this smell bother you? It's just a seasoning, like salt. I don't know how you eat food without it.

MUG: Ee vanna corpso! [I want to die!]

Rehearsing a scene involves memorizing lines, considering physical movement (blocking), and practising proper delivery of lines (diction, articulation, pronunciation, projection).

NICK: You don't have to make those faces. If you tasted it, you'd probably like it.

MUG: Chay vanch may tastay? [Does he want me to taste it?]

MENCH: Goo fo shtat. [Go for it.]

MUG: Sue vanch may tastay? [You want me to try it?]

The director initiates and controls all aspects of the presentation. He or she analyzes the script, casts the roles, sets the basic floor plan for the sets, supervises the design of the costumes, decides on the scenery and lighting, conducts rehearsals, and assists actors with the interpretation of their characters.

NICK: Yeah, here. Taste it.

MUG: Nax! [No!]

MENCH: Oo, chargit, nerd noggin. Tastay. [Oh, come on, big mouth. Taste it.]

MUG: (angrily) Nax taka, Mencha! [No thanks, Mench!]

MENCH: Ooooo. Nicknick, Mog ein igg squirter. [Ooooo. Nick, Mug's a chicken.]

MUG: …Sue-she. [All right then.] Skay may doma dis? [How do I do this?]

NICK: Just take a little bit, like this.

(NICK demonstrates, holding a little food with his thumb and index finger.)

See? Just take a little bit in case you don't like it.

(MUG takes a bit in his fingers with much disgust and trepidation. Suddenly he turns and shoves the food he's holding at MENCH, who jumps away. They laugh. Then MUG turns serious, saying to MENCH:)

MUG: See ee corpso, dito mee moom-eye et pop-eye. [If I die, tell my mom and dad.]

MENCH: (solemnly) Bo bo. Tra La. Bee bee. [Goodbye, good luck.]

(MUG takes the tiny amount in his fingers and places it in his mouth.)

(Slight pause. He seems to enjoy it.)

(But then he starts to react, he goes into convulsions, he is gasping, and screaming.)

(He is hamming it up for MENCH and she loves it.)

(Finally, after many death rattles, groans, and spasms he is "dead.")

(MENCH takes his pulse and pronounces him "dead.")

MENCH: Chay corpso. [He's dead.]

(Suddenly MUG is up again. The dead have risen; he is a horrible ghoul.)

MUG: Ee bee Zombo! [I'm a Zombie!]

(He is a walking corpse, sniffing the air angrily.)

Ee vancha da gourda da Nicknick... Ee vancha da gourda da Nicknick... [I want the bowl of Nick... I want the bowl of Nick.]

(Before NICK can react, MUG has grabbed the bowl and holds it over his head.)

MUG: Sisco la glowba. Corpsa la gourda da Nicknick!

[Save the world. Kill the bowl of Nick!]

(MUG bangs the bowl on the top of his head. It breaks in two.)

(He is startled for an instant, but quickly sees the humour in it. MENCH starts laughing too.)

The breaking of the symbolic prop (the bowl) increases the tension.

NICK: You broke it.

MUG: Gros bos. [Big deal.]

(MUG tosses the pieces to NICK.)

MENCH: Ee bee joost ein gourda, Nicknick. [It's just a bowl, Nick.]

NICK: You broke my bowl!

MUG: Aw, Poost a itsi Nicknick. [Oh, poor little Nick.]

NICK: You don't know what that was, you idiot!

(NICK grabs MUG. MUG throws NICK on the floor.)

Do you feel that the characters in this play are portrayed as stereotypes rather than as unique individuals? Would you need to see a performance of the play before answering this question? How might seeing the actors in action affect your opinion?

MUG: Sue es logo. Toota des Homelander say logo. Sue sgak. [You're crazy. All the Homelanders are crazy. You Sgak.]

MENCH: *(shocked)* Mog! [Mug!]

MUG: Sgak!

(MUG exits.)

NICK: ...He broke my bowl.

MENCH: Donax regretto. Mog joost tantra. [Don't worry about it. Mug just got mad.]

NICK: Why did he do that?

MENCH: Or bay sue-she? [Are you okay?]

NICK: That was my good bowl.

MENCH: Ee besta zet nama. Tra la. [I'd better go now. Bye.]

(*MENCH exits.*)

NICK: (*to the audience*) I just went home. I didn't wait for school to get out. I just left.

(*NICK's MOTHER enters and sits by the window.*)

(*NICK looks in at her through the window, then decides to go in, hiding the broken bowl…*)

Activities

Responding To and Creating Scripts

1. Prepare a critical written response to the excerpt from *New Canadian Kid*. In your response, make sure you consider the title, to what extent the characters are portrayed as round characters, and how effectively the theme has been conveyed.

2. In a small group, discuss the use of gibberish in this play. Evaluate this *dialogue* device and suggest other ways in which Foon might have achieved his goals. Present your ideas to the class.

3. Write a monologue that the character Mug might give after he resolves his differences with Nick. However, write the monologue entirely in English. Be prepared to explain the choices you made regarding voice and style.

4. Think of a fairy tale, myth, fable, or nursery rhyme that might be the basis of a play for young children. As a group, write the script and present your play to an elementary class in your community.

5. Write a script for a dramatic work (for example, a monologue or short one-act play) to be presented to the class. The drama might arise from a theme that is important to you, a personal experience, a news clipping, or an anecdote. Incorporate the elements and devices of drama discussed in this chapter, and choose a form suitable to your audience and purpose.

Communicating Through Media

The World Beyond the Classroom

In this chapter we will examine public communication and the role of **mass media** in our society. Media messages provide information, entertainment, and advertising. They occur in print in newspapers, magazines, and books; they are found in visual form on posters, billboards, and corporate **logos**. They are heard on radio and audio CD; they are seen on television, film, videotape, and DVD; and increasingly, because of its ability to integrate a wide range of media products, they are available on computer via the World Wide Web.

Global communication networks have provided a dramatic increase in accessible information. Now we need to develop strategies to analyze and respond to this information explosion. We must go beyond the headlines, the surface meaning, and the sixty-second **sound bites** to probe the background, deeper causes, and personalities behind specific events. This means developing **media literacy**—a critical awareness of media products and an interpretation of their construction. It also means keeping up with the changing values and trends that influence our lives.

Becoming Media Literate

Print, television, film, radio, and the Internet are powerful sources of information and opinion in our lives. What we read, view, and hear in the **media** shapes how we think about ourselves, what we believe, what we value,

LEARNING FOCUS
- understand what it means to be media literate
- reflect on the role of media in contemporary culture
- investigate topics for media research

how we behave, and even how we dress. Rather than passively absorbing each media message, it is important to

- assess the point of view being expressed.
- understand how the form of media used affects the impact of the message.
- evaluate the accuracy and balance of its presentation.
- interact with, debate, and respond critically to the message.

Ask yourself the following critical questions as you experience the media around you:

WHAT IS THE MEDIUM OF THE MESSAGE? The form of media has a definite bearing on its meaning. Each **medium** offers its own construction of reality. For example, a television program and a news article covering the same event may provide very different messages.

WHO IS THE AUDIENCE? Each media message is intended for a specific **target audience**—a group of people of a particular age, gender, and economic background who have similar needs and values. When media are constructed, assumptions about the target audience are carefully considered. For example, advertisements related to automobiles are targeted by driver age group. Ads for vans are commonly directed at twenty-five to forty-year-old drivers who have young families. Luxury sports cars may be targeted at the young professional. Our unique situations will influence the way we interpret and react to the same media message.

HOW WAS THIS MEDIA TEXT CONSTRUCTED? Media texts are carefully constructed by writers, photographers, creative designers, and in some cases, by musicians. Creators of media shape their content in specific ways to *re-present* rather than *present* reality. As the audience, we may assume that what we see is "the way it is," but we never see what was edited out of the news release, the audio recording, or the picture. Deconstructing media texts—examining how media is put together, what is omitted, and how the media shape our perception of the world —will allow us to become more critical thinkers and viewers.

WHAT ARE THE CONVENTIONS USED? Each form of communication has its own media **conventions** (big headlines indicate significance, camera close-ups convey intimacy). Visual texts communicate symbolically through their use of colour, gesture, setting, objects, and so on. A Web site that displays an icon of a red maple leaf is likely to contain Canadian content or be authored by a Canadian entity. Understanding these conventions increases our appreciation of the media experience and helps us to be less susceptible to manipulation.

WHAT VALUES ARE BEING CONVEYED? Media texts express either *explicitly* or *implicitly* a wide range of social, political, and ideological values. They may reinforce current beliefs on consumerism, lifestyle, or social status. They may be linked to social change or political activism. It is therefore important to identify the values reflected in the media texts around you and to question whether they are consistent with what *you* value and believe in. Consider which voices are expressed as well as which ones are absent from media messages.

WHO OWNS THE MEDIA CONSTRUCTION AND WHAT IMPACT DOES THIS HAVE? Many of the editorial and creative decisions made in media construction are driven by commercial interests. Newspapers are relatively inexpensive because their production cost is subsidized by numerous advertisers who pay for space in them. It is possible to receive a free Internet service connection, but with it come the **banner ads** that border the computer screen. The vast majority of media texts are designed with the profit motive in mind; it is important to consider who is trying to sell what to whom when assessing the specific message.

Activities

Taking Stock of the Media

1. Keep a diary for a week to evaluate what you read, view, or hear in the media. Record instances where you feel the media had a positive, creative, informative impact on your thinking and learning as well as those where you felt manipulated in some way. Indicate the medium of each media text you note down. Share your diary entries as part of a general class discussion on the theme: "Media for Better or for Worse."

2. By phone or e-mail, contact government departments or independent bodies such as Industry Canada's Office of Consumer Affairs, Statistics Canada, the BBM Bureau of Measurement, or A.C. Nielsen to research media consumption by type of media. Try to find information that reflects changing trends and differences by age, gender, education, and so on. Show your results in graph or chart form. (Refer to the section on graphs in Appendix A to help you.) Present your findings in a visual presentation to the class.

3. Complete some research on the trend of *media convergence* (corporate mergers, consolidations, acquisitions) to determine who controls

the media (the radio, television, and newspapers) in your province, in Canada generally, or in North America. In a speech to the class, examine the blending of print, aural, and visual media currently taking place. Outline some advantages and disadvantages of media conglomerates. Discuss, as well, the role of the Canadian Radio-television and Telecommunications Commission (CRTC) and the Canadian Broadcast Standards Council in monitoring the media in this country.

Thinking and Communicating Clearly

LEARNING FOCUS
- analyze the role of logical fallacies in communication
- evaluate ideas critically
- practise clear thinking and communicating

Clear thinking involves an openness to different perspectives and new-found information. It requires an acknowledgment of our own biases and those of others. Even though there are agencies such as the Advertising Standards Council to guide advertisers and the CRTC to regulate radio and television broadcasting, it is important to evaluate for ourselves whether the information we are receiving via the media is reasoned, objective, and responsible.

The following chart illustrates ways in which clear thinking can be jeopardized by inappropriate or misguided logic. These are referred to as **logical fallacies**. See if you recognize any of these illogical *pitfalls* (either deliberate or unintentional) in the media texts you read, view, or hear, or in your own interactions with family or friends.

COMMON LOGICAL FALLACIES

FALLACY TYPE	DEFINITION AND EXAMPLE
Arguing in a Circle	When we repeat a claim rather than provide actual evidence for it, we wrongly imagine that repetition acts as proof. As an example, saying "Orange juice is necessary for breakfast because oranges are a part of a good breakfast" reflects this fallacy.
Weak Analogy	Analogies become weak or questionable when the arguer assumes that because two things are similar in one way, they must also be in others. For instance, if someone says, "That coffee tastes like sewage; if you drink that, you'll get sick," the speaker is assuming that, just because the drink has a foul taste, it will have the toxic qualities associated with sewage.
Attacking the Person	Sometimes we resort to the bad habit of attacking the person instead of what he or she says. For example, if someone is arguing for increased conservation in a region threatened by deforestation, and you respond with "but you would say that, you're a tree-hugging hippie radical," not only have you offended your opponent, you've also strayed from the real issue.

COMMON LOGICAL FALLACIES (CONTINUED)

Presumed Cause and Effect

We may draw conclusions by presuming a cause without having enough evidence to see it as the *only* or *actual* one. The statement "Jodi received more birthday cards than Sandra, so Jodi must be more popular" illustrates this fallacy. What if Sandra's friends choose to share their time with her instead of sending her cards? What if Jodi dropped numerous hints about her own upcoming birthday the previous week?

Slippery Slope

This extension of presumed cause and effect may occur in the following situation. If you are trying to convince someone to save money, you might say, "If you don't start saving now, when you're older and the government's pension funds dry up, and all your immediate family has passed away, and you have no one to support you, you'll end up on the street begging for pennies." It appeals to the listener's fears. Although the situation *could* happen, in refuting it, you need to point out why things don't *have* to slip in that particular direction.

Two Wrongs

This fallacy is illustrated by the attempt to defend or excuse one's behaviour by saying that someone else is doing the same thing. For example, even if the people who are advising you not to smoke are smokers themselves, you cannot justify your own behaviour by pointing to theirs.

False Dilemma

Here we misuse the *either/or* construction by presenting a situation as though there are only two possible positions, one clearly desirable and the other weak or ludicrous. For example, "What's wrong with a curfew? Would you rather have kids up all night vandalizing the neighborhood?" The speaker avoids considering alternative outcomes to not having a curfew.

Hasty Generalization

Some people make a habit of forming sweeping generalizations on too little evidence. For example, although a person may sincerely believe that he or she is speaking from experience, to say something like, "Teenagers today have no respect for authority," is to paint *all* teenagers with the same brush. It is easy to see how one can eventually start believing in the unqualified truth of such statements if used often enough.

Misuse of Statistics

Imagine that a random group of teenagers is asked how many hours per week they spend surfing the Internet and the answers in a sample of fifty teens range from zero to thirty-one hours. Depending on if we are given the *mean* (the total of all responses divided by the number of responses), the *median* (the middle number in the series) or the *mode* (the most frequently occurring number), the statistic will reflect a different emphasis. When quoting or interpreting statistics, you need to know how the information was gathered, by whom, under what conditions, and exactly what kinds of questions were used.

COMMON LOGICAL FALLACIES (CONTINUED)

Bandwagon Approach

Advertisers using this approach hope that our desire to be part of the crowd will override our better judgment. Think of such enticements or appeals as "Join the Now Generation, buy ____" or "Do you want to be the last one on the block to get one of our ____?" The more independence of mind you have, the less susceptible you will be to this approach.

Snob Appeal

Here the object is to convince people that they will become part of an elite group if they buy into your line of reasoning. Many specialty products and exclusive organizations play on people's status-seeking desires. This kind of message flatters the audience that they will acquire prestige and be the envy of others by purchasing what is offered.

Questionable Authority

The most common instance of this is the use of celebrities in advertising. Having a basketball star recommend a court shoe or a famous guitarist endorse an amplifier is fine, since these are within each of their areas of expertise. However, if one of these individuals tells us how his or her dog prefers Brand X Chow because of its enhanced chewability, we need to investigate the basis of his or her authority on the subject. Otherwise, we believe the celebrity's claim out of blind faith rather than reasoned evaluation.

Activities

Practising Clear Thinking

1. Identify the kind of logical fallacy in each of the following statements:
   - A recent study indicated that teenagers who watched situation comedies rather than music videos received higher scores on their final exams. Therefore, sitcoms must be more educational than music videos.
   - If you don't try Ultima Shampoo for yourself, how will you know whether you're getting the shiniest, most beautiful hair you deserve?
   - Our educated young people are our most precious natural resource. Having them go to other countries to work is like sending orphans into slavery.
   - Why should homeowners stop using pesticides on their lawns when commercial farmers are still allowed to spray them on their crops?

2. Create four of your own examples of logical fallacy or find examples from the media. Exchange your list with a partner and ask him or her to identify which is which. Share your lists with the class.

Formal Debate

LEARNING FOCUS
- review debating styles, formats, and techniques
- analyze and evaluate elements of oral presentations
- plan and participate in a debate

A **formal debate** is a structured discussion between opposing individuals or teams with the objective of establishing the superiority of one view over another. Important issues and questions are often debated in the media. Newspapers, magazines, and radio and television programs invite experts to debate contentious topics in print or on the air. Political debates of representatives from different parties are broadcast close to election time so that viewers and listeners have the opportunity to understand the issues of importance to various candidates.

Principles and Guidelines for Debate

1. For every argument there should be a counter-argument.

2. Every debate has two sides, an affirmative side that supports the **resolution** (question) and a negative side that contests the validity of the resolution or proposes an alternative solution to the problem.

3. In preparing for a debate, each side must determine how much it knows about the topic and how much research is needed. Debaters on each side should also research the opposing side's arguments as this enables them to better defend their own position.

4. Each debate is chaired by a **moderator** or speaker. In televised or radio debates, a prominent television anchor or radio host might fulfill this task. It is the moderator's role to maintain order and enforce rules and procedures fairly for all participants. He or she does not take an active part in the debating itself, unless it is necessary to protect the rights of a particular debater. Decisions of the moderator are final and cannot be appealed.

5. Debaters must present concrete information, not so much to convince their opponents but to convince the judge and audience of the merits and soundness of their case.

6. Debaters must conduct themselves with dignity and behave in a courteous manner toward other debaters and officials. Judges will penalize debaters guilty of rudeness, flippancy, or any attempt to belittle another debater.

DEBATING STYLES Two major debating formats are the **parliamentary debate** and the **cross-examination debate**. Both styles require a range of skills, including research, public speaking, critical listening, and thinking clearly on demand. The type of debate outlined below is the cross-examination style because, in addition to the above skills, it requires each debater to ask probing questions of another debater and in turn be cross-examined in the role of **witness**. Whereas parliamentary debates begin with a resolution (e.g., "Be it resolved that Government should assume responsibility for reducing violence in schools"), cross-examination style debates begin with a question (e.g., "Should Government assume a responsibility for reducing violence in schools?").

The table below shows the order of speakers (see circled numbers) for a cross-examination debate, the expectations of each speaker, and the suggested time limits. (A televised or radio debate format may vary somewhat from the format below in terms of order and time frames. However, even these debates have opening and summary speeches and times when the candidates are questioned by an opponent.)

CROSS-EXAMINATION DEBATE

AFFIRMATIVE SIDE (SUPPORTING)

① 1st Affirmative Debater (5 min)
- presents **constructive speech** including all definitions and any plan of action
- is cross-examined by 1st Negative Debater (3 min)

③ 2nd Affirmative Debater (5 min)
- presents constructive speech building on points made earlier by colleague
- is cross-examined by 2nd Negative Debater (3 min)

⑤ Rebuttal Speech from Affirmative Side (3 min)
- **rebuttal speech** presented by an individual or affirmative team
- looks at question from several points of view and refutes arguments made by opponent

NEGATIVE SIDE (OPPOSING)

② 1st Negative Debater (5 min)
- presents constructive speech, challenging any definitions at issue and introducing any possible counter plan
- is cross-examined by 2nd Affirmative Debater (3 min)

④ 2nd Negative Debater (5 min)
- presents final constructive speech, building on points made earlier by colleague
- is cross-examined by 1st Affirmative Debater (3 min)

⑥ Rebuttal Speech from Negative Side (3 min)
- rebuttal speech presented by an individual or negative team
- looks at question from several points of view and refutes arguments made by opponent

Activities

Conducting a Debate

1. Evaluate the debaters in a televised or radio debate, taking notes as you view or listen. Consider the following questions and provide support for your responses:

- Did the debaters present their arguments clearly and logically?
- Did the debaters provide reasonable and sufficient evidence to support their positions?
- Did each debater recognize and expose the weaknesses in their opponent's evidence and reasoning?
- Did the debaters demonstrate knowledge of and make effective use of the rules?

2. Conduct a cross-examination debate following the guidelines below:
   - Work in small groups to formulate possible questions for a debate.
   - Ensure that each question is debatable, focuses on *one* topic, and contains no confusing or ambiguous words.
   - One team of two students should take the affirmative side. Two other students should take the negative side. Another student should act as a moderator.
   - Take a week to research the topic thoroughly before presenting your group's debate.
   - Ensure that you appoint a timekeeper and judges who will evaluate the performance of each debater and decide which side wins.
   - The remaining class members will be the audience for the debate. Sometimes a **straw vote** or opinion poll allows the audience to take on the role of judge.
   - If possible, allow time at the end of each debate for the judges to give their verdict and for the audience to ask questions.

An Introduction to Journalistic Media

The news media are guided by the public's *right to know*. An effective press foresees trends, alerts the public to potential problems, and helps ensure that government, public agencies, and corporations operate *in the open*. Whether they work for newspapers, magazines, or radio or television stations, journalists have a responsibility to cover *and* uncover the truth of what is happening.

Unfortunately there are some journalists who lack compassion, invent news, distort the truth, or quote out of context, either deliberately or due to lack of investigation and research. The tragic death of Diana, Princess of Wales in 1997 highlighted the brazenness of the **paparazzi**— photographers who will engage in a high-speed chase in pursuit of the quick snap and the even quicker dollar from editors and publishers of **tabloids** willing to pay exorbitant fees for a single photograph. For the most part, however, journalists adhere to the principles and codes of behaviour of their profession. The Canadian Association of Journalists (CAJ) is a professional body that monitors and upholds standards of journalism.

✓ CHECKLIST GOOD JOURNALISM

- ✓ Be an accurate observer of events and issues.
- ✓ Do not allow personal **bias** to distort the objectivity of your reporting.
- ✓ Aim to inform and to stimulate discussion of newsworthy issues.
- ✓ Avoid reporting that tries specifically to shock or sensationalize.
- ✓ Establish whether the interviewee's statements are *on the record* or *off the record*.
- ✓ Avoid profanity and invasion of privacy.
- ✓ Avoid bias toward, and stereotyping of, members of groups (e.g., ethnic, gender, sexual preference, disability, age, geographical).
- ✓ Check the reliability of your sources; be careful not to print or broadcast false information that might result in **libel** or **slander**.
- ✓ Avoid plagiarism and attribute credit to your sources of information.

The Newspaper

Newspapers provide us with information on international, national, and local events. There are daily national and large city papers that are broad-based in coverage as well as smaller community papers focusing primarily on municipal concerns. Newspapers provide immediate news coverage (**hard news**) of current events such as sports and political contests, war, or natural disasters. They also examine in depth the issues behind the news, in special features. These, along with lifestyle, arts, and entertainment articles are referred to as **soft news**. Regularly featured **columns** providing insight and opinion on a wide range of topics from financial advice to parenting skills as well as comics and **editorials** round out the content of the newspaper.

LEARNING FOCUS

- review the purpose and format of newspapers
- research job opportunities in the newspaper industry
- read and respond to newspaper articles

The format of newspapers is changing all the time in order to compete with television news and the World Wide Web. Newspapers today cater to an extremely busy audience with little time to read. As a result, news stories tend to be shorter than in the past, with more summaries, short lists, and boxes of facts. There is also an increase in coloured visuals, graphs, and charts.

Many newspapers are now available on-line. Some are free of charge, while others require subscribers to pay a fee to gain on-line access. Note the Web page for the *Calgary Herald* on the following page.

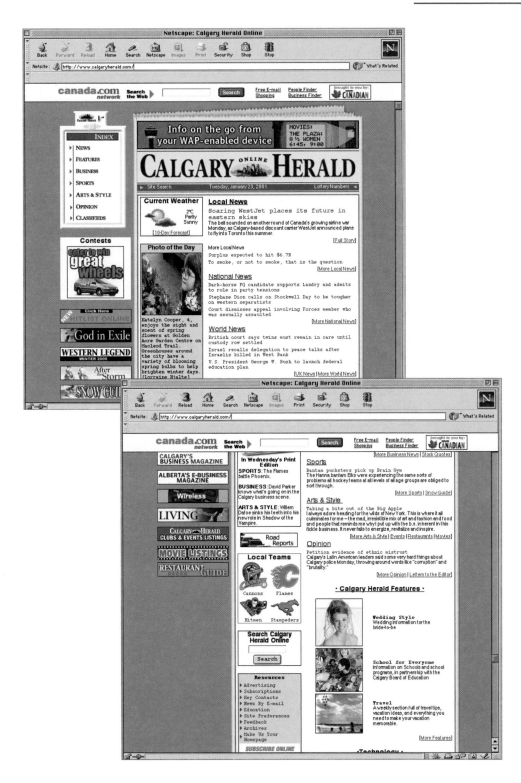

The organizational structure of many school newspapers resembles that of their larger commercial counterparts. The publisher of a school newspaper, typically the principal, sets the direction and has the final say on what is published. A teacher-advisor serves as a liaison between principal and student reporters. A managing editor gives out story assignments and fulfills the **gatekeeper** role by deciding which stories will be published. An advertising manager is responsible for advertising and possibly also for circulation of the school paper. Editors work with reporters to construct headlines and ensure the accuracy and consistent style of what is written. Reporters on school papers tend to have general assignments and cover various beats, whereas commercial papers have general, specialist, and freelance reporters. If student photographers are available, they help capture the visual side of the story. Typically in a student newspaper there is no dedicated layout artist to arrange stories, headlines, and visuals on the page, as there would be in a commerical paper. This job may be done by the managing editor.

Activities

Learning About the Newspaper

1. Conduct a poll in your school or neighbourhood to determine which newspapers people are reading and which sections of the paper they prefer. Create a graph or table to illustrate your findings. Share your information with the class.

2. Visit a local newspaper and interview some of the individuals who work there. Use the information from the interview to create a career profile of at least one of the following personnel: a publisher, a columnist, an editor, a cartoonist, a photojournalist. Share the information gathered with your class.

3. Read some local and national newspapers to find a news story of interest to you.
   - Write a précis of the story.
   - Compare the newspaper coverage of the event in your chosen story to coverage of the same event received on local or national radio or television.
   - Share your summaries and comparisons with the class.

Analyzing Newspaper Writing

LEARNING FOCUS
- understand the form, purpose, and style of news articles
- analyze and assess ideas expressed in news stories

News stories are written for a variety of purposes: to narrate or chronicle events, to inform or instruct, to describe, to argue and persuade, and to entertain. They provide concise coverage of the who, what, where, when, why, and how (**W5H**) of a story, with complementary graphics.

A reporter must decide what order and format a news story will take. Important information is presented first in the **lead** (introductory sentence or paragraph) with non-essential news coming toward the end of the article. Leads are intended to grab the readers' attention, to entice them to read on, and to inform the reader on the subject.

Many news stories follow an **inverted pyramid** sequence. This format provides factual, objective (third-person style) information in descending order of importance, with the most vital information coming in the introductory paragraph. A busy reader can thereby get the essential points without reading the full story. As the pyramid narrows at the bottom, the facts are less significant. If an editor finds that a story is too long, the less significant information occurring at the end of the article can easily be cut.

Not all news stories follow this style: some start with a lead paragraph summarizing important details and then, in chronological order, give an account of the event. The reporter may also incorporate a more subjective first-person style (referred to as **New Journalism**) in which personal opinions and perceptions are part of the story.

Reporters from different papers often focus on different angles of a story. Sometimes, too, within the same paper you will find **sidebars** on the same subject adding additional information on some aspect of the story. For example, in May 2000, residents of Walkerton, Ontario, fell ill as a result of deadly E. coli bacteria that contaminated the town's water supply. The article that follows, from the *National Post*, focuses on the water-testing facilities and who was responsible for notifying the public about the contaminated water. A sidebar might have consisted of an interview with a medical health officer discussing the E. coli outbreak.

Note the headline for this national news story.

E. COLI LAB HAD NO DUTY TO RAISE ALARM

TOWN TRIES TO COPE WITH WATER CONTAMINATION DEATHS

Law does not require private testing facilities to notify health officials of dangerous results

By Paul Waldie and Jonathon Gatehouse

The subtitle and first paragraph provide the lead. It has direct appeal to the reader in terms of the subject of personal health and safety.

The article makes use of the W5H technique as well as the *inverted pyramid* in its presentation of information.

The head of the laboratory hired to test drinking water in Walkerton, Ont., says he had no duty or obligation to alert medical officials even though he knew the supply was contaminated nearly a week before a public health warning was issued.

In an interview yesterday, Greg Patterson, president of A&L Laboratories Canada East Inc., also suggested town officials were informed about the contamination earlier than they have let on because his company provides test results within a day.

"There are no laboratories existing anymore in the government to do this," Mr. Patterson said from his London, Ont., offices. "I suppose at one time if a provincial lab saw something they might say something to the health office, but we are an independent laboratory getting samples from all over the place, and we just report back to our client."

Note the short paragraph length found in newspapers. Such clear, concise writing caters to a wide, general audience with a range of reading skills.

Mr. Patterson said his office has been inundated with calls about the testing. "We've been threatened," he said.

Water testing has become the central issue in the growing scandal surrounding Walkerton, where five people have died and hundreds are ill because the town's water supply was contaminated with a strain of E. coli bacteria.

Since the Ontario government privatized water testing in 1996, laboratories have not been required to notify health officials about contamination, a senior Environment Ministry official confirmed. Under the old system, the government labs that did the bulk of the water testing would report health concerns to a district manager in the ministry who then alerted medical officials.

Front page stories are often continued on inside pages. Page numbers indicate where to find the continuation of the story or related articles.

Private contractors such as A&L now only have to report their results to the municipality that requested the tests, according to Dale Henry, a manager in the Ontario Environment Ministry.

See *WATER* on Page A6

Activities

Reacting to News Stories

1. Reread the *National Post* article on page 226. Now, in writing, answer the questions that follow:
   - How does this news article answer the questions who, what, where, when, why, and how?
   - Does it convince you that something needs to be done? If so, how?
   - What role do direct quotations play in the article?
   - Does the article present a balanced view of the Walkerton situation?

2. Complete some research on newspaper articles at your library or on the Internet:
   - Find stories on the Walkerton issue in various papers. Write a comparative report to examine how two papers may approach the same story from different angles.
   - Find an article (on a subject of your choice) in which the reporter has presented a story in chronological sequence and has included personal perceptions and emotive (evoking emotions) descriptions.

3. Check out three news stories in your local newspaper. Answer the questions below:
   - Does each lead provide the main information concisely? How is this achieved?
   - What evidence can you find of the journalist's opinions within each story?
   - Is the journalistic style engaging? (Consider sentence structure, diction, and tone.)
   - Is each article free of errors in spelling and mechanics?

The Editorial Pages

The editorial pages stimulate thought and debate on local, national, and international issues. They aim to influence readers by providing analysis of major news stories and persuasive *calls to action*. It is now common practice for columnists with **opinion pieces** in the editorial section and elsewhere in the paper, to provide their e-mail addresses so that readers can respond instantly on-line.

The editorial pages of any newspaper typically contain the following:

THE MASTHEAD This is found at the top of the editorial page. The **masthead** gives the name, owner, publisher, and mailing address of the paper.

LEARNING FOCUS
- analyze and assess the content and style of editorial writing
- understand values and ideas expressed in opinion pieces
- create various kinds of opinion pieces

Sometimes it includes the names of the management team. Although a newspaper has an editorial board that sets editorial policy and often takes a consistent political stand on issues, the paper must be seen as presenting all sides of an issue or at least a balanced view over time.

EDITORIALS An **editorial** represents, in approximately 300 to 500 words, the official stance of the newspaper. It is written by a staff editor (the editorial page editor) and is endorsed by the editorial board. Editorials can grow out of immediate happenings in the community or wider world or can be reactions to headlines and stories in the news.

The editorial below comments on the news story of the E. coli outbreak in Walkerton, Ontario. This outbreak spawned numerous news stories, other editorials, editorial cartoons, and letters to the editor in the weeks and months following the tragedy.

MODEL: EDITORIAL

Answer the Question

This editorial uses specific facts and statistics to support opinion. Note the **rhetorical question** at the start and the use of strong emotional language. Consider the editorial stance on the issue.

This topic at the time was current and extremely relevant. The major news story on the front page of the *National Post* (see page 226) also dealt with the E. coli outbreak. This editorial comments on and further questions the causes of the outbreak.

'What did you know and when did you know it?' For 72 hours now, reporters have put that Watergate-esque question to the health authorities of Walkerton, Ontario, in hope of getting to the bottom of the worst E. coli outbreak in Canadian history. Five people have died, several more are in critical condition and hundreds have been stricken with preliminary symptoms since E. coli 157:H7 mysteriously contaminated the town's water supply. The potentially fatal bacteria strain produces a potent toxin that binds with various cells in the body, causing them to die.

Officials' answers have been evasive and Greg Patterson, president and co-owner of the private laboratory that tested Walkerton's water samples, says he performed his duty by sending the results to the local Public Utilities Commission (PUC): "We just report back to our client." The law does not require the laboratory to report abnormalities to anyone other than the utility commission, unless previously specified under contract. Before 1996, when the province devolved water safety to the municipalities, publicly run laboratories did the tests, and were required to alert the local government authorities if they found abnormalities. Voluntary industry protocols insist that even private labs must notify city councils, but the law does not appear to demand it.

Stan Koebel—Mr. Patterson's "client" and the manager of the utility—has said nothing to explain his actions or lack of them, and David Jacobi, a municipal councillor, commented glibly: "Hey, we all make mistakes no matter what business we are in." To be sure, most of us do make mistakes, but the purpose of public health is, at least in part, to prevent mistakes.

Note the extent of research carried out by the editorial team. We are provided with a contrast between a reaction time in Ireland and the reaction time in Walkerton. Note, as well, the careful chronology of facts.

How should things have happened? An outbreak of an E. coli infection last year near Dublin suggests an answer. Ten children at a crèche were infected by a relatively new strain, E. coli 026. All 29 children at the crèche were immediately screened along with their family members. When staff suspected one child had contracted E. coli, they quickly notified the health board. Only one child was admitted to hospital, and soon released. The Food Safety Authority of Ireland later commended the health authority's vigilance.

Although the facts were doubtless different, the basic point is that early detection and quick action are crucial to controlling outbreaks. A one-day delay can mean the difference between life and death. In Walkerton, however, there was a 13-day delay, according to dates supplied by the Owen Sound Health unit. On May 12, heavy rain flooded the local well creating conditions conducive to the spread of E. coli from manure. On May 15, the PUC drew a water sample and on May 18 received a fax from its laboratory saying the water was contaminated. But the utility did not advise the Owen Sound Health unit until May 23, and then only after Dr. Murray McQuigge, the chief medical officer of health, had run his own tests, found evidence of the dangerous pathogens and confronted the PUC. What's more, the PUC insisted from May 19–20, despite being in possession of the fax, that the water system was safe and secure.

The editorial concludes with a persuasive call for action. It clarifies who should do what and why. The last paragraph basically restates (for emphasis and unity) the title of the editorial.

A bipartisan inquiry is needed. David Thomson, the mayor, would be wise to bring in the world's leading experts, from the Centers For Disease Control in Atlanta, to trace the etiology of this outbreak. Today, our sympathies are with the victims' families, but official efforts must be directed immediately toward finding out the answer to the question. "Who knew what, and when?"

OPINION PIECES While an editorial presents the official voice of the paper, an **opinion piece** on the editorial page or elsewhere reflects the viewpoint of a particular columnist. It presents a personal perspective based on fact and appeals to the reader with logic and emotion. Such columns, with accompanying **bylines**, may be written by staff writers, guest writers, or **syndicated columnists** whose writing appears in one or several different papers or magazines on a regular basis. They use a persuasive style, establishing a thesis at the start and supporting it with examples and evidence. The opinion piece below, by a student columnist, discusses the issue of high salaries paid to professional athletes.

STUDENT SAMPLE: OPINION PIECE

This column begins with a rhetorical question to catch the reader's interest.

The content of this paragraph makes it obvious that the student writer has completed research to gather accurate facts and statistics. It also provides a hint of which side of the argument the writer is supporting.

In the next two paragraphs the writer acknowledges possible counter argument(s) against the thesis that baseball players are overpaid. This shows the student has looked at both sides of the issue.

Note the effective word choice and the combination of short and long sentences that work to convince the audience of the validity of the writer's arguments.

Are they in it for the love of the game or the love of the dollar?

This is the question many baseball fans are asking themselves this season.

With an increasing number of players breaking the $10-million mark, it is becoming much more apparent that this is not the same baseball game we all know and love. In this elite, but ever-growing club, you have Pedro Martinez, who is pulling in over $12 million a year. There is also Greg Maddux ($11.5 million), Barry Bonds ($11.45 million), and Sammy Sosa ($10.625 million).

When the topic of baseball payrolls comes up, many will argue that players deserve these salaries because professional athletes act as role models, entertaining millions of sports fans worldwide, and providing many jobs. Among these jobs are those held by sports reporters, coaches, managers, and promoters. However, what these people forget is that these wonderful things can be achieved without a huge payroll. An athlete is just as much a good role model when he is not making $10 million a year. I have never really thought of pro ball players as entertainers. To my mind they should be considered as athletes. When an athlete turns into an entertainer...well just look at wrestlers.

No matter how much the owners gripe, they keep paying these enormous salaries. There is no end in sight. Long ago, pro sports stopped being just a game. It became a business. The difference between now and then is that it is no longer just a business, it is a form of commercial entertainment. When each star in the sitcom *Friends* can command close to $1 million a television episode, then ball players start feeling justified in asking for a comparable amount per season to provide entertainment in the form of professional baseball.

It is obvious that today's baseball players are overpaid. When you look back on great players of the past such as Ted Williams, Willie Mays, or Mickey Mantle, players who in every way deserved to be paid just as much as today's players, you can plainly see that they were not. Even when you increase their salary to the equivalent of that amount today (with inflation and so on) you arrive at an amount far under what today's star athletes are making. These players are examples of truly great ball players. They received no outrageous salary and enjoyed the game just as much, if not more. However, they lived in a time of real baseball where the true incentive to play the game came from the heart and not the paycheque. This is what baseball is supposed to be like.

Before concluding this piece of persuasive writing, this writer could have included another pro argument or two to add evidence to the thesis.

By using a *closing by return* technique the student returns to the opening question and concludes that players today are into baseball for the money.

EDITORIAL CARTOONS Like opinion pieces, **editorial cartoons** are often linked to specific stories in the news: they enhance news stories and editorials. Notice how the editorial cartoon from the May 27, 2000, *National Post* complements the paper's coverage of the Walkerton E. coli contamination.

Gary Clement/National Post

LETTERS TO THE EDITOR These are found in the editorial sections of all newspapers, and in many magazines as well. **Letters to the editor** are also aired as *feedback* features on radio and television. They provide a forum for readers, listeners, and viewers to respond to what they read in newspapers and magazines and what they hear on radio and view on television. They are reactions to headline news stories, editorials, editorial cartoons, and to letters to the editor written by other people. The letter that follows appeared in the October 2, 2000 issue of *Maclean's* as a reaction to a cover story on the Olympics.

MODEL: LETTER TO THE EDITOR

Sometimes writers suggest a title for their letters or editors will provide a headline to capture the essence of the response.

Letters are edited for clarity and length. Although copyright for all letters submitted to the publisher remains with the author, the publisher may freely reproduce these in print and electronic form.

Olympian Ads

Are the Olympics a huge sporting event or just an endless marathon of advertisements and product placements ("Eyes on the prize," Cover, Sept. 18)? It seems that this ancient tradition of pitting the world's best athletes against one another has changed into a two-week-long commercial for Coca-Cola and Visa. And it's not just commercials either, it's billboards that distract viewers from the actual event. I am not saying that there shouldn't be sponsorship, but that the sponsors need to step back and let the real stars, the athletes, have the spotlight for longer than a minute and 30 seconds between commercials.
Rachel Stephenson, Whitby, Ont.

CHECKLIST   WRITING A LETTER TO THE EDITOR

✓ The letter should be relatively short (between 100 and 300 words).

✓ If responding to an article, give the title of the article, the writer, the date published, and the name of the newspaper or magazine.

✓ Summarize the article, editorial, or letter if responding to a piece of writing, because readers may not have read the original or may have forgotten the content.

✓ Present your view in a logical, persuasive manner and quote from the article as needed.

✓ You may agree with some points but disagree with others: begin with the positive and then proceed to the negative.

✓ Be sure to provide support for any arguments you raise.

✓ Conclude with a call to action (persuasion) or a statement that will linger in the minds of the readers.

✓ Sign the letter—the newspaper must have the writer's name and address on file, even if it does not appear in print.

Activities

Working with Editorial Pages

1. Reread the editorial "Answer the Question" found on pages 228 to 229. In writing, respond to the following questions:
   - What is the main point being made?
   - How is this editorial different from the news story on the same subject found on page 226 of this text? (Consider content *and* style.)

2. Write an opinion piece on a current issue reported in the paper or an occurrence in your school or community. Consider the characteristics of persuasive writing before you begin; try to appeal to your reader's logic and emotions. Have a peer read and edit your article.

3. Think of an idea for an editorial cartoon about a global, national, or local issue. Sketch your ideas or use computer to help you design it. Effective word choice should complement the pictures and reinforce the central message of your cartoon.

4. Write your own letter to the editor responding to a story you have been following in the newspaper or other media. Use the checklist above for writing a letter to the editor to guide you.

Magazines

LEARNING FOCUS
- analyze and assess the form and content of magazine articles
- analyze the relationship between magazines and their readers
- write a magazine article for a specific audience

Take a look at the wide range of magazines on display at a bookstore or convenience store: the covers tell us a great deal about subject matter and focus. We read magazines for pleasure, for information, and for critical examination of current issues. Whereas newspapers are published daily on large sheets of inexpensive newsprint, magazines are published weekly or monthly on high quality paper. Newspapers, radio, and television report the news *as it happens*, keeping their audience current. Magazines treat a topic in an extensive, thorough manner, often using interviews with individuals associated with a story to give the headlines more background and depth.

When we consider magazines, we might think first of major news magazines with a large circulation, like the American *Newsweek*, which features international news stories or its competitor *Time*, which provides **split-run** segments of content and advertising tailored to specific geographic areas (e.g., Canada). In Canada, our largest weekly newsmagazine is *Maclean's*, published by Rogers Media, owner of Canada's largest cable company and publisher of other magazines, including *Chatelaine*, which focuses on topics of interest to women.

Large circulation magazines have found it increasingly difficult to compete with television for the advertising dollar. The number of ads a magazine can sell determines its size. Magazines must strike a balance between ads and editorial content; so if they cannot sell enough ads, they cannot publish many articles. The trend, therefore, has been to specialty publications that target specific markets and contain advertisements tailored to small-circulation interest groups. The magazine *Popular Science*, for example, explores high-tech subjects and advertises goods and services that electronic enthusiasts crave. *Seventeen* provides fashion and fitness tips for young women. There are specialty magazines for the home decorator, sports enthusiast, the business-minded, the traveller, the entertainment buff, the intellectual.

Numerous magazines come into existence annually and many disappear after a couple of years due to intense competition and disappointing circulation. Those that last do so because they fit a particular *market niche* not being addressed elsewhere: they carefully tailor their product to that readership. These magazines are able to guarantee their advertisers that they can deliver a message to the target audience the ads have been designed to reach. Some specialty magazines, such as scholarly or arts publications, receive subsidies from local, provincial, or national councils to help keep them afloat.

Many magazines are now available via the Web, though they may appear in an abridged version, tailored to fit the Web medium. Magazines, in both their print and on-line versions, give readers the opportunity to send e-mail responses to writers and editors, and to become part of on-line chat groups discussing articles featured in the magazine. This user group is a potentially useful resource for magazine publishers when researching customer preferences and priorities.

The Internet also allows for the creation of electronic magazines or **e-zines** that provide an alternative to print media. These e-zines vary greatly in their level of sophistication. Some mimic the style of print magazines; others contain text and graphics in simple newsletter format. Some are written as information fact sheets on specific subject areas; some feature comic writings, poetry, and cartoons; others may be created to lobby government and private agencies to bring about social or economic improvements.

Regardless of the type of magazine, readers need to apply some standard of critical analysis regarding the acceptability of content and style. As readers we have an opportunity to voice our opinion on magazine coverage of an issue, through guest editorials or letters to the editor. Ask yourself these questions as you read:

- Is the cover of the magazine appealing? If so, why?
- Are the articles accurate, timely, informative, well researched, thought-provoking?
- Are the articles unbiased and fair?
- Are creative titles (**heads**), explanatory subheads (**decks**), and leads used to catch reader attention?
- What proportion of the magazine is devoted to advertising? Where is it placed? Is this placement effective?
- What kinds of products are advertised and to what target audience do they appeal?
- Are many visuals used? What purpose do the visuals serve? Do they stimulate interest and complement the written text?

The larger magazines have a staff of editors, who also write occasional articles. Their primary responsibility is to commission and edit articles by **freelance writers** (referred to on the masthead as contributing editors) who are used on a regular basis. On smaller magazines, usually the staff both write and edit most of the articles published.

The article that follows appeared in the Canadian edition of *Time*. It addresses the pervasiveness of advertising as it might become in the not-too-distant future.

MODEL: MAGAZINE ARTICLE

HOW WILL ADVERTISERS REACH US?

by Jay Chiat

Jay Chiat writes with a high degree of expertise, having co-founded Chiat/Day, an advertising firm that created ads for Nike and Apple ("1984"), among others. He now heads ScreamingMedia Inc.

IT'S SUPER BOWL LIVE IN 2020, RECORD-SETTING NUMBERS of viewers are tuned in to watch the game, but not on television and not over the Internet. Instead they are using handheld broadband devices that allow them to project the transmission onto any flat surface. And in 2020, just as today, viewers are interested in the game, but they're even more interested in the advertising.

The commercials, of course, are great—surprisingly better than they are now. Directors make sure the commercials are moving, exciting, entertaining; research and planning make sure they are relevant; technicians make sure the effects are breathtaking.

It's not the commercials that are the most interesting part, though: the really important advertising is hiding in plain sight on the field. The Microsoft Mustangs are playing the GM Generals at Cisco Stadium in a town called Ciscoville—formerly known as Philadelphia. Corporations will pay big money for the right to digitize logos onto the T-shirts of the fans in the stands. Logos of sponsors won't be painted on stadium signs or on the field anymore. Thanks to a trend that is already happening, they'll be digitally embedded in the image on your screen. The logos you see will depend on your personal interests and profile, and they'll be different from the ones seen by your next-door neighbours.

Advertising will change profoundly over the next couple of decades, although there's a good chance you won't notice the difference, since the most meaningful changes won't be visible to the casual observer. It's the changes that are happening underground that will count, and they're the ones we should be aware of. Advertising in the future will be surgically, stealthily, and eerily targeted, and disturbingly omnipresent.

Technology, naturally, will be the engine. User-tracking software that records your TV-and Internet-viewing habits in minute detail—and crosses it with your purchasing history—will allow the advertiser to know that you have children, that you eat meat, that your native language is Spanish and that your dishwasher is however many years old. That way you will be shown commercials for minivans, cheeseburgers and replacement dishwashers, all in Spanish, and not for roadsters, tofu and replacement refrigerators, in English. (In fact, this technology already exists.) Refined with data that track what kinds of on-line ads you tend to click on—funny, sentimental, fact laden—every commercial will hit home.

Say what you will, that's a nifty trick. In the future people won't be bothered with advertising messages irrelevant to them. They'll tend to like advertising better because it's so carefully tailored to their tastes. It will begin to feel less like an intrusion. This works for the advertiser too because fewer dollars will be wasted. While it's a little dispiriting to think we can be so predictably

Note the parallel structure—the repetition of the adverbs "surgically," "stealthily," "eerily," and "disturbingly" to emphasize the manipulative *tricks* of advertisers.

Again in this paragraph the writer uses parallel structure ("that you have children, that you eat meat, that you…") to emphasize how well advertisers will know their target audiences.

Narrowcasting is the term used to describe the strategy of focusing television programs and their advertisements on particular demographic groups (e.g., teenagers, parents, young professionals).

manipulated, maybe that's a fair price to pay to avoid the pollution of messages you don't care about.

Nevertheless, it seems clear that the advertising outlets that exist today—TV and radio commercials, print ads, billboards and taxi tops—will not be plentiful enough to accommodate all the commercial messages that are agitating to get out. Advertising will therefore necessarily slip beyond the boundaries of the thirty-second commercial and the full-page ad and migrate to the rest of the world, including entertainment, journalism, and art.

You can glimpse the future now. Product placement in movies is an obvious instance of advertising having slipped outside its traditional container into entertainment. MTV—an entertainment medium designed expressly to sell records—is another classic example. Every time a rapper mentions a brand of anything in a song, advertising slips into art. If you have a Harley-Davidson tattoo, you're there already. If you wear a T-shirt with a logo on it, you're also there, but with less pain. Eventually, every surface that can display a message will be appropriated for advertising.

A backlash is inevitable. Perhaps people will pay a premium to live in "advertising-free zones," just as, perhaps, they will be willing to pay a premium to live in cell phone-free zones.

The Internet will accelerate the phenomenon. The browser page and the LCD screen on your cell phone or your PalmPilot are still contested territories, allowing new relationships among the different kinds of content that appear there. The Pampers Web site provides parenting information and advice—and, presumably, not the kind that the Pampers people wouldn't want you to see. In a less obvious kind of relationship, marketing execs can enter chat rooms under assumed names and praise their company's product, service, or stock: that's just advertising masquerading as conversation. And more directly, consumers are excited about an emerging technology that allows them to click and buy as they consume journalism or entertainment—say, to buy Frasier's couch as they watch the show. That's not entertainment with advertising: that's entertainment as advertising.

People get very nervous when they see the line blurring between advertising and other forms of content; they think advertising is some kind of infection that pollutes the purity of art, ruins the objectivity of editorial, and distracts from the pleasure of en-

---

Note the creative use of verb choice in the following two paragraphs. What is effective about "agitating," "migrate," "slips," "appropriated"?

In the last sentences of this paragraph just a change of a preposition—"with" to "as"—alters the meaning of the sentences.

tertainment. As usual, however, people are nervous about the wrong thing. Consumers are smart and perfectly aware when they're being sold; surely parents who go to the Pampers site are happy to find worthwhile information there and are capable of distinguishing between a commercial message and an editorial one. Art and journalism, until they became pretentious in the late 20th century, always relied on direct subsidy from private sources. Don't think for a minute that commercial interest didn't enter into it.

In Canada, as well, corporations have purchased the naming rights for large civic centres. Examples are the Air Canada Centre in Toronto, GM Place in Vancouver, Molson Centre in Montreal, and Skyreach Centre in Edmonton.

The only genuinely disturbing aspect of the ubiquity of advertising—the real reason to get nervous—is that it has begun to supplant what was formerly civic and public. There's no Candlestick Park anymore, just 3Com Park, and now there's a PacBell Park to match. The venerable Boston Garden was replaced not too long ago by the Fleet Center: a city erased, its role played by a bank. A little town in the Pacific Northwest just renamed itself after a dot-com company in return for a generous donation. I won't mention the name here, since I figure advertising should be paid for. That's when advertising has gone too far: when it's become something we are, rather than something we see.

Activities

Learning About Magazines

1. Bring several kinds of magazines to school. In small groups discuss their common features and any unique features that are evident. Consider each magazine's purpose, appeal, content, and appearance. Would you take out a subscription to any of these magazines? Why or why not? Identify the following as you evaluate each magazine: (i) name of the magazine, (ii) publisher, (iii) country of publication, (iv) subscription rate, (v) frequency (weekly or monthly), (vi) **target audience**, (vii) style of writing (and level of language), (viii) articles (feature articles, editorials, letters to the editor), (ix) amount and kinds of advertising, (x) quantity and quality of the visuals.

2. Reread the article from *Time* beginning on page 235 for a deeper understanding of its style and content. In small groups, brainstorm ways in which advertising techniques will change in the future. Share your ideas with the class.

3. Compare a popular magazine for women (e.g., *Chatelaine*) with a similar magazine for men (e.g., *Esquire*). Examine the topics of the articles and the accompanying advertisements. What conclusions can

you draw about the way each magazine targets its audience? What are the similarities and differences in the kinds of articles and advertising in each magazine? Summarize your findings in a written report.

4. Find a magazine or e-zine that is published for a special interest audience and that appeals to your own particular tastes. Write an article and send it to the magazine publisher or editor.

Communicating Through Visual Messages

Whether you are looking at a poster, advertisement, photograph, or comic strip, watching a television show, or exploring an icon-rich Web site, you are engaged, both *consciously* and *subconsciously*, in deriving meaning from a visual message. The more critical awareness we develop about the *whys* and *hows* of visual information, the better we can understand *what* we are seeing.

The skill of *visual literacy*—how well we interpret the world of colours, shapes, lines, and symmetries—is becoming increasingly important in the twenty-first century. Some of the general strategies used to make sense of print texts (determining purpose, audience, content, and context) will help us to analyze visual messages. However, like critical reading, critical viewing has some unique requirements of its own.

Posters

Posters have varied purposes, which include promoting upcoming events, presenting social commentary, persuading the viewer to purchase a service or product, and displaying art, photographs, or reproductions. The designer of a poster must ensure that the poster's message is

LEARNING FOCUS
- analyze and assess the form and content of visual texts
- explain how a visual text conveys meaning
- design and evaluate a visual text

consistent with its purpose, its target audience, and the location in which it is placed. Posters are often on display in public areas where they compete for the viewer's attention with other posters and the immediate surroundings. A range of colours, various font styles and sizes, and diverse background patterns can serve to draw attention to the message.

In the following poster advertising Canadian rock-legends the Guess Who, notice the bright yellow background and *retro* appeal with its psychedelic lettering. A humorous touch is added by having the moose (a Canadian icon) peeking out of the "O," with his Blues-Brothers-style sunglasses. The group's song titles unobtrusively border the poster, reminding fans of the broad range of hit songs the Guess Who produced over a long career.

MODEL: POSTER

Running Back Thru Canada Tour

THE GUESS WHO

BURTON CUMMINGS JIM KALE GARRY PETERSON RANDY BACHMAN

WEDNESDAY MAY 31
MEMORIAL STADIUM
TICKETS ON SALE AT ALL REGULAR OUTLETS!

GUNS, GUNS, GUNS · CLAP FOR THE WOLFMAN · UNDUN · RUNNING BACK TO SASKATOON · DO YOU MISS ME DARLIN'

NO SUGAR TONIGHT · NEW MOTHER NATURE · HANG ON TO YOUR LIFE · FOLLOW YOUR DAUGHTER HOME · ALBERT FLASHER

BUS RIDER · LAUGHING · HAND ME DOWN WORLD · SHARE THE LAND · AMERICAN WOMAN · RAIN DANCE

The House of Blues Concerts logo and trademarks are under license from House of Blues Brands Corp. (USA).

✓ CHECKLIST CREATING POSTERS

- ✓ Come up with an idea (product, service, event) and a specific message.
- ✓ Identify your audience and purpose.
- ✓ Determine what kind of competition there is, particularly if advertising a product or service.
- ✓ Research locations where the poster is likely to appear.
- ✓ Identify the human and material resources needed to create the poster.
- ✓ Decide on the exact information you would like to communicate.
- ✓ Simplify your message and avoid unnecessary **jargon**.
- ✓ Decide on a size, shape, and orientation (horizontal or vertical).
- ✓ Create a reasonable balance between words and images.
- ✓ Use the **rule of thirds** to help with the placement of images and text.
- ✓ Select a **typeface** (font) that is appropriate for the tone of your message.

Activities

Communicating Through Posters

1. Bring three posters to class and write a brief personal response to each one. Include comments about each, as to whether you like it, and why, how it makes you feel, what stands out, what purpose it serves, what message it communicates, and what makes it successful or ineffective. Share your responses in a class discussion.

2. Examine the poster "Math Is Power."
   - What is its purpose?
   - Why has the designer chosen the image of the clenched fist?
   - What message do the words "Demand it" communicate?
   - Explain the effectiveness of the typeface(s).
   - Who is the intended audience for this poster?

   Now create a "Language Is Power" poster suitable for a high school audience.

3. Create a poster to advertise an upcoming event at your school. Contact the group sponsoring the event (your client) to determine its needs. Research the conditions that may affect the design of your poster. Decide on the poster's size and shape. Produce at least *three* different **thumbnail sketches** for your client to choose from. Ensure that your poster is informative and persuasive—your goal is to encourage as many people as possible to take part in the advertised event.

Advertisements

LEARNING FOCUS

- analyze and respond to the form and content of advertisements
- explain the relationship between ads and consumers
- explore the relationship between the advertising industry and government regulations

For a moment, imagine what your life would be like without advertising—no photos of clothing or food in your newspaper, no perfume smells wafting from your favourite magazine, no flyers in your mailbox, no roadside billboards, no commercials on television. How would you learn about new products? How would you know which store had the new snowboard you wanted? Where would you find information about the new digital camera you're anxious to purchase?

To advertise, in its most fundamental sense, is simply to call attention to something. If we keep this basic definition in mind, we are then free to judge both the effectiveness of the presentation and the value of the message itself. Many ads simply wish to provoke a stimulus-response reaction (e.g., supper-time ads asking "Hungry?—try our mouth-watering, easy-to-prepare pizza-rolls."). Others may use attention-getting elements to prompt us to civic and humanitarian action or to urge us to become better informed.

Advertising is often viewed as a negative medium that persuades people to buy things they don't really want or need, or do things they don't want to do. If you don't have an interest in high-tech "toys," can ads create one for you? More often, advertisements try to convince you to choose one brand of product over another for a purchase you were likely to make anyway. There may be little real difference between one product and the next; it is the effectiveness of the advertising techniques that often tips the scales in favour of or against a particular purchase.

Companies spend a lot of time studying the desires, motivations, and **demographics** of a particular target audience. These factors are strong predictors of consumer preference. Advertisers sell *image* and *lifestyle* as much as they sell any individual product. As consumers, we tend to choose products or services consistent with an image of ourselves or with a lifestyle we have or want to have.

✓ CHECKLIST | VIEWING AN ADVERTISEMENT

- ✓ Examine the advertisement as a whole.
- ✓ Determine the target audience and the needs being appealed to.
- ✓ Identify the product or service being promoted.
- ✓ Identify the setting, the people (if any), and the action taking place.
- ✓ Decide if you have a pre-existing desire for what is being advertised.
- ✓ Consider the kinds of images being used to convey excitement, social status, improved health, and so on.
- ✓ Determine what normally holds your attention and how this particular ad keeps you interested.
- ✓ Look for **buzzwords** (e.g., "free," "easy," "safe," "new and improved").
- ✓ Decide how you feel about the product being advertised.

Consider the advertisement below, taken from a snowboarding magazine. It provides an image of the human brain as it supposedly looks when experiencing the emotion of exhilaration. By showing us the image in association with the **slogan** "Technical Clothing = Performance = Exhilaration," we are likely to associate the desired feeling with the product being advertised. The truth, of course, is that just wearing Helly Hansen clothing will not make you perform better, nor will it cause the neurons in your brain to fire. The ad is effective because viewers who desire this sensation are more likely to succumb to the **logical fallacy**, and purchase clothing and equipment that they feel is consistent with achieving the supposed effect.

MODEL: ADVERTISEMENT

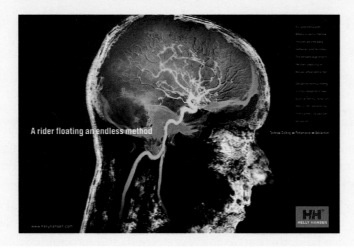

ADVERTISING STANDARDS When viewing advertisements, be on the lookout for subtle manipulation or **propaganda**. In its most positive sense, propaganda is "spreading the word"; in a more negative sense, it may be used to mislead and manipulate. Any time an advertisement requests our unquestioning allegiance or compliance, it is a type of propaganda.

In Canada, both consumers and producers are protected by the Canadian Code of Advertising Standards. The Code is administered by Advertising Standards Canada and is designed to help set and maintain standards of honesty, accuracy, fairness, and propriety in advertising. It forms the basis upon which advertising is evaluated in response to consumer or business complaints. It is widely endorsed by advertisers, advertising agencies, media that exhibit advertising, and suppliers to the advertising process. The full text of the Code is available from Advertising Standards Canada at their Web site (please refer to the Pearson Canada Web site: <www.pearsoned.ca/referencepoints/links>).

✓ CHECKLIST | DESIGNING AN ADVERTISEMENT

- ✓ Decide on the product or service you will advertise.
- ✓ Establish your purpose and your target audience.
- ✓ Consider the values you wish to convey visually and verbally.
- ✓ Determine the size and shape of the advertisement.
- ✓ Catch your viewers' attention with effective design techniques (images, colours, shapes, and layout).
- ✓ Create a desire in your viewers by addressing what is important to them.
- ✓ Ensure that the text and images work together to create the effect you want.
- ✓ Produce a number of sample layouts before you select one you prefer.

Activities

Working with Advertisements

1. Scan newspapers and magazines to find *five* print advertisements focused on different products or services. In chart form, evaluate each ad in terms of the following:
   - what kind of behaviours and attitudes are made to appear desirable
   - how effective each advertiser was in influencing your thinking
   - how your personal values compare with the values being promoted in each of the ads

2. A typeface is an artistic element that sends a visual message. For example, a fine, script-like typeface communicates elegance and expense; a bold, thick style conveys strength and forcefulness.

Bring to class a number of newspaper and magazine ads. With a partner, examine each one to identify the typefaces used. Discuss with your partner how each typeface reflects or reinforces the content or image of the product or service being advertised.

3. With a group of your peers, create a set of criteria for what you think makes an effective advertisement. Search through current issues of magazines to find examples and non-examples of your criteria. Give each advertisement a rating based on your criteria. Present your ads to the class, justifying your recommendations and choices.

Photographs

A well-constructed photograph allows us to stop and think; it may create a sense of stillness or an impression of action. The skilled photographer can capture a range of moods, make the ordinary extraordinary, and supply a fresh angle on the familiar. Black-and-white photographs may even cause us to look more carefully at scale, outline, and meaning, enabling us to go beyond the immediate sensual appeal of colour.

Photographs are media constructs—they have a subtext of who or what the photographer thinks is important. With current technology it is easy to change and manipulate a photograph without the viewer being aware of such *tricks*. Once a photograph is digitized, it can be altered in such a way that the change is virtually undetectable. We need to question the accuracy of the photographic information we encounter.

LEARNING FOCUS
- explain the choices made in the design of a photograph
- analyze the messages conveyed through photographs and photo essays

✓ CHECKLIST   VIEWING A PHOTOGRAPH

✓ Find out something about the photographer.

✓ Examine the title (if there is one) for clues to direct your interpretation.

✓ Identify the form (portrait, photo journalism, advertising, fine art, documentary film), as each form has a specific purpose.

✓ Determine the historical or cultural context of the photograph, i.e., where and when it was taken and the resulting impact on the visual message.

✓ Consider how the photograph is framed and what is included in the image you see.

✓ Identify the **focal point**, often the main subject in the image.

✓ Determine the **aesthetic elements** used (light and shadow, camera angle, colour, focus, composition, and shape).

✓ Identify both the emotion found within the photograph itself and your own emotional response to it.

In this photo by Pam Coristine, we see the power of photography to reveal the mysterious and beautiful in otherwise commonplace settings. The hints of debris, the wind-strewn boughs, and the muddy patches exposed by footprints in the snow all help build atmosphere. The open space in the bottom third of the photo draws us in as viewers. In addition, the camera angle trains our eyes upwards, providing the impression of movement in the stillness, and reinforcing the sense that we, as viewers, are *in* the picture.

MODEL: PHOTOGRAPH

Activities

Communicating Through Photographs

1. "V-J Day in Times Square" is a famous **still image**. Use the following questions to guide your viewing of it:
   - What people are shown? How are they placed? What is the setting?
   - What do you know about the situation and time period shown?
   - Who are the people and what are they doing? What is the function of the objects? What can you conclude from what you see?

2. The image below captures a Sufi dancer engaged in ritualistic whirling.
   - In what ways does the photo project a sense of movement?
   - How might the picture's impact be different if it were a black-and-white image?
   - What can you find out about the culture to which this image belongs? How do your discoveries enrich your appreciation of the photograph?

3. A **photo essay** is a series of images linked by a common technique, concept, or theme. The relationship between the photos may be explicit, as in a sequence of images of a war-torn village, or less obvious, requiring you to look for a connection. At your local library or on the Internet, search for photo essays on current events. Before you begin, ask yourself what kinds of topics you'd like to see explored in pictures: political conflicts, technological advances, cultural trends, or changing social customs. Bring your findings back to class and discuss the photo essay that you find most compelling. Or, if you wish, create your own photo essay on a theme of personal interest.

Cartoons and Comic Strips

LEARNING FOCUS
- analyze the messages and meanings conveyed by cartoons
- understand and analyze the techniques of cartooning
- design and evaluate a cartoon

Cartoons combine words and visuals to create a message. The impact of a **cartoon** is similar to that of a memorable line from a poem: it says a lot by doing a little. In a compact, meaning-rich image, or series of images in a **comic strip**, the cartoonist communicates a point of view that might take a writer pages to express as effectively.

Cartoon drawings may be used for pure amusement, to draw attention to an issue, or for advertising purposes. Sometimes they are based on observational humour, much like the style used by stand-up comedians. Cartoons may also spark debate about our values and the messages we receive through the media. By viewing or—if one has talent for sketching—creating cartoons, we can heighten and refine our sensitivity.

A cartoon can serve to illustrate the absurdities of everyday behaviour. Cartoonists often highlight the ridiculous with carefully aimed **satire**. Observe on the next page how Scott Adams satirizes the self-importance of the manager.

CREATING CARTOONS Understanding the techniques of cartooning can help you to interpret and create cartoon messages more effectively. Cartoonists use several of the following:

- Communication Balloons—**speech balloons** and **thought balloons** are used to indicate what a character is speaking or thinking. They are usually connected to the character using arrows or tails (for speech) and small circles (for thoughts).

- Coined Language—fashionable jargon and buzzwords may be presented in a humorous way to make a point. Cartoonists may also make use of **puns** and figures of speech.

- Contrasting sizes (huge and tiny)—distortions of size (people and objects) are used to emphasize a situation or problem.

MODEL: COMIC STRIP

DILBERT reprinted by permission of United Feature Syndicate, Inc

- Caricature—features of a well-known person or object are comically distorted for satirical effect.
- Ridiculous exaggeration (**hyperbole**)—this goes well beyond the boundaries of reality to stress a point. For example, an image of a government leader towering over a map of the nation may show the power of this one person in comparison to the entire country.
- Symbolism—one thing is used to represent another. For example, a heart is a common symbol for love, a lion for courage.
- Reversal—the usual or expected situation is reversed to catch the reader's attention and make a point. An example might be a group of professional sports players selling chocolate bars door-to-door to raise money for their team.
- Understatement and irony—these devices express the opposite of something's literal meaning. For example, to illustrate understatement a character in a cartoon might say that there is a minor, insignificant problem with acid rain, while all around the speaker the environment is disintegrating. Irony may be created by using a

249

hidden element, not evident to a character in the cartoon, but obvious or visible to the reader.

- Surprise ending—the action or sequence of events (usually presented in four to eight panels) proceeds in a logical manner. In the last panel there is an unexpected twist that emphasizes the point the cartoonist wishes to make.

✔ CHECKLIST | DRAWING CARTOONS

✓ Look for cartoon ideas in the funny things that happen to you and others.
✓ Determine the characters, the *joke*, and the setting for your cartoon.
✓ If you are developing a comic strip, decide how many frames are needed.
✓ Provide a logical sequence (beginning, middle, and end) to your frames.
✓ Use pencil to sketch your cartoon, to allow for easy revisions.
✓ Keep your drawings simple: the fewer lines per scene, the better.
✓ Make your dialogue and written text consistent with your visual message.
✓ Create your final cartoon version by going over the sketch in ink.
✓ Add colour if you wish.

Activities

1. Search the Internet, recent newspapers, or magazines for a cartoon or comic strip you find effective. Write an analysis of the cartoon in which you include the following:
   - an explanation of the issue—what is the event or issue that inspired the cartoon? Who is the target audience(s)? What is the message? What do you think the cartoonist's opinion is about the topic? Do you agree with the cartoonist? Why?
   - a discussion of the techniques used—are any real-life personalities depicted? What type of person is being featured? What characteristics of society are reflected? Are symbols used? What are they and what do you think they represent? What other techniques have been used? Are these techniques effective?
   - your emotional reaction to the cartoon—does it make you laugh, smile, groan, or think?

2. Create your own single-frame cartoon or cartoon strip. You might begin by imagining some absurd situations or bizarre personalities you've encountered and try to render these in cartoon form. You could also consider creating a cartoon in the style of one of your favourite cartoonists.

Communication Through Electronic Messages

At the beginning of the twentieth century, communication in the industrialized world was carried on through surface mail and telegraph, with telephone technology just starting to make an impact. A hundred years later, phones are something we can carry in our pockets, and we can send a written message around the earth in seconds via the Internet. The better we understand the major features, benefits, and shortcomings of communication technology, the better prepared we will be to cope with the increasingly complex world we're creating.

Pause for a moment to think how electronic technology has permeated our everyday lives: many of us wake up to clock radios or switch on our television to the weather channel; others rub the sleep from their eyes while they boot up their computers to check for e-mail; some may pick up the phone to see if they've got any voice messages; next, when they arrive at work or school, they may check their day's agenda on an electronic organizer or receive messages over the intercom, by fax machine, by video billboard monitor, or perhaps by pagers attached to their belts.

For those with the income and inclination, there is now a universe of entertainment options available on cable and satellite television. In addition, the Internet features **Webcasts**—mini-video programs—sometimes with the added feature of interactivity allowing users to search and participate actively with other users through chat groups and e-mail. Internet radio has similar benefits, in that one can always find a station that caters to one's specific interests and tastes.

The following sections are designed to help you reflect on the various electronic media we all experience. Preparing yourself not to be taken in, not to be carried away, not to be overwhelmed, will permit you to take advantage of the wonderful possibilities and benefits of each.

Radio Broadcasting

LEARNING FOCUS
- compare public and private radio broadcasting
- understand the relationship between radio programs and their audience
- plan and create a radio broadcast

Radio, the first electronic form of mass media, has become so pervasive in our lives that we tend not to realize its daily impact. Most homes have two or more radios; a radio is standard equipment in automobiles, and we listen to radios as we walk, jog, work, and mow the lawn. Radio provides the background music in office buildings and we sometimes hear the radio on the telephone as we wait for our phone call to be answered.

Since radio's inception in the 1920s, its technology and programming have undergone significant changes. In Canada today we have public radio (CBC) and numerous private stations that are owned locally or form part of an extensive broadcasting network.

PUBLIC RADIO The Canadian Broadcasting Corporation (CBC) is owned and operated by our federal government and paid for by Canadian taxpayers. Its mandate is to provide coast-to-coast information and entertainment programming that is predominantly Canadian in its content and character. CBC has a role as a nation-builder, contributing to our sense of national unity, helping listeners to understand the unique cultures of our different regions and the common links that make us one. CBC radio promotes the music, drama, news, and special events that define us as a people. It airs shows that focus on science, on comedy, on sports. It promotes discussion on talk shows like *As It Happens* and *This Morning* and on **open-line shows** such as *Cross Country Checkup* that give citizens an opportunity to express their views on current topics and themes. There are programs that broadcast the voices of youth and minority groups providing time for talk-back and debate of issues relevant to these groups. Public radio allows us to hear the speeches that our political leaders make in the House of Commons, while on-air commentators provide thought-provoking analysis of national events.

The commentary below was delivered by CBC radio host Michael Enright on *This Morning—Sunday Edition* on October 1, 2000. It is that commentator's reflection on the life and death of Pierre Elliott Trudeau, broadcast when our former prime minister was lying in state on Parliament Hill.

MODEL: RADIO COMMENTARY

This commentary (monologue) has a distinct purpose: to inform and to offer praise of the late prime minister. Such writing is referred to as a **eulogy**, a speech of high praise or commendation for someone who has died.

The Week of Looking Back
by Michael Enright

We were all so much younger then. Middle age was a far country and in our arrogance, everything was happening for the first time.

And it was happening to us.

Expo '67 on the islands of Montreal had turned us outward to the world.

Québec was burning with a refiner's fire that English Canada didn't understand. But we knew in Québec there was no turning back.

Young people marched in the streets and chanted on campuses and felt the tantalizing pulse of power. The country was prosperous. We were still in a party mood.

Our prime minister was Lester Pearson, much honoured and nice, but too Uncle Fudd.

We looked for someone new. Someone to match the mood and momentum of the times.

Pierre Trudeau came onto the scene like, in Gordon Donaldson's memorable phrase, "a stone through a stained-glass window."

The physicalness of the man, the eyes, blue beyond blue, the fierce focus of his attention, was something never seen in a politician.

To be around him, even for a moment, felt almost dangerous. This was a man who made things happen and to whom things happened. And you knew you wanted to be there if either occurred.

In fact he didn't seem to be a politician at all. More an outlaw, a statesman/highwayman of some kind.

Well, it turned out he was a politician after all—one of the toughest we've seen.

He was like one of those old British actor-managers—he picked the play, hired and fired the actors, blocked out the movements, and took the lead role for himself.

We in the press were extras; what the script would call "others."

His vision of a strong country had at its core a powerful, coherent federal government with a willingness to do things on a national scale.

That part of his vision has been carefully, systematically, dismantled over the past 20 years in cries of devolution and more power to the provinces.

In the silent lineups that snaked across Parliament Hill, we mourned the passing of this singular man.

I wonder if, in some way, we also mourn the passing of his vision.

Enright's writing style could be called poetic. Note the concise one-line and one-sentence paragraphs, the comparisons, the use of parallel structure, the vivid verbs and descriptive language.

Note the effectiveness of Enright's use of similes to describe Pierre Elliott Trudeau.

This monologue has a discernible plan:
- a beginning (discussion of the past)
- a middle (a description of Pierre Elliott Trudeau)
- an ending (an apt quotation to summarize)

Pierre Trudeau is described as "a man of words," "an accomplished essayist" who "read widely" and "liked the company of writers." Consider why these are important traits in a leader and prime minister.

Yes Pierre Trudeau was a man of action. But he was also a man of words. He was an accomplished essayist and commentator. He read widely and always.

He liked the company of writers.

He gravitated to French writers and one of his favourites was Edmond Rostand.

Trudeau loved Cyrano de Bergerac and it's not too much of a stretch to think that he might have identified with the romantic hero.

What does this concluding quotation tell us about Pierre Trudeau?

This is from Cyrano:

> To sing, to laugh, to dream
> To walk in my own way
> Free to cock my hat where I choose
> To fight or write. To travel any road
> Under the sun or stars
> And if my nature wants that which grows
> Towering in heaven, like the mountain pine
> I'll climb not high perhaps but all alone

Consider the tone used in this monologue. Why is it appropriate, given the circumstances?

PRIVATE RADIO Private radio stations rely heavily on advertising revenue to cover operating costs and ensure profits for the owners. Private stations keep listeners up-to-date with the latest news, weather, sports, traffic reports, and exact time. Those stations also reserve time for special programs, open-line programs, and for editorial commentary. However, private radio's main appeal is in its music area—its instantly-filled requests and Top 40 hits.

Just as magazines have had to compete with television for advertising dollars, private radio has had to tailor its products and advertisements to specific target groups. There are specialty radio stations and programs that provide one type of music predominantly (some play all country, some mainly rock, some, classical or jazz, some, hits of the '60s and '70s). There are stations that provide only news and talk, others that offer multicultural programming catering to particular ethnic groups, and still others that offer inspirational music and messages.

Radio-style transmission is now available through the computer. Numerous sites allow listeners to get the latest in news and entertainment as well as customized niche-market audio shows via their Internet connections. With advances in digital technology, both the quality and nature of what we receive from radio will continue to change considerably.

Activities

Exploring Radio

1. Interview representatives of various demographic groups (e.g., a senior high student, teacher, parent, grandparent) to determine their favourite radio station and the features of its broadcast that are most appealing to them. Chart your results by demographic group using graphs or tables.

2. In a small group visit a local radio station.
   - Interview a station official to determine who owns the station, what the transmitting range is, who the target audience is, and what its advertising fees are.
   - Interview a disc jockey (DJ) to determine the range of responsibilities and training required for the job.

3. Create a thirty-minute radio show for broadcast at your school. Write scripts that include
   - brief introductions, thank-you comments, and station identifications.
   - news briefs.
   - advertisements (for pizza, clothes, school supplies, etc.).
   - public service announcements (e.g., school announcements promoting upcoming events).
   - sports news.
   - music.
   - an editorial, commentary, or monologue on some timely issue.
   - interviews (e.g., a school athlete or student council president).

   Consider the equipment (e.g., tape recorders, PA system, patch cords) and personnel (e.g., audio technician, disc jockey, news reader) you will require to produce this show.

Television Broadcasting

LEARNING FOCUS
- reflect on your television viewing habits
- understand and evaluate the various kinds of television programs
- plan and create a music video

We are bombarded daily with **moving images** on television, which provide us with entertainment and information. Sometimes we respond to these images without really thinking about them. As critical viewers, we must understand that television both reflects the values of a society at a particular time and influences those values. We must also question whether or not everything we see is real. Television frames society, constructing a perception so close to reality that sometimes we accept what we see as being real when, in fact, it is often a distortion of reality.

Use the following questions to reflect on your television viewing:

- Where and with whom do you prefer to watch television? How do these factors affect the way you watch?
- When do you choose to watch TV? What do you watch, and why?
- Do the programs you watch have commercials? If so, do you watch them? If not, why not?
- What are the genres (e.g., sitcom, sports, cartoon, television drama, news program, documentary) you prefer? What do you know about these genres? What expectations did you have of these types of programs? Are these usually met?
- Do you have a favourite program or series you watch regularly? Why do you like it?

TELEVISION DRAMAS Both **television dramas** and **soap operas** develop our ideas of what society is, what it should be, or what it could be.

Marriage, divorce, death, medical problems, and financial woes make up the everyday lives of the characters revisited on a daily or weekly basis by the viewers.

The following are some common features of the television drama and soap opera genre:

- The plots are slow-paced and constructed in such a way that a viewer's full attention is not necessary.
- The focus is on the effect of the events on the characters, not on the events themselves.
- The passage of time reflects real time for viewers. The implication is that the action goes on whether or not we are watching the program.
- Flashback sequences in the minds of the characters serve to fill us in on key plot developments we might have missed.
- There are many characters, and none are indispensable.
- There are usually one or two settings, such as a hospital and someone's home.
- Viewers have an omniscient (all-knowing) point of view—they know more than the characters do.

SITUATION COMEDIES (SITCOMS) This type of show is a storytelling forum for society's concerns, values, and priorities. Although their content changes to reflect the trends of the time, **sitcoms** deal with relationships and how characters fit into a family or a group. With their underlying optimistic vision of the family, we are encouraged to both laugh at and laugh with the characters, whose antics poke fun at society's failings.

Characteristics of sitcoms include the following:

- They have a standard plot structure with rising action, resulting complications, and a resolution that can be easily discerned.

- The themes and plots typically represent the idealized North American middle class with the characters adhering to, or departing from, the status quo.

- Viewers identify with the characters and are sympathetic to their problems.

- Characters (whether main, supporting, or transient) tend to be stereotyped.

- They rely on comic suspense created through pretence, disguise, misunderstanding, ignorance, and comic **situational irony** where the viewer knows more than the characters.

- Laugh tracks are often employed to simulate a live audience.

REALITY-BASED TELEVISION Reality television is based, or claims to be based, on real-life truths. Such shows do present reality, but it is highly crafted to make the program fit the desires of the audience. The producers set the stage, choose the actors, set up the cameras, and eventually show us only selected portions of what they film.

The genre probably has its origins in hidden-camera programs like *Candid Camera*. The popularity of home-video cameras and spinoff shows like *Funniest Home Videos* have also spurred its growth. Reality-based television now includes several sub-genres such as courtroom shows; emergency, rescue, and dating shows; mystery and the unexplained.

Every reality-based television story has heroes and villains. It also includes the rising and falling action that we expect in a plot. In addition, the unscripted, and therefore unpredictable, drama that unfolds creates tremendous suspense. We see real people exposing the dramas of their lives in front of us as entertainment. As viewers, we are fascinated with the genuine emotions of the ordinary people who become the show's "stars." As television invades formerly private zones, it provides a safe way for us to see something that we've never been allowed to see before.

Why participate in a reality TV show? Fame—the camera is a seductive medium that provides one with exposure to a national audience. It is estimated that fifty million viewers watched the final episode of *Survivor* in the summer of 2000. In addition to becoming instant celebrities, participants are paid—and there are financial spinoffs, such as lucrative endorsements. Reality-based television often has huge pay-offs for the networks as well. Such programs are relatively inexpensive to produce, at $400,000 per hour as compared with the $1.2 million price tag attached to a typical hour-long drama such as *ER*. Advertisers are also easily attracted to such shows as they realize what a massive audience they can reach.

MUSIC VIDEOS When stations such as MuchMusic in Canada and MTV in the United States first aired in the early 1980s, some critics were puzzled by their core programming: music videos. Were these videos extended advertisements? Mini-documentaries? Art films?

Music videos are primarily an entertainment medium. With their fast pace and kaleidoscope of images, they offer us continuous visual and aural stimulation. Anyone who has watched a series of videos for a lengthy period knows how hard each video strives to keep our attention by rarely pausing for more than a second on a single image. Sometimes, in addition, they attempt to teach us or to show us new ways of envisioning the world (for example, Bruce Cockburn's "If a Tree Falls" or Alanis Morissette's "Thank U"). We may be treated to thought-provoking lyrics and visuals showing the highs and lows of human interaction—passion, courage, jealousy, hardship, for example.

Music videos provide a way to put a face to a voice; to anchor a song's sound appeal with visuals and a story; to establish a *look* or total image for the performing act; to distinguish an act and song from all the others vying for the audience's attention and dollars. Videos can be categorized as *performance* (with, for example, live-concert footage or synchronized dance) or *concept* (developing a theme or image from the lyrics).

For performers and recording companies, stations like MuchMusic are promotional alternatives to radio stations. Many recording companies submit videos to the stations for free in hope that their videos will be chosen to air. How can a music video stand out at a station's programming meeting *and*, if chosen, capture the viewers' attention? The stakes are high and the possible pitfalls numerous: individual videos have gained negative publicity for the portrayal of excessive sexism or violence. In addition, industry insiders have raised the concern that the importance of music videos has heightened the industry's preference for *visually* appealing music acts while placing less emphasis on the aural. Still, music videos continue to be produced despite their considerable cost (in 1999, $30,000 to $80,000 per video in Canada, and $60,000 to $300,000 in the United States) and the form continues to grow in popularity worldwide.

✓ CHECKLIST │ VIEWING A MUSIC VIDEO

- ✓ Examine the video's content and effect. Is it a performance or concept video? Does it illustrate a song, tell a story, give insight into the performers, present a movie soundtrack?
- ✓ Identify conventions used (e.g., live-concert footage, backstage footage, lip-synching, dance, computer special effects, black-and-white film) and their effects.
- ✓ Describe the image or look of the performer(s) that the video promotes.
- ✓ Identify the target audience and what appeals to this group.
- ✓ Examine the video for its implicit message and underlying values.
- ✓ Consider the context of your viewing (e.g., on music television, in a music store, on a purchased video) and your purpose.

Activities

Responding to Television Programming

1. Over a period of a month, watch several episodes of *three* television sitcoms. Analyze how these shows portray various characters. Is this depiction realistic? Identify any stereotyping you notice. Bring your observations to class to share in a discussion of character portrayal in situation comedy.

2. Watch a couple of episodes of a police, legal, or hospital show. Even though such shows are not strictly based on reality, how are producers achieving similar results to actual reality-based programs? What techniques do they employ to enhance reality? Make notes as you watch the episodes and share your reactions in a class discussion.

3. Interview your friends and family to find out how many of them watch reality television shows. Generate a list of questions to investigate *why* they find them compelling and perhaps more engrossing than scripted fictional dramas and sitcoms. Offer your findings in a brief oral presentation to the class.

4. Write a review of a music video using the checklist above to guide you. View each other's choice of videos and discuss the reviews in small groups. Finally, as a group, prepare a television show in which a video jockey presents all of the videos to the class.

5. Try making your own music video. You might sing one of your favourite songs, lip-synch to it, or produce a completely original song and video script. Decide whether it will be a performance or concept video, what conventions you will use, and how the video will combine art and commercial appeal. Using **storyboards**, present your plan to the class. (See Appendix A for tips on video creation.)

Television News Reporting

LEARNING FOCUS
- analyze the choices made in the production and design of television news
- compare print and non-print news reporting
- use critical thinking skills to identify bias in news reporting

News-related programs consume more time on television than in past decades when they were primarily restricted to two newscasts—the 6 p.m. supper slot and the 11 p.m. pre-bedtime slot. Some channels now provide a twenty-four-hour news service so that we can watch and follow developments in events anywhere in the world. News programs *appear* to be the most *real* or least constructed programs on television. They aim to be a reliable source of news by presenting an unbiased and balanced review of significant events. However, some news reports are less credible than others. For example, in the "reality" of tabloid journalism, news events are often sensationalized and facts about celebrities distorted. In this form of reporting, individuals are often paid for their stories, whereas traditional news programs do not pay for stories.

A typical news program is divided into segments that include global, national, and local stories, politics, and the economy, followed by sports and weather information. **Feature stories** may be added in instalments over a week's duration, causing viewers to return to the particular news program each day. Throughout the program, *teasers* are thrown in to encourage us to keep watching until the story that we've been teased about is eventually shown later in the broadcast. The final piece in most news broadcasts usually ends on a positive note. The inclusion and order of each part in the presentation reflects the priority news producers assign to each story or segment.

The newsreader, or anchor, functions somewhat like a story narrator, reading the news in a neutral, friendly, and reassuring manner. We come to trust these people and, by association, the view of the news they provide as they directly address us from the television screen. When they use emotion-laden or stereotyped language to tell us the stories, we sometimes overlook the impact of this. Viewers must separate facts from opinions when watching the news in order to determine the accuracy, quality, and relevance of what they are seeing and hearing through the newsreader.

News stories often include interviews gathered by reporters, and video images shot by camera operators who have been at or close to the scene of an event. Both these elements add authenticity to the news. However, entire interviews are rarely seen by the viewers, and the raw film footage is reduced to a manageable length, often a few seconds, for inclusion in the news program. If the editing of interviews and video is not done ethically, the result can be a biased or incomplete news clip that does not reflect the truth.

News is *selective*, so it is important to consider not only what's been included, but also what has been left out of the news. Criteria such as the following are used to help editors decide which stories to include and how much time to dedicate to each one:

- Importance—how much does the event matter to the target audience?

- Timeliness—when did the events happen? Viewers want up-to-the-minute reports.

- Proximity—did the events happen close to where viewers live? The closer to home, the more relevant an issue generally is. It is also less expensive and easier for producers to report on such events.

- Uniqueness—is there something unusual or novel about the event? Sudden, violent, or unexpected events are newsworthy.

- Prominence—are noteworthy people involved in the event? Although a significant event is the impetus for any news story, more time is often spent on what important people have to say about the event rather than the event itself. People can *make* the news: names and personalities sell news.

- Suspense—is the outcome still to be determined?

- Conflict—who is opposing whom: in sports, politics, unions, racial disputes, and so on?

- Emotion—does the event trigger an emotional response in viewers?

- Innovation—is the news reporting on scientific, medical, technological breakthroughs or other advances?

Activities

Analyzing Television News Stories

1. Choose a local or national news story from the newspaper. Watch one or more television news reports about the same story. In a written report, use the questions below to compare and contrast how the two media sources covered the story:
   - How much time or space was given to the story in each report?
   - What are the "who, what, where, when, why, and how" details from each report?
   - Were any sources quoted in the reports? If so, who were they?
   - How were the reports similar?
   - How were they different?
   - What do you think was missing from either report?
   - Which reporting on the story do you prefer? Why?

2. Videotape a single news story and analyze it in terms of objectivity. What is the topic of the story? How long is the segment? Determine whether or not it has received appropriate coverage in the time allotted it. Where has it been placed in the newscast? Why? Is bias evident through verbal or visual cues? Are any of the words *weighted* in tone or meaning? Does the material that has been selected for viewers appear to have been manipulated? How have framing and camera angles been used? What message is suggested by the way the visuals (camera shots, camera angles, and framing) have been filmed?

Present your news story to the class, accompanied by a critical talk.

Television Commercials

LEARNING FOCUS
- analyze how television commercials are constructed
- understand the relationships among form, purpose, and audience in the design of commercials
- plan and create a television commercial

Successful television commercials combine *visual effects* (colour, images, camera angles, camera movement, lighting, characters, and locations) with *audio effects* (music, voices, sounds, and silence) to play on our emotions, *not* our logic. Therefore, when we view television commercials, a high level of critical awareness is crucial.

Commercials are an efficient and effective way to reach a specific target audience. Advertising spots that fall during the peak viewing hours between 5:30 p.m. and 10:30 p.m. generally cost the most because of the large audience watching television during those hours. Marketers match their commercials with certain programs in order to gain access to their target audience. Children's programs, for example, are often accompanied by commercials for toys, cereal, and snack foods.

ANALYZING A TELEVISION COMMERCIAL Consider taping a commercial in order to analyze it: you can then replay it a number of times to get to its essence. As you view it, consider each element in terms of its mood and effect, and how it relates to the target audience.

- Watch the commercial *once through without stopping*, to determine the product or service being advertised, the target audience, the specific slogan, and the feeling evoked. What emotions or needs are being appealed to?

- Replay the commercial *without the sound*, this time focusing on the characters, the actions, and the setting. Who are the people (gender, age, race, etc.)? Is anyone stereotyped? What are the people doing? How and why are people and things placed in relationship to each other? Is a company **logo** included? If so, is it effective? What are the predominant colours used in the logo? In the commercial?

- Rewind and play the commercial for a third time, *again without sound.* Examine the types of camera shots (close-ups, medium shots, long shots) and angles (high, normal, low) that have been used. How many cuts (changes of shot) can you count? How many cuts per second? Is the pace of the action related to the cuts?

- Now play the commercial *without looking at the images* and concentrate on the sound and music. Describe what you hear. Is the pace slow or fast? Does it change? Are transitions achieved using sounds or music? Which, if any, words are included?

- View the commercial again *with both sound and visuals,* focusing on any special effects used. How have they been used to communicate the message?

- During which television program has this commercial been run? Why?

Activities

Analyzing and Creating Commercials
"FUNERAL"

VIDEO: Open on the Meal Maker Express, seen from behind, with lid up. Chicken #1 stands in front, looking at the grill. He walks off.

SFX: Funeral music.

SFX: Sniff, sniff.

VIDEO: Chicken #2 enters, looks at the grill and shakes head.

CHICKEN #2: He went so quickly.

VIDEO: Reverse angle of grill. We see a beautifully cooked chicken with veggies arranged around it.

ANNOUNCER: From freezer to table in minutes. The Meal Maker Express, from Hamilton Beach.

LOGO: Hamilton Beach.

SUPER: Smarter than the average appliance.

1. Analyze the award-winning commercial above by addressing the following points:
   - What is the name of the product?
   - Who is the target audience?
   - How does the advertiser get the viewer's attention?
   - How does the advertiser create viewer interest in the product?
   - What motivates the viewer to buy the product?
   - How might a vegetarian react to this commercial?

2. Over the course of a week, view various television commercials. Select one that strikes you as particularly effective and analyze it. Consider the name of the product, the target audience, the style of language, the methods used for maintaining viewer interest, and the sound and visual effects. Share your thoughts in a critical talk to the class.

3. In small groups, decide on a product you are going to sell. Determine your target audience and plan a commercial to entice viewers to purchase your product. Include your product's name, a description, and a slogan and logo for it. Create a script for your commercial and storyboard your visuals and sound effects. Indicate what television show it would accompany and why it is the right choice for your target audience. Try filming your commercial and show it to the class. (See Appendix A: Producing Videos for suggestions on preparing a storyboard and shooting script.)

Introduction to Film

Films both reflect and shape our lives. They reveal our hopes and dreams, our relationships with others, even the things that scare us. They can influence the way we act, speak, and dress. Although we often watch a film purely for pleasure and escapism, a good film can also make us think seriously about important personal and social issues.

Movies are also a remarkable expression of human creativity. They combine words, pictures, and music so seamlessly that we often forget the highly specialized techniques (writing, editing, directing, acting, and photography) behind what's on the screen.

When we enter a video store, we see hundreds of movies, sorted by film genre. The more common film genres include the following:

ACTION/ADVENTURE Whether it's Humphrey Bogart and Katharine Hepburn in *The African Queen* (1951) or Harrison Ford in *Raiders of the Lost Ark* (1981), the ingredients are the same: heroes and heroines, good versus evil, daring escapes, close disasters, and sometimes, exotic locales.

COMEDY Comedies are among the oldest and most popular movie genres. Early comedy actors include Charlie Chaplin and Laurel and Hardy, and the comic tradition continues in such contemporary hits as *Mrs. Doubtfire* (1993) and *The Nutty Professor* (1996). It is a genre in which Canadians, such as Mike Myers and Jim Carey, have been particularly successful.

ROMANCE Judging from the continued popularity of this movie genre, love, at least at the movies, is alive and flourishing. Movie romance may not always run smooth—in fact, the writers and directors of this kind of movie seem to delight in inventing obstacles for couples to endure, and, usually, overcome. The happy ending is seldom in doubt (*Sleepless in Seattle*, 1993) but may be short-lived (*Love Story*, 1970).

DRAMA Films that explore the lives of other people—their conflicts, their relationships, their failures and successes—are part of the genre of drama. These films may examine the experiences of ordinary people in extraordinary circumstances, such as in *The English Patient* (1998), the Academy Award-winning film based on the acclaimed novel by Canadian writer Michael Ondaatje. They may depict personal triumph over tragedy as in *The Color Purple* (1985). They may sometimes have a historical setting such as the American Civil War period, which provided the backdrop for *Gone With the Wind* (1939).

FAMILY FILMS Because these films are aimed at families, they avoid serious violence, adult situations, and strong language. They explore relationships and conflicts but usually end happily. They may include live action such as *Honey, I Shrunk the Kids* (1989) and *Home Alone* (1990), or animation such as Disney's *Snow White* (1937) and *The Lion King* (1994).

HORROR Many of us love to scare ourselves. Horror films such as *Dracula* and *Frankenstein* (both made in 1931) were among the earliest movie successes. *Psycho* (1960) remains a classic of film horror. One the most remarkable recent successes in this genre was *The Blair Witch Project* (1999), a low-budget movie about some students who encounter unknown terrors in the making of a documentary film.

MUSICALS Though this genre may explore concerns and conflicts, its main goal is to provide musical entertainment. Often the success of a musical is tied directly to the original cast recordings that are sold at the time of its release. From *The Jazz Singer* (1927), *The Wizard of Oz* (1939), and *Singin' In the Rain* (1952) to *The Sound of Music* (1965), *Saturday Night Fever* (1977), and *Evita* (1996), musicals have enhanced the careers of their stars and contributed to the music of their generation.

SCIENCE FICTION This genre features time travel, future worlds, fantasy, scientific inventions, aliens, robots, and artificial intelligence. It has become closely associated with Steven Spielberg and George Lucas, two of the most innovative and successful directors working in the industry. Recent movies in this genre range from the heart-warming exploration of what it means to be human in *Bicentennial Man* (1999), to the speculation about the nature of reality in *The Matrix* (1999).

WESTERNS Classic westerns feature "good guys" and "bad guys," frontier towns and landscapes, gunfights and saloon brawls. From *Stage Coach* (1939) and *High Noon* (1952) to *A Fistful of Dollars* (1964), *Dances With Wolves* (1990), and the science-fiction-slanted *Wild Wild West* (1999), they have defined an image of themselves that North Americans have chosen to present to the rest of the world.

As well as being an influential form of entertainment, movie making is a huge industry that involves millions of dollars and employs thousands of people. In 1999, *Star Wars: Episode 1—The Phantom Menace* grossed an incredible $425 million (U.S.) at the box office. In the same year, *The Blair Witch Project,* made for the paltry sum of $40,000, grossed over $138 million (U.S.). Behind the glamorous actors, directors, and producers there are, for example, cinematographers, camera operators, and costume designers. Beyond the people employed directly on the film set, there are those involved in promotion, advertising, and distribution. As you learn more about the movie industry, you may begin to identify a career for yourself.

Activities

Learning About the Movie Industry

1. Visit a local movie entertainment complex. Describe the various elements that have been brought together in one location (e.g., the number and kinds of screens, the type of sound systems, other forms of entertainment such as video games, restaurants, and food sales). Interview the manager to discuss these elements, and also to find out about the kinds of advertising used to promote the movie theatre complex. Discover the age and characteristics of the people who patronize it, and any potential plans for development and marketing in the future. Present your findings in an oral report.

2. Prepare a video collage of film clips from different genres. (Download clips off the Internet, and use computer video-editing equipment or two VCRs for tape-to-tape dubbing.) Use your collage to research the effect of films on viewers. Ask the participants in your study to jot down their thoughts as you show them excerpts from different genres. Analyze your results according to age group and gender. Consider the differences and similarities in the responses and try to account for these. Present your findings in a multimedia presentation to the class. (See Appendix A for video production tips.)

3. Explore the relationships between filmmaking and the film industry. Pick a favourite film and research its making. Consider such elements as the studio that developed it, other financial interests of the studio and how these relate to the film, previous projects of its director and producer, the marketing and distribution of the film, the target audience and the elements of the film that appeal to that particular market, the kinds of advertising that were used to promote it, and reasons for the success (or failure) of the film. Prepare a written report based on your findings.

Reviewing Movies

LEARNING FOCUS
- respond personally and critically to a movie
- understand the form, style, and content of a movie review
- write and assess a movie review

Whether it's "two thumbs up," "three stars," "or "buy some popcorn and wait for the video," a movie review is essentially an evaluation and a recommendation. Did you like it? Did you not? What appealed to you? What didn't you like? Would you suggest that others see it? Why or why not?

An effective movie review, however, goes beyond simple likes and dislikes. It introduces the story and its characters and deals with the elements of filmmaking in a thoughtful, entertaining, and sometimes provocative manner. (Professional examples may be found in magazines, on radio, or via the Internet.) A movie review typically provides the following information:

- the film's title, director, and genre to which the film belongs
- the major issue, theme, or message of the film
- a summary of the plot, without giving too much away
- an introduction to the main characters and an evaluation of the actors who portray them
- the impact of the film on the audience
- the effectiveness of the musical score or soundtrack
- the quality of the script
- the use of special visual or sound effects
- the cinematography (e.g., camera work, lighting)
- background information about the making of the film
- comparisons with other films by the same director or its major stars

Canadian movie critic Brian Johnson wrote the following review of the Academy Award-winning film *Shakespeare in Love* (1998) as part of a year-end article in *Maclean's* on the best films of the year.

MODEL: MOVIE REVIEW

The reviewer concisely introduces the film, its premise, its setting, the main characters, and the actors that portray them. He also manages to provide some historical and literary background.

Shakespeare in Love is another romantic masquerade, but one set in the days when love letters flowed from a quill instead of a keyboard. It is the summer of 1593 in Elizabethan London. A young, hot-blooded William Shakespeare (Joseph Fiennes) is paralyzed by writer's block as he tries to meet a deadline for a new play, a romantic comedy titled *Romeo and Ethel, The Pirate's Daughter*. The man needs a muse. And he finds one in Lady Viola (Gwyneth Paltrow), a comely aristocrat who has a desperate ambition to be an actor in a society that prohibits women from appearing onstage. Disguising herself as a man, she wins the part of Romeo, then tumbles into an illicit affair with Will, who draws on their passion to turn his comedy into the tragedy, *Romeo and Juliet*. Viola is also the Dark Lady who inspires his sonnets and the Viola of *Twelfth Night*.

This paragraph deals mainly with the author and his script. Note the phrase "riff of iambic pentameter," which combines contemporary and traditional terms in a fresh way.

Co-written by playwright Tom Stoppard—who turned *Hamlet* inside-out with *Rozencrantz and Guildenstern Are Dead*—the script is truly ingenious. Jiving with wit, wordplay and the odd riff of iambic pentameter, the dialogue trips off the tongue like ersatz Shakespeare. The movie, which skips between buoyant farce and flat-out romance, has terrific fun at the Bard's expense, without making a mockery of him. It portrays Shakespeare as a journeyman actor who writes by the seat of his pants. He borrows plot ideas from his rival, dramatist Christopher Marlowe (Rupert Everett). And on the set his producers treat him with a dismissive scorn worthy of Hollywood—"he's just the writer."

Johnson reviews the acting by referring to the ways in which the actors present their characters, their presence on the screen, and their previous work. Note his effective choice of words and images to convey the quality of Judi Dench's portrayal of Queen Elizabeth.

The review concludes with his overall assessment of the film, and a punchy closing.

The notion that being madly in love makes writing a snap requires a major leap of poetic licence (ask any writer). But Paltrow and Fiennes (Ralph's kid brother) make a hot couple.... The top-notch cast also includes Geoffrey Rush as a brow-beaten theatre manager, Ben Affleck as a star actor, Colin Firth as Viola's venal fiancé—and Judi Dench, who blows everyone off the screen as a shrewd, crisply sardonic Queen Elizabeth. The film's director, John Madden, first cast Dench as Queen Victoria in last year's *Mrs. Brown*, and she holds court with terrifying authority and Solomonic wisdom. Her brisk performance is the royal icing on a sublimely clever confection that manages to be substantial and frothy all at once. Virtual Shakespeare.

Here are some stylistic points to consider when assessing professional reviews or when writing a review of your own:

 CHECKLIST WRITING A MOVIE REVIEW

✓ Hook the reader at the start by describing a particularly interesting or provocative aspect of the film.

✓ Keep the tone and style lively and witty.

✓ Be balanced in your appraisal of the film, considering both strengths and weaknesses.

✓ Use effective diction and images to make your comments vivid.

✓ Include some quotes and examples from the film to back up your observations.

✓ Provide convincing reasons for your assessment.

✓ End with a summary evaluation statement and recommendation.

Activities

Reviewing Movies

1. Search for recent film reviews in newspapers or magazines or by visiting Web sites on the Internet. (See the Pearson Canada Web site: <www.pearsoned.ca/referencepoints/links>.) Bring the reviews to class for discussion or to use as review models. Be prepared to discuss the strengths and weaknesses of the reviews you find.

2. Write a one-page movie review that could be used in your school or community paper. You may wish to view a new film in a theatre setting, so you should take notes as you are watching, for later reference. As an alternative, rent a copy of your movie selection so that you can rewind the tape to examine particular elements more closely.

   • Organize your notes under such headings as acting, directing, the script, the musical score, editing, special effects, and camera work.
   • Write a rough draft in paragraphs according to the various elements you have chosen to consider.
   • Exchange your review with a partner and ask for style and content revision suggestions.
   • Rewrite your review using the suggestions provided.
   • Publish a class movie review journal.

Documentary Films

LEARNING FOCUS
- respond personally and critically to a documentary film
- analyze documentary film techniques
- explore the relationship between the making of a documentary film and its audience

Documentaries give us windows on worlds we may never see in our daily lives. Like the best investigative journalism, many documentaries reveal ideas and situations that raise difficult questions or draw attention to issues not routinely covered in the daily news, standard television programming, or commercial movies.

Canada has an international reputation for producing some of the most insightful and groundbreaking documentaries in the world. A good place to begin exploring the world of Canadian documentaries is the National Film Board. (Check the Pearson Canada Web site: <www.pearsoned.ca/referencepoints/links> for their Web address.)

Before viewing a documentary, ask yourself what, if anything, you already know about the topic of the film. What are your attitudes toward the topic? Interest? Fear? Indignation? Hope? What might you expect to learn from a documentary on the topic?

While viewing a documentary, pay close attention to the points of view expressed. Does the director focus on one person, family, or side of an issue? If multiple perspectives are offered, do any dominate? How might the sequencing of scenes affect how you view each segment of the film?

After viewing a documentary, jot down your initial impressions. Did it make you aware of anything you didn't know already? Did it offer an alternative perspective on any of your attitudes? Could you detect any **bias** on the part of the filmmaker? Does the film conflict with or contradict anything you already thought about the topic? Are you inclined to think differently about the topic, or did the film reinforce your previous views?

DOCUMENTARY FILMMAKING TECHNIQUES

Omniscient voice-over	A narrator with no evident connection to the topic of the film is used. The use of **voice-over** tends to provide an objective tone.
Interviewee narration	Commentary is made on the film's subject(s). This allows the filmmaker to explore scenes without having the interviewees on camera all the time.
Interview	These can range from formal, scripted sit-down studio interviews with experts, to **walkabouts** with the participants, or snippets of their casual conversations.
Dramatic re-enactment	Filmmakers may interweave fictional recreations of events with a factual account, either to tell part of a story or to emphasize a point of view.

DOCUMENTARY FILM MAKING TECHNIQUES (CONTINUED)

Concealed camera footage	Documentary makers may act like surveillance cameras, trying to catch people in unguarded moments. It may be necessary to obtain the people's permission to use the footage afterwards.
Close-up	**Close-ups**, particularly of faces, can give viewers a chance to study a face carefully, interpreting nuances of expression and specific reactions.
Extreme close-up	Here a particular area or physical feature is highlighted; this is a staple technique in nature documentaries.
Panoramic scan of location	These wide scans provide the viewer with a context for the film topic. A balance must be struck between the depiction of the location and the investigation of the subject matter.
Background music and sound	Many filmmakers use music for transitions between scenes, as well as for opening and closing sequences. In addition, the amount of **ambient sound**, or "natural" background noises, is often manipulated during the production process to enhance the dramatic effect of specific scenes.

Remember, that although many documentaries rely on the spontaneous remarks of those they interview, filmmakers play a large role in selecting and arranging these remarks and effectively placing them in context. Although documentaries appear to be a reflection of fact, they are the product of a person with a certain perspective and, perhaps, a specific *agenda*. The art of skilled documentary makers lies in their ability to summarize issues without trivializing or distorting them.

Activities

Communicating Through Documentary Movies

1. View two documentaries on the same topic to see how perspective gives a different *version* of the truth (e.g., hunting advocates versus non-advocates). Identify the perspective of each and examine how this influences the film's construction of reality. Summarize your findings in a written report.

2. Think of a topic for your own documentary film. How might you go about collecting information? Try filming a segment or a sequence of shots that explores the topic.

Communicating in the World of Work

Preparing for the World of Work

Chapter 1 provided information and activities to improve literacy, helping you learn to read, write, listen, and use technology with greater precision. This chapter focuses on the importance of a *workplace literacy*—those skills and attitudes required to *learn a living* and earn a living in the workplace of the twenty-first century. Actually, all the skills emphasized throughout this text (e.g., note taking, précis writing, paraphrasing, discussion, debating, research) have direct relevance to the workplace. The leadership role and the skills needed to conduct a meeting of a school club or meet the budget guidelines for a school yearbook, for example, are no different from those you will require on the job.

Understanding Yourself

LEARNING FOCUS
- complete a personal inventory
- assess your workplace skills
- reflect on your personal learning style

Before you look for a job, you need to be clear about your own aspirations and skills. A good way to do this is to create a **personal inventory** of your interests, aptitudes, skills, abilities, values, goals, and personality traits. When you put in writing what you like and what you *are* like, you may even surprise yourself with what you discover.

Once you have begun your self-assessment, ask yourself what careers might interest you. Begin by reflecting on the kind of activities you find most rewarding. Then explore what you value, asking yourself: Is it important to me to make a lot of money? Do I like variety? Risk? Creativity? Teamwork?

Remember that it is quite common to be indecisive about what career you want. As you begin to actively research options, realize that as long as the choices you make fit your true preferences, abilities, and opportunities, they will lead to the best outcome. What matters is that you take the first steps.

There are no limits on sources of ideas about careers: guidance counsellors, friends and family; job ads in newspapers and on the Internet; university and college calendars. Finally, never underestimate the value of your own imagination—in today's economy, more and more young people are creating jobs for themselves, deciding to be their own boss.

Activities

Taking Stock of Yourself and Your Experiences

1. One way of learning more about yourself is to reflect on things you have done that you enjoyed and felt good about. Think of *three* experiences you have had, at any age, where you felt satisfied with what you achieved. Write a brief description of each one, including: the purpose of the activity, who was involved, what took place, what you achieved, and how you felt. Then ask yourself these questions:
   - What do these experiences tell me about my major areas of interest?
   - What skills or abilities did I use in each one that enabled me to succeed?
   - Were these skills dealing primarily with things, with information, or with people?
   - What do these experiences say about what is important to me?

   Next, exchange your written descriptions within a group. Tell your classmates what interests, skills, and values you can see in their experiences. Find out what they see in yours.

2. Now create a personal inventory of your interests, skills, and values. On a sheet of paper write down your answers to the questions below:
   - What are my major interests?
   - What are my major skills and abilities?
   - What motivates me to learn?
   - Do I like to work with my hands?
   - Do I enjoy helping others?
   - Do I enjoy settling conflicts between team members?
   - Do I like organizing activities?
   - Am I a naturally curious person?
   - Am I a creative person?
   - Do I enjoy leading?

- Am I methodical and detail-oriented?
- Do I have good reading, writing, speaking, and listening skills?
- Do I like working with numbers and statistics?
- How strong are my computer skills?
- What is really important to me?

Now exchange your sheet with a classmate's. Role-play a career counselor, and make suggestions about careers that fit your partner's skills, aptitudes, and interests. Your classmate can then do the same for you.

3. School activities often reinforce workplace skills. Using a format similar to the one below, assess the relationship between school and the workplace. A set of index cards or a template made on the computer can help you with this activity.

Name of School Activity _____

Group ☐   Individual ☐
In-Class ☐   Co-curricular ☐

Reflect on the workplace skills that were evident in this activity.

_____

_____

Building a Career Portfolio

LEARNING FOCUS
- prepare a career portfolio
- compile and assess your work-related experiences
- reflect on your educational and career-related goals

A **portfolio** is a collection of representative work samples, *best pieces*, which has been compiled during a specific time period. You may be familiar with its use in writing, art, and photography. The portfolio represents a set of decisions made about what to collect, what to select, and what this reflects about the individual and the work. A **writing portfolio**, for example, might contain the best piece of writing in process, often a creative piece.

A **career portfolio** is a collection of career-related material that you gather to represent your skills and accomplishments. Although it displays your abilities and interests in a broad sweep, it also has a central focus, with each item contributing to build a portrait of the individual.

A career portfolio can include

- a statement of career goals, both personal and educational. (Include occupations of particular interest to you.)

- a course selection sheet, showing both courses you already have and those (high school and post-secondary) you will need to qualify for a particular field.

- the latest transcript of your school marks.

- a current resumé (see pages 286 to 290).

- documentation of co-operative education, school-to-work placements, job shadowing, and volunteer work experiences.

- a list of part-time jobs (include your specific assignment and responsibilities).

- letters of reference or appreciation (from teachers, employers, etc.).

- lists of awards or badges (athletic, public speaking, writing, science-related, etc.).

- copies of certificates or diplomas (first aid, technology courses, etc.).

- a brief description of co-curricular activities and hobbies.

- a collection of projects or exemplary assignments completed.

- photographs (especially those related to work and achievement).

- a list of books you are currently reading (showing your varied reading interests).

Your career portfolio will need constant revising and upgrading. Share it with peers and family for constructive feedback. It can be organized in an attractive folder, and should include your name, phone number, and a title page with an appropriate graphic. A career portfolio provides you with information you can draw on when applying for a job or for admission to a post-secondary program. Look on it with pride: it enables you to showcase your accomplishments.

Activities

Preparing for a Career

1. Begin designing a folder for your career portfolio, and select information to include. Start with your statement of career goals, your course selection sheet, and a list of your accomplishments to date. Over the high school year as your ideas percolate and your experience and education broaden, revise the content and organization of your portfolio.

2. Create a list of jobs in a range of areas (sales, education, health care, media, technology, banking, etc.). Prepare a short oral or written report on a career that interests you.

Understanding the Workplace

As you enter the workforce, the one constant will be change—in attitudes, technologies, work expectations, and, according to the Conference Board of Canada, in full-time jobs—as many as *five* times over the course of a career. In view of these rapid changes, it is crucial to understand workplace trends so you can conduct an effective job search. Read the selections below on current practices in the global workplace.

LEARNING FOCUS

- analyze and interpret information about changes in the workplace
- investigate work-related topics for oral and written communication
- communicate in small groups to research and write about the workplace

READING SELECTION: MAGAZINE ARTICLE

Recruiting on the Web
In a highly competitive labour market, employers are turning to the Net to find new people

by Ross Laver

Two decades ago—far back in the mists of time in high-tech terms—Gerry Stanton was vice-president for human resources at Mitel Corp., a telecommunications equipment maker. Those were heady days at the Ottawa company: revenues were soaring and the firm had a reputation as a technology superstar, so there was no shortage of people clamouring to work for it. "On an average day," Stanton recalls, "we'd get 150 resumés." The problem, of course, was that no one had time to read them all, let alone examine them carefully to identify promising applicants. Says Stanton: "I used to joke that I was VP in charge of buying filing cabinets. Every time we placed career ads in the newspaper, we knew that 70 per cent of our needs were already sitting there in those cabinets—yet there was no efficient way to screen them."

Thanks to the Internet, that has changed. As has Stanton: after a stint as an independent corporate headhunter, he now runs an Ottawa-based firm called E-Cruiter.com Inc., which develops software for companies in Canada and elsewhere that want to use the Internet to recruit new employees. It's a fiercely competitive field, but the market is growing so rapidly that, for now at least, Stanton probably needn't worry about his own career prospects. "The forecasts for this industry differ," he says, "but one thing everyone agrees on is that on-line recruiting is destined to become a multibillion-dollar business...."

There's a simple reason for this development, and it's one that corporate bean-counters readily understand: done properly, on-line recruiting is far less expensive than the traditional method of finding new employees. The savings start with the cost of advertising. A typical career ad in a daily newspaper can cost thousands of dollars a day, while an on-line posting generally costs a few hundred dollars at most and runs for several weeks. To drive down the bill even further, many large companies opt to become sponsors or partners of job boards, which gives them the right to post an unlimited number of on-line career ads for a fixed yearly or quarterly fee....

The savings are even greater for companies that choose to automate part of the hiring process by eliminating or reducing their use of printed resumés. Increasingly, job applicants are being encouraged to fill out "electronic" resumés that are collected in on-line databases, either on an employer's own Web site or on a site operated by one of the big job boards. Using customized search terms and sophisticated filtering software, employers can then screen tens of thousands of applications in a single go, instantly narrowing the field to a shortlist of potential candidates....

And what about those career ads in the newspapers? The consensus seems to be that they will continue to be a fat source of profits for dailies such as the *Globe*, but that increasingly they will be used not to publicize specific openings but to promote the company as a place to work—a necessary function in an era of low unemployment and growing competition for talent. Thanks to the buoyant economy, Stanton says, "for the first time in history individuals have acquired more control over the hiring process than companies. It's almost as though skilled people are in a position to hire the companies, and not the reverse." Nice work if you can get it.

Forming a business is part of a planned decision-making process:

i. Identify the business goal or define the problem.

ii. Gather information about the goal or problem.

iii. Identify possible solutions or alternatives.

iv. Identify the consequences of each alternative and make a decision.

v. Take action.

vi. Evaluate the results of the decision(s).

As you read this second selection, look up the meaning of any unfamiliar words. Note how these words enhance the impact of the article.

Mighty is the Mixture
by G. Pascal Zachary

People can argue about what makes a 50-mile stretch of Northern California so successful. But certainly no one can argue that Silicon Valley is a monoculture...the mixing of people is central to its success. "If you subtracted that," says Anna Eschoo, a member of Congress who represents the area, "the Valley would collapse." Indeed, at least one-third of the Valley's scientists and engineers are immigrants. They come from Europe, Latin America, and the Middle East, and, in particular, Asia. Since 1980, Chinese and Indian immigrants alone have founded 2,700 companies, which in turn employ 58,000 people.

Silicon Valley is not an aberration. Throughout the United States, hybridity pays off in higher-quality ideas, in greater flexibility, and in closer ties to places and people around the world. The United States offers the best example of what happens economically when an entire business class exploits hybridity. The new economic paradigm turns hybrids into a signal economic weapon. And, because the United States has more hybrids than anywhere else, it gets a bigger bang from hybridity than any other country.

But the idea is spreading. Edgar van Ommen, managing editor of Sony's unit in Berlin, believes in the "principle of United Nations." His prime directive is to recruit the best people for his team, regardless of their nationality. Sure, that makes life tougher for managers. But what's the alternative? For the most idea-driven enterprises, a focus on one nationality is too limiting. Ommen grew up in Austria, married a German, holds a Dutch passport, and keeps a second home in Bangkok. Two-thirds of the 60 people on his team come from outside Germany; they represent more than a dozen nationalities. "The engineering of a concept is a lot easier because each person shows a different emotion as to what's being presented," Ommen says. "Maybe the Turkish lady likes it, but the Sri Lankan doesn't." To think great thoughts, he says, employees must contribute their "whole being," not just their mind. Heated argument may spur fresh ideas. Passion matters.

At Work, Less Is More...

by Charles Fishman

On the surface, Norway seems to be a moderate place. The climate can be intemperate, but the people and the lifestyle are just the opposite—the picture of restraint and judiciousness. Oh, there are some unassuming little oddities: Norwegians eat fish for breakfast, and often for lunch and dinner. Very few people are overweight. Unusual, but hardly alien.

The workplace, too, seems familiar: computers, cubicles, bullet-point slides. Familiar, that is, until you look more closely.

Every weekday at 6:10 a.m., Morte Lingelem boards a train at Sandefjord for the 90-minute ride to his job in Oslo. Mr. Lingelem, 42, a process-technology manager, has a standing reservation in the train's "office car," where he can power up his laptop and work in quiet comfort. That office car serves a purpose that's exactly the opposite of what it would be in North America: it enables Mr. Lingelem to hold down a demanding engineering-management job, to spend more than three hours a day commuting, and still be home by 6 p.m.

Atle Taerum lives on a farm 90 minutes west of Oslo. And two days a week that's where he is, taking care of his 10-month-old daughter. On those days customers—perhaps calling from Africa or the Middle East—often reach him while he's plowing his fields, or chaperoning his son's kindergarten class.

Norway is, in fact, a sort of alternative universe of work. The workplace setting and language and the profit imperative all seem familiar. But Norwegians have a singular view of what work can become.

The vision is rooted in the notion that balance is healthy. The argument: work can be redesigned to promote balance. More than that, balance can become a source of corporate and national competitive advantage. Working less can, in fact, mean working better....

Balance shapes life for Norwegians, who long ago discovered sane responses to the tension between work and family. Norway is a place, after all, where people typically leave work between 4 p.m. and 4:30 p.m. Working women get at least 38 weeks of paid maternity leave; men get as many as four weeks of paid leave.

In a series of experiments, Norsk Hydro, the company for which Mr. Lingelem and Mr. Taerum work, is testing an ambitious vision of balance in the workplace. In these tests, the company has given hundreds of employees varying combinations of flexible hours, home offices, new technology, and redesigned office space.

What has Hydro learned?

The company believes it can help employees find a better balance by redesigning physical work spaces—and by redesigning work itself, it can free people from old restrictions on where and when they work. That flexibility makes workers more productive and jobs more appealing, and more appealing jobs attract more talented people.

New business laying mosaic chips on the table
Two young people use their skills to start their own business

by Pat Doyle
The Telegram

When a magazine picture of a mosaic table caught the eye of Natasha Squires a few months ago, it changed her life.

Squires, 17, who had been "messing around with mosaic" for some time, converted her inspiration into a new business venture: Mosaics and Modern Furnishings.

She runs the business in Portugal Cove–St. Philip's with her friend Jason Mercer, 22, a woodworker and furniture maker.

Mosaics is the art of making pictures or designs by inlaying small bits of coloured material, such as stone, crockery, or glass, in an object like a table or other piece of furniture.

Mercer builds furniture and accessory pieces while Squires adds the finishing touches by creating an artistic, mosaic design unique to every piece. All kinds of broken crockery, glass, ceramic, and marble are worked into the one-of-a-kind images.

Hooked at first sight

Squires said when she saw the picture in the magazine, she was hooked.

"I just loved it and thought I'd like to do that," she said.

She then thought of Mercer, who had previously made furniture for her, and the plan was hatched.

"I suggested to him we work together on it and that's how it all got started."

Before launching the business, the partners approached the YMCA–YWCA Enterprise Centre for advice and assistance through its Youth Ventures Program.

Michelle Barney, a Youth Ventures co-ordinator for the Northeast Avalon area, thought it was an excellent idea but wasn't sure how they could make it work.

She invited them to the enterprise centre to work on their business plan.

Enthusiastic and talented

Squires and Mercer were enthusiastic, talented, and committed, Barney said, and had done considerable work on their business plan.

"This is a new product to Newfoundland and I think they are going to do excellent with it," said Barney, who also helped secure a loan for the new business.

The company will start out making end tables, night tables, odd-size tables, and hope chests, Squires said.

She noted she is fixing up a shed in her yard for a workshop, while Mercer works from his own workshop.

"Jason will make the furniture in Portugal Cove and bring it to me in St. Philip's where I will do the mosaics," she said.

Confident but anxious

Squires is confident and excited about the new venture, but also anxious.

"I'm quite nervous, I don't know how people will react," she said. "But I think it's

281

going to be all right. Everybody I talk to about it likes it."

In fact, she's already received 10 orders from friends and acquaintances.

Customers can select from a variety of designs on display or bring in their own design, she said.

"It will generally take three to four days from the time of ordering for a piece to be ready."

The company will have a phone line, e-mail address, and hopefully a Web site, Squires said.

Now look closely at the list of skills outlined on page 283 in the Conference Board of Canada's Employability Skills 2000+ chart. According to the board, these skills are critically important for workplace success.

EMPLOYABILITY SKILLS 2000+

The skills you need to enter, stay in, and progress in the world of work—whether you work on your own or as a part of a team.

These skills can also be applied and used beyond the workplace in a range of daily activities.

FUNDAMENTAL SKILLS

The skills needed as a base for further development

You will be better prepared to progress in the world of work when you can:

Communicate

- read and understand information presented in a variety of forms (e.g., words, graphs, charts, diagrams)
- write and speak so others pay attention and understand
- listen and ask questions to understand and appreciate the points of view of others
- share information using a range of information and communications technologies (e.g., voice, e-mail, computers)
- use relevant scientific, technological, and mathematical knowledge and skills to explain or clarify ideas

Manage Information

- locate, gather, and organize information using appropriate technology and information systems
- access, analyze, and apply knowledge and skills from various disciplines (e.g., the

PERSONAL MANAGEMENT SKILLS

The personal skills, attitudes, and behaviours that drive one's potential for growth

You will be able to offer yourself greater possibilities for achievement when you can:

Demonstrate Positive Attitudes and Behaviours

- feel good about yourself, and be confident
- deal with people, problems, and situations with honesty, integrity, and personal ethics
- recognize your own and other people's good efforts
- take care of your personal health
- show interest, initiative, and effort

Be Responsible

- set goals and priorities, balancing work and personal life
- plan and manage time, money, and other resources to achieve goals
- assess, weigh, and manage risk
- be accountable for your actions and the actions of your group
- be socially responsible, and contribute to your community

TEAMWORK SKILLS

The skills and attributes needed to contribute productively

You will be better prepared to add value to the outcome of a task, project, or team when you can:

Work with Others

- understand and work within the dynamics of a group
- ensure that a team's purpose and objectives are clear
- be flexible: respect, be open to and supportive of the thoughts, opinions, and contributions of others in a group
- recognize and respect individual differences and perspectives
- accept and provide feedback in a constructive and considerate manner
- contribute to a team by sharing information and expertise
- lead or support when appropriate, motivating a group for high performance
- understand the role of conflict in a group to reach solutions
- manage and resolve conflict when appropriate

EMPLOYABILITY SKILLS 2000+ (CONTINUED)

FUNDAMENTAL SKILLS

Manage Information (cont.)

arts, languages, science, technology, mathematics, social sciences, and the humanities)

Use Numbers

- decide what needs to be measured or calculated
- observe and record data using appropriate methods, tools, and technology
- make estimates and verify calculations

Think and Solve Problems

- assess situations and identify problems
- seek different points of view and evaluate them based on facts
- recognize the human, interpersonal, technical, scientific, and mathematical dimensions of a problem
- identify the root cause of a problem
- be creative and innovative in exploring possible solutions
- readily use science, technology, and mathematics as ways to think, gain, and share knowledge, solve problems and make decisions
- evaluate solutions to make recommendations or decisions
- implement solutions
- check to see if a solution works, and act on opportunities for improvement

PERSONAL MANAGEMENT SKILLS

Be Adaptable

- work independently or as part of a team
- carry out multiple tasks or projects
- be innovative and resourceful: identify and suggest alternative ways to achieve goals and get the job done
- be open, and respond constructively to change
- learn from your mistakes and accept feedback
- cope with uncertainty

Learn Continuously

- be willing to continuously learn and grow
- assess personal strengths and areas for development
- set your own learning goals
- identify and access learning sources and opportunities
- plan for and achieve your learning goals

Work Safely

- be aware of personal and group health and safety practices and procedures, and act in accordance with these

TEAMWORK SKILLS

Participate in Projects and Tasks

- plan, design, or carry out a project or task from start to finish with well-defined objectives and outcomes
- develop a plan, seek feedback, test, revise, and implement
- work to agreed quality standards and specifications
- select and use appropriate tools and technology for a task or project
- adapt to changing requirements and information
- continuously monitor the success of a project or task and identify ways to improve

Activities

Understanding the Workplace

1. Reread the articles on pages 277 through 282. In your own words, précis the information in each one. What employment trend is featured in each article? Discuss your thoughts and written summary with a partner.

2. In small groups, discuss your lifestyle expectations in terms of: career goals, earning power, division of household duties, and child care responsibilities. Share your group's ideas in a class discussion.

3. Think of a business venture that you would like to start on your own or with a group of friends to generate summer employment. Write a ten- to fifteen-minute script, and deliver a multimedia sales presentation (individually or as a group) to convince a Youth Ventures Program in your area to provide professional or financial backing, to get your enterprise started.

   Include the following information in your presentation:
   - an introduction to your goods, services, or ideas
   - positive aspects of the idea
   - areas you see as potential hurdles, where outside expertise is needed (e.g., in writing and organizing a business plan)
   - solutions to these hurdles
   - a persuasive summary

4. Use a **jigsaw** process to discuss the Employability Skills chart. Place three students in each home group. Each member of a home group will be responsible for investigating one of the subtopics (Fundamental Skills, Personal Management Skills, Teamwork Skills).

   The members of each home group will then join other class members to form three expert groups to focus on their specific subtopic. Each expert group will
   - read information on this topic.
   - decide on the most important points through discussion.
   - decide on an interesting way to present information in the home groups.

   Members of the expert groups will then return to their respective home groups. They will present their subtopics, allowing time for questions and comments.

5. Invite someone to class who, in your view, has a successful and interesting career. Conduct an interview focusing on the fundamental, personal management, and teamwork skills required in his or her particular field. Determine from the interview what educational requirements you would need to pursue such an occupation.

Communicating for Employment

In the world of work, the ancient maxim "know thyself" has an additional requirement: "and make sure others know all about you too." Since most of us are surrounded by friends and family who are familiar with our habits, attitudes, values, and abilities, we may find it intimidating and artificial to have to explain ourselves to strangers in a resumé or interview. Nevertheless, the *process* of creating your resumé and letter of application, and the *preparation* for a job interview are crucial in today's competitive workplace. Remember that employers are often as anxious as the candidates they are interviewing, since they need to find the best person for a position.

The Resumé

A **resumé** is a written summary of your qualifications, paid and unpaid work experience, and personal information. It is essentially a *word picture* of yourself and your achievements.

LEARNING FOCUS

- analyze the purpose and structure of a resumé
- organize your own work-related experience
- draft, revise, and edit a resumé for an employer

✓ CHECKLIST PREPARING A RESUMÉ

- ✓ Be brief and to the point (no more than two pages).
- ✓ Customize the information to suit the job you are applying for.
- ✓ Present a positive image in both design and content.
- ✓ Do not misrepresent yourself or exaggerate your qualifications.
- ✓ Use action verbs (planned, produced, organized, etc.) to describe your accomplishments.
- ✓ Use clear, everyday language.
- ✓ Proofread for spelling, grammar, and typing errors.

CHRONOLOGICAL RESUMÉ This is the most common format, which employers often prefer. The **chronological resumé** is useful when someone has had several years of employment experience in a particular field, and has demonstrated steady progress there. For instance, if you were to leave high school with an interest in biology, enroll in university studies in marine biology, work summers at marine research institutes, graduate from university, and find a job in a government fisheries' office, you would benefit from using a chronological format for your resumé. Chronological style usually begins with a list of work experience (most recent first), followed by education, then lists of awards, volunteer work, or special training.

Below are examples of two drafts of a chronological resumé. Notice how the second version is an improvement on the first.

MODEL: CHRONOLOGICAL RESUMÉ–FIRST DRAFT

Boldface is overused in this heading: the name doesn't stand out.

This is irrelevant information, data that the employer, by law, should not request.

Education should be placed before work experience only if it is a key qualification for the job.

Key responsibilities and accomplishments are missing.

Details of volunteer responsibilities are missing.

Reference names are provided at the time of interview *only* if requested.

Alain Leduc
34 East Blvd.
Ottawa, ON
K1K 0V2
(613) 555-9876

Sex: Male
Age: 18
Height: 178 cm
Weight: 68 kg

Education

Grade 12 Diploma
Laurier Academy
Ottawa, ON

Work Experience

Sales Clerk   September 2000-present
Grover's Shoes   (part-time)
Ottawa, ON

Service Station Attendant   July-Aug 2000
Petro-Plus   (summer)
Vanier, ON

Volunteer Work

Multiple Sclerosis Annual Telethon, Oct. 1998, 1999

References

Irene Bailey, Manager
Grover's Shoes
Phone: (613) 555-9652
Fax: (613) 555-9655

Ivan Andronovich, Coordinator
Multiple Sclerosis Society
Phone: (613) 555-7675

MODEL: CHRONOLOGICAL RESUMÉ—FINAL DRAFT

The heading includes the name (in large, bold type), address, telephone number, and e-mail, if available.

This provides a clear statement of the applicant's job goal.

The formatting is simple and clear, with consistent use of typeface. This allows the resumé to fit on one page, when possible.

List the most recent job first, with responsibilities and accomplishments. Use qualitative adverbs such as *promptly* and *cheerfully*.

Include any special honours and awards.

This section lists details of community service.

Reference names are not actually provided here.

Alain Leduc
34 East Blvd.
Ottawa, ON
K1K 0V2
(613) 555-9876
aleduc@sympatico.com

Objective
Summer employment in the retail industry

Relevant Employment Experience

September 2000-present
Retail Sales Assistant (part-time)
Grover's Shoes
Ottawa, ON
- manage cash deposits and operate computerized register
- awarded "Salesperson of the Month" during holiday rush
- work unsupervised on weekends

July-August 2000
Service Station Attendant
Petro-Plus
Vanier, ON
- opened and closed station on Sundays
- served customers promptly and cheerfully
- performed oil and fluid checks

Education

June 2000
Awarded Grade 12 Diploma (Honours Standing)
Laurier Academy
Ottawa, ON

Volunteer Work

October 1998, 1999 Multiple Sclerosis Annual Telethon
- helped build cable television stage
- processed pledges

References
Available on Request

MODEL: FUNCTIONAL RESUMÉ

The heading includes the name (in slightly larger, bold type), address, telephone number, and e-mail address, if available.

The job goal.

Skills and accomplishments are placed in a prominent position, highlighted with bullets.

Employment history lists the most recent job first, with responsibilities and accomplishments.

Formatting should be simple and clear, with consistent use of boldface type, for example. This plain style allows the resumé to fit on one page if possible.

Note information on additional special courses taken.

Community-service work experience.

Reference names are not actually provided here.

Phoebe Kestenbaum
989 Bay St.
Victoria, BC
V8T 3R4
(250) 555-9874
pkestenbaum@saanich.bc.ca

Objective   Summer Employment as Research Assistant

Summary of Accomplishments and Skills
- 81% average in grades 11 and 12
- two summers working in a deadline-driven environment
- familiar with Corel WordPerfect and Microsoft Excel
- experience with search engines, including Metacrawler and Dogpile

Work Experience

July-August 2000   **Retail Bookstore Clerk**
Fern's Book Nook, Victoria, BC
- helped customers find titles
- processed searches and sales for special orders
- operated computerized cash and inventory system

June-August 1998, 1999   **Bicycle Technician**
G & B BikeWorks, Saanich, BC
- unpacked and assembled new bikes from wholesaler
- repaired various types of bikes
- met demanding schedules in busy shop
- created floor displays and checked inventories
- trained replacement worker before leaving the job

Education

1997-99	Arbutus High School, Victoria, BC
Summer 1999	Received National Lifeguard certification
Fall 1999	Completed a desktop publishing course

Volunteer Work

1997, 1998	Hospital Volunteer, Victoria General Hospital

References Available on Request

FUNCTIONAL RESUMÉ This format places less emphasis on *when* and *where* you received your job experience. A **functional resumé** works best if you have little job experience (like most high school students) or if you have gaps in your work history. A **targeted resumé** is a version of the functional resumé tailored to one specific job. Some job advertisements are very specific in their requirements, so you can use a targeted resumé to show exactly how your skills and experience match the needs of the available position.

Notice in the example on page 289 how the writer provides a summary of her most relevant accomplishments and skills *before* providing details regarding her work experience and education. This way, she emphasizes her strengths and shows the employer that she understands what the job requires. Remember: employers may have dozens, sometimes hundreds, of resumés to review, so by summarizing your major skills near the top of your resumé, you are doing them—and yourself—a favour.

Activities

Creating a Resumé

Start building your resumé:

- List all the paid and unpaid work you have done. (Do not underestimate work such as child care, gardening, painting, small home-repairs, or any other chores that you do.)

- Imagine the kind of summer job you would ideally like to have. Write an objective statement for it, then list the top three skills, achievements, or educational qualifications you have that match your objective.

- Organize your information on-screen to put together a one-page resumé. (Review the resumé samples presented here for ideas on how to organize your information.)

The Application Form

LEARNING FOCUS

- analyze the purpose and structure of an application form
- draw on personal experience to complete a writing task
- complete, revise, and edit a job application form

When applying for either part-time or full-time jobs, you will typically be asked to complete a job application form. This form, though always available from the job site itself, may be downloaded on your computer if your potential employer has it posted on a Web site. An application form is designed to gather information about your work experience, education, and general interests. Remember that your completed form creates an impression of you as a potential employee. Here are some pointers you can use to ensure this impression is a positive one:

✓ CHECKLIST | COMPLETING AN APPLICATION FORM

✓ Read the entire application form before you start. This will help you gauge the length of your answers.

✓ Read and follow the directions carefully.

✓ Write neatly—always in pen.

✓ Give accurate, honest answers to all questions.

✓ Be specific as to the job you want, and use a specific job title if possible (e.g., write *administrative assistant* as opposed to *helping around the office*).

✓ Provide complete information, even if it means rewriting part of your resume.

✓ Read it carefully when you are finished to check for possible errors or omissions.

Activities

Working with Application Forms

1. Obtain an application form for a part-time job of your choice (e.g., from a retail store, a restaurant, a recreation centre, a movie theatre). Complete the application form, attending carefully to the information required. Exchange the application form with a partner and evaluate each other's form for completeness and accuracy.

2. Locate (at the Pearson Canada Web site: <www.pearsoned.ca/referencepoints/links>), download, and following the instructions given, fill out the application forms for the following programs:
   - Federal Public Sector Youth Internship program, which places interns aged fifteen to thirty in federal government departments for up to a year
   - Student Work Abroad Programme (SWAP), an initiative of the Canadian Federation of Students that helps students gain work experience outside Canada
   - Federal Student Work Experience Program (FSWEP), which provides summer jobs for students between the ages of sixteen and eighteen, at selected national parks and historic sites across Canada.

   Print out your completed application forms and share them in small groups.

The Letter of Application

LEARNING FOCUS

- analyze the purpose and structure of a letter of application
- write a letter of application
- work with others to revise, edit, and evaluate a letter of application

You may be able to use copies of the same resumé (perhaps with minor modifications) when applying for a number of similar jobs. You must, however, customize a **letter of application** (sometimes called a covering letter) for the particular employer to whom you are submitting your resumé. Letters of application are similar to sales letters: both are intended to *persuade* or *convince* those who read them.

A letter of application gives you the chance to expand on your most significant skills and experience. If carefully written, it will give the employer a glimpse of your work attitude and personality. As well, the application letter provides an opportunity to tell employers *why* you want to work for them. Having at least some knowledge of the company before you apply is not only useful, but also shows the potential employer that you are not just sending your resumé around at random. Try to find out as much as possible about the company to which you've applied. Your local library's business files, newspaper archives, and magazines are good places to begin. Current information about specific companies is also usually available on their Web sites.

The length of your application letter is important. For part-time or entry-level positions it should be brief and to the point: ideally, one page. Candidates applying for more senior positions may need to write more detailed letters, but should still stay within two pages. Your letter should be simple and direct, but not stilted—leave a little room for your personality to show through.

The two most common types of application letters are the *solicited* and the *unsolicited*. A **solicited letter of application** is written in response to a direct request from an employer or to an advertised position. In this case, a job vacancy has already been identified by the employer.

An **unsolicited letter of application** goes to employers who have not actually advertised jobs. These are letters asking employers to consider you if and when there is an opening.

MODEL: SOLICITED LETTER OF APPLICATION

The sender's address.	345 Portage St. Winnipeg, MN R3M 0G5
The date line.	March 4, 2001
Make especially sure you have the *correct* name and position of the person you are writing to.	Ms. Stella Santos Human Resources Expanding Minds Research Inc. Suite 323, 534 Kingsway St. Winnipeg MN R2L 9H4
The salutation uses a colon at the end.	Dear Ms. Santos:
The subject line, in boldface, indicates the job title and file number as advertised.	**Re: Junior Researcher; Competition #14295**
The first paragraph refers to the job being applied for, enclosure of resumé, and where you saw job advertised or heard about it.	Please accept this application for the position of Junior Researcher advertised on March 2 in the *Winnipeg Free Press*. Enclosed you will find my resumé and list of three references, as requested.
The second paragraph outlines what you have to offer the employer.	My summer of part-time employment at the Huntington Children's Hospital, together with my high academic standing in high school, has prepared me well for a job as a Research Assistant. While at the hospital, I was responsible for assisting a team of five registered nurses and three intern doctors. Helping these professionals by organizing and typing their proposals trained me to become more organized myself. As a result of this employment, I also understand the "need to work to strict deadlines" mentioned in your job advertisement.
It is important to highlight why you are interested in this employer.	I'm aware that your company deals in medical research and I feel the familiarity with Internet and hospital record searches I gained in my last job will serve me well in becoming a junior member of your research team.
The letter ends with a request for an interview.	Please contact me at your earliest convenience for an interview. I look forward to discussing my interest in the position in greater detail.
This is referred to as a complimentary closing.	Sincerely,
The signature block.	*Amy Tremblay* Amy Tremblay (204) 475-9874 atrem@hotmail.com
This is referred to as enclosure notation.	Enclosed resumé and references

MODEL: UNSOLICITED LETTER OF APPLICATION

The sender's address.	45 Willow St. Leamington, ON M5T 7Y8 (519) 672-8491
The date line.	May 27, 2001
The receiver's name and position title. This is referred to as the inside address.	Ms. Jennifer Dowling Manager, Human Resources Department Eastern Foods 435 Winter Ave. Windsor, ON M4L 5G9
The salutation (with a colon).	Dear Ms. Dowling:
The first paragraph gets attention with a question that highlights two personal qualities.	Could Eastern Foods use an energetic and well-organized helper on the factory floor this summer?
Information about current education and work situation focuses on skills of interest to the employer.	I'm currently enrolled in Grade 12 at Angus Young Collegiate in Windsor and am seeking employment for the coming summer. For the past three summers I've worked on my uncle's farm, planting tomatoes, harvesting corn, and making small machinery repairs. On some weekends, I worked by myself, so I had to solve any problems that came up on my own and remain aware of the importance of planning and trying to do things right the first time.
The applicant re-emphasizes his chief strengths, and shows awareness of the company's reputation. Notice the action-oriented approach in the final paragraph.	With my experience and my positive attitude, I feel that I would fit in well with your summer bakery crew. Two of my friends have worked for your company, and both liked the busy atmosphere of the plant. I would be grateful if you would consider me for an interview. I have enclosed my resumé with this letter. You may reach me at the above phone number. I look forward to your call. Yours truly, *Brian Hutchinson* Brian Hutchinson
The signature block.	
The enclosure notation.	Enclosed resumé

STRUCTURE OF A LETTER OF APPLICATION As you can see from the models provided, you need to address your letter to someone in a department even if you are not sure which department might employ you. (Phoning the company will give you a name and position title, often in Human Resources.) In your letter, let the prospective employer know what job you want—then the company will be able to forward your letter of application to the right person or department. If you are sending a solicited letter, you should also indicate in your first paragraph where you found out about the job. That will help the employer to identify which newspaper, Web site, or other media advertisements are the most successful in attracting applicants.

The second paragraph is the most important and the most difficult to compose. Here, you need to be brief but informative. Focus on specific skills and achievements (e.g., your exact course average or academic awards). You should also point to your greatest strengths here, and briefly describe the nature of the work you've done. A statement such as, "I worked as a camp assistant last summer" does not tell a prospective employer very much. Instead try, "As a camp assistant last summer, I planned and supervised wilderness field trips for a group of 50 seven- to ten-year-olds."

The third paragraph enables you to show that you have done research on the employer. You should find out enough about the company to be able to say succinctly why you would be a suitable addition to the company's staff. Try to emphasize *what you can offer the company*, rather than *what you hope it can do for you*.

In your final paragraph, ask politely but directly for an interview. Strictly speaking, the whole purpose of submitting your cover letter and resumé is to get an interview, not a job. It is only after the interview that the employer will consider hiring you. Also, it is only then that you can know if you really *would* like to work for them.

Activities

Writing a Letter of Application

Write a letter of application for one the following job advertisements:

> **Office Assistant.** Busy downtown office requires summer replacements for secretarial duties. Must have basic experience with word processing and e-mail. Pleasant phone manner an asset.
>
> **Stockroom Help.** Large wholesale warehouse near airport requires help in taking inventory and reorganizing space. Some heavy lifting required. Valid driver's licence desirable, but not essential.

Tutorial Assistants. Language laboratory needs tutors/assistants to manage language lab for small groups. Must have written or oral fluency in French, Spanish, or Mandarin.

Assistant Graphic Designer. New Web-based firm seeks energetic personality with knowledge of HTML, JavaScript, Photoshop 5.5, Illustrator 9, and Dreamweaver 3. Experience working in teams a definite asset.

Market Research Assistant. Major recording company is in search of an assertive, results-oriented person with knowledge of recent popular music trends. Excellent oral and written communications required, as well as a readiness to work to tight schedules. Must be willing to travel occasionally.

Retail Sales. Cutting-edge fashion boutique requires personable, stylish salesclerks. Must be confident, eager to learn product line, and able to work split shifts and weekends.

Retail Sales. Computer Store needs knowledgeable sales representatives for summer employment. Must be willing to work in a fast-paced environment and be able to explain product specifications to novice computer users.

Help for Family-oriented Restaurant. Cashiers, line-cooks, and wait-staff needed for non-smoking establishment. Must enjoy working with the public.

- Exchange your letter of application with a classmate's and discuss each other's letters.
- Revise your letter based on the discussion.

The Job Interview

LEARNING FOCUS
- analyze the characteristics of an effective interview
- prepare for a job interview
- work with others to evaluate and enhance your interview skills

An interview is an effective way for an employer to discover if you have the best skill and personality match for a job opening. What many interviewees do not fully appreciate, however, is that it is also an opportunity for *them* to interview the employer. When you attend an interview, you frequently have a chance to see where you might be working, meet some of the staff, and, most important, ask direct questions of your prospective employer.

BEFORE THE INTERVIEW Prepare yourself by taking the steps below:

- Take stock of your own goals, your strengths and weaknesses, and your reasons for wanting the job.
- Know your rights as an employee and the obligations of your potential employer. (It is useful to check federal and provincial human

rights codes for current legislation on discrimination as it pertains to gender, religion, or disability.)

- Collect as much information as you can about the company: its business goals, its products or services, its personnel policies, and so on.

- Consider your potential employer and why he or she might be interested in you. Try to anticipate questions that might be asked, and rehearse suitable answers. Be ready to give a figure or a range if asked what pay you are expecting.

- Gather additional information (names and addresses of references, samples of work completed, volunteer projects not on your resumé) to submit during the interview if requested.

- Make a list of your own questions about, for example, working conditions and job advancement prospects.

- Dress in a style that is neat and that suits the job you are applying for (e.g., banks and insurance companies tend to be more conservative than advertising agencies or design studios).

- Make sure you carefully record the time, place, and directions for reaching the interview so that you arrive as scheduled.

AT THE INTERVIEW Use the following checklist to help you at the interview:

✓ CHECKLIST INTERVIEW SUCCESS

✓ Be on time for your interview, and enter the office alone.

✓ Introduce yourself to any office staff, and wait patiently until your interview begins.

✓ Be enthusiastic, and show interest in the interview process.

✓ Be courteous, pleasant, and sincere.

✓ In answering questions, clearly indicate your relevant qualifications, skills, and experience.

✓ If you have trouble understanding a question, rephrase it in your own words so that both you and the interviewer are starting from the same point.

✓ Watch for signs that the interview is coming to an end so as not to draw out the process unnecessarily.

✓ Finish the interview on a positive note by confirming your interest in the position.

AFTER THE INTERVIEW Soon after you finish your interview you need to write or e-mail a follow-up letter. The letter should begin with a thank-you comment. Include a confirmation of your interest in the position and a comment that shows you are willing to answer additional questions if needed. When closing the letter, provide your phone number and an indication of when you will be available in the next few days.

In general, it is appropriate, both before and after an interview, to contact a potential employer in writing. If you do use the telephone, however, ensure that you observe some basic telephone etiquette:

✓ CHECKLIST | USING THE TELEPHONE OR VOICE MAIL

- ✓ Rehearse what you are going to say before you call.
- ✓ Know the name or title of the person whom you want to speak to.
- ✓ Give a brief reason for your call.
- ✓ Speak clearly, and not too quickly or slowly.
- ✓ Be pleasant and courteous.
- ✓ Choose a practical time to phone (i.e., not close to lunchtime or the end of the day).
- ✓ Identify the job you are interested in as specifically as possible.
- ✓ Leave your full name, phone number, and a detailed message if the person is unavailable.

Activities

Preparing for a Job Interview

1. Choose an industry in which you have a personal interest. Pretend you are an employer looking for someone to fill a specific job at your company. Write a paragraph explaining the kinds of skills and abilities you feel would be a perfect fit for this job.

2. In groups of three, find or create a job advertisement for the kind of summer or long-term job you would like to have. One member of your group should then prepare a resumé and letter of application for the job. The other two members of your group (the interviewers) should then prepare a list of ten questions to ask the group member (the interviewee) who has applied for the job (e.g., "Tell me about yourself," "What might give you the edge over other qualified applicants?" "Explain what you would do if you had to intervene in a dispute between two co-workers.").

You now have the opportunity to role-play an interview situation. The group will set up a ten- to fifteen-minute **panel interview**, in which each of the two interviewers takes turns asking questions of the interviewee. This way, each interviewer can take notes while the other maintains eye contact with the interviewee.

The interviewers should refer to the chart below to assess the interviewee:

Preparedness	1	2	3	4	5
Alertness/eye contact	1	2	3	4	5
Reasonable/logical answers to questions	1	2	3	4	5
Demonstrated awareness of strengths	1	2	3	4	5
Willingness to respond to questions	1	2	3	4	5
Conciseness in responding	1	2	3	4	5
Consistency/accuracy	1	2	3	4	5
Energetic presentation/enthusiasm for job	1	2	3	4	5
Use of non-verbal cues while listening and speaking	1	2	3	4	5
Positive/genuine tone	1	2	3	4	5
(Evaluation Key 1=poor; 2=adequate; 3=good; 4=very good; 5=excellent)					

The interviewers can discuss their assessment of the candidate between themselves. They should then present a short, informal oral report to the interviewee.

Written Communication in the Workplace

Once you are actually in the workplace, you will need to communicate in numerous ways: through writing and speaking to individuals and groups; through reading and viewing such job-specific materials as technical manuals, **trade magazines**, and company reports; through the use of electronic technology to prepare, transmit, and receive information.

Memos, e-mail messages, letters, and business reports are common forms of written communication, both within an office environment and from business to business.

Memos and E-mail Messages

A **memorandum** or memo, as it is commonly called, is a brief document (one paragraph to two pages) used to convey messages within an organization. With the advent of e-mail, most offices now send many of their internal memos electronically as opposed to using the more traditional system of paper-based inter-office mail.

An effective memo

- covers one main topic.
- identifies people who should receive a copy.
- indicates what action needs to be taken, when, and by whom.

Ensure that any memos and e-mails you write contain the above features. Take a look at the following inefficient request for a common meeting time.

LEARNING FOCUS

- analyze the characteristics of effective memos and e-mails
- practise writing for the workplace
- assess the effectiveness of written memos and e-mail messages

MODEL: INEFFECTIVE MEMO

MEMORANDUM

TO: Janet Franz, Ivy Lang, Keith, Sam Li, Judy, Fred, Olive
FROM: Ike
DATE: Sept. 7, 2000
RE: Committee Meeting

Hi Guys,

It's that time of year again when we have to start thinking about how we're going to set up the open house for this year's celebration in November. I know that Keith had some really good ideas last year, so let's hope that he doesn't let us down this year (just kidding, Keith, I know you'll come through for us).

Anyway, we really need to meet sometime to discuss what we'd like to do this year, so give me a call or drop by my office, or send me an e-mail to tell me when you'd be free for a get together to talk this out. We probably should meet early in October, so let me know as soon as possible what's good for you. And maybe we can also use that time to talk about the sales figures and the possible layoffs that have been rumoured lately.

Take care,
Ike

This message is typical of the kind of overly informal memo that a rushed or careless worker might send. Besides the tactless and unnecessary humour, the memo writer, Ike, is making more work for himself than he imagined, since he must now wait for an unspecified time period for a list of possible dates from his co-workers. Then, if he receives a list of dates that conflict, he will have to re-contact each person individually to see if he can negotiate a suitable time for all.

In addition, Ike has made the mistake of introducing new topics at the end of the memo. This is a problem for three reasons:

- It distracts readers from the key request in the memo.
- It makes the memo difficult to file under a single topic.
- It switches to a negative topic (layoffs), when the focus of the message is a positive event (company open house).

Notice in the rewritten example how the writer tells his audience, politely and concisely, exactly what he needs to know, and when.

MODEL: EFFECTIVE MEMO

MEMORANDUM

Use the full names of each employee.

Indicate your job title, if applicable.

No opening salutation is required.

Place the main idea first, indicating precisely and clearly any relevant times, deadlines, and meeting places.

No formal closing is required.

TO: Janet Franz, Ivy Lang, Keith Mercer, Sam Li, Judy O'Grady, Fred Tripp, Olivia Torano

FROM: Ike Toulany, Manager, Public Relations

DATE: September 7, 2000

RE: Open House Promotion Committee

Please let me know by Friday, September 14 if you are free to attend a meeting at 2:30 p.m. on Thursday, October 2 in Boardroom C of the Hart Building.

An agenda of the items to be discussed at this open house committee will be forwarded early next week.

If you have any questions, give me a call at extension 514 or drop me an e-mail.

When sending e-mail messages either within or outside the office, observe certain courtesies, known in the workplace as **netiquette**.

 CHECKLIST E-MAIL NETIQUETTE

✓ Notify the e-mail sender if you have received a message by mistake.

✓ Before forwarding important messages, ask the sender's permission.

✓ Include a brief and informative title for each e-mail to save recipients time, and to allow everyone to file the messages appropriately.

✓ Avoid writing long paragraphs which go beyond a single screen.

✓ Do not use all uppercase or all lowercase letters (the former implies shouting, the latter suggests laziness).

✓ If including graphics or specially formatted text, send the file as an attachment, since your receiver's e-mail software may not be able to interpret the original formatting.

✓ When sending messages with attached files, paste the text into the message itself as a precaution, in case the attachment cannot be opened.

✓ Do not assume that everyone will respond immediately: if you require an immediate response, mark the e-mail "URGENT!"

✓ If you want to be sure your message was received, include a request for the recipient to confirm that the message arrived.

In addition, it is important to remember that there are *no guarantees* when it comes to e-mail messages. The message may be intercepted, lost, incomplete, or corrupted in some way; more important, it may contain a computer virus. It is a good idea to install an anti-virus program on your computer to monitor for possible infection.

Activities

Writing Short Messages

1. Assume the role of a company office manager. You must inform all employees of an upcoming power shutdown on November 30 due to the installation of new fibre optic cable in your building. This installation had been scheduled to take place during the end-of-year holidays but, unfortunately, the contractors were unable to get enough staff to work over that period. Since this will be a major inconvenience to several of your workers, you must decide whether they need to know why the power will be shut down. You also need to find out if there are any employees who are away on vacation currently so that they can be informed. Finally, you need to know if anyone will be working overtime on the weekend prior to the shutdown in order to meet project deadlines.

Write a memo or e-mail message to your employees, communicating the necessary information.

2. You have just been hired for the summer by a software training company to help assemble their training manuals. After working twelve hours voluntary overtime each weekend for the last month, you feel you need a break. It has been particularly difficult lately because the air conditioning in the photocopy room has been malfunctioning and the automatic binding machine has been sent out for repairs. As a result, you have had to spend long hours in a hot room using the manual binder, which involves a painstaking process. And even though you really like the people you work with, you are exhausted. In addition, a close friend wants very much for you to attend her cousin's wedding this weekend. Since you are newly hired, you are a little nervous about asking for time off so soon, but you really feel you owe it to yourself.

Write a memo or e-mail to your supervisor, requesting the time off.

Letters—External Business Correspondence

Many of the same guidelines you apply to writing memos and e-mails apply as well to external business correspondence:

LEARNING FOCUS
- analyze the characteristics of effective business correspondence
- practise writing and evaluating business letters
- use techniques of persuasion in oral and written communication

✓ CHECKLIST │ EFFECTIVE LETTER WRITING

- ✓ Be courteous and considerate.
- ✓ Be clear and logical.
- ✓ Be concise, and avoid wordy, repetitious, clichéd language, or **jargon**.
- ✓ Include accurate and specific dates, locations, and details so that people can respond quickly and appropriately to your messages.
- ✓ Avoid overusing "I" or write in the third person.

Below is a multi-purpose format for a business letter. Since organizations typically use individualized letterheads and customized formats, this format is designed to show the main components of a business letter. Note the use of the **full block style** (all elements aligned at the left-margin). It is the easiest to type and the most popular format for most business correspondence. This is a model for a **letter of inquiry**, one in which you make a business request.

MODEL: LETTER OF INQUIRY

The sender uses her workplace letterhead with its preprinted company name and address.

The date line.

The name of the recipient. The position title should be accurate.
The department and company name and address.

The salutation.

The subject line.

The opening paragraph includes a brief introduction and clearly stated request.

The second paragraph explains the reasons for the inquiry.

Questions or items are numbered for ease of reference.

A target date is politely suggested for fulfillment of the request.
The complimentary closing can use "sincerely" or "yours truly."
The sender's title is included in the signature block.

Yukon Community College
899 Landsdowne Rd.
Whitehorse, YT
Y5K 1R4

March 5, 2001

Dr. Sheldon O'Neil
Coordinator
Research and Development
Trinark Corporation
Red Deer AB
T5N 3T4

Dear Dr. O'Neil:

RE: QUESTIONS REGARDING ERGONOMIC RESEARCH

As an instructor in the Business Administration program at Yukon Community College, I'd be grateful for any answers you could supply to my concerns listed below.

I became acquainted with your research through your article "Current Health Concerns in the Workplace" published in *Canadian Business* magazine. My department has just received approval for extensive renovations and for the purchase of new equipment, and I feel that your expertise could be of great assistance in our efforts to build optimal working spaces for our students. Here are my primary concerns:

1. What are the major spine- and neck-related injuries that are suffered by office workers, particularly by those who must spend up to eight hours seated at computer terminals?
2. What, in your opinion, is the best way to combat the eye fatigue caused by long hours viewing a monitor?
3. Apart from posture and visual complications, what are the other key dangers faced by office employees?
4. Do you have any statistics on the cost in lost wages due to sick leave caused by poorly constructed offices and inferior working conditions or routines?
5. Are there any particular brand names or product lines of ergonomically designed office furniture that you would recommend?

Thank you for any assistance you can provide. Since we need to submit our plans by April 30, I'd appreciate if you could respond before this month's end. I look forward to your opinions.

Sincerely,
Helena Cheung

Helena Cheung
Senior Instructor, Business Administration

When writing a **letter of refusal**, be especially careful not to offend the reader. Note how the writer of the following letter refuses a request for an interview but still maintains interest and goodwill. Note also that the writer does not apologize for refusing. Apologies are unnecessary and add an inappropriate negative tone to a business letter of refusal.

MODEL: LETTER OF REFUSAL

Delmar Technologies
36 Erin Mills Rd.
Mississauga, ON
L5C 2V4

The date line.	June 15, 2000
The name and address of the letter's recipient (referred to as the inside address).	Ms. Cecilia Chambers Utopia Research Associates 47 Grosvenor Rd. Toronto, ON M6S 9B2
The salutation.	Dear Ms. Chambers:
This paragraph contains the *buffer statement*, a polite acknowledgement and re-statement of the request. Note the transition between the buffer statement and the reasons to be provided for the refusal. An explanation is given as to why the request cannot be met.	Thank you for your interest in interviewing Anna Soyinka, our manager of Human Resources, for your research on the hiring practices of major corporations. We are pleased that you thought of us as worthy to include in your research. Judging by the lengthy questionnaires and research methods you had mentioned in your letter, I'm certainly confident that you are conducting a thorough and unbiased study. However, it is unfortunate that your request comes at this time, since we are in the process of hiring over a dozen new employees this summer, all of who will require Ms. Soyinka's attention for their company orientation sessions.
The refusal itself is accompanied by an alternative or suggestion.	Although Ms. Soyinka cannot take part in your study in the next two months, she has told me that she is certainly willing to provide a brief telephone interview later this month, if that will be of any assistance or interest to you.
An expression of good wishes is used in closing.	Given the comprehensiveness of your project, I trust that your study will be of great interest to anyone interested in the hiring process. I wish you all the best in your worthwhile research.
	Sincerely,
The signature block.	*Jeri McKinney* Jeri McKinney, Executive Assistant, Human Resources

Whenever you are communicating to persuade—for example, in job application letters, sales letters, posters, advertisements, oral presentations—consider following the Attention Interest Desire Action (**AIDA**) **sequence.** The AIDA chart below provides some strategies for getting and keeping attention.

COMMUNICATING TO PERSUADE: ATTENTION-INTEREST-DESIRE-ACTION (AIDA)

Attention Begin by getting your audience's favourable attention. Consider carefully their background and interests as well as the kind of ideas, humour, cultural references, and emotional appeals to which they would relate.

Interest Cultivate your audience's interest in what you have to offer. Highlight your skills and strengths in a job application letter, for example, or the key features of a product or service in a sales letter.

Desire Try to create a desire by convincing your audience that they really need what you have to offer. Show them, for example, why they must have you as an employee or why the product you describe would be beneficial to their specific consumer group.

Action Finally, as a persuasive communicator, you need to strive for what retail salespeople call the *close*. In a job application letter, this may be done by requesting an interview and mentioning how you will follow up your letter. In a sales letter, this may be done by encouraging the sale by providing a toll-free phone number, by enclosing coupons for limited-time discounts, or by referring, in the letter, to the location of a nearby outlet.

A **sales letter**, as the model on page 307 shows, is a business letter intended to convince potential customers to buy a product or use a service. Sales letters are most effective when they follow the AIDA sequence.

Activities

Writing Business Correspondence

1. Assume that you will soon be moving to Halifax from Calgary and are looking for a new computer. You plan to sell your old computer, 15-inch monitor, scanner, and laser printer to your brother-in-law, whose children will use it to play games. With the money from this sale and a moving bonus from your new employer, you want to purchase a computer from a reputable vendor in Nova Scotia. Because you will need a home Internet connection within a week of your arrival in Halifax, you want a vendor who can supply you with a reasonable package deal with an Internet service provider, and an

MODEL: SALES LETTER

Homesteader's House and Garden Care
342 Dauphin St.
Winnipeg, MN
G3I 5S7

The company's letterhead.

Date and inside address.

Address of the recipient.

An attention line is used if individual names are not available or are difficult to obtain. This is better than using *generic salutations such as* "Dear Friend" *or* "Valued Customer."

An attention *grabber*, such as questions, anecdotes, or thought-provoking statistics helps gain reader attention.

September 4, 2001
Box 9000
Winnipeg, MN
G4T 0N8
(204) 786-9898

Attention: Home Owner
- Do you have pets whose routine you don't want to upset by placing them in a kennel while you're away?
- Do you have valued tropical house- or outdoor plants that require careful attention?
- Are you concerned about leaving your home unoccupied during your next vacation?

If you're asking yourself any of these questions, we may have an affordable solution for you. At *Homesteader's House and Garden Care*, we offer house and pet minding services at a variety of prices to suit your exact needs and budgets.

An explanation of the value of the service is given, with some concrete examples.

Some customers simply don't want to trouble their neighbours to check their mail each day, or water and mow their lawn as required. Others have several pets, ranging from gerbils to German shepherds, that may demand feeding, walking, and the attention of alert and caring animal lovers.

This paragraph highlights the company's experience and reputation.

Here the customer receives a *call to action*, with incentives offered.

At *Homesteader's House and Garden Care*, where we have a fully bonded and reliable staff, we've been tailoring our services for satisfied clients over the last seven years.

We're enclosing with this letter a coupon for a free in-person estimate of your home and pet-care needs. Feel free to call us during regular business hours; or leave a message on our answering machine, and we'll return your call at a time convenient for you.

The final line reinforces the name and value of the service.

At *Homesteader's*, we understand that part of a relaxing vacation is knowing that you can rest assured that your home is not alone.

Sincerely,

Tony Rulli

Tony Rulli,
President

IBM-compatible computer with a Pentium III chip, a 15-inch monitor, and a high-quality ink-jet printer. Jerome Mercer, a long-time business associate, has suggested that you try Hitek Computers on 117 Regina St., Halifax, NS C5S 2T4. You would not normally purchase a computer sight unseen, but given your need for an Internet connection, you are willing to take a chance, provided that the price is right and the computer has a three-year warranty.

Write a letter of inquiry to Hitek Computers, requesting price quotations on the items you need. Let them know that you need the information as soon as possible for your move on the 15th of December.

2. Assume that you are a plant operations manager for Anton Foods Corporation. You have received a letter from Rita Gopalsingh, president of the Saskatoon Community Association. Ms. Gopalsingh writes at the suggestion of Rhonda Burke, the supervisor of your night crew. Ms. Burke is the coordinator of the association's walk-a-thon and has been a member in good standing for almost a decade. She mentioned over the telephone to Ms. Gopalsingh that Anton Foods might be able to donate the use of its picnic tables and other lunchroom supplies for the walk-a-thon finish-line reception. You would like to help the association and show appreciation of their efforts in the community. However, company materials cannot be lent to outside organizations, even for charitable purposes, because your liability insurance limits property coverage to on-site use only.

Write a letter of refusal to Ms. Gopalsingh.

3. Imagine that you have been unsuccessful in searching for a summer job, so you have decided to start your own summer business. Consider one of the following ventures or think of your own alternative: exterior housepainting, landscaping, computer instruction for kids. Create a sales letter or flyer describing your services. Use the **AIDA** sequence and incorporate eye-catching visuals and graphics.

Business Reports: An Introduction

LEARNING FOCUS
- analyze the purpose of business reports
- learn how to conduct primary research
- practise writing and presenting an informal report

Reports take various forms in the workplace, depending on their purpose. There are **informal reports** such as short one-page **progress reports** and **incident reports**, five-page **proposals**, and much longer recommendation reports and **feasibility studies**. Although shorter reports are used primarily for record keeping, many reports are written in order to solve a problem or initiate change. The best reports often make clear recommendations.

Whatever the purpose, the principles of report writing are usually the same for both shorter and longer reports. In general, report writers strive for

- purposefulness—defining what needs to be done or achieved, and by whom.

- objectivity—presenting all relevant viewpoints fairly.

- clarity—ensuring that terminology is clearly defined, and appropriate background information is supplied or referenced.

- accuracy—double-checking all facts and figures, and verifying credible sources of information.

- consistency—maintaining a uniform tone and format throughout the report.

RESEARCH TECHNIQUES Novice report writers frequently ask how a long formal report differs from a research essay (see Chapter 2). The biggest single difference is that research essays seldom advocate specific action or make detailed recommendations. Another distinction is that most research essays are based mainly on **secondary research**; that is, information and analysis found in published books, journals, Web sites, videos, and other sources. Business reports, on the other hand, rely more on **primary research**, typically undertaken by the report writers themselves. This primary research is done using various methods, including phone surveys, questionnaires, interviews with experts, experiments, and on-site inspections.

Review the checklist below on how best to conduct primary research using the methods listed:

✓ CHECKLIST | CONDUCTING PHONE SURVEYS

- ✓ Arrange a suitable time with your interviewees. Never assume that they will have time to answer your questions immediately.
- ✓ Keep your questions as brief as possible. Test them on friends or colleagues before you use them on your intended audience.
- ✓ Avoid asking multiple-choice questions over the phone. It is difficult for listeners to remember all the choices.
- ✓ Leave room on your question sheet for additional comments from interviewees.

✓ CHECKLIST CREATING AND ADMINISTERING A WRITTEN QUESTIONNAIRE

- ✓ Draft questions on everything you would like to know. Then you can edit to prioritize them and eliminate possible duplication.
- ✓ Use open-ended questions sparingly. Although they provide the most detailed information, they are time-consuming to evaluate.
- ✓ Give respondents options, using rankings and multiple-choice questions, but also include space for *other* categories so that they can mention options you haven't considered.
- ✓ Ask *personal information* (age, occupation, salary, gender, etc.) questions at the *end* of your survey. This section should be considered optional.
- ✓ Have several people fill out your survey to test it for clarity and length. If a survey takes more than ten minutes to complete, it is unlikely people will do it unless they are given a special incentive.
- ✓ Consider how you will administer the surveys. If you leave them with people, you must provide a convenient way to collect them. Never assume people will mail them back to you.

✓ CHECKLIST CONDUCTING AN INTERVIEW

- ✓ Brainstorm as many questions as possible, and then refine and list them in logical sequence.
- ✓ Prepare clear, written questions. Be ready to ask follow-up questions that you may not have considered in your original interview plan.
- ✓ Let the interviewee know the purpose of your research before you begin questioning.
- ✓ Take point-form notes and rewrite them as soon as possible after the interview.
- ✓ If you plan to make a follow-up call to verify information, be sure to clear this with your interviewee before the end of your session.
- ✓ Avoid debating issues: you are there to listen and gather information only.
- ✓ Write a follow-up thank-you letter to your interviewee to show formal appreciation for assisting you.

PROGRESS REPORTS These are informal reports written whenever a long-term project requires the coordination of several people's schedules and efforts. Such reports allow for clearer lines of communication among staff as a project develops. Some organizations have streamlined styles of weekly progress reports. For example, one high-tech company uses what it calls RAG (Red, Amber, Green) **progress reports**, which correspond to the colours of a traffic light. If a progress report is tagged red or red-filed it requires immediate attention. A report tagged amber signals that a situation must be closely monitored. Green indicates that all is progressing as planned.

INCIDENT REPORTS These are written to provide details of a specific event and to outline any follow-up action required. Like most informal reports, **incident reports** are usually presented in memo format.

MODEL: INCIDENT REPORT

The information at the top is in a format similar to a memo.

The opening sentence summarizes the incident, with specific details to clarify the explanation.

The explanation of events is stated objectively, from the point of view of both of those involved. The information includes the actions each has taken.

The report records each party's judgment as to who is responsible for the accident.

The current status of the follow-up to the incident is given. The recipient is invited to contact the sender for more information.

TO: Rhonda Wenqi, Regional Manager
FROM: Ken Urlich, Human Resources
DATE: March 10, 2001
RE: Possible Liability for Vehicle Damage in Loading Bay

On March 4 at approximately 2:30 p.m., our night supervisor, Derek LeBlanc, accidentally backed a tractor-trailer into Nancy Riordan's personal vehicle, causing damage estimated at $2,789. Nancy is requesting that our company, or Derek himself, pay the insurance deductible portion of the damages to her 1999 Trans Am. (She has a $500 deductible.) She has informed her insurance company and has also consulted a lawyer on the matter.

Derek, who has also spoken to his insurance agent, explained to me that he was showing one of the delivery staff how to back out of the loading bay properly when the incident occurred. (Incidentally, Derek does have the proper class of driver's license to operate a vehicle with air brakes.) However, as he was backing the truck out of loading bay 3, he assumed that the driver's energetic waving of his arms back and forth was encouragement when, in fact, the driver was trying to warn him that Nancy had temporarily parked her car at the entrance to the loading bay while she dropped in to pick up her pay cheque.

Ignoring the warning, Derek backed the tractor-trailer into the passenger side of Nancy's vehicle, much to her amazement as she stepped out of the front office. They exchanged some angry comments, which ended in the on-looking driver stepping in to drive Nancy to her mother's house until she calmed down.

Derek insists that he is not to blame for the incident since Nancy had no business parking her car at the entrance to the loading bay, even if only for a few minutes. Nancy is willing to pay the fine for the parking infraction, but does not feel this permits anyone to demolish her vehicle through their carelessness. In addition, she does not feel she should have to pay for the deductible portion of the damages.

At this time, we are waiting to hear from Nancy's insurance agent and lawyer, and as we discussed in our conversation, she will be contacting you personally to talk about this. If you require further details or clarification, please contact me at extension 397 or drop me an e-mail.

Activities

Working with Informal Reports

1. Find a news story about an accident or crime and imagine you are a police officer called to the scene. Write an incident report about what happened, what action has been taken, and what still needs to be done.

2. For your next major project in any subject area, plot the steps necessary to its completion (e.g., finding resources; reviewing the collected materials; meeting with classmates or teachers). Next, after the midway point of your assignment's due date, write a one-page progress report (in memo format) to your teacher. Indicate what you have completed, what remains to be done and when, and any obstacles to completing the report.

Structure of the Formal Business Report

LEARNING FOCUS

- analyze the structure and organization of a business report
- work independently and in small groups to conduct research
- practise writing and evaluating a formal report

Although a formal business report is usually long, a reader should be able to see its main points and structure easily. Unlike most essays, a formal report should use headings, subheadings, lists, and graphics as signposts for the reader. The key elements required for all formal reports are examined below. Excerpts from several reports demonstrate the *range* of business reporting conducted and highlight characteristics of each report element.

COVER OR TRANSMITTAL LETTER The **cover** (transmittal) **letter**, addressed to the appropriate person and organization, should be paper-clipped to the front cover of the report.

FRANK & ERNEST reprinted by permission of Newspaper Enterprise Association, Inc.

TITLE PAGE This should include a brief informative title, your name, the date, and the names of the persons for whom the report is prepared.

SUMMARY This section is commonly called an **executive summary** or **abstract**. It is about half a page in length and written in plain English—free of any jargon, or technical language—so that a wide range of readers can understand the gist of the report. Be sure to use information from your introduction, discussion, conclusions, and recommendations in the summary.

MODEL: EXECUTIVE SUMMARY

This is a summary taken from a formal report entitled "Electives in Canadian High Schools."

The first paragraph indicates the purpose of the report.

This indicates the report's scope and the research methods used.

This paragraph identifies the key findings of the research.

The final paragraph includes any major recommendations, identifies limitations, and mentions any other further actions to be taken.

Our curriculum review committee initiated a three-month study of Canadian high schools to discover what electives are offered to students. The study was commissioned by a deputy minister of education to discover how our province compares with others in Canada.

Over thirty telephone interviews were conducted with high-school administrators, and seventy-four written surveys were completed of the hundred that were distributed to various schools. Informal interviews with high-school students were held each month to verify and clarify certain information supplied by administrators.

Our study reveals that we offer five per cent fewer electives than Quebec, and three per cent fewer than Manitoba schools, thus ranking third out of the eight provinces and two territories surveyed.

Since our schools offer a reasonable selection of electives, our chief recommendation is that no immediate changes be made to the curriculum with regard to students' course choices. In addition, we suggest that a brief follow-up study be conducted to further investigate the two provinces that could not meet our survey deadlines.

TABLE OF CONTENTS This section contains all major headings and subheadings to be used in your report. It uses the same format and numbering system as the table of contents for a research essay (see Chapter 2).

INTRODUCTION Make sure your introduction contains the following:

- Background—events leading up to the present situation and an explanation of why the study is necessary
- Purpose—what the study is designed to achieve and for whom

- Scope—an outline of limits on the study, set by yourself or the people authorizing it. These may include restrictions on time, depth of study, and sample populations, as well as omissions for confidentiality or other practical reasons

DISCUSSION This section, also referred to as the body, begins with your first major heading from the table of contents, and arranges your points logically. The following model is excerpted from the discussion section of a report on the benefits of Integrated Pest Management versus the use of toxic pest-exterminating chemicals.

MODEL: REPORT—DISCUSSION

The main results of the survey are presented at the beginning.

The views of those willing to spend more money are compared with those who are not.

Highly detailed information is relegated to an appendix.

The concluding sentence implies a direction for the future based on the report's findings.

About 70% of the 45 customers surveyed at six garden centres in Vancouver indicated that they had never heard of IPM (Integrated Pest Management).

Of those surveyed, 38 indicated they would be willing to spend more money on less toxic forms of pest control as a replacement of chemical pesticide. The most popular response for how much more the consumer would be willing to pay was 10%. The 7 who were unwilling to spend more on the less toxic forms stated that effectiveness was far more important than price when determining what product to purchase.

In the same survey, 21 remarked that they were informed of IPM alternatives the last time they purchased pesticides, 18 indicated they were not, and 6 did not answer. All 21 that were informed of IPM the last time they bought pesticides did indicate that they chose pesticides again over IPM alternatives because of their familiarity with pesticides. (See Appendix D for complete survey questions and results.)

Clearly, after also interviewing the salespersons/dispensers, one reason for the continued reluctance of customers to try IPM is that dispensers lack the training to promote the products effectively; dispensers also regretted that they just couldn't spend enough time with each customer explaining the merits of IPM.

CONCLUSION This section presents your primary conclusion first, followed by less significant conclusions, as seen on the next page:

MODEL: CONCLUSION

The writer clearly restates the general purpose of this formal report on computer buyers. The key issues are summarized concisely in the second sentence.

In researching the needs of home-use consumers of computers, the area that requires the most attention is the extensive research expected of the buyer. Buyers must be aware where to begin in determining their computing needs, the type of system that best meets those needs, and how to compare the huge variety of systems available in today's market.

The research methodology is indicated and the results are clearly highlighted.

After surveying thirty recent computer buyers in the Ottawa Valley, it was evident the majority—72%—were unsatisfied with the system they had purchased. They felt unqualified to make such a purchase, and when it came to the final decision, it was the sales person who decided for them. Buyers felt that the computer retailers provided ample service, but 80% felt intimidated because of their own lack of technical knowledge.

The writer uses the conclusion as a *bridge* between the body of the report and its final recommendations section.

The following recommendations are intended to help consumers educate themselves and to outline the varying merits of six of the most popular and affordable computer products.

RECOMMENDATIONS This section of a formal report

- arranges points in descending order of importance or in chronological sequence if appropriate.
- appears in point form if several recommendations are being made.
- advocates specific action.
- uses the active **voice**.

MODEL: RECOMMENDATIONS

This set of recommendations, from a formal report on cellular phone use, is provided in order of importance.

To prevent health and safety problems, cellular phone users should:

1.1 Avoid operating cell phones for prolonged periods within .5 km of base station towers.

1.2 Purchase protection devices such as the RayAway (approximate cost $25) to absorb as much RF radiation as possible before it reaches the user.

1.3 Lobby the Canadian government for an independent study into the long-term effects of RF radiation.

Suggestions are made for the organization's future direction. These are action oriented and include estimated costs.

To ensure responsible manufacture and use of cellular phones, government and industry should:

2.1 Increase co-sponsored research into RF radiation and health, at a cost of $800,000 per year over a three-year period.

2.2 Initiate an information campaign warning the general public of the health risks involved in frequent cellular phone use, at a one-time cost of $350,000.

REFERENCES AND BIBLIOGRAPHY Ensure that all material from primary and secondary sources quoted or paraphrased in your report is referenced using proper source documentation. (See Appendix A for information on citation of sources.)

APPENDICES (OPTIONAL) This section is used for any information that would interrupt the reading continuity if included in the body of the report. Such information as complex data analysis, statistics, large drawings and illustrations, maps, detailed test and survey results, sample copies of surveys, and cost comparisons, for example, could appear as appendices. If you have more than one **appendix**, arrange them in the sequence in which each is referred to in the report. Give each one an informative title, and assign an identifying letter to each appendix, starting with Appendix A. Ensure that every appendix is referred to in the discussion. Otherwise, readers may feel you are simply padding the report with unnecessary information.

MODEL: APPENDIX

This survey used in a formal report on fast-food franchises is provided in the appendix for information, and also for potential future use.

The purpose of the survey is included.

Appendix D - Copy of survey sent to franchise owners

Please take a few minutes to fill out the following survey.

I am a student at Lansdowne Secondary School, currently taking a course in business studies. I will be using the information gathered to complete a formal report analyzing the rationale for opening fast-food franchises. You may attach your handwritten answers on the spare sheet provided if you wish.

1. Are you the original owner? If yes, please answer the following questions. If no, please skip to question 4 and continue from there.

2. Did you choose the location yourself or did a Vendex staff member advise you?

3. What factors led you to set up a Vendex franchise in your current location?

4. What prompted you to buy a Vendex franchise instead of another franchise?

5. What are the key benefits of owning a Vendex franchise?

6. Are there any disadvantages to owning a Vendex franchise?

7. In the last three years, have your profits increased, decreased, or stabilized?

Thank you for taking part in this survey.

GLOSSARY (OPTIONAL) If you cannot avoid using technical terms in your formal report, provide a brief glossary, which includes a list of abbreviations and **acronyms**, either after the table of contents or at the end of your report.

Activities

Researching and Writing Formal Reports

1. In small groups, research businesses or government agencies in your area you would like to contact. Write a proposal, outlining where your group is going, why, when, and indicate any minor expenses that might be associated with the visit. After conducting your site visit, write a brief travel report, indicating the purpose, highlights, and your assessment of the organization. If the business/agency has copies of a formal annual report, bring one back to class for discussion.

2. Write a ten- to fifteen-page formal report on one or more specific career-oriented jobs, using both primary and secondary research. The report should include the following information, where applicable:
   • full job titles and descriptions (including salary range, if available)
   • educational and experiential qualifications required for each position
   • full name, address, and phone number of each employer
   • names (and position titles, if available) of all contact people (interviewed by phone, letter, e-mail, fax, or in person)
   • detailed description of duties involved in the selected job(s)
   • brief company or department histories and other relevant background information (e.g., number of employees locally, domestically, and internationally; overview of benefits package)

- your personal analysis of the positions in the organizations (i.e., after gathering your information, would you be interested in any of the positions? why or why not?)
- a detailed explanation of what further education and experience you would need to be competitive in the fields (you can present these requirements as recommendations)

Oral Communication in the Workplace

Much of the decision-making in business occurs through oral communication—whether in one-on-one discussions, telephone conversations, or in larger group meetings. Effective oral communication is a major part of daily work activities and is important in problem-solving and team building situations. An employee's effectiveness, success, and morale can be deeply affected by how well he or she communicates orally with co-workers and clients. Employers have learned, too, mostly through trial and error, that employees are much happier when they are kept *in the loop* through regular oral (and written) information sharing and when the channels for feedback are kept free and open.

The more you can learn from seasoned professionals, gifted talkers, and anyone in your personal life who you feel is a good oral communicator, the better prepared you will be as you enter the world of work. The sections that follow are intended to help enhance your communication skills in any business situation.

Communication and Leadership

In a business environment, you will be required from time to time to take on a leadership role. This is not so different from the school environment where you may be called upon to lead a student council meeting, or to run a school newspaper or graduation ceremony. In business, as in school, some followers will be unhappy with your decisions; others will not even complete their portion of the work. There will be difficult decisions to make regarding advertising, public relations, personnel management, and consensus building. The ideal follower (employee) is one who is loyal, offers constructive and creative criticism, and contributes his or her share of the workload and possibly more. Few projects reach successful completion in business unless both leaders and followers understand their roles and work as a team.

LEARNING FOCUS

- identify the characteristics of effective leadership
- practise participating in a meeting
- improve your oral communication skills

There are various leadership styles, with distinct characteristics:

- Autocratic (despotic) leaders give their followers or employees little voice in decision-making. This is a dictatorial leadership style that can cause considerable dissatisfaction among the followers. However, when the autocrat is the most knowledgeable of a group and needs to act quickly, this style can be effective.

- Laissez-faire leaders let their followers do things on their own. Such leaders permit employees to establish their own goals and objectives with little interference. However, they also provide little structure, frame of reference, or direction in their leadership.

- Democratic leaders encourage followers or employees to participate by sharing authority and responsibility with the group. Such leaders allow two-way communication and welcome the input of group members but do not relinquish their leadership role. They use a judicious combination of pressure and support to ensure that group or company objectives are achieved.

RUNNING A MEETING One of the major functions of a leader is planning and conducting meetings. Discussion groups, subcommittee meetings, and annual general meetings are the *engines* that drive business decisions. In some committees, you will be assigned the role of leader. At other times you will assume the role of a follower, helping to achieve co-operation and team commitment and consensus. Rotating the role of leader (**chairperson**) enables you to see the important role leaders and followers play in an effective business operation.

Before a meeting leaders must consider such details as

- the purpose of the meeting.
- the time and location of the meeting.
- arrangements for refreshments and equipment.
- preparation of an **agenda**.
- invitation to guest speakers.
- preparation of necessary handouts.

During a meeting leaders are responsible for

- welcoming meeting members.
- setting the tone of the meeting.
- maintaining control.
- balancing input from different participants.
- showing empathy and concern for all participants.

- resolving conflicts.
- making **motions**.
- conducting votes.
- posing questions for clarification.
- synthesizing conclusions based on the discussions.
- ensuring accurate **minutes** are kept.
- bringing the meeting to a close.

After the meeting the chairperson must ensure that minutes of meetings and any follow-up action plans are distributed to participants.

Activities

Understanding Leadership

1. Organize a role-play scenario involving a leader and some followers (employees) in a job situation. Have three groups perform different role plays in front of the class, each one demonstrating an example of one of the leadership styles described in this section.

   After you have viewed the three scenarios, conduct a whole-class reflective session on what you have seen to compare and contrast the different leadership styles. You might construct a chart that looks at the pros and cons of each type from the point of view of leader and follower.

2. Write an essay defining or analyzing the qualities and characteristics of an effective leader. You may focus on a specific business leader or look at the concept of a leader generally. Begin by sketching an outline of some of the traits you wish to discuss (e.g., decision-making skills, dependability, ability to work with others, ability to resolve conflicts, high energy).

3. Interview, in the classroom, someone from the business world or the wider community who you feel exemplifies the qualities of a leader. You might tape the interview instead and play it for the class to hear or view at a later date, or provide a written transcript like those in newspapers and magazines. If you are unable to arrange an interview with a leader, do some research on some famous business leader (present or past) and present his or her profile to the class.

4. For your next group project in any subject area, conduct a semi-formal meeting. Arrange a mutually agreeable time, location, duration, and agenda. Decide on a chairperson and a recorder to take notes and type up the minutes. Be sure to distribute the agenda at least one day before the meeting, and invite members to suggest new business to be

discussed. Remember that the chairperson is not only responsible for opening and closing the discussion, but must also ensure that members stay on topic and that all members who wish to speak get a chance.

Oral Business Presentations

An oral presentation can be impromptu and informal, such as being asked by three co-workers in the corridor what your new project involves. At the other end of the scale, it can be complex and formal, such as presenting a two-hour global marketing proposal to a company's shareholders via videoconferencing technology.

Participating in informal speaking situations helps you in the more formal ones, and vice-versa. For instance, when you speak casually to co-workers, you learn to listen closely to their questions to ensure they understand what you are saying. An attentive formal presenter will try to do the same, no matter what the size of the audience, by building time into a presentation for listeners to ask questions. In addition, the experience of speaking to large groups increases your sensitivity to an audience's range of knowledge and experience. This means that you will be less likely to assume that all members of even the smallest group will understand your message in the same way.

When giving an oral presentation, consider using the eight-step approach below:

SELECT A TOPIC Choose a subject in which you are interested. Your enthusiasm will be infectious. (Remember the AIDA formula mentioned earlier.) Make sure that you are able to find enough information so that you appear knowledgeable and well prepared to discuss all aspects of the content.

PURPOSE Do you want to entertain, to inform, to persuade, to summarize, to advocate action? Clarify your purpose before you begin work on your presentation.

IDENTIFY YOUR AUDIENCE AND VENUE Before you even begin research into your topic, ask yourself two basic questions: "Who is my audience?" and "What might they already know about my topic?" Be sure to find out as much about your audience as possible *before* the presentation. If you are unable to find out about their knowledge level on your topic, it is helpful at least to find out general background information such as the audience's age range, educational levels, gender, and cultural backgrounds.

Once you have established whom you will be addressing, you need to determine how much time you have for your presentation. Most novice presenters discover they have prepared far more information than they need for the amount of time available. It is also useful to find out how many other speakers will be preceding you. If you are at the end of a full afternoon of speakers, for example, you will need to be especially lively to keep your listeners' attention.

It is important to find out exactly *where* you will be speaking. (This is referred to as a **venue** or delivery environment.) Check out the room, if possible, to determine the number of electric outlets. Ask the organizers if they have the equipment you need for your presentation such as overhead projectors and presentation software. On the day of your presentation, try to arrive early to ensure that all the materials you need are on hand. If you can't arrive early, contact people who can, and ask them to check for you.

PREPARE YOUR OUTLINE Use point-form notes. Your outline should be a guide to lead you through your presentation. It should not be read verbatim. Consider the following when writing the outline:

- The introduction should capture the attention of the audience, define the topic and thesis statement, and provide a brief preview of what approach the presentation will take.

- The body of the presentation should support and explain the thesis, and use examples and illustrations to clarify and strengthen your point of view.

- The conclusion should re-emphasize the thesis and major points of the presentation.

ORGANIZE YOUR INFORMATION Once you have gathered most of your information together, experiment with different ways to organize it. When you have settled on a general structure, start writing note cards.

✓ CHECKLIST | USING NOTE CARDS

- ✓ Use large print, as it is easy to see in any lighting.
- ✓ Hold note cards (not full-size sheets) in one hand to allow for hand gestures to emphasize points.
- ✓ Limit each card to no more than *three* point-form phrases. This fosters a conversational tone and more eye contact with your audience.
- ✓ Number and colour-code your note cards to prevent you from losing your place.

✓ CHECKLIST USING VISUALS

✓ Use nothing smaller than a sixteen-point font when presenting to a room of over thirty people using an overhead screen.

✓ Introduce only one point at a time. Otherwise, your audience may read ahead and not listen while you expand on your first point.

✓ Do not use overly complex illustrations or lists of statistics onscreen as your audience will not have time to understand them.

✓ Reserve lengthy information for a handout.

✓ CHECKLIST USING TECHNOLOGY

✓ Keep your presentation simple when using presentation software. It is easy to get carried away with graphics and produce a presentation that is overdone.

✓ Don't overuse *drop-in* characters or animations. These can slow down your presentation and can quickly become tedious to your audience.

✓ Avoid using pre-timed sequencing for your slides. It is too easy to fall out of synchronization with the computer.

✓ Test your slides to see if they are easy to read on a large screen. Dark text with a light background is best for moderately lit rooms.

PRACTISE YOUR PRESENTATION Even a single rehearsal of your presentation can make a tremendous difference. Some presenters use audio- or videotape for a practice run. Many people report that they cringe at seeing and hearing themselves, but once they overcome the initial self-consciousness, they find it extremely useful. Taping your rehearsal, or even having a friend, colleague, or family member critique your presentation, can be constructive as well as confidence-building. Listen to that person's comments about your rehearsed performance and think about how you can improve it, if necessary, before the actual presentation.

USE WARM-UP STRATEGIES Just as athletes never jump into a game without a warm-up, think about what most relaxes you before you get up to speak. Sometimes reminding yourself of an amusing story can help to put things in perspective. Physicians recommend yawning to reduce nervousness. Posture is also important. *Keeping your chin up* actually helps you project your voice better and makes people feel more confident.

If you are ever overcome by nervousness, you might also try **visualization techniques**. Find a quiet space; then close your eyes and imagine the sounds and sights of a favourite place for a few minutes. This strategy works for many people.

MAKE YOUR PRESENTATION As you stand up to speak, remember the following:

- Give the audience a few minutes to settle down. You can even make a few casual remarks before beginning your topic.

- Be sure to maintain eye contact with the entire audience. If you're speaking to a large group, ensure that those on the far sides and in the back can hear you.

- Use **body language** to your advantage. Walk from side to side occasionally and use purposeful hand and facial gestures to emphasize points.

- Avoid reading long passages of text, either from note cards or overheads. Keep notes as much as possible in point form, as this will encourage you to speak in your own words.

- Inject as much enthusiasm into your voice as you can muster. Vary the pitch of your voice to emphasize key points.

- Be conversational but not overly informal: avoid *ahs* and *ums* to fill up silences. Practise leaving brief pauses between phrases, as it allows your listeners time to reflect on what you're saying, and gives you time to collect your thoughts.

- Invite your listeners to ask questions if they need something clarified.

- Plan your conclusion for maximum impact.

Activities

Oral Presentations and Business Issues

1. In small groups, choose a recent important business news story that has made the evening television news. Check several newspapers, magazines, and Web sites for related coverage. Prepare a business presentation for the class, noting and analyzing differences in how various media cover the story. Do newspapers from different parts of the country supply significantly different perspectives? Use presentation software and other technology as appropriate.

2. Use the research from your formal recommendation report prepared earlier to create a formal oral presentation for your classmates. Consider using presentation software, videos, audiotaped interview excerpts, or handouts.

3. Organize a small group discussion or debate on a business-related issue, such as
   - the North American attitude toward the balance of work and personal life versus that of other continents.
   - contributing factors to job satisfaction (competitive salary, travel, co-operative co-workers, professional development opportunities).
   - the increased earning and spending power of teens and the effects on the economy and new businesses or services.
   - shopping via the Internet and e-commerce.
   - policies that ensure equality in the Canadian workplace. (Check Statistics Canada and prepare charts and graphs to illustrate trends and use in discussion.)
   - business' responsibility to workers, to consumers, to global society, and to the environment.

4. In small groups, make up a set of thirty cards for a business game called "Be Decisive." Each card should contain a scenario requiring a decision, such as the one below. Players will be asked to choose a card and explain to the group what they would do in that scenario.

> You have a summer job at an ice-cream parlour. The owner has treated you well, providing training, promotions, and a graphics course for designing flyers. However, you have now been offered a better paying job at a hospital as a pharmacy assistant. You plan to study pharmacy in university, so this new job would be useful experience and good on a resumé. What will you do?

Producing, Presenting, and Documenting Your Work

A

Appendix A: 1—Elements of Effective Writing

Good writing has specific, identifiable qualities. Some qualities are unique to one type of writing (e.g., supporting evidence in expository writing or strong plot development in narrative writing). Others (e.g., clarity, precision, standard spelling) are qualities shared by all good writing.

To help you write effectively

- read widely.

- analyze what you read in order to identify qualities of good writing.

- find out the criteria for evaluation for assigned writing, *before* you start to write.

- attend to these criteria during the relevant stages of the writing process.

The information that follows provides an overview of the qualities of good writing. Use it to guide you in producing your written work.

The Writing Process

Generate ideas, make jot notes, and create a tentative outline. Brainstorming, talking, reading, freewriting, interviewing, observing, and listening all help you to generate the content of your writing.

DRAFTING/COMPOSING Decide on the purpose of the piece, its audience, and the subject's focus. Consider a suitable genre, mode, and tone. Work your notes into sentences and paragraphs.

REVISING Ask yourself what content needs to be changed, expanded, and deleted, and how parts can be combined to make your topic and purpose more clear. Think also about how you might increase your audience's interest. Use a thesaurus, and confer with classmates and your teacher to help you with diction. Consider your style carefully.

EDITING/PROOFREADING Pay attention to the mechanics of writing (punctuation, spelling, capitalization), grammar (subject–verb agreement, use of tenses, pronoun–antecedent agreement), and usage.

PUBLISHING Post your work in its final draft form on a bulletin board, submit copies to a class or school newspaper, or forward it to readers outside the school.

Expository Writing

PURPOSE Expository writing informs, enlightens, persuades, and sometimes entertains the reader. Produce pieces of writing (critical essays, opinion pieces, formal reports, instructions) that are clear and well focused, and that develop a controlling idea.

AUDIENCE Know your audience and write for that target group. Anticipate potential misunderstandings and possible counter-arguments on a particular topic. Provide sufficient information to answer potential questions.

CONTENT/MEANING Provide details that are relevant, accurate, substantive; that enhance your thesis statement; and that show independence of thought. Convey knowledge of your subject through evidence, definition, comparison or contrast, and logical reasoning. Support judgments and generalizations through persuasive examples and appropriate references to secondary print or non-print sources, or to personal experience.

ORGANIZATION/STRUCTURE/FORM Include a strong introduction to spark the reader's interest and frame the topic. Establish a focus (unity) and exclude extraneous or inappropriate content. Arrange your ideas in a logical order (coherence) and provide smooth transitions between sentences and paragraphs. In longer papers, section headings and subtitles can help establish transitions. Clearly convey a different aspect of the general topic in each paragraph. Rework any paragraphs that seem too short or too long. Emphasize the most important information and differentiate main ideas from supporting ones. Provide a strong conclusion that re-emphasizes your thesis statement.

SENTENCE STRUCTURE Produce clear, relevant, carefully considered sentences. Pay attention to subject–verb agreement, particularly when the subject is separated from the verb (e.g., The <u>computers</u> purchased by our office manager <u>are</u> networked.). Create sentence variety (simple sentences, compound sentences, complex sentences, combinations of short and longer sentences). Use some sentences that make statements, others that ask questions, convey surprise, or give commands. Longer compound or complex sentences should be used to express complicated ideas and to illustrate and provide examples as evidence. Omit run-on sentences and sentence fragments (except when used for effect).

VOICE Demonstrate voice (the personality you wish to project in the writing) suited to your subject, purpose, and audience. If appropriate, it should reveal your individual stance on the subject.

WORD CHOICE Use a precise, active vocabulary that conveys your thoughts accurately and concisely. Avoid vague terms, especially adjectives and adverbs such as *good*, *many*, or *quite*. Define specialized vocabulary and avoid unnecessary jargon.

CONVENTION Attend to the conventions of usage, grammar, punctuation, spelling, and capitalization. Errors in these elements of style can interfere with the clarity of your writing; they are stumbling blocks to comprehension and enjoyment.

Descriptive Writing

PURPOSE Clarify your purpose (e.g., to describe a scene, a particular character, a type of exotic bird) before you begin writing. Regardless of whether your purpose requires objective or subjective description, use *all* your senses to convey an impression of your subject to the reader. If the writing task involves factual, scientific description, avoid expressing personal thoughts and impressions.

AUDIENCE Keep your audience in mind when making decisions about word choice, figurative language, and imagery. Transmit images of persons, places, or objects in a clear and interesting manner.

CONTENT/MEANING Demonstrate a keen observation of persons and things. Provide well-chosen details to create a vivid word picture. Attend to details that convey a dominant impression (positive or negative) of a particular person, place, or object. Decide on the impression you want to give before composing the first draft so that the details all build toward that impression.

ORGANIZATION/STRUCTURE/FORM Just as expository writing is arranged in a rational logical order, descriptive details should be arranged in an identifiable sequence. The order or sequence of descriptive writing orients objects for the reader (with words such as *near*, *below*, *far away*). Chronological order, often used in narrative writing, provides a temporal sequence (with such words as *then*, *next*, *later*). Details may also be arranged according to their order of importance using such words as *significant*, *unimportant*, *redundant* to orient the reader. Use topic sentences to focus the reader.

SENTENCE STRUCTURE Use longer, more complex sentences with adjectives, adverbs, participial phrases, and subordinate clauses to add a pictorial quality. Include longer sentences as well, to convey a slower pace or more contemplative mood.

VOICE In objective description, the object being seen or heard ideally dominates the description. The writer's voice is more detached, the tone more factual. In subjective description, the perceptions, personal reactions, and emotions of the writer convey a specific tone and evoke (connote) a mood. For example, *a large house* states a fact while *a magnificent mansion* suggests a feeling. *Voice* in descriptive writing should convey what the object, person, or scene *means* to the writer who observes it.

WORD CHOICE Of all forms of writing, description perhaps best illustrates the power of words. Include figures of speech that appeal to the reader's senses (e.g., metaphors, similes, onomatopoeia), as well as those that evoke emotion. Use vivid adjectives, adverbs, participles, and compound modifiers. Use allusions and implied comparisons to enhance and clarify the description. Create description that is precise, concise, accurate, and honest. Avoid using ornate language or adjective piled on top of adjective.

CONVENTION Errors in written mechanics can be addressed by referring to a good style guide, large dictionary, spell checker, or thesaurus.

Narrative Writing

PURPOSE Narrative fiction (short stories, novels, plays) can both entertain and enlighten the reading audience. Although it may provide factual information, that is not its primary goal. Narrative non-fiction (autobiography, memoirs, personal-experience narratives) has both an informational and entertainment focus.

AUDIENCE Your narrative writing should engage and affect the reader. The tone of the narrative (humorous, wistful, sarcastic) is important because it directs the reader's response.

CONTENT/MEANING For fiction, think of a situation that lends itself to narrative, and use ingenuity to create a rich, interesting plot with an identifiable sequence of events. Provide a vivid and believable setting, develop varied characters, and attend to the various meanings or themes your story might convey.

For narrative non-fiction, accurately render the sequence of events (the who, what, where, when, and how) into words. Demonstrate the significance (the why) of those events.

ORGANIZATION/STRUCTURE/FORM Narrative writing requires a chronological order. Use transitional words (e.g., *that morning, later, the following Sunday*) to convey a flow of events. Because unity of thought and impression is important, remove unnecessary details or inconsistencies.

SENTENCE STRUCTURE Short sentences are often used deliberately in narrative fiction to describe rapid action, express strong feelings, or create dramatic effect. Such sentences should be balanced by longer sentences to avoid a choppy or monotonous tone. Long sentences extend the description of setting and character and can build suspense.

WORD CHOICE In narrative writing, words must convey strong images. Use sensory details and concrete language to develop plot, and describe characters and setting. Well-chosen verbs animate the story and lend power to the action. Draw on conversations between friends and family, as well as those of complete strangers you might overhear, to write realistic, believable dialogue.

VOICE Make sure that your narrative has a distinctive style and personality. Consider the narrative perspective carefully (first-person, third-person limited-omniscient or omniscient, or rarely, a second-person point of view) as this helps shape the voice, tone, and mood.

CONVENTION Narrative writing requires you to follow standard conventions of spelling, capitalization, usage, and grammar. Ensure that punctuation and paragraphing, particularly for dialogue, are correct.

Appendix A: 2—Documenting Sources

It may seem like a tedious task to copy out source information (e.g., authors, publishers, publication dates, URLs). However, this is an important part of the research process for several reasons:

- Secondary sources lend weight to your research paper by giving your argument extra strength and credibility.
- Source information enables readers to follow up on points only touched on in your paper.
- Since books go out of print, are republished with changes, or are sometimes substantially revised, it is crucial that you let your readers know the *exact* edition of a source you are using. With electronic sources, this becomes even more important since Web sites are so easily modified.
- Accurate citations in a research paper can prevent charges of plagiarism. Plagiarism detracts seriously from a writer's credibility; it is a kind of intellectual theft.

It is better to cite too many sources than too few or to try to pass others' ideas off as your own. Remember to analyze the quotations you use and to judge their validity in light of other research. By including your own perspective on the quotations you select, you avoid the patchwork effect of merely threading others' ideas together. You also establish your writing as alert and purposeful.

The two most popular formats for academic documentation are the MLA style (Modern Language Association) and the APA style (American Psychological Association). At the post-secondary level, MLA is most often used for literature and other disciplines in the humanities, such as history. The APA format is favoured by science and social science researchers. Ask your teacher which form of documentation he or she prefers, or whether to use a different style of citation: don't mix methods.

Bibliography

A bibliography is a complete list, alphabetized by author's last name, or title if no author is named, of every source you have used in your research. Even if you do not quote directly from a book you have consulted, it should be included in the bibliography if you feel it has in some way contributed to your knowledge of the topic.

The key elements required for all bibliographical entries are as follows:

- Name of author(s) (last name, then first name) (period)
- Full title of publication (underlined, or italicized if your teacher prefers) (period)
- Edition of publication (if multiple editions exist) (period)
- Place of publication (city, usually *not* country, province, or state) (colon)
- Name of publisher (comma)
- Date of publication (period)

Variations on this format apply if you are citing, for example, a journal, audio tape, Web site, or interview. When you have an unusual source, consult specific MLA or APA reference sources available at local libraries or find MLA and APA sites on the

Internet. Refer to the Pearson Web site at <www.pearsoned.ca/referencepoints/links> for relevant URL references.

MLA STYLE FOR A BIBLIOGRAPHY OR WORKS CITED LIST Note that the first line of any entry is flush with the left margin but all subsequent lines are indented. For further examples of this style, see Chapter 2.

A book with one author:
Richards, David Adams. <u>The Coming of Winter</u>. Toronto: Oberon Press, 1974.

A book with two authors/two editors (eds.):
Ryan, D.W.S., and T.P. Rossiter, eds. <u>Poetic Insight</u>. St. John's: Jesperson Press, 1987.

A book with more than two authors: (note the use of the Latin phrase *et al* meaning *and others*)
Flachmann, Kim, et al. <u>Reader's Choice</u>. 3rd ed. Scarborough: Prentice-Hall, 2000.

A signed article in a newspaper:
Jawhra, Barbara. "Politics and Revolution." <u>Ottawa Citizen</u> 10 Sept. 2000: B7.

An article in a magazine:
Schofield, John. "Back to School Online." <u>Maclean's</u> 6 Sept. 1999: 22-26.

An article in an on-line periodical:
Roberts, Alasdair. "Access Denied." <u>Media Magazine</u> Spring 1998
  <http://www.caj.ca/mediamag/spring98/media98.html>.

An audio recording (Compact Disc):
Dion, Celine. "It's All Coming Back to Me Now." <u>Celine All the Way…A Decade of Song</u>. Toronto: Sony Music Canada, 1999.

A television advertisement:
The Terry Fox Run Promotion. Advertisement. <u>CBC Newsworld</u> Aug. 23, 2000.

A cartoon/comic strip:
Larson, Gary. "The Far Side." Cartoon. <u>The Globe and Mail</u> 12 Dec. 1993: R16.

A video recording: (note that "Dir."is short for "Director"and that the medium, in this case, videocassette, is named)
Salt. Dir. Amber Goodwyn. Videocassette. National Film Board of Canada, 2000.

APA STYLE FOR A BIBLIOGRAPHY OR REFERENCES LIST In this format, only the first word and any proper nouns in the title of the cited work are capitalized. Note that the date of publication is written in parentheses after the author's name. In addition, in APA style the first line of each entry is indented five spaces, while subsequent lines are flush left.

A book with one author:
  Richards, D.A. (1974). <u>The coming of winter</u>. Toronto: Oberon Press.

A book with two author/two editors (Eds.):

Ryan, D.W.S., and Rossiter, T.P. (Eds.) (1987). <u>Poetic insight</u>. St. John's: Jesperson Press.

A signed article in a newspaper:

Gilstrap, E. (2001, January 4). Why education still matters in Canada. <u>The Vancouver Sun</u>, p. A14.

An article in a magazine:

Schofield, J. (1999, September 6). Back to school online. <u>Maclean's</u>, 22-26.

An article in an on-line periodical:

APA provides the following general template for on-line formats: Author's name, author's initial. (Year, month, day). Title of article. <u>Name of Periodical</u> (underlined or italicized according to teacher preference) (on-line serial) volume number (if available) issue number. Available URL.

Hagawa, R. G. (1998, April 2) Psychological effects of vitamins. <u>Psychology Round-up</u>, 12 (4) [on-line] Available WWW: http://www.psychround.edu.ca.

Source Citation

There are *two* ways in which to indicate the exact page location of a quotation or reference from the original source: parenthetical references, and footnotes or endnotes. Use one of these methods to credit precisely (with the exact page reference) the source of each quotation, idea, or paraphrase or précis of information that did not originate with you.

PARENTHETICAL REFERENCES Embedded directly in the text of your discussion, the author's last name and the page number are given in parentheses immediately after the quotation or paraphrase referred to. Note the excerpts below, from a student paper on *The Lord of the Rings*, by J.R.R. Tolkien.

- *MLA Method* (name–page method): If only one work by the author is referenced, only the author's last name and page number are given; if two or more books by the author are cited, the title must also be given. When the author's name is included in the text sentence, the parenthetical reference gives the page number only. Include a period *after* the parentheses (or, if the reference follows an indented quote, put the period after the quote).

  "The fame and success that <u>The Lord of the Rings</u> brought Tolkien...both surprised and perplexed him" (Grotta-Kurksa 8).

  Daniel Grotta-Kurska tells us that in 1896, when Tolkien was four years old, his father died of acute peritonitis (16).

- *APA Method* (name–date–page method): For paraphrased or summarized sources, APA requires only the name of the author and the date cited in parentheses. However, some teachers expect page numbers for any sources cited, so determine this *prior* to essay submission. If the author's name is included in the text, only the date of publication and page number need to be included in the parenthetical reference.

"The fame and success that <u>The Lord of the Rings</u> brought Tolkien...both surprised and perplexed him" (Grotta-Kurksa, 1976, 8).

Daniel Grotta-Kurska tells us that in 1896 when Tolkien was four years old, his father died of acute peritonitis (1976, 16).

FOOTNOTES AND ENDNOTES A footnote is a numbered note placed at the bottom of your page, whereas an endnote is a numbered reference note that appears in a list at the end of your whole document. MLA style includes footnotes and endnotes as options (although parenthetical references are now preferred). Both footnotes and endnotes use identical formatting (i.e., identical indentation, parentheses, italics, and commas). Footnotes and endnotes are *not* part of APA style for documenting sources.

Keep the following in mind when constructing footnotes or endnotes:

- Number the notes consecutively.
- Leave a space after the raised superscripted number.
- Indent the first line of each entry five spaces.
- Align all subsequent lines of the same footnote with the left-hand margin.
- Single-space lines within each entry, but double space between entries.
- Place the author's first name and initials first.
- List the title of the book with no punctuation following.
- List the publication facts in parentheses in the following order (city, colon, publisher, comma, year of publication), then page number(s).
- For notes citing a work referred to earlier, use only the last name of the author unless you are referring to two or more works by the same author.

Footnote/endnote reference for a book with a single author:
 [1] Graham Swift, <u>Last Orders</u> (Toronto: Vintage, 1997) 76.

Footnote/endnote reference for a book with two or more authors:
 [2] Robert Graves and Alan Hodge, <u>The Reader Over Your Shoulder</u> (New York: Macmillan, 1943) 227.

Footnote/endnote reference for a book that has been previously referred to:
 [3] Graves 232.

Appendix A: 3 — Producing Videos

Schools today make use of a wide range of technology. Video technology allows us to recreate reality with a series of camera images. Videos can be used, for example, to explore a day in the life of a school, to examine a topic in science, or to retell a historical event. Video productions can enliven existing dramatic scripts (e.g., the balcony scene from *Romeo and Juliet*) or capture dramatic scenes we create ourselves.

As with all presentations, video production requires both good planning and countless on-the-spot decisions. However, more than with many other presentation formats, video production is a *team* effort; it involves writers, directors, camera technicians, actors/announcers, sound technicians, and editors. Use the following tips to guide your team during the production process.

PRE-PRODUCTION STAGE

- Determine your purpose and your target audience.
- Choose a topic that will encourage your audience to think and respond.
- Assess the resources available, including time, equipment, and people.
- Develop a **storyboard** of the video's key scenes and events. This includes a series of sketches, arranged in order, to allow you to plan and preview what the camera will shoot.
- Develop a **shooting script**. This includes the written text or dialogue to be videotaped. It also provides descriptions of scenes, sounds, actions, and camera techniques to aid in the actual shooting.
- During rehearsals and **shoots**, adjust scenes as needed as you move from storyboard to on-location shots.

PRODUCTION STAGE

- Practise with the camera—learn how to use it before you begin.
- Use your storyboard and shooting script to guide you as you film.
- Use a steady hand when filming. Ensure that your subject is in focus and appropriately framed.
- Tape as many shots as you can (e.g., **close-ups**; **medium** and **long shots**; **panoramic shots**; shots that **pan** or **zoom in**). Scenes can be shot out of sequence and edited later.

POST-PRODUCTION STAGE

- Screen your raw film footage to determine its strengths and weaknesses.
- Delete, add, and rearrange the visual and audio components of your video.
- Use desktop video-editing tools (e.g., to create **jump-cuts** or dissolves).

PUBLIC SCREENING

- Show your edited production to your audience to gauge their reaction.

The partial storyboard sample and shooting script that follow are for a short promotional video to orient students and parents to Millennium High School.

MODEL: PARTIAL STORYBOARD

① EXTERIOR OF MILLENNIUM HIGH SCHOOL

② BUS ARRIVING AT SCHOOL

③ NARRATORS IN SCHOOL LOBBY

④ SCIENCE LAB WITH TEACHER AND STUDENTS

⑤ LEARNING RESOURCE CENTRE

⑥ STUDENTS PRACTISING LAYUPS

⑦ ART ROOM

⑧ CAFETERIA

MODEL: SHOOTING SCRIPT

PROMOTIONAL VIDEO

TITLE: Millennium High School—We Hope You Enjoy Your Stay

FADE IN: EXTERIOR MILLENNIUM HIGH SCHOOL—DAY

PANORAMIC SHOT OF high school to establish setting and to orient viewers.

BACKGROUND MUSIC to accompany shot.

PAN CAMERA (MEDIUM SHOT) of bus arriving and students leaving bus to enter school as VOICE-OVER (VO) narration starts.

> ANGELA LU (VO): What makes our high school unique is the people—teachers and students—who call this school home for six hours a day, one hundred and ninety days a year.

DISSOLVE TO: INTERIOR SCHOOL LOBBY SCENE.

ZOOM IN from LONG SHOT to CLOSE-UP SHOT of pair of student narrators (SALVADOR LOPEZ AND ANGELA LU).

> SALVADOR: Hello, my name is Salvador Lopez...

> ANGELA: ...and I'm Angela Lu. We're here to give you an orientation to our school...

> SALVADOR: ...not just the building, but its people and programs. Around here, we take pride in the ethic of care we have for each other.

DISSOLVE TO: LAB. Lighting should be bright in all shots to create a warm, inviting atmosphere. Narration continues as VOICE-OVER above sounds of laboratory activity.

PAN CAMERA (LONG SHOT) and ZOOM IN for MEDIUM SHOTS and CLOSE-UPS of activity. Narration continues as VOICE-OVER above sounds of laboratory activity.

> ANGELA (VO): Our teaching staff at Millennium High are well qualified. They teach us the concepts and skills we will need to become lifelong learners.

DISSOLVE TO: RESOURCE CENTRE.

MEDIUM SHOTS of individual students gathering books, using computers, while VO narration continues.

> SALVADOR (VO): Our Learning Resource Centre is well stocked with books and periodicals and we are connected via computers to the World Wide Web.

CUT TO: GYMNASIUM.

LONG SHOTS of girls practising layups...then CLOSE-UP of face of boy lifting weights, while VO narration continues.

ANGELA (VO): Our philosophy at Millennium High promotes a sound mind and a healthy body. Students keep fit by accessing programs in our gymnasiums and weight room.

CUT TO: THEATRE for MEDIUM SHOTS of students rehearsing play, while VO narration continues, synchronized with series of JUMP-CUTS to art room and music room.

SALVADORE (VO): Millennium High also offers top-notch instruction in the Arts. We have facilities here where students can showcase their creative talents in theatre, the visual arts, and music. Millennium provides a good balance between curricular and co-curricular programs.

CUT TO: ART ROOM

CUT TO: MUSIC ROOM

CUT TO: CAFETERIA

CLOSE-UP SHOT of students in cafeteria, while VO narration continues.

ANGELA (VO): We Millenniums relax in the cafeteria and enjoy refreshments, or just socialize with friends.

CUT TO: CREDITS run as background music (high energy) plays and slowly increases in volume as VO narration ends.

ANGELA (VO): Sure, high school prepares us with those skills we'll need for further study and work in the outside world. But it is also an important part of our happiness and well-being in the here and now....

SALVADOR (VO): At Millennium we feel motivated to do well. We also feel a sense of safety and belonging. So join our Millennium family. We hope you enjoy your stay.

THE END

Appendix A: 4—Working with Graphs

Graphs are essentially pictures of information. We are exposed to them in the newspaper, in reference materials we read for reports and research papers, and on the computer when we search for data on a given topic. Often a written paragraph of factual information or a numerical table with rows and columns of data can be made more interesting and easier to grasp when set up in visual form.

Examine the following table, which shows Canada's population by province. Note how it *changes shape* in the discussion of kinds of graphs that follows and how each graph type has its own unique strengths.

CANADIAN STATISTICS—POPULATION, CANADA, THE PROVINCES AND TERRITORIES

Statistics Canada Canada Statistique	1996	1997 Shown in thousands	1998	1999	2000
Canada	29,671.9	29,987.2	30,247.9	30,493.4	30,750.1
Newfoundland	560.6	554.1	545.4	540.8	538.8
Prince Edward Island	136.2	136.9	136.9	137.6	138.9
Nova Scotia	931.2	934.5	936.1	939.2	941.0
New Brunswick	753.0	754.2	753.4	754.3	756.6
Québec	7,274.0	7,302.6	7,323.5	7,349.1	7,372.4
Ontario	11,100.9	11,249.5	11,386.1	11,517.3	11,669.3
Manitoba	1,134.3	1,136.6	1,137.9	1,142.6	1,147.9
Saskatchewan	1,019.5	1,022.0	1,024.9	1,025.7	1,023.6
Alberta	2,780.6	2,837.2	2,907.0	2,959.4	2,997.2
British Columbia	3,882.0	3,959.7	3,997.5	4,028.1	4,063.8
Yukon	31.9	32.2	31.5	31.1	30.7
Northwest Territories	x	41.8	41.1	41.1	42.1
Nunavut	x	25.9	26.5	27.0	27.7

x data unavailable, not applicable or confidential.
1. On July 1 of each year.
Source: Statistics Canada, CANSIM, Matrices 6367–6378 and 6408–6409.
Last modified: November 15, 2000.

There are three major kinds of graphs:
- the line graph
- the bar graph
- the pie graph

LINE GRAPH This kind of graph illustrates information in a continuous line. Line graphs are often used to show changes (in quantity) over some variable, usually time. The vertical axis shows the subject of the information (i.e., what is changing). The horizontal axis indicates the passing of time (e.g., in years, decades, centuries).

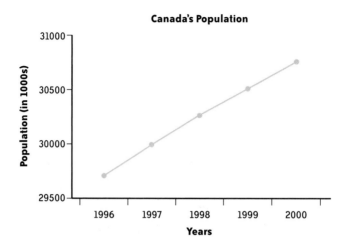

Canada's Population

BAR GRAPH In this kind of graph, each column represents a category of information. A bar graph could be used to compare different categories at the same point in time (i.e., a snapshot comparison). Alternatively, as in the case below, it could show the change (in quantity) of a given category over time. A stacked bar graph, with different colours or shading within each bar, compares various subcategories within a particular category.

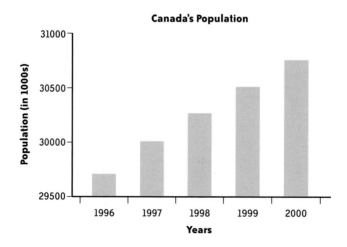

Canada's Population

PIE GRAPH Also referred to as a circle graph, a pie graph shows relationships of parts to other parts and to the whole, often at a given point in time. The graph following uses the information from the table on page 339 of Canada's population by province and territory in the year 2000. These figures have been converted to percentages to represent population proportions for each province or territory relative to the population of the country.

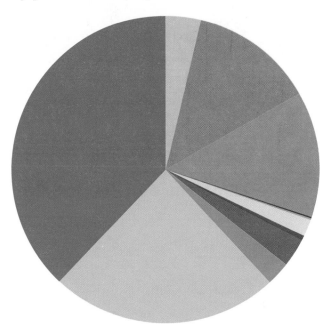

- **Manitoba** 3.73%
- **Saskatchewan** 3.33%
- **Alberta** 9.75%
- **British Columbia** 13.22%
- **Northwest Territories** 0.14%
- **Yukon** 0.10%
- **Nunavut** 0.09%

- **Newfoundland** 1.75%
- **Prince Edward Island** 0.45%
- **Nova Scotia** 3.06%
- **New Brunswick** 2.46%
- **Québec** 23.98%
- **Ontario** 37.95%

Grammar, Usage, and Mechanics

B

Common Writing Problems and How to Solve Them

Reviewing the Basics to Improve Your Writing

Common Writing Problems and How to Solve Them

Run-on Sentences

PROBLEM: Two main clauses written as one sentence, either without punctuation or with only a comma between them. (A *clause* is a group of words with a subject and verb.)

ERROR: *In many maps North America seems larger than Africa this is a distortion of the Mercator projection.*

Add a period and a capital letter to create two separate sentences.

REVISION: *In many maps North America seems larger than Africa. **This** is a distortion of the Mercator projection.*

Add a semi-colon between the two clauses.

REVISION: *In many maps North America seems larger than Africa; this is a distortion of the Mercator projection.*

Use a comma and a coordinating conjunction (*but*) between the two clauses.

REVISION: *In many maps North America seems larger than Africa, **but** this is a distortion of the Mercator projection.*

Introduce one clause with a subordinating conjunction (*while*) and use a comma before the other clause.

REVISION: ***While** in many maps North America seems larger than Africa, this is a distortion of the Mercator projection.*

Sentence Fragments

PROBLEM: A sentence is missing a subject:

ERROR: *Canada is the largest country by area in North America. Also boasts the most fresh water.*

Add a subject to make the sentence fragment into a sentence.

REVISION: *Canada is the largest country by area in North America. **It** also boasts the most fresh water.*

Combine the sentence fragment with a sentence, rewording it if necessary.

REVISION: *Canada is the largest country by area in North America, **and** also boasts the most fresh water.*

PROBLEM: A sentence is missing a verb:

ERROR: *Mount Denali is the highest mountain in North America at 6194 m Mount Logan, in the Yukon, a close second at 5951 m.*

Make the sentence fragment a sentence by adding a verb.

REVISION: *Mount Denali is the highest mountain in North America at 6194 m. Mount Logan, in the Yukon, **is** a close second at 5951 m.*

Join the sentence fragment to a complete sentence, rewording if necessary.

REVISION: *Mount Denali is the highest mountain in North America at 6194 m, **but** Mount Logan, in the Yukon, is a close second at 5951 m.*

Lack of Subject–Verb Agreement

PROBLEM: Verb does not agree with the main part of the subject:

| | **ERROR:** | *A chain of mountains separate B.C. and Alberta.* |
| Make the verb agree with the main part of the subject (*chain*). | **REVISION:** | *A **chain** of mountains **separates** B.C. and Alberta.* |

PROBLEM: Using the incorrect form of a verb with a subject that has two parts:

	ERROR:	*The Pacific Ocean and Alaska borders B.C. on the west.*
If the parts of the subject joined by *and* name more than one thing, use the plural form of a verb.	**REVISION:**	***The Pacific Ocean and Alaska border** B.C. on the west.*
	ERROR:	*Alberta's capital and largest city are Edmonton.*
If the parts of the subject joined by *and* refer to the same thing, use the singular form of a verb.	**REVISION:**	***Alberta's capital and largest city is** Edmonton.*
	ERROR:	*Neither Edmonton nor Calgary are as cold as Fort McMurray.*
If the subject has two parts joined by *or* or *nor*, make the verb agree with the part of the subject closer to *or* or *nor*.	**REVISION:**	*Neither Edmonton nor **Calgary is** as cold as Fort McMurray.*

PROBLEM: Using the incorrect form of a verb with a subject that has two or more parts preceded by *many a, every,* or *each*:

| | **ERROR:** | *Every skier and nature lover enjoy the Rockies.* |
| Use the singular form of a verb. | **REVISION:** | ***Every** skier and nature lover **enjoys** the Rockies.* |

PROBLEM: Using the incorrect form of a verb with a subject separated from a verb:

| | **ERROR:** | *The peregrine falcon as well as the eastern wolverine is an endangered species.* |
| Make the verb agree with its subject, avoid phrases like *as well as, in addition to,* and *together with*. | **REVISION:** | *The peregrine falcon **and** the eastern wolverine **are** endangered species.* |

PROBLEM: Using the incorrect form of a verb with a subject that is an amount:

	ERROR:	*Six months of winter make life difficult above the Arctic Circle.*
If the amount is considered a single unit, use the singular form of a verb.	**REVISION:**	***Six months of winter makes** life difficult above the Arctic Circle.*
	ERROR:	*The last few winters has been slightly warmer than usual.*
If the amount is considered as separate units, use the plural form of a verb.	**REVISION:**	*The last few **winters have** been slightly warmer than usual.*

PROBLEM: Using the incorrect form of a verb with the number or a number as the subject:

| | **ERROR:** | *A number of unusual birds nests in northern Manitoba.* |
| If *number* is preceded by a, use the plural form of a verb. | **REVISION:** | ***A number of unusual birds nest** in northern Manitoba.* |

| | ERROR: | *The number of caribou are decreasing.* |
| If *number* is preceded by *the*, use the singular form of a verb. | REVISION: | **The number of caribou is** *decreasing.* |

PROBLEM: Using the incorrect form of a verb when the subject is a noun referring to a group:

	ERROR:	*The herd gather every summer.*
If the subject is considered to be the whole group, use the singular form of a verb.	REVISION:	**The herd gathers** *every summer.*
	ERROR:	*The herd moves in different directions.*
If the subject refers to individual group members, use the plural form of a verb.	REVISION:	**The herd move** *in different directions.*

PROBLEM: Using the incorrect form of a verb when the subject is a singular pronoun that refers to no specific person, place, or thing:

	ERROR:	*Each of Canada's provinces have extensive water resources.*
If the pronoun is singular, use the singular form of a verb.	REVISION:	**Each** *of Canada's provinces* **has** *extensive water resources.*
	ERROR:	*Some of the hydro power are sold to the United States.*
Use the singular form of a verb when the pronoun refers to a singular noun.	REVISION:	**Some of the hydro power is** *sold to the United States.*
	ERROR:	*Some of the provinces sells hydro power cheaply to the United States.*
Use the plural form of a verb when the pronoun refers to a plural noun.	REVISION:	**Some of the provinces sell** *hydro power cheaply to the United States.*

Verb Tenses and Shifts

PROBLEM: Forming an irregular verb incorrectly:

| | ERROR: | *He buyed the shirt in Goose Bay.* |
| Consult a dictionary to find the correct form of irregular verbs. | REVISION: | *He* **bought** *the shirt in Goose Bay.* |

PROBLEM: An incorrect shift in tense (the time—past, present, future—shown by a verb):

| | ERROR: | *When the storm hit St. John's, the electricity immediately goes off.* |
| When events occur at the same time, use the same verb tense. | REVISION: | *When the storm* **hit** *St. John's, the electricity immediately* **went** *off.* |

PROBLEM: Failure to shift tense to show that one event preceded another:

| | ERROR: | *Many people already collected extra food and water before the storm hit.* |
| Shift tenses to show clearly the sequence of events. | REVISION: | *Many people* **had already collected** *extra food and water before the storm hit.* |

Pronoun Shifts and References

PROBLEM: An incorrect reference in gender when the antecedent (the noun or pronoun to which a pronoun refers) can be male or female:

	ERROR:	*Everyone has his favourite writer.*
Use both male and female pronouns.	**REVISION**:	*Everyone has **his or her** favourite writer.*
Eliminate the pronoun.	**REVISION**:	*Everyone has **a** favourite writer.*
	ERROR:	*The nature lover may find that Jack London's works interest him.*
Make both the noun referred to (the antecedent) and the pronoun plural.	**REVISION**:	*Nature **lovers** may find that Jack London's works interest **them**.*

PROBLEM: An incorrect shift in person or number (the singular and plural forms of nouns and pronouns):

For more information on the person of pronouns, see page 362.	**ERROR**:	*The reader enjoys* The Call of the Wild *because we admire Buck.*
Use an antecedent in the same person and number as the pronoun.	**REVISION**:	***We** enjoy* The Call of the Wild *because **we** admire Buck.*
	ERROR:	*Jaye likes Farley Mowat because you can learn about the North from his works.*
Use a pronoun in the same person and number as the antecedent.	**REVISION**:	*Jaye likes Farley Mowat because **she** can learn about the North from his works.*
Use a noun, not a pronoun.	**REVISION**:	*Jaye likes Farley Mowat because **readers** can learn about the North from his works.*

PROBLEM: An incorrect shift in person when the antecedent is a singular pronoun that refers to no specific person, place, or thing (an indefinite pronoun):

	ERROR:	*Each of the students makes notes in their journals on* Never Cry Wolf.
Use the singular form of the pronoun.	**REVISION**:	***Each** of the students makes notes in **his or her** journal on* Never Cry Wolf.
Change the pronoun antecedent to a plural form.	**REVISION**:	***All** the students make notes in **their** journals on* Never Cry Wolf.
Replace the indefinite pronoun antecedent with a noun antecedent.	**REVISION**:	***The students** make notes in **their** journals on* Never Cry Wolf.

PROBLEM: A vague or weak pronoun reference:

	ERROR:	Never Cry Wolf *is very descriptive, which most readers enjoy.*
Reword the sentence to show a clear antecedent.	**REVISION**:	Never Cry Wolf *is filled with **vivid descriptions, which** most readers enjoy.*

PROBLEM: Indefinite use of *you* or *they*:

> **ERROR:** *In Never Cry Wolf, they [or you] have detailed information about wolf behaviour.*

If *number* is preceded by *the*, use the singular form of a verb.

> **REVISION:** **Never Cry Wolf provides** *detailed information about wolf behaviour.*

PROBLEM: A pronoun that could refer to either antecedent:

> **ERROR:** *When the writer met the exhausted hunter, he asked him many questions.*

Use a noun and an adjective instead of the pronoun.

> **REVISION:** *When the writer met the exhausted hunter, he asked* **the weary man** *many questions.*

Misplaced or Dangling Modifiers

PROBLEM: Misplacing a modifier (a word or group of words that helps describe or clarify another word or group of words):

> **ERROR:** *Iqaluit, in the east Arctic, is warmer than Resolute with a normal January temperature of −25°C.*

Move the modifier as close as possible to the word or group of words modified.

> **REVISION:** *In the east Arctic,* **Iqaluit, with a normal January temperature of −25°C,** *is warmer than Resolute.*

PROBLEM: Lack of clarity as to what the modifier is describing (dangling modifier):

> **ERROR:** *Having an ice-free port, winter does not close down shipping.*

Reword the sentence to include the word or group of words modified.

> **REVISION:** **Having an ice-free port, the town** *does not close down shipping in winter.*

Missing or Misplaced Possessive Apostrophes

PROBLEM: Missing apostrophes ('); singular nouns:

> **ERROR:** *The Arctics animal life is part of our biology classes studies.*

Use an apostrophe (') and *s* to form the possessive of every singular noun.

> **REVISION:** *The* **Arctic's** *animal life is part of our biology* **class's** *studies.*

PROBLEM: Missing and misplaced apostrophes; plural nouns:

> **ERROR:** *The student's voices were very quiet.*

With a plural noun ending in *s*, use an apostrophe after *s*.

> **REVISION:** *The* **students'** *voices were very quiet.*

> **ERROR:** *The savagery of wolves is exaggerated in some peoples minds.*

With plural nouns not ending in *s*, use an apostrophe and *s*.

> **REVISION:** *The savagery of wolves is exaggerated in some* **people's** *minds.*

PROBLEM: Missing or misused apostrophes; possessive forms of pronouns:

ERROR: *Everyones view of wolves is negative.*

Use an apostrophe and *s* to form the possessive of a singular pronoun that refers to no specific person, place, or thing.

REVISION: ***Everyone's*** *view of wolves is negative.*

ERROR: *Because wolves affect animal populations, their's is an important role.*

Do not use an apostrophe to form the possessive of a pronoun that refers to a specific person, place, or thing.

REVISION: *Because wolves affect animal populations,* ***theirs*** *is an important role.*

PROBLEM: Confusion between *its* and *it's*:

ERROR: *A deer eating it's way through a field of crops is a problem.*

Do not use an apostrophe in the possessive personal pronoun *its.*

REVISION: *A deer eating* ***its*** *way through a field of crops is a problem.*

ERROR: *Its an important role of wolves to limit deer populations.*

Use an apostrophe in the contraction of *it is* and *it has.*

REVISION: ***It's*** *an important role of wolves to limit deer populations.*

Missing Commas

PROBLEM: Missing commas in introductory phrases or clauses:

ERROR: *To be sure they also eat smaller animals.*

Use a comma after introductory words.

REVISION: *To be sure, they also eat smaller animals.*

PROBLEM: Missing commas in a series:

ERROR: *Wolves are found in northern Canada Alaska and northern Russia.*

Use commas to separate words in a series.

REVISION: *Wolves are found in northern Canada, Alaska, and northern Russia.*

PROBLEM: Missing commas in compound sentences:

ERROR: *Wolves once ranged throughout North America but human activity has limited their habitat.*

Use a comma between the main clauses of a compound sentence, unless they are very short.

REVISION: *Wolves once ranged throughout North America, but human activity has limited their habitat.*

PROBLEM: Missing or misplaced commas; adjectives:

ERROR: *Years of being hunted have made them elusive wary creatures.*

If adjectives have equal importance, separate them with a comma.

REVISION: *Years of being hunted have made them elusive, wary creatures.*

PROBLEM: Missing commas; non-essential or essential groups of related words:

> **ERROR:** *Wolves in pairs or sometimes in packs hunt mainly large animals.*

If a related group of words adds information that is non-essential, i.e., it could be deleted without changing the meaning of the sentence, set off the group with commas.

> **REVISION:** *Wolves, **in pairs or sometimes in packs,** hunt mainly large animals.*

> **ERROR:** *Wolves which usually kill weak or unhealthy animals help control the populations on which they prey.*

> **REVISION:** *Wolves, **which usually kill weak or unhealthy animals,** help control the populations on which they prey.*

> **ERROR:** *The wolf, that is found in Alaska, is called the grey wolf.*

Do not set off a related group of words that is essential to the meaning of a sentence. If such a group of words were deleted, the sentence would make no sense, or change in meaning.

> **REVISION:** ***The wolf that is found in Alaska** is called the grey wolf.*

> **ERROR:** *The well-known writer, Farley Mowat, describes its habits in several books.*

> **REVISION:** ***The well-known writer Farley Mowat** describes its habits in several books.*

Reviewing the Basics to Improve Your Writing

The alphabetized terms listed here provide definitions of grammatical elements and examples of usage. Follow the cross-references after each definition to see more detailed information on a topic.

Adjectives

adjective—a word that modifies or describes a noun or pronoun

For more about nouns, see page 356. For more about pronouns, see page 362.

Adjectives can be used to make nouns and pronouns more vivid and precise by telling how many, which one, or what kind.
> <u>Two</u> burglars came through <u>that</u> window and stole my <u>antique</u> vase.

- **determiner:** tells which one or how many and includes the following:
  - article *the, a, an*
  - demonstrative adjective *this, that, these, those*
- **proper adjective:** is formed from a proper noun and begins with a capital *British monarchy, Chinese diplomat*

  For more about proper nouns, see page 356.

- **compound adjective:** combines two or more words to form an adjective, usually with a hyphen *two-year-old child, well-researched essay*
- **comparative adjective:** compares two items, whereas the **superlative adjective** compares more than two items. Most one-syllable adjectives and some two-syllable adjectives add *-er* to create the comparative form, and *-est* to create the superlative form *slow, slower, slowest*. Others use *more* and *most* or *less* and *least*, as in *beautiful, more beautiful, most beautiful*. Still others are irregular, such as *little, less, least*.

COMMON USAGE PROBLEM: Using the superlative when comparing two things, or the comparative when comparing more than two.
Which is bigger, Saturn or Jupiter?
Which is fastest—a Ferrari, Porsche, or Lamborghini?

COMMON USAGE PROBLEM: Using *more, most, less,* or *least* if the *-er* or *-est* ending has been used.

ERROR: *She was more faster than the other runners.*

REVISION: *She was faster than the other runners.*

COMMON USAGE PROBLEM: Using comparative or superlative forms with adjectives that are already absolute, such as perfect, ideal, unique, and true.

ERROR: *He has the most unique sense of style.*

REVISION: *He has a unique sense of style.*

STYLE TIP   Avoid vague adjectives such as *good, nice, awful,* and *interesting.* Use more precise adjectives to make your writing more vivid.

Adverbs

adverb—a word that modifies a verb, an adjective, another adverb, or a whole sentence or clause

conjunctive adverb—a word that connects ideas between clauses
  Adverbs can be used to give more detail, for example:

For more about conjunctive adverbs, see page 355.

- **when used with verbs** to answer: how? when? where? to what extent?
  Zoki was <u>fully</u> aware of the risks involved.

- **when used with adjectives or other adverbs** to answer: to what extent?
  He was <u>very</u> determined to achieve his goal.

  Many adverbs are **formed from adjectives** by adding *-ly clearly.* Sometimes the spelling of the adjective must change when *-ly* is added *eerie–eerily, happy–happily*
  Other adverbs serve as conjunctions *indeed, meanwhile, moreover, nevertheless, therefore.* **Conjunctive adverbs** are often used in formal writing and are usually preceded by a semicolon and followed by a comma.
  Like adjectives, adverbs have **comparative** and **superlative forms**. Most one-syllable adverbs and some two-syllable adverbs add *-er* to create the comparative form and *-est* to create the superlative form *fast, faster, fastest.* Others use *more* and *most* or *less* and *least,* as in *often, more often, most often.* Still others are irregular, such as *well, better, best.*

For more about comparative and superlative forms of adjectives, see page 349.

COMMON USAGE PROBLEM: Confusing an adjective with the adverb that is formed from it. Use an adverb to modify a verb.
  Come ~~quick~~ quickly, before someone sees you!

COMMON USAGE PROBLEM: Confusing adjective and adverb forms such as *good–well* and *bad–badly*. *Good* and *bad* are always adjectives. *Well* and *badly* are adverbs, although *well* can also be used as an adjective to describe someone's health.

> It's a <u>good</u> idea to rest if you don't feel <u>well</u>.

NOTE ON USAGE: An adverb that modifies a verb can usually appear in various positions in a sentence without changing the meaning of the sentence. Some adverbs that tell *to what extent* (such as *only, nearly, almost,* and *merely*) must be placed next to the words they modify, or the meaning of the sentence will change.

> *I nearly fell and hit my head.* [I didn't fall and hit my head.]
>
> *I fell and nearly hit my head.* [I did fall but didn't hit my head.]

STYLE TIP

Use strong adverbs to describe actions clearly and concisely, and to indicate precise degrees of certain qualities or conditions. Take care, however, not to overuse vague adverbs such as *actually, truly,* or *really.*

Apostrophes

For more about possessive forms, see page 358.

Apostrophes are generally used to show **possession** or to show that letters are missing in **contractions**. Apostrophes are also used to **pluralize** abbreviations having more than one period. *Simone's, sister-in-law's, spring of '99, I.D.'s.*

NOTE ON USAGE: The apostrophe is now rarely used to pluralize numbers and letters, except when eliminating it causes confusion.

> *1990s, MPs, 8s, but s's, no's*

Clauses

clause—a group of words that contains a subject and a verb

Clauses (and phrases) are the building blocks of sentences. There are two major types of clauses.

- main clause: a group of words that makes sense as a sentence on its own
- subordinate clause: a group of words that contains a subject and verb but does not make sense on its own, and so must be linked to a main clause

> **main clause**
> *I signed up for the seminar on effective study strategies,*
>
> **subordinate clause**
> *which should help me to improve my marks.*

There are three types of subordinate clauses.

- **noun clause:** used as a noun in the sentence and introduced with words such as *that, which, whomever, how, where, what, who, whose, when, why*
  > <u>*How long the seminar will be*</u> *is still not clear.*

- **adjective clause:** used as an adjective in the sentence and often introduced with words such as *that, which, what, whom, whose, whoever, where, when*
  > *The seminar leader,* <u>*whom I met yesterday*</u>*, is highly regarded.*

— **adverb clause:** used as an adverb in the sentence and introduced with such words and phrases as *after, as soon as, where, because, so that, although, unless, as if, as though*
Unless more people sign up, the seminar may be cancelled.

COMMON USAGE PROBLEM: Using commas to set off **restrictive clauses** from the rest of a sentence. Use commas to set off **non-restrictive clauses**.

- **restrictive clauses:** groups of words that are necessary to identify or complete the meaning of the sentence. These words or word groups define or limit the meaning of the word to which they relate.
The athlete who was injured was rushed to hospital.

The underlined clause is restrictive because it identifies which athlete is being referred to.

- **non-restrictive clauses:** groups of words that are not essential to the meaning of the sentence and could be omitted without trouble. They do not define or limit the meaning of the word to which they relate.
The coach, who seemed upset by the injury, devised a new game plan.

The underlined clause is non-restrictive because the sentence would still make sense if the clause were omitted.

STYLE TIP

To achieve a variety of sentence lengths when you are revising a piece of writing, look for short, simple sentences that can be subordinated to main clauses in other sentences.

Two simple sentences: *She might make the Olympic team. She should try harder.*

One (combined) sentence: *If she tries harder, she might make the Olympic team.*

Look also for long sentences with strings of clauses that can be separated into shorter sentences with fewer clauses.

Long sentence, string of clauses: *David, who has just returned from Asia, now volunteers one hour a week at the museum, which is on Laurier Street, where I met him.*

Shorter sentences, fewer clauses: *David has just returned from Asia. He now volunteers one hour a week at the museum, which is on Laurier Street. That's where I met him.*

Colons

In general, a **colon** calls attention to what follows it. Use it

- to introduce a **list**, especially a list preceded by the words *these, following,* or *as follows.*
The recipe calls for these spices: salt, pepper, and cumin. The directions are as follows: Chop the onion....

- **between main clauses** if the second clause restates, clarifies, or illustrates the first clause. For more about main clauses, see page 351.
Beans and rice are natural complements: they are part of many Latin American dishes.

- before a long or formal **quotation**. For more about quotations, see page 364.
Shirley Jackson starts her story "The Lottery" as follows: "The morning of June 27th was clear and sunny...."

- after the **salutation**, or greeting, of a business letter. *Dear Manager:*

Also, use colons with **numerals** in the following circumstances:

- between the hour and minute *8:45, 5:15*
- between chapter and verse references to sacred texts
  Jerusalem Talmud, Sotah 3:16a, Matthew 4:2-4, Koran 6:115

Commas

Commas are used to make writing clear and to allow the reader to pause. Wrongly omitting them can confuse readers; using them incorrectly or too often will make writing unclear or disjointed. Commas are used in the following ways:

- to **separate three or more words or word groups** in a series
  After the holiday, Martin had mosquito bites, sunburn, and heat stroke.

NOTE ON USAGE: The use of the **series comma**, which places a comma before the last group of words, is usually optional. Whatever you do, be consistent, and always use a comma if omitting it would confuse the reader, as in the following sentence:
  Jazz, blues, rhythm and blues, gospel, and country music all played a part in the birth of rock and roll.

Without the serial comma here, someone might read "gospel and country" as a single category like "rhythm and blues."

- before a **coordinating conjunction joining two main clauses**   For more about main clauses, see page 351.
  Elvis Presley and Buddy Holly came from the world of country music, but they won fame in rock-and-roll.

COMMON USAGE PROBLEM: Using commas between two or more verbs with the same subject.
  <u>S   V</u>   <u>V</u>
  *A tragic **plane crash** cut short Buddy Holly's career and **claimed** the lives of several other rock stars.*

COMMON USAGE PROBLEM: Using commas to set off a noun clause.
  <u>That rock-and-roll was born in Cleveland</u> is not disputed.

NOTE ON USAGE: If the clauses are short, you may omit the comma if the meaning of the sentence would still be clear.
  My mother loves music from the 1950s and I also love it.

In the following sentence, a comma is necessary for clarity.
  My father worshipped Elvis, and millions of others did too.

- to set off **non-essential, or non-restrictive adjective clauses**   For more about non-restrictive clauses, see page 352.
  Chuck Berry, <u>who had studied to be a hairdresser,</u> had an early hit called "Maybelline."

COMMON USAGE PROBLEM: Setting off essential, or restrictive, adjective clauses with commas.
  The rock singer who first recorded "La Bamba" was Richie Valens.

- to set off **non-essential, or non-restrictive, phrases**
  The Chords, <u>an African American group,</u> recorded "Sh-Boom" in 1954.

COMMON USAGE PROBLEM: Setting off essential, or restrictive, phrases with commas.
  The Canadian group the Crew Cuts recorded the song two months later.

- to set off an **introductory adverb clause**
  <u>When a film was made about Valens,</u> Los Lobos recorded a new version of "La Bamba."

For more about adverb clauses, see page 352.

- after **long introductory prepositional phrases or a string of introductory prepositional phrases**
  <u>For both the Chords and the Crew Cuts,</u> "Sh-Boom" was a huge hit and a big seller.

For more about prepositional phrases, see page 358.

NOTE ON USAGE: After a short introductory prepositional phrase, a comma is not necessary unless it is needed for clarity or for emphasis.

> To teenagers the new music was fresh and exciting.

In the following sentence, a comma is used for emphasis.

> <u>In 1954,</u> disk jockey Alan Freed began calling the music rock-and-roll.

- between **adjectives of equal importance**
  <u>Compelling, dangerous</u> waves drew the mainly young crowd.

For more about adjectives, see page 349.

COMMON USAGE PROBLEM: Using a comma if the adjectives do not have equal importance, that is, if it does not make sense to insert the word *and* between them, as in the following sentence.

> Some singers today have done their own versions of <u>great old</u> songs from the 1950s.

- after **expressions that interrupt** such as "for example," "that is" (or their abbreviations, e.g., i.e.), "by the way," and "on the other hand."
  Female groups (<u>e.g.,</u> the Shirelles and the Supremes) rose to fame in the 1960s.

  <u>By the way,</u> Diana Ross first won fame with the Supremes.

- to set off **terms of direct address**
  <u>Chris,</u> do you know about the Platters?

- to set off **tag questions** such as "didn't you?" or " have you?", which suggest an answer to the statement that precedes it.
  You also liked the Beatles a lot<u>, didn't you</u>?

- to separate the parts of a **place name or address**
  <u>Toronto, Ontario,</u> was the first Canadian city the Beatles played.

- to separate the parts of a **date**, except when only two elements of the date are given
  <u>Friday, February 7, 1964,</u> marks the Beatles' landing in New York.

NOTE ON USAGE: No comma is needed if only the month and day of the month are given.

> That February 7 was a crazy day in New York.

Conjunctions

conjunction—a word that links two or more words or groups of words

Conjunctions are the links that can connect related information in sentences in meaningful ways. They can help the writer avoid stringing together a series of short, choppy sentences.

- **coordinating conjunctions:** link two or more words or groups of words of equal importance *and, but, or, nor, for, yet, so*
  Travelling to distant countries is exciting <u>but</u> can be expensive.

- **subordinating conjunctions:** make a clause within the sentence subordinate (less important) and link the clause to the rest of the sentence *after, although, because, even though, if, since, so that, unless, when, while*

  For more about clauses, see page 351.

  > *It is important to get the appropriate vaccinations <u>so that</u> you don't become ill while you're away.*

- **correlative conjunctions:** work in pairs to link two words or groups of words of equal importance *both...and, just as...so (too), not only...but (also), either...or, neither...nor, whether...or*

  > <u>*Whether*</u> *you plan a short trip <u>or</u> a long one, check with your doctor to see that your vaccinations are up to date.*

- **conjunctive adverbs:** link main clauses and clarify the relationship between clauses *also, as a result, besides, consequently, for example, for instance, however, indeed, meanwhile, nevertheless, on the other hand, similarly, therefore, thus*

  > *Some people are squeamish about getting shots; <u>nevertheless,</u> the discomfort of a vaccination is preferable to a serious illness.*

COMMON USAGE PROBLEM: Using *like* as a subordinating conjunction. Use *like* to make a comparison; use the subordinating conjunction *as* or *as if* to introduce a subordinate clause. Note that *as* sometimes introduces clauses in which all or part of the verb is omitted but understood, as in the third sentence below.

PREPOSITION: *My sister drives <u>like</u> a maniac.*

SUBORDINATING CONJUNCTION: *She drives <u>as if</u> she were in a race.*

SUBORDINATING CONJUNCTION: *She does not drive <u>as</u> a good driver should [drive].*

NOTE ON USAGE: *So* is acceptable as a coordinating conjunction in informal English, but in formal writing this usage is discouraged.

AVOID: *My computer had a virus, <u>so</u> I borrowed a laptop.*

BETTER: *I borrowed a laptop <u>because</u> my computer had a virus.*

Also discouraged in formal English is the use of *so* for the subordinating conjunction *so that*. In general, replace *so* with *so that* whenever *so that* makes sense in a sentence.

AVOID: *I bought virus-protection software <u>so</u> my computer would be protected.*

BETTER: *I bought virus-protection software <u>so that</u> my computer would be protected.*

STYLE TIP

In the past, starting a sentence with a coordinating conjunction was discouraged in formal writing. Today, however, many professional writers begin sentences with coordinating conjunctions to create transitions, achieve a dramatic effect, or make dialogue more realistic.

DRAMATIC EFFECT: *I raced for the ball. <u>And</u> then I tripped.*

DIALOGUE: *"<u>But</u> you made a heroic effort," the coach said.*

Ellipses

Use ellipses

- to show an interruption in dialogue.
  "Let me think…It must have been last week that he called."

- to identify an incomplete quotation or other incomplete thoughts.
  The quotation "All the world's a stage…" comes from Shakespeare.

NOTE ON USAGE: When ellipsis points fall at the end of a sentence, follow them with a period or, if appropriate, a question mark or an exclamation point.

Exclamation Points

An exclamation point is a form of end punctuation. Use it

- at the end of a sentence that expresses strong feeling or a strong command.
  Don't touch that dial!

- after an interjection meant to show strong feeling.
  Ugh! That was a dreadful film.

 **STYLE TIP**   Do *not* overuse exclamation points. Using too many reduces the effectiveness of those that ought to be used. Get into the habit of using expressive words to show strong feelings.

Nouns

noun—a word that names a person, place, thing, or idea

- **concrete noun:** names something physical that can be perceived by one or more of the five senses *lion, flute, perfume, salt, silk*

- **abstract noun:** names something that cannot be seen, heard, smelled, tasted, or touched *hope, dedication, hatred, health, separation*

- **proper noun:** names a particular person, place, thing, or idea. Proper nouns begin with capital letters. *Wilfred Laurier, Saskatoon, Rideau Canal, Judaism*

- **common noun:** names a person, place, thing, or idea in a non-specific or general way. Common nouns do not start with capital letters.
  man, city, canal, religion

- **compound noun:** consists of more than one word and is written as one word, joined with a hyphen, or written as separate words
  letterhead, eyesight, mother-in-law, well-wisher, Rolling Stones, pencil sharpener

- **singular noun:** refers to one of something *antelope*

  Most nouns have singular and plural forms. To form the plural of most nouns, just add *-s*. Some nouns have irregular plurals that require other spelling changes. *crutch - crutches, crisis - crises, wife - wives*

  If you are uncertain about a plural form, consult a dictionary. Dictionary entries usually indicate plurals formed in ways other than adding *-s* or *-es*.

- **plural noun:** refers to more than one of something *antelopes*

- **possessive noun:** shows ownership or possession *Jorge's, class's*

For more about possessive nouns, see page 359.

STYLE TIP Good writers usually avoid general, abstract nouns and instead choose specific, concrete nouns that make their writing clearer and more precise. On the following word lines, notice how vague and dull the more general words are:

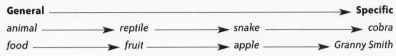

Objects and Other Complements

- **direct object (DO)**—something that receives the action the subject performs; usually a noun or pronoun answering the question *what* or *whom* after the action verb *Leonardo writes* **poetry**.

For more about action verbs, see page 368.

- **indirect object (IO)**—a noun or pronoun that answers the questions *to what, for what, to whom,* or *for whom* after the action verb

             V   DO   IO
  He **submitted** *some* **poems** *to a* **magazine**.

- **subject complement (SC)**—a noun, pronoun, or adjective that follows a linking verb (LV) and describes or renames the subject

             LV   SC
  His poems **were** *always* **long** *and* **mournful**.

- **object complement (OC)**—a noun, pronoun, or adjective that follows and describes or renames the object

            V   DO   OC
  The editor **found** *his* **poems tedious**.

Parallelism

Parallelism (also called **parallel structure**) refers to the use of equivalent grammatical forms to express a series of ideas of equal importance. Parallelism can help to give your sentences rhythm, balance, impact, and clarity of expression.

- **parallel words**

  ERROR: *She loved to jog, swimming, and skiing.*

  REVISION: *She loved <u>jogging</u>, <u>swimming</u>, and <u>skiing</u>.* [parallel *-ing* verbs]

- **parallel phrases**

  ERROR: *I skydive to relieve boredom and for getting over my fear of heights.*

  REVISION: *I skydive <u>to relieve boredom</u> and <u>to get over my fear of heights</u>.* [parallel phrases beginning with *to*.]

- **parallel clauses**

  ERROR: *The movie is successful because it is very funny and it features a popular star.*

  REVISION: *The movie is successful <u>because it is very funny</u> and <u>because it features a popular star</u>.* [parallel clauses beginning with *because*]

Check to see that you have used parallel grammatical forms when joining elements with coordinating conjunctions (such as *and, but,* and *or*) or with correlative conjunction (such as *either…or, both…and,* and *not only…but also*).

ERROR: *Smoking not only can lead to heart disease but also to cancer.*

REVISION: *Smoking not only <u>can lead to heart disease</u> but also <u>can cause cancer</u>.*

Parallelism should also be used for comparisons using *than* and *as.*

ERROR: *Reading a novel can be more enjoyable than a movie.*

REVISION: *<u>Reading a novel</u> can be more enjoyable than <u>seeing a movie</u>.*

Periods

A **period** is a form of end punctuation. Use it

- to end all sentences except direct questions or exclamations.
  Careful planning is the key to success.

- as appropriate, in many abbreviations. *Wed., St., Nfld.*

- in decimals and to separate dollars and cents. *7.5 per cent, $199.95*

- after a person's initials. *Mr. C.S. Lewis*

Phrases

phrase—a group of words that serves as a single part of speech and does not contain both a subject and a verb

Using phrases effectively can clarify meaning, create variety, and enliven writing.

- **absolute phrase:** includes a noun or pronoun modified by a participle or participial phrase. Absolute phrases have no grammatical relationship to the sentence and are always set off by commas to open, interrupt, or conclude a sentence. For more about participles, see page 372.
  <u>Her face brushed by the wind</u>, the athlete stood at attention.

- **appositive phrase:** appears near a noun or pronoun to give more information about it
  The other skater, <u>tall and triumphant</u>, accepted the gold.

- **prepositional phrase:** begins with a preposition and includes a noun or pronoun as object For more about prepositional phrases, see page 360.
  The country <u>with the best team</u> won.

- **verbal phrase:** includes a verb form functioning as a noun, adjective, or adverb For more about verbal phrases, see page 372.
  <u>To win ten golds</u> was an amazing achievement.

Possessive Forms

Keep in mind that possessive forms do not always show true possession. For example, while *Eduardo's watch* means "the watch that Eduardo possesses," *Eduardo's lawyer* merely means "the lawyer that Eduardo visits regularly."

POSSESSIVE NOUNS

- To form the possessive of singular nouns, add an apostrophe and *s*.

  bike →   *the bike's chain*
  Chris →   *Chris's cat*

- To form the possessive of a proper noun with two or more syllables and ending in *s*, add an apostrophe and *s* or an apostrophe only, for smoother pronunciation.

  Marcos →   *Marcos's attitude*
  Pericles →   *Pericles' predicament*

- To form the possessive of plural nouns that end in *s*, add an apostrophe only.

  dogs →   *the dogs' barking*
  teachers →   *teachers' lounge*

- To form the possessive of plural nouns not ending in *s*, add an apostrophe and *s*.

  children →   *children's shouts*

- To form the possessive of hyphenated compound nouns, make the last word possessive.

  runner-up → *runner-up's prize*
  sit-ups →   *sit-ups' value*

NOTE ON USAGE: The possessive form of a noun is the same whether it comes before the word it possesses or stands alone.

For more about compound nouns, see page 356.

> My *dentist's* sign has a big tooth on it.

> The sign with the big tooth on it is my *dentist's*.

Possessive Pronouns

For more about personal pronouns, see page 362.

Personal pronouns have possessive forms that use apostrophes. In addition, most have two possible forms, depending on whether the possessive comes before the word it possesses or stands alone.

	PRONOUN → POSSESSIVE	EXAMPLE
First person singular	I → **my** [before] → **mine** [alone]	*My* sunglasses are here. Those are not **mine**.
First person plural	we → **our** [before] → **ours** [alone]	*Our* camp is nearby. This tent is **ours**.
Second person singular or plural	you → **your** [before] → **yours** [alone]	*Your* water is over there. You haven't touched **yours**.
Third person singular masculine	he → **his** [before and alone]	He rolled up **his** sleeping bag. That sleeping bag is **his**.
Third person singular feminine	she → **her** [before] → **hers** [alone]	She lost **her** toothbrush. This toothbrush is **hers**.
Third person singular neuter	it → [before] [can't stand alone]	Camping has **its** challenges.
Third person plural	they → **their** [before] → **theirs** [alone]	***Their*** boots are muddy. These muddy boots are **theirs**.

- **The pronoun _who_** also has a possessive form that does not use an apostrophe: _whose_. It has the same form whether it comes before the word it possesses or stands alone. _Whose knapsack is it? Whose is it?_

- **Indefinite pronouns** such as _anybody_ and _someone_ form the possessive by adding an apostrophe and _s_, and use the same forms whether or not they stand alone. _Is this anybody's canteen? Is this canteen anybody's?_

  For more about indefinite pronouns, see page 363.

COMMON USAGE PROBLEM: When two or more nouns jointly possess the same thing, using the possessive form for both. Only the last one requires the possessive form: _The father and son's tent is the largest._

If two or more nouns possess separate things, use the possessive form for each: _The brother's and sister's tents are both quite small._

COMMON USAGE PROBLEM: Using apostrophes with _who_ and with personal pronouns. Do not confuse such forms with similar-sounding contractions of pronouns plus verbs.

POSSESSIVE: _Whose X-ray is this? Its image is unclear._

CONTRACTION: _Who's [Who is] on the phone? It's [It is] the dentist._

STYLE TIP Possessive forms can help streamline sentences, saving the reader's time, avoiding repetition, and making the meaning clearer.

EXAMPLE: _The nickname of that dentist is Dr. Painless._

STREAMLINED WITH POSSESSIVE: _That dentist's nickname is Dr. Painless._

Prepositions

preposition—a word that relates a noun or pronoun to another word in the sentence

prepositional phrase—a group of words that begins with a preposition and includes the object of the preposition

Prepositions help connect key words in a sentence. Many are single words, such as _against, about, above, along, among, between, but, except, like, over, since, through, to, toward, without._ Some consist of more than one word, such as _by means of, because of, according to._ Like adjectives and adverbs, prepositions can be used to make writing more precise, clear, and vivid.

The object of the preposition (OP) is the noun or pronoun that the preposition (PREP) relates to another word in the sentence.

            PREP   **OP**
    They strolled **along the shore**. [along relates shore to strolled]

For more about nouns, see page 356. For more about pronouns, see page 362.

Prepositional Phrases

For more about phrases, see page 358.

A group of words that begins with a preposition and includes the object of the preposition is called a **prepositional phrase**. The phrase may also include one or more words, such as _the_ and _green_ below, that modify the object of the preposition.

    The coat with the green stripes was a real bargain.

The entire prepositional phrase acts as a modifier. An **adjective phrase** is a prepositional phrase that modifies a noun or a pronoun.

> The coat _with the green stripes_ was also incredibly ugly. [Adjective phrase modifying the noun _coat_]

An **adverb phrase** is a prepositional phrase that modifies a verb, an adjective, or another adverb.

> _For slightly more money_, I bought a much nicer coat. [Adverb phrase modifying the verb _bought_]

> The green stripes were unsuitable _for daily wear_. [Adverb phrase modifying the adjective _unsuitable_]

For more about adjectives, see page 349.

For more about verbs, see page 368. For more about adverbs, see page 350.

COMMON USAGE PROBLEM: Using the wrong preposition after certain words. Sometimes this depends on the meaning intended:

> We agreed _on_ a price range.

> You agreed _with_ my opinion.

At other times, the correct preposition is determined by common usage.

> comply with   meddle in   distaste for   prejudiced against

Watch for two words with the same object but different prepositions. In such a case, use both prepositions.

> What more can I say about my discomfort _with_ and sheer distaste _for_ the coat?

COMMON USAGE PROBLEM: Incorrect use of _between_ and _among_. Use _between_ to show a relationship between two items at a time. Use _among_ to show a relationship among more than two items at a time.

> In the checkout line, I stood _between_ two angry shoppers. [two items]

> I was _among_ the many customers who complained. [more than two]

NOTE ON USAGE: Traditionally, ending a sentence with a preposition has been discouraged in formal English.

INFORMAL: _What credit card are you paying with?_

FORMAL: _With what credit card are you paying?_

However, speakers and writers disregard this rule so often that many sentences now sound more awkward when the prepositions are moved from the end.

Like adjectives and adverbs, prepositional phrases add descriptive details that make your writing more precise, clear, and vivid. In addition, opening sentences with a prepositional phrase is one way to vary sentence beginnings.

Pronouns

pronoun—a word that takes the place of a noun, another pronoun, or a group of words

antecedent—the word or group of words to which a pronoun refers

antecedent   pronoun   pronoun
*Cecile wants a pet tarantula, but **she** is afraid **her** roommate will object.*

- **personal pronoun:** refers to a specific person, place, thing, or idea by indicating one of the following:
  - the person(s) speaking or writing, called the **first person**
  - the person(s) being addressed, called the **second person**
  - the person(s), place(s), thing(s), or idea(s) being discussed, called the **third person**

Personal pronouns have different forms depending on their **number** (i.e., singular or plural) and their **gender** (i.e., masculine, feminine, or neuter). Most also have different **subject** and **object forms**, which reflect how they are used in a sentence.

For more about subjects, see page 366. For more about objects, see page 357.

She ran away. [she - third person feminine singular, subject form]

PERSONAL PRONOUNS

Person	Gender	SINGULAR		PLURAL	
		Subject	Object	Subject	Object
First Person:		*I*	*me*	*we*	*us*
Second Person:		*you*	*you*	*you*	*you*
Third Person:	Masc.	*he*	*him*	*they*	*them*
	Fem.	*she*	*her*		
	Neut.	*it*	*it*		

- **possessive pronoun:** shows ownership or possession *my, your, yours, our, ours, his, her, hers, its, their, theirs*
  Franco scratched <u>his</u> head.

Use the possessive form of a personal pronoun to modify a gerund.
  <u>His playing</u> in the slow movement impressed the judges.

- **reflexive and intensive pronoun:** is formed by adding *-self* or *-selves* to the object or possessive form of a pronoun *myself, ourselves, yourself, yourselves, himself, herself, itself, themselves*

A **reflexive pronoun** refers to the subject and is necessary to the meaning of the sentence.
  Mr. Ho often asks <u>himself</u> that question.

An **intensive pronoun** emphasizes a noun or pronoun mentioned earlier and is not necessary to the meaning of the sentence.
  Mr. Ho <u>himself</u> wonders about that.

- **interrogative pronoun:** is used to form a question *who, whoever, whom, whomever, whose, what, whatever, which*
  To <u>whom</u> did she give the envelope?

- **relative pronoun:** introduces an adjective or noun clause and usually serves as subject, object, or subject complement in that clause
  who, whoever, whom, whomever, whose, what, whatever, which, whichever, that
  > Vina, *who delivered the envelope, could not remember.*

For more about clauses, see page 351.

- **demonstrative pronoun:** refers to a specific person or thing
  this, that, these, those
  > <u>This</u> *is the one I want.*

- **indefinite pronoun:** refers to a noun or pronoun that is not specifically named
  - **singular** *another, anybody, anyone, anything, each, either, everybody, everyone, everything, much, neither, nobody, no one, nothing, one, other, somebody, someone, something*
  - **plural** *both, few, many, several*
  - **singular or plural** *all, any, most, none, some*
    > <u>All</u> *of us were relieved.*

COMMON USAGE PROBLEM: Using apostrophes with possessive forms of personal pronouns. Be especially careful not to confuse the possessive form *its* with *it's*, a contraction of the pronoun *it* and the verb *is* or *has*.

> **yours   it's (it is)**
> *Is this essay* ~~your's~~ *No,* ~~its~~ *mine.*

For more about personal pronouns, see page 362.

COMMON USAGE PROBLEM: Confusing *whose*, which shows possession, with *who's*, a contraction of *who* and the verb *is* or *has*.

> **Whose   Who's**
> ~~Who's~~ *essay is this?* ~~Whose~~ *willing to argue with the point it makes?*

COMMON USAGE PROBLEM: Lack of agreement between verbs and indefinite pronouns used as subjects.

> <u>Each</u> *of the ideas* <u>comes</u> *while interviewing.*

> <u>Many</u> *of the ideas* <u>come</u> *from her journal.*

 **STYLE TIP**

Pronouns are useful writing tools that help you tie ideas together without unnecessary repetition. It's always important, however, to keep the meaning of a pronoun clear. For more on clarifying pronouns, see pages 346–47.

Question Marks

A **question mark** is a form of end punctuation. Use it

- at the end of a direct question. *Have you seen my pen?*

- at the end of a direct question appearing within a sentence. *Lila lost her pen—or was it a marker?—in Biology class.*

- in the quotation of someone's direct question. *Noah asked, "Is this your pen?"*

For more about punctuating quotations, see page 365.

Whether or not a question mark appears within quotation marks depends on whether the question is part of the quoted material. If it is, place the question mark inside the quotation marks.

George asked, "This is your pen, isn't it?"
BUT
Did you say, "Yes, that's my pen"?

Use a question mark when a question is quoted indirectly.
She asked whether anyone had seen her laptop computer.

Quotation Marks

Use **quotation marks**

- to enclose a direct quotation.
  Emilio cried, "This math homework is tough!"

  "I'll help you," said his sister.

Note the use of punctuation between the speaker tag (which identifies who is speaking) and the quotation, as well as the quotation's end punctuation.
  Using quotation marks for an indirect quotation.
  Emilio said that he had finally finished his math homework.

- to enclose names of short works, such as short stories, essays, poems, and songs.
  "The Lottery" is one of my favourite short stories.

- to call attention to words or a phrase used in a special sense, including nicknames, slang, or words used ironically. However, do not overuse this device.
  On the football field, he was known as "Touchdown Tom."

NOTE ON USAGE: Use quotation marks to quote one or two lines of a poem or play. Do not use quotation marks when quoting more than two lines, or with prose, more than forty words. Set off the lines below the introductory statement by indenting left, or both, margins. You may also use a smaller typeface for the quotation.
  Thinking of murder, Macbeth says:
  Is this a dagger which I see before me,
  The handle before my hand? Come, let me clutch thee:
  I have thee not, and yet I see thee still.

Quotations

Direct and indirect quotations can add substance and authority to an essay or report. When using quotations in a report or essay

- make sure the person or document you are quoting is a reliable source of information about your topic.

- choose direct quotations carefully. Use only quotations that illustrate or support your point effectively, or that paraphrase other ideas.

- if you are using a direct quotation, make sure that you have accurately quoted your source.

- if you are using an indirect quotation, make sure your rewording does not change the meaning of the original source.

- identify the speaker or writer of every quotation and state the book or other source from which you obtained it.

Punctuating Quotations

For more about quotation marks, see page 364.

PUNCTUATION	EXAMPLE
• comma ending the quotation and preceding the quotation mark	*"The merger will be advantageous for both companies," stated the executive.*
• comma before and after the tag when the speaker tag interrupts the quotation	*"Yes," he said, "some layoffs will be inevitable."*
• question mark inside the quotation marks because it's part of the quotation	*The reporter asked, "How many workers will be laid off?"*
• exclamation mark outside the quotation marks because the person quoting is exclaiming	*I couldn't believe my ears when he said, "Only ten per cent"!*
• as above, because the person quoting is questioning	*Did he really say, "Only ten per cent"?*
• in a quoted passage of more than one paragraph, quotation marks opening all paragraphs but not ending any except the last	*"Layoffs are to be expected in a merger of this type," said the executive. He went on to explain, "This will enhance profitability.*
	"However, the potential for future growth is great. In a few years, we may well need to expand our workforce."

STYLE TIP

When using direct quotations in your reports or essays, try to vary the way you work them into your writing. For example, it would probably not be a good idea to have two long, set-off quotations back to back. Try to separate the longer quotations with your own ideas and analyses, with indirect quotations, or with short quotations that can be embedded, or included, within a paragraph of your writing.

Another way to achieve variety is to use different methods of inserting quotations in your running text. Sometimes quoting only part of a statement can make your sentences flow more smoothly. Here's an example:

Good: *The director said, "In my opinion, good actors are the ones who know their lines and don't knock over the stage furniture."*

Better: *The director said he admired actors "who know their lines and don't knock over the stage furniture."*

Semicolons

A **semicolon** is used to separate major sentence elements of equal rank. Use it

- between **two main clauses in a compound sentence** when they are not connected by a coordinating conjunction.

  For more about main clauses, see page 351. For more about coordinating conjunctions, see page 354.

  That new house-cleaning company with the amusing name is doing quite well; its name is Everything but the Kitchen Stink.

- to separate **items in a series when the items already contain other punctuation.**

  They travelled to Montreal, Quebec; Lime Rock, Connecticut; and New York City to pursue their interests.

Sentences

sentence—a group of words that expresses a complete thought and that contains a subject, a verb, and any necessary complements

subject—who or what the sentence is about, consisting of at least one noun or pronoun and any modifiers

predicate—the verb of the sentence, plus its objects, complements, and modifiers

direct object—something that receives the action the subject performs; usually a noun or pronoun answering the question *what* or *whom* after the action verb

indirect object—a noun or pronoun that answers the questions *to what, for what, to whom,* or *for whom* after the action verb

subject complement—a noun, pronoun, or adjective that follows a linking verb and describes or renames the subject

object complement—a noun, pronoun, or adjective that follows and describes or renames the object

For more about objects and other complements, see page 357.

The **parts of a sentence** include the **subject (S)** and the **predicate (P)**, with the predicate consisting of a combination of **action verb (V)**, **linking verb (LV)**, **helping verb (HV)**, **direct object (DO)**, **indirect object (IO)**, **subject complement (SC)**, and **object complement (OC)**.

Each sentence structure depends on its parts and on how they are combined. Note, for example, the following five common **sentence patterns**:

COMMON SENTENCE	PATTERN EXAMPLE
subject—action verb	*Hurricanes* [S] *destroy* [V].
subject—action verb—direct object	*Hurricanes* [S] *destroy* [V] *ports* [DO].
subject—action verb—indirect object—direct object	*Hurricanes* [S] *bring* [V] *outports* [IO] *misfortune* [DO].
subject—action verb—direct object—object complement	*Hurricanes* [S] *make* [V] *ship captains* [DO] *anxious* [OC].
subject—linking verb—subject complement	*Hurricanes* [S] *are* [LV] *treacherous* [SC].

 **STYLE TIP**

Adding modifiers to the basic elements will expand sentences but maintain the same pattern.

ORIGINAL: *Hurricanes destroy ports.*

EXPANDED: *On the North Atlantic, treacherous <u>hurricanes</u> in their most deadly month of September <u>destroy ports</u> with abandon, leaving ships and houses gutted.*

Most frequently, the subject comes before the verb. However, some sentences are written in **inverted order**—i.e., with the subject after the verb. Inverted order can be used to build suspense and to create a poetic effect.

REGULAR ORDER: *A swarm of mosquitoes came through the camp.*
                 (S)   (V)

INVERTED ORDER: *Through the camp came a swarm of mosquitoes.*
                  (V)   (S)

Sentence Types

- **simple sentence:** has one main clause, consisting of a subject and predicate

      S   **P**
  Karen gathered raspberries on the hillside.

- **compound sentence:** has two or more main clauses linked by a coordinating conjunction or a semicolon

      main clause   **main clause**
  She filled the bowl, and then she looked out to the harbour.

- **complex sentence:** has one main clause and one or more subordinate clauses

      subordinate clause   **main clause**
  As she scanned the horizon, she saw a sailboat.

- **compound—complex sentence:** has two or more main clauses and one or more subordinate clauses

      subordinate clause   **main clause**
  By the time the Coastguard arrived, Karen had already rowed out and

      main clause
  the desperate sailors had clambered aboard.

Spelling

When to Check and Correct Spelling

Incorrect spellings are acceptable only at first draft or in private writing. Incorrect spellings in final drafts and other public writing distract the reader from the content and style and leave a poor impression. You should therefore check and correct spellings just prior to the final draft. In writing that you will not be redrafting, check and correct spellings immediately.

Strategies

- **Troubleshoot:** Keep a list of words you often misspell. Refer to your list each time you are about to complete some writing.

- **Read:** Regular reading will help you recognize correct and incorrect spellings. Use a dictionary for spellings that strike you as odd, unique, or easily confused. Add these to your word list.

- **Create memory devices:** Think of ways to remember spellings that you stumble over.
  (Bill Eats Apples Upside-down- tiful)
  You are so B - E - A - U -tiful!

- **Proofread:** Proofread everything you write and check suspicious spellings in the dictionary, even if you're almost sure they're right. In a first draft, mark tricky words to check later.

- **Spell check:** If you are word processing your writing, use the spell check function as one of your many checks. Note, however, that it won't alert you to spellings that are incorrect for the meaning you intended but that are correct in other contexts, such as *rite* for *right*, *form* for *from*, *no* for *know*, *weigh* for *way*.

- **Learn rules and patterns:** Get to know how words work so that you can see patterns and note their exceptions.

Rules and Patterns

syllable—unit of pronunciation spoken without interruption, making up part or all of a word, usually with one vowel sound and often a consonant or consonants before or after, or both

prefix—word part added to the beginning of a word *anti-, de-, semi-*

suffix—word part added to the end of a word *-like, -ful, -ness*

base form—form of the word without any prefixes or suffixes

Dividing words into syllables may help with spelling. Each syllable makes up a single beat and generally consists of a vowel or a vowel with a consonant before or after, or both. So by sounding out a word, you can often guess at the spelling or at least get close enough to find it in the dictionary.

Patterns also often emerge when you examine the word's **prefix**, **suffix**, and **base form**. The following are some rules and patterns.

- Use *i* **before** *e*, as in *achieve, hieroglyphic,* and *niece;* **except after** *c*, as in *ceiling, conceived,* and *deceit;* or when sounded as *eh,* as in *eighth, freight, sleigh, neighbour,* and *weigh.* *Exceptions: caffeine, either, foreign, forfeit, height, heirloom, leisure, neither, protein, seize, weird*

- **If the base word ends in** *ie,* change the *ie* to *y* before adding *-ing* *die + -ing = dying*

- **The suffix** *-able* is added to words when there is a clear base word *agree + -able = agreeable.* When there isn't a clear base word, use *-ible permiss + -ible = permissible*

Dictionaries

When checking and correcting your writing for spelling, make consistent use of one current, authoritative Canadian dictionary. It will include variant spellings that are U.S. or British spellings.

Verbs

verb—a word that expresses action or being

- **action verb:** expresses physical or mental action and tells what the subject does
  The telephone <u>rang</u> incessantly. He <u>considered</u> leaving it off the hook.

  Action verbs can be either of the following:
  - **transitive verbs**, which have a direct object, meaning something receives the action the subject performs
    The batter <u>hit</u> the ball right out of the stadium.

  - **intransitive verbs**, which have no direct object
    The crowd <u>cheered</u> wildly.

    For more about direct objects, see page 357.

- **linking verb:** expresses a state of being and tells what the subject is by linking the subject to other words that further identify it
  The pitcher <u>was</u> clearly discouraged.

  The most common linking verb is *be* (including the forms *am, is, are, was,* and *were*). Others include *become, seem, appear, feel, look, taste, smell, sound, stay, remain,* and *grow.* Some linking verbs also can function as action verbs.

Sometimes two or more verbs function together, in which case,

- the most important verb is called the **main verb**.
- the other verb or verbs are called **helping verbs**.

helping verb   main verb
The coach may decide to use the relief pitcher.

COMMON HELPING VERBS	EXAMPLES
forms of *have*	*has, have, having, had*
forms of *be*	*am, is, are, was, were, be, being, been*
other helping verbs	*do, does, did, may, might, must, can, could, will, would, shall, should*

Verb Forms, Number, and Person

Verbs may change to agree with a subject in **number** (i.e., **singular** or **plural**) and in **person**.

	SINGULAR	PLURAL
First person	*I <u>sway</u>*	*we <u>sway</u>*
Second person	*you <u>sway</u>*	*you <u>sway</u>*
Third person	*he/she/it* [or any singular noun] *<u>sways</u>*	*they* [or any plural noun] *<u>sway</u>*

Check that singular subjects have singular verbs and plural subjects have plural verbs.

Common usage problems: Making errors in subject–verb agreement. Use the following tips to avoid common errors in agreement. For more about subjects, see page 366.

- Don't be confused by **words that modify the subject** and come between it and the verb.
    The <u>box</u> of pencils that they bought <u>was</u> missing.
- Don't be confused by **the subject following the verb**; make the verb agree with the subject anyway.
    There <u>are</u> few good <u>skiers</u> in my class.
- Don't be confused by **subject complements**; make the verb agree with the subject.
    A major <u>concern</u> among homeowners <u>is</u> property taxes.
- When **subordinate clauses start with *who*, *which*, or *that*,** use the antecedents as guides. For more about subject complements, see page 366. For more about subordinate clauses, see page 351.
    Abdul is just one of my <u>friends who speak</u> several languages.
- **Phrases beginning with prepositions like *as well as, in addition to, accompanied by, together with,* and *along with* do not change a singular subject to plural.**
    The <u>house</u>, along with its contents, <u>was</u> destroyed.

- Treat most **compound subjects joined by** *and* as plural.

  My <u>sister and brother want</u> to go to Newfoundland.

  However, when the parts form a single unit (name one thing) they take a singular verb.

  <u>Alberta's capital and largest city is</u> Edmonton.

- With **compound subjects joined by** *or* or *nor*, make the verb agree with the part of the subject nearer the verb.

  If heavy rain or <u>high winds are</u> forecast, do not go sailing.

- Treat most **indefinite pronouns** as singular. For those that may be singular or plural—*all, any, most, none, some*—choose the verb form based on the noun to which the pronoun refers.

  <u>All</u> of the <u>hikers are</u> hungry, but <u>all</u> of the <u>food</u> <u>is</u> gone.

  For more about indefinite pronouns, see page 363.

- With **collective nouns**, use singular verbs unless the noun's meaning is clearly plural. Words such as *class, jury, committee, herd, audience, crowd, family*, and *couple* usually emphasize the group as a unit. However, when the individual members of the group are to be emphasized, use the plural verb.

  The <u>committee wants</u> you to present your findings.

  The <u>herd scatter</u> when the predators approach.

- For amounts, treat those considered as a single unit as singular and those considered as separate units as plural.

  <u>Two years of experience is</u> a requirement for the job.

  The last <u>few kilometres</u> of the marathon <u>seem</u> endless.

- In general, treat words such as *athletics, economics, mathematics, physics, measles*, and *news* as singular.

  <u>Measles is</u> a common childhood disease.

- Treat titles of works and words mentioned as words as singular.

  <u>The Grapes of Wrath</u> <u>is</u> one of my favourite novels.

  <u>Calisthenics is</u> a word not often used today.

Verb Tenses and Principal Parts

tense—verb form to show the time of its action

Verbs also change form to show time. The four **principal parts of the verb** are used to form the six main **tenses**.

PRINCIPAL PART	EXAMPLE	DESCRIPTION
base form	*climb, bake, return*	basic form of the verb
past form	*climbed, baked, returned*	adds *-ed* or *-d*
present participle	*climbing, baking, returning*	adds *-ing*
past participle	*climbed, baked, returned*	adds *-ed* or *-d*

Regular Verbs and Tensing

Verbs that form tenses in the regular way follow these patterns:

- **present tense:** shows an action or a condition that exists at the present time or that is generally true. To form the present tense, use the base form without any helping verbs, and change the verb form to agree in number with its subject if necessary. *The door opens right now. I scream.* You can also express present action by using a form of *be*, plus the present participle. *The door is opening. I am screaming.*

STYLE TIP   Use the present tense when writing about literature or summarizing an author's views.

- **past tense:** shows an action or a condition that began and ended at a given time in the past. Use the past form without any helping verbs, and check the subject–verb agreement. *The door opened. I screamed.*
- **future tense:** shows an action or a condition that has not yet occurred. Use the helping verb *will* or *shall* before the base form of the main verb.

    The door will open in the future, and I will scream!

    You can also express future time by using a form of *be* with *going* or *about*, plus the infinitive. *I am going to scream.*
- **present perfect tense:** shows an action or a condition that occurred at an unnamed, indefinite time in the past or one that began in the past and has continued into the present. Use the helping verb *have* or *has* before the present participle of the main verb. *The door has recently opened. I have screamed.*
- **past perfect tense:** shows a past action or condition that ended before another past action began. Use the helping verb *had* before the past participle of the main verb. *The door had opened in the past. I had screamed.*
- **future perfect tense:** shows a future action or condition that will have ended before another begins. Use the helping verb *will* or *shall* before the past participle of the main verb. *The door will have opened before another event begins. I will have screamed.*

Voice

Action verbs change to indicate voice.

- **active voice:** a verb form in which the subject of the sentence performs the action *The strange figure terrified me.*
- **passive voice:** a verb form in which the subject of the sentence receives the action, using a form of the verb *be* *I was terrified by the strange figure.*

STYLE TIP   Overuse of the passive voice makes writing flat, wordy, and hard to follow. The active voice is generally more lively, concise, and easier to understand. Therefore, choose the active voice in most cases.

Flat, wordy: *The farmlands were devastated by the flood.*

Lively, more concise: *The flood devastated the farmlands.*

STYLE TIP   Strong, precise verbs make writing lively and imaginative by appealing to the senses.

Weak, vague, unimaginative: *The heavy rain <u>fell</u> on the roof.*

Strong, precise, imaginative: *The heavy rain <u>hammered</u> the roof.*

Verbals

verbal—a verb used as a part of speech other than a verb

Well-placed **verbals** can help combine sentences (and thus help vary sentence lengths and structures), can make writing less wordy, and can make writing clearer.

- **participle:** verb form that can be used as an adjective to modify a noun or pronoun and that falls into two categories:
  - **present participle**, which ends in *-ing*
    The movie had a <u>surprising</u> ending.
  - **past participle**, which usually ends in *-ed* or *-d*
    Many people now drink <u>filtered</u> water.
- **gerund:** verb form that is used as a noun and always ends in *-ing*
  <u>Swimming</u> is her favourite sport.
- **infinitive:** the base form of the verb, usually preceded by *to*, and used as a noun, adjective, or adverb
  <u>To graduate</u> is his immediate goal.

Verbals can act alone or can be expanded into **verbal phrases**.
  <u>Quickly ducking into an alley</u>, she avoided being caught.

The Development of the English Language

In the year 2000, Pope John Paul II gave a historic speech to an audience of Christians, Muslims, and Jews in the city of Jerusalem. The Pope addressed the crowd not in his native Polish, nor in Latin, the traditional language of the Catholic Church, nor in Hebrew or Arabic, the predominant languages in Israel. He delivered his message in English. For observers like David Crystal, an internationally recognized scholar of the English language, this event confirmed their belief that English is well on its way to becoming the global language.

The facts on the use of English around the world are undeniably impressive:

- Some 400 million people worldwide speak English as their mother tongue. For 375 million others, English is their second language.

- English is an official language in more than seventy-five countries.

- Most of the world's technical and scientific periodicals are written in English.

- English is an important language of world trade and one of the principal languages of international diplomacy.

Fifteen hundred years ago, only a few thousand people on one island spoke a language they called *Englisc*. And this ancient tongue probably had only a few thousand words. How did a language with such humble beginnings rise to the prominence and variety it enjoys today? To answer this question, you need to go even further back in time.

The Origins of English

About six thousand years ago, peoples living in northeastern Europe or near the Black Sea spoke a language or group of languages that historians call *Proto-Indo-European*. European languages such as English, French, German, Russian, and Spanish; Asian languages such as Bengali, Hindi, and Persian; and classical languages such as Greek, Latin, and Sanskrit can all be traced back to this ancient tongue.

ENGLISH	FRENCH	SPANISH	GERMAN	SANSKRIT	GREEK	LATIN
mother	mére	madre	Mutter	matar	meetera	mater
three	trois	tres	drei	trayas	tria	tres
night	nuit	noche	Nacht	nakta	nichta	nox

Language scholars established the links between Indo-European languages by comparing words and identifying similar patterns of sounds.

Proto-Indo-European changed and evolved as people migrated across Asia and Europe over the next four thousand years. Some of the languages that developed at that time—Celtic, Anglo-Saxon, Latin, Greek, and French—became the ancestors of modern English.

The development of the English language falls roughly into three periods.

- Old English (CE 450 to 1066)
- Middle English (1066 to 1485)
- Modern English (1485 to the present)

Old English

Old English began with the *Angles*, *Saxons*, and *Jutes*, tribes who lived along the North Sea coast in what is now Holland, Germany, and Denmark. Around CE 450, they began to invade the islands then known as Britannia.

THE SOURCES OF OLD ENGLISH

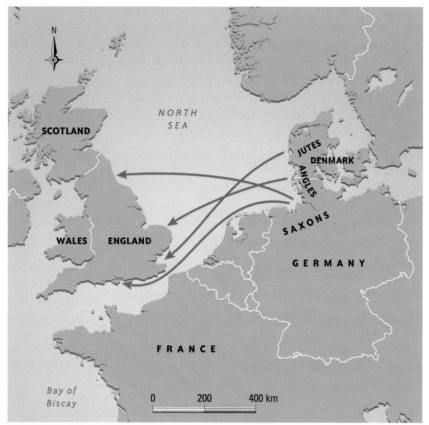

The *Celts*, who had been living in Britannia for some thousand years, fled to what is now Wales, Ireland, Scotland, and northern France, where Celtic languages survive to the present day. Eventually, the Angles settled north of the Humber River (Northumbria); the Saxons, south of the Thames River (Mercia and Kent); and the Jutes occupied the territory in the middle (Essex, Wessex, and Sussex).

The invaders brought with them a Low Germanic tongue that, in its new setting, became *Anglo-Saxon*, or Old English. In CE 827, King Egbert first named Britannia *Engla-land*, "land of the Angles" and by about CE 700, people had begun calling the language they spoke *Englisc*. (The letters *sc* were pronounced like our modern *sh*.) Although Old English is extremely different from modern English, we can recognize a number of Anglo-Saxon words: *bedd, eorth, moder, nama, healp, mann,* and *waeter.*

The Story of Beowulf

Long before there were books, stories and poems were passed along by word of mouth. In Anglo-Saxon England travelling minstrels known as *scops* captivated audiences with presentations of long narrative poems. One of these poems was *Beowulf*, which was told and retold to audiences throughout England over hundreds of years. When *Beowulf* was finally set down in writing in the eleventh century, it marked the birth of English literature.

The excerpt below from *Beowulf* describes the arrival of the monster, Grendel, at the banquet hall of the Danish king Hrothgar.

Old English
Ðā cōm of mōre   under mīst-hleopum
ʒrendel ʒonʒan,   ʒodes yrre bær;
mynte se mān-scaða   manna cynnes
sumne besyrwan   in sele pām hēan.
Wōd under wolcnum,   tō pæs pe hē wīn-reced,
ʒold-sele ʒumena,   ʒearwost wisse,
fǣttum fāhne;

Most Anglo-Saxon poetry contained lines with regular rhythms, usually four strong beats or stresses to a line. A sound break, called a *caesura*, appears in the middle of each line, indicating a pause for breath in the reading. The caesura was probably a useful device for scops who had to recite hundreds of lines of poetry.

A close translation (by Benjamin Thorpe)
Then came from the moor,   under the misty hills,
Grendel stalking;   he God's anger bare:
expected the wicked spoiler   of the race of men
one to ensnare   in the lofty hall.
He strode under the clouds,   until he the wine-house,
the golden hall of men,   most readily perceiv'd,
richly variegated.

A verse translation (by Burton Raffel)
Out from the marsh, from the foot of misty
Hills and bogs, bearing God's hatred,
Grendel came, hoping to kill
Anyone he could trap on this trip to high Herot.
He moved quickly through the cloudy night,
Up from his swampland, sliding silently
Toward that gold-shining hall.

Outside Influences on Anglo-Saxon

The language of the Anglo-Saxon conquerors was influenced by that of their neighbours. The *Celtic* influence on Old English is evident from such borrowed words as *cradle, griddle, glen,* and *whisky. Latin* words entered Old English through contact between the Romans and the Anglo-Saxon tribes on the European continent (e.g., *street* from *strata,* meaning *paved road, wine* from *vinum,* and *cup* from *cuppa*). In addition, there was a rich legacy of Latin words left by the Romans who had occupied Britannia for 350 years before the Anglo-Saxons arrived. Words such as *port* (from *portus,* meaning *harbour*), *mountain* (from *mons,* meaning *hill*), *tower* (from *turris,* meaning *tower* or *rock*), and *village* (from *vicus,* meaning *village*) originated at that time.

The arrival of Christianity in Britain in CE 597 was also important in the development of English. Christian scribes—priests, monks, and nuns—were the first to write in Old English. They used the *Roman alphabet* and added extra symbols to stand for sounds that did not exist in Latin. Words that date back to this time are *altar, priest, apostle, pope, school,* and *candle.*

A later invasion from Scandinavia by the seafaring Vikings (around CE 850) introduced elements of the *Norse* language into Old English. The most notable additions were the pronouns *they, their,* and *them,* and the verb *are.* A great deal of our everyday English vocabulary is of Norse origin (e.g., *happy, fellow, leg, low, sky, take, window, sister,* and *wrong*).

Activities

Work with a partner to create a time line of the history of England from 55 BCE to 1066, noting the dates of events that you consider important in the development of the English language. Record a list of the resources you found most helpful. Present your work to the class and explain the choices you made. If possible, use visual aids, charts, and maps to clarify your ideas.

Middle English

A dramatic step in the evolution of the English language came after yet another conquest of England, this one by the French in 1066 at the Battle of Hastings. The new conquerors came from Normandy, a province of France across the English Channel. For three hundred years after the invasion, French was the official language of the English court, of government, and of art, society, and literature. French words flooded into the English language. Many of them dealt with government, feudalism, and the Church—words like *parliament*, *law*, *judge*, *armour*, *prisoner*, *homage*, *fealty*, *chivalry*, *tournament*, *pardoner*, and *penance*.

Because both conqueror and conquered had different words for similar things, English is incredibly rich in synonyms providing fine shades of meaning. English can draw upon its Anglo-Saxon and French ancestry to choose between pairs of words like *home* and *mansion*, *work* and *labour*, *speed* and *velocity*, *stir* and *agitate*.

Chaucer and *The Canterbury Tales*

The poet Geoffrey Chaucer was the most important writer in Middle English. By Chaucer's time, the influence of the French was waning in England and the Anglo-Saxons were rising in the ruling class. His writings helped to establish Middle English, a mix of French and Old English, as the prevailing language of England.

Chaucer's masterpiece, *The Canterbury Tales*, written in 1380, consists of stories told by characters on a religious pilgrimage to the cathedral of Canterbury. Gathering together people from many different walks of life, Chaucer takes the reader on a journey across medieval society.

Here is the prologue of *The Canterbury Tales* in Middle English and in a modern translation.

Middle English
Whan that Aprill with his shourës sootë
The droghte of March hath percëd to the rootë
And bathëd every veyne in swich licour
Of which vertu engendrëd is the flour,
Whan Zephirus eek with his sweetë breeth
Inspirëd hath in every holt and heeth
The tendrë croppës, and the yongë sonnë
Hath in the Ram his half cours y-ronnë,

Modern verse translation
When in April the sweet showers fall
And pierce the drought of March to the root, and all
The veins are bathed in liquor of such power
As brings about the engendering of the flower,
When also Zephyrus with his sweet breath
Exhales an air in every grove and heath
Upon tender shoots, and the young sun
His half-course in the sign of the Ram has run,

Activities

1. Read the original of the prologue from *The Canterbury Tales* without looking at the translation. How much of it can you understand? What words are similar to modern English? Is there consistency in spelling and meaning within Chaucer's text? What other things do you notice about his writing? Share your observations in a group.

2. Pronunciation of Middle English was very different from modern English pronunciation. With a partner, try reading the original poem aloud in rhyming couplets. What do you notice about the pronunciation of certain words in the poem that is different from modern English? Choose examples that illustrate your point.

The Invention of Printing

The era of Middle English corresponds roughly to the historical period known as the *Middle Ages* or *medieval period*. This was a time of great upheaval in Europe, including the Hundred Years' War between England and France, and the Black Death, which claimed millions of lives. But by the fifteenth century, the Middle Ages had given way to the great flowering of culture that was the *Renaissance*.

Crucial to the spread of the civilizing influence of the Renaissance was the invention of the printing press. In 1456, Johann Gutenberg of Mainz, Germany, printed a complete edition of the Bible using movable type on a machine called a printing press. On the heels of Gutenberg's success, printing presses sprang up across Europe. By 1500 they had turned out more than twenty million volumes. The printing revolution brought immense changes. Printed books were cheaper and easier to produce than hand-copied works, and with books more readily available, more people learned to read. William Caxton brought printing to England in 1474. From that time on, English spelling became more fixed and grew less and less phonetic.

Latin and Greek Roots

During the Renaissance there was a great resurgence of interest in the writings and scientific knowledge of the ancient Greeks and Romans. As Greek and Latin texts began to be translated into English, writers often found that no English words existed to adequately express the ideas. These scholars added Latin and Greek words to English at a furious rate.

Many English words were created by adding prefixes and suffixes to Latin and Greek stems. About sixty-five per cent of words in modern English dictionaries are of Latin or Greek origin.

LATIN OR GREEK WORD	ENGLISH WORDS
struere, to build up	structure, construction, reconstruct, constructive
credere, to believe	discredit, creditor, incredible, credulous
monere, to warn	admonish, premonition, monitor
monos, one	monogamy, monotheism, monologue, monopoly
poly, many	polyglot, polygon, polytheism

Activities

1. We can discover how a word has acquired its present meaning by looking up its derivation in the dictionary. Here is an example:
   word: confer
   derivation: Latin *com* together + *ferre* to bring, carry
   literal meaning: bring together
   current meaning: meet for discussion

   Now look up the following words to trace the derivation of their meaning:

except	telephone	dictator	bicycle
photograph	proficient	convene	

2. Work with a partner to create a list of twenty words in which the following prefixes are used at least once: *sub-*, *super-*, *con-*, *trans-*, *syn-*, *inter-*, *post-*, *extra-*, *non-*, *dys-*, *mis-*, *peri-*, *anti-*. Share the list with your classmates.

Modern English

The next major step in the development of the English language took place between 1400 and 1600. No one really knows why the *Great Vowel*

Shift happened, but over the course of 200 years, a change in vowel sounds altered the pronunciation of many words. This difference in vowel sounds is one of the main things that distinguishes Middle English from Modern English. Compare the selection from *The Canterbury Tales* on page 378 with the speech below from Shakespeare and you will see the dramatic effect of the Great Vowel Shift.

Shakespeare's English

William Shakespeare is universally recognized as the foremost dramatist in the history of English literature. But what is not well-known about Shakespeare is his contribution to the development of English. He was, quite simply, the greatest word-maker who ever lived. Of the 20,138 different words that Shakespeare employed in his plays, sonnets, and other poems, 1,700 received their first known use through his writings. The most verbally innovative of English authors, Shakespeare invented an estimated 8.5 per cent of his written vocabulary.

> These are some of the words that, so far as we can tell, Shakespeare was the first to use in writing.
>
> aerial bedroom critic frugal dishearten generous lapse perusal invulnerable monumental amazement bump assassination castigate dislocate gloomy laughable pious auspicious countless dwindle hurry lonely sneak baseless courtship exposure impartial majestic useless

In the soliloquy below, from Shakespeare's *Hamlet*, the hero expresses his deep despair over his father's death.

Hamlet. O that this too too solid flesh would melt,
Thaw and resolve itself into a dew,
Or that the Everlasting had not fix'd
His cannon 'gainst self-slaughter! O God, God,
How weary, stale, flat, and unprofitable
Seem to me all the uses of this world!
Fie on't, ah fie! 'tis an unweeded garden
That grows to seed; things rank and gross in nature
Possess it merely. That it should come to this!

(1.2.129–37)

Activities

1. Take turns reading the speech aloud with a partner. What do you notice about the language Shakespeare uses? How is it similar to contemporary English? How is it different? Look up unfamiliar words in a dictionary to find out their origins. Work with a partner to paraphrase the speech in contemporary English. Compare your version with that of another group.

2. Without rival in his ability to invent words, Shakespeare is also unequalled as a phrase-maker. Complete the following expressions, each of which first saw the light in one of his plays.
   - Neither a _____ nor a _____ be
   - All the world's a _____
   - Eaten me out of house and _____
   - Too much of a good _____
   - With bated _____

Johnson and His Dictionary

On April 15, 1755, *Dr. Samuel Johnson*—impoverished, poorly educated, and blind in one eye—produced *The Dictionary of the English Language*, the first modern dictionary. Johnson set himself the task of creating a different kind of dictionary, one of the first to include all the words in the English language, not just the difficult ones. With little financial backing and working almost alone in an attic room, Johnson defined some 43,000 words and illustrated their meanings with more than 114,000 supporting quotations drawn from every area of literature.

Below are some definitions from Johnson's dictionary.

dedication. A servile address to a patron.

gambler. (A cant word, I suppose, for game, or gamester.) A knave whose practice it is to invite the unwary to game and cheat them.

opera. An exotic and irrational entertainment.

parasite. One that frequents rich tables, and earns his welcome by flattery.

Activities

1. How do these definitions differ from those you find in current dictionaries? What opinions is Johnson expressing in these entries? How would you describe Johnson's style? Discuss in a group.

2. Locate a copy of Johnson's dictionary (*Johnson's Dictionary: A Modern Selection*, edited by E.L. McAdam, Jr., and George Milne). Browse through it and report any interesting and unusual definitions to the class.

The Age of Exploration and Colonialism

Beginning in the 1400s, advancements in navigation and shipbuilding allowed British and European navigators to travel the globe in search of spices, jewels, perfumes, and fabrics. As they voyaged, British explorers and merchants left the language of the home country in their wake, but they also returned from foreign ports laden with cargoes of words from other languages. English continues to be the most hospitable language in the world, unique in the number and variety of its borrowed words.

Over the centuries Britain extended its language and influence over every continent. *Colonies* were established in Canada, the United States, Australia and New Zealand, and large parts of Africa and Asia fell under British rule. At its height in the late 1800s, one quarter of the world was part of the *British Empire*. Although most of these territories eventually became independent from Britain, the English language had firmly taken root as the language of government and commerce.

The following are some words that became part of the English language as a result of England's great economic expansion.

COUNTRY	BORROWED WORDS
India	bandanna, bungalow, calico, cashmere, cot, curry, polo
Asia	gingham, indigo, mango, typhoon
Australia	boomerang, kangaroo, koala
Africa	banana, boorish, gorilla, gumbo, zebra, okra
Canada	moccasin, raccoon, squash, toboggan, kayak, parka, wigwam

The New Englishes

In every new country, English took on a distinctive local flavour. Today, linguists talk about the *"New Englishes"* that have developed all over the world. Caribbean English, for example, contains elements of Creole, local Amerindian languages, and West African languages; other European languages such as Dutch, French, Portuguese, and Spanish; and South Asian languages.

Canadian English can be divided into subvarieties or dialects such as Newfoundland dialects, British Columbia dialects, an Ottawa Valley dialect, and so on. Many of these can be traced back to the migration patterns of the early settlers. The population of the Maritimes, for example, was composed largely of Acadians, Britons, and Scots until the American Revolution drove thousands of United Empire Loyalists north into Canada. In spite of the massive influx, however, the speech of Maritimers continued to reflect the influences of the early settlers.

Everywhere that English travelled, local people made changes to the language. Here are some Canadian equivalents for British words.

BRITISH	CANADIAN
lift	elevator
pram	stroller
chemist	drugstore
dust bin	garbage can
queue up	get in line
macintosh	raincoat
sweets	candies
crisps	potato chips

Activities

1. With a partner, study the following list of Canadian words and try to guess their origin. Use a dictionary of Canadian English to verify your answers.

   McIntosh   tuque   sugaring off   fiddlehead   voyageur   skidoo

2. Work with a group to make a list of ten place names across Canada and research their origins. Share your findings with the class.

The Global Village

Until the twentieth century, print was the medium of *mass communication*. But the burst of electronic technology in the modern age—telephone, radio, television, communication satellites, movies, computers, faxes, the Internet—changed all that. Canadian media guru Marshall McLuhan coined the phrase "the global village" to describe the effect of mass media. Time and space were no longer important, McLuhan said; it has become a world of "all-at-once-ness." Through the miracle of technology, everyone around the world has access to the same information.

The electronic revolution and the creation of a global economy have helped spread the English language faster than ever. British linguist Caroline Moore explains the importance of English in the *information age* this way: "As people interact with more people in different ways, they need a language in common. And in many countries, to be seen as a player, you need English."

COMPUTER LANGUAGE

Many thousands of words entered the English language as a result of advancements in science and technology in the twentieth century. The advent of the computer alone brought with it an extensive new vocabulary. Use the following list to test your knowledge of *computerese*:

toolbar	attachment	modem
menu	Internet	download
e-mail	login	virus
browser	Web	mouse
Web site	hotlinks	pop-ups
bookmark	scroll bar	search engine

In the past fifty years, the United States has overtaken England as the primary disseminator of the English language. *American English* and culture have infiltrated every corner of the globe through American television, movies, music, and the rise of multinational companies like Nike, Coca-Cola, and McDonald's. In the words of writer Pico Iyer, "Pop culture makes the world go round, and America makes the best pop culture."

A SAMPLING OF ENGLISH WORDS OF AMERICAN ORIGIN				
airline	flowchart	radio	teddy bear	xerox
disco	OK	soup	UFO	zipper

The Future

So what lies ahead for English? Will it become the global language? David Crystal predicts that the use of English will become even more widespread in the years to come. He believes that something called "ISSE" International Spoken Standard English, a mixture of traditional English and the new Englishes, will eventually be the umbrella language of the twenty-first century. Other experts point to the fact that there are three times as many native speakers of Chinese in the world as native speakers of English, and to the possibility of a backlash against American culture in places like the Middle East and Asia, and predict a very different future for the English language. Only time will tell.

Activities

1. "The English language is the sea which receives tributaries from every region under heaven." Use this quotation from Ralph Waldo Emerson as a starting point for an essay about the development of the English language.

2. View, with a partner, a video of a movie from an English-speaking country outside North America. Make note of any words and expressions that are new to you and, if possible, provide a translation of them.

Glossary

abstract A summary of the contents of a scholarly work, or a condensed presentation of a business report at the report's beginning as in an **executive summary**.

acronym A word created from the initial letters of other words, usually pronounced as a word (e.g., laser for **l**ight **a**mplification by **s**timulated **e**mission of **r**adiation; NATO for *North Atlantic Treaty Organization*).

act A major division in a dramatic work, larger than a **scene** or **episode**.

aesthetic element An aspect of a work's artistic quality or beauty (e.g., composition, colour, and light and shadow in **visual media**).

agenda A list of topics to be considered or things to be done in a meeting.

AIDA sequence A format for persuasive communication consisting of getting the audience's **a**ttention, cultivating its **i**nterest, creating a **d**esire, and persuading the audience to take **a**ction.

alliteration The repetition of the same sound *at the beginning* of nearby words (e.g., the falcon took flight with flair).

allusion A direct or indirect reference in one work to another work or to a historical person or event (e.g., In Shakespeare's play of the same name, Hamlet compares his dead father to the ancient Greek god, Apollo).

ambient sound Surrounding or background noise (e.g., the sound of a siren recorded as part of an interview with a firefighter).

analogy A comparison based on partial similarity for the purpose of making something clearer (e.g., the growth of a tree as an analogy for the growth of human beings).

analytical essay A **critical essay**.

anecdote A brief story about a single humorous or interesting event.

antagonist A **character** who is the **protagonist**'s main opponent.

anti-hero A **protagonist** who, though obviously unheroic, or lacking typical qualities of a **hero,** may be a sympathetic character as portrayed by the author (e.g., the wolf in Hermann Hesse's short story in Chapter 3).

APA style (name–date method) An approach (developed by the American Psychological Association) to documenting research sources with **parenthetical** (in-text) **references**—e.g., (Abrams, 1998)—and a later list of **bibliographical information.**

appendix An addition to lengthy written material, which appears at the end of the work so as not to interrupt the flow of the body of the work; examples might be survey results or a glossary.

arena stage An open stage at floor level surrounded by raised seating.

aside A **monologue** in which a **character** speaks directly to the audience as though unheard by the other characters onstage.

assonance The repetition of the same or similar vowel sounds *within* nearby words for musical effect (e.g., We chatted and laughed as we ambled along.).

autobiography A person's story of his or her own life.

backdrop A painted curtain hung at the back of a stage set as scenery.

ballad A **narrative poem** telling a popular, emotional story, typically with four-line **stanzas** and a **refrain**; the term is also used broadly to mean romantic songs.

banner ad A long, horizontal advertisement, like a large headline across the front page of a newspaper, which often appears on commercial **Web sites**.

bias A prejudice; a narrow, subjective perspective.

bibliographical information Publication details for sources of information and opinion (e.g., title of work, author(s) of work, publisher, place of publication, date of publication).

bibliography A central list of **bibliographical information** for all sources cited in a work (e.g., in **footnotes** or **parenthetical references**) and any others consulted.

biography The story of a person's life as told by another. A brief biography is called a **profile**.

blank verse A type of unrhymed verse that closely resembles everyday conversation, is always in **iambic pentameter**, and is used in Shakespearean plays and other forms of **drama**.

blocking The directing of actors' movements and positions onstage.

body language Non-verbal gestures, expressions, postures, and movements made consciously or unconsciously, which communicate messages to others.

bookmark Saving a link to (or flagging) a **Web site** so that a computer user can return to it easily; also the name of a marked site, which is also called a favourite.

Boolean operator Effective database searches combining elements with *and, or,* and *not* to define and narrow a search (e.g., for student work-abroad programs, try *student* AND *job* OR *work* NOT *Canada*).

brainstorming A fast-paced technique of stimulating and recording a free, uncritical flow of ideas independently or in groups.

browser A computer program that enables a computer user to look at and interact with the **World Wide Web** and other **Internet** resources.

buzzword A slogan or expression, especially one that is inexact and used for effect (e.g., *multitasking* when used to refer to a person's job rather than to a computer operation).

byline The line at the top of an article giving the writer's name. It acknowledges the effort made by the journalist.

career portfolio A portfolio related to one's work, goals, and experience.

caricature A **flat character**, who is identified by a comic, absurd, or grotesque exaggeration of characteristics.

cartoon A humorous drawing (e.g., **editorial cartoon**, frame in a **comic strip**).

cause and effect chart A **graphic organizer** with two vertical columns, one for specific causes and another for their outcomes, sometimes aligned horizontally.

CD-ROM **c**ompact **d**isc-**r**ead **o**nly **m**emory; a device similar to the audio compact disc that stores computer data and that cannot be erased, revised, or rewritten. A recent alternative is the CD-R (**c**ompact **d**isc-**r**ecordable), which is sold blank, ready for recording.

chairperson The person who oversees or leads a meeting, often referred to as the *chair.*

characters The people in a story—either in narrative **prose** or **drama** (e.g., **round characters, stereotypes, stock characters, protagonists, foils, heroes**).

chat room An **Internet** feature, a *virtual* conversation in which users with a common interest write each other messages that are displayed in **real time**.

chorus In song lyrics, the **refrain** or repeated phrases or lines; in **drama**, one or more **narrator**-like **characters**, particularly in Classical Greek drama, who comment on the action of the drama or voice a character's thoughts.

chronological resumé A **resumé** organizing work experience in order of occurrence (starting with the most recent), often by category.

cliché An overused, time-worn phrase, usually avoided unless used for effect in **dialogue**. **Diction** and **characters** can be called clichéd.

climax In a **plot**, the height of the tension in the **conflict**; the turning point in the plot; sometimes called the crisis.

close-up A photographic, filmed, or videotaped **image** made close to the subject (e.g., showing a person's face only).

cluster chart A **graphic organizer** that groups similar things or ideas.

coherence The quality of being logical, consistent, articulate, and easy to follow.

colloquial language Words, phrases, and expressions used in everyday conversation; it is relaxed and informal rather than literary and formal.

column In a periodical publication, an article written regularly by one writer, sometimes a **syndicated columnist**.

comedy A **drama** (e.g., **farce**, **satire**, **parody**) that may include mishaps but ends happily. Its intention is to entertain, but sometimes also to educate or persuade.

comic character A **character** who makes audiences laugh, who lightens the **mood.**

comic strip A sequence of drawings (cartoons) that tell a humorous story.

comparison and contrast chart A **graphic organizer** used to show ways in which two or more things are similar *and* different; similar to a **Venn diagram**, but columnar (e.g., for two **characters**, a column for each in which to list the character's unique qualities, plus a column showing shared qualities).

complication The rising action of a **plot** leading to its **climax** in which **conflict** is introduced and developed.

concrete poem A poem that experiments with the visual effects, and sometimes sound, of words and their arrangements (e.g., a poem about forests arranged in the shape of a tree).

conflict The central struggle or problem of a **narrative**, which moves the **plot** forward and motivates the **protagonist**.

connotation An implied meaning of a word or phrase that can be derived from association or frequent use (e.g., dove as a peace-loving person).

constructive speech An opening speech in a **cross-examination debate**.

context The surroundings or circumstances of something (e.g., the words before and after a phrase, the imagined world that an author creates).

convention A customary practice, feature, characteristic, or pattern of a text, often arising from the **medium** (e.g., **sound bites** in television news).

cover letter The transmittal letter that accompanies a **formal report**, addressing it to its intended reader.

creative writing Written imaginative work in which the writer crafts his or her ideas, feelings, and perceptions artistically.

critical essay A formal **essay** (e.g., **research essay**, academic essay) that carefully examines and evaluates a subject; also called an analytical essay.

critical response A written or spoken reaction to a text that involves commenting on the text's content, **style**, quality, effectiveness, and so on, and giving supporting evidence.

cross-examination debate A type of **formal debate,** involving **constructive speeches**, questioning of **witnesses**, and **rebuttal speeches** about the question or **resolution**.

deck In a periodical publication, a line explaining (and following on) the head of an article, acting as a subtitle.

demand writing Required written work, as for a timed test.

demographics Statistics (e.g., on age, income level) resulting from the study of a particular population's characteristics, used for various purposes (e.g., to identify consumer groups).

denotation A literal, dictionary meaning of a word or phrase (e.g., dove as a bird of the Columbidae family).

dénouement In a **plot**, the story's end or conclusion; also called the **resolution**.

descriptive writing Writing that creates **images** of people, places, and objects using carefully observed, expressed, and arranged details; it can range from objective and scientific, to subjective and impressionistic.

deus ex machina An improbable or forced device that resolves a **plot**; Latin for *the god from a machine*, the phrase alludes to the Classical practice of lowering (with a machine) a god **character** to the stage to solve the problems of the human characters in a **drama**.

dialect A way of speaking or a variation on language unique to a particular people or to one region or social group.

dialogue The conversation of two or more **characters** involving an exchange of ideas or information.

dial-up The method of making a telephone connection to the Internet using a **modem**.

diction The choice of words and phrases. In literature, a term used to describe the *level* of language used (e.g. slang, colloquial, formal).

diorama A three-dimensional replica, usually small scale, with a painted background and figures.

direct quotation A word-for-word repetition of what was said.

docudrama A **drama** based on real events, based in fact.

drama An artistic form in which performers assume roles to enact imagined, usually scripted, events.

dramatic irony A type of **situational irony** contrasting what a character perceives and what the audience and one or more of the characters know to be true (e.g., a student believes a classmate has taken her calculator, but the audience knows it has been tidied away by an efficient maintenance worker).

dramatic monologue A poem in which the **speaker** addresses an unseen, silent listener. This form is related to the **soliloquy**.

editorial An article (with no **byline**) written to present the official opinion of a periodical publication (e.g., newspaper).

editorial cartoon A **cartoon** in a periodical publication that presents a particular point of view about a topic, often a current event.

e-mail Electronic mail, a method of sending messages (usually text) between computer users via telecommunications; also the actual messages.

emphasis The stress or focus on a part of a whole. In writing, emphasis can help specific elements (e.g., key ideas) stand out for the reader.

endnote A note giving full **bibliographical information** for a source at the end of a work and keyed to the text, usually with a number. Endnotes are an alternative to **parenthetical references** or **footnotes**.

enjambment In poetry, the continuation of a unit of syntax (sentence, phrase) over the end of a line, couplet, or stanza without pause (e.g., in Keats's lengthy poem *Endymion* "Who, of men, can tell / That flowers would bloom. Or that green fruit would swell / To melting pulp…"). The term is French and means *a striding over*.

epic A type of **narrative poem** that is long and is about historic or legendary people. Thus it is like a **legend** but not **prose** (e.g., Homer's *Iliad*).

epilogue A closing or concluding section of a **drama**.

episode A division within a dramatic work, within a **scene**.

essay A **prose** form of writing that explores a topic in detail and is primarily informative. Essays can be *personal, expository, persuasive*, and so on.

eulogy A speech or essay written in praise of a person, usually soon after the subject's death.

executive summary A type of **abstract** used in formal business **report** writing.

exposition The segment of a work that introduces the **characters** and their situation, and so explains the **complication** to come (e.g., the feuding between the Montagues and Capulets in the early scenes of *Romeo and Juliet*).

expository writing Writing that is systematically explanatory, and communicates information, as in an expository **essay.**

expressive writing Written work that primarily explores and records the writer's feelings and thoughts (e.g., **personal journal**).

e-zine An electronic magazine, which is a collection of written and other texts regularly published on the **Internet**, often at the publisher's **Web site.**

fable A brief **folk tale** (often with animal characters) told to illustrate a truth or widely held belief (the **moral**), which is usually explicit.

fairy tale A **folk tale** involving supernatural powers, focused on a **hero**, and typically ending "happily ever after" for that **character**.

farce An obvious, unsubtle **drama** using exaggeration and improbable happenings to evoke laughter.

feasibility study A long **report** that examines and evaluates an idea or **proposal** for whether it can be achieved and for its predicted effects.

feature story A distinctive article in a newspaper or magazine, or a special segment of a television news program that is focused on one topic.

fiction A general term for an imaginative, written work in **prose**.

figurative language Language that uses figures of speech, such as **simile**, **personification**, and **alliteration** (e.g., "Like a pinball in an arcade, she ricocheted again and again down the avenue."), which are used extensively to create **imagery**.

first-person narration Storytelling in which one **character** of the story serves as the storyteller or **narrator**, telling the **narrative** from his or her **point of view**.

flashback A device used to depict events of the past (e.g., a story of a teenage heroine might flash back on her early childhood).

flat character A **character** lacking complexity, often built on one unchanging characteristic.

flowchart A **graphic organizer** used to show a sequence (e.g., of stages, episodes in a **plot**).

focal point The area of greatest interest, emphasis, or focus.

foil A **character**, usually minor, who contrasts with, and so sheds light on, the **protagonist.**

folk tale A traditional written or oral story told in **prose** (e.g., **legend**, **fairy tale**, **fable**, **tall tale**). Unlike **myths**, folk tales are not part of a culture's mythology or system of stories.

footnote A note giving full **bibliographical information** for a source at the bottom of a page and keyed to the text; footnotes are an alternative to **parenthetical references** or **endnotes**.

foreshadowing A device of hinting at the future or events occurring later in the work (e.g., a discovery of an injured bird might foreshadow the main character's accident).

form Broadly, the shape of a communication (e.g., one form of **poetry** is the **haiku**, one form of business communication is the **memorandum**); with **literary texts**, **genres** are the larger divisions and forms are the smaller divisions.

formal debate A discussion or argument on a topic (a **resolution**) that follows a format and for which each side prepares.

free verse Poetry that is close to natural speech and that has no regular pattern of line length, **rhyme**, or **rhythm.**

freelance writer A self-employed writer who writes for publications or for the broadcast media on a piece-by-piece basis**.**

freewriting A **brainstorming** technique involving writing whatever comes to mind without concern for content or correctness.

full block style A format for letters in which all elements start at the left-hand margin.

functional resumé A **resumé** that organizes experiences according to the skills that they demonstrate; a **targeted resumé** is one type of functional resumé.

gatekeeper Someone who controls the access to, and flow of, information or resources.

genre A type or class of **literary texts** (e.g., novel) within which there are categories of **forms** (e.g., historical novel, science fiction, fantasy). Broadly, genre means any type or class, so can refer, for example, to media products (e.g., **sitcoms**, quiz shows) and formal speeches (e.g., sales presentations, **eulogies**).

graphic organizer A tool for organizing ideas and information visually to find order in a mass of information, see relationships, plan, etc. (e.g., **flowchart**, **Venn diagram**).

haiku A short, traditional, Japanese form of poem requiring five syllables in the first line, seven in the second, and five in the third.

hard news News that is of immediate interest to the broadest audience and typically focused on events and actions (e.g., politics, wars, disasters).

head The headline, or title, of an article in a periodical publication; sometimes followed by a deck.

hero The central **character** or **protagonist** of a work of fiction, who *may* show heroic qualities. Some protagonists are anti-heroes.

hyperbole Intended exaggeration, a device often used to create **irony**, humour, or dramatic effect.

hyperlink A connection (indicated with a highlighted word, phrase, or even visual **image**) in one document that a computer user can choose to retrieve and display another document in the **World Wide Web**; sometimes called a *hotlink*.

iambic pentameter In **poetry**, a pattern of ten syllables (five **metrical feet**) per line, each foot (pair) beginning with an unstressed ($\cup$), and ending with a stressed ($\diagup$) syllable.

image A picture. In writing, images are words or combinations of words that help the reader form a mental picture. Images can also appeal to the sense of smell (*olfactory*), hearing (*auditory*), taste (*gustatory*), and touch (*tactile*). They can be descriptive (*literal*) or evocative (*metaphorical*). For visual images (i.e., those that can be literally seen), see **visual media**.

imagery Both the pattern of **images** in a work *and* all language used to represent objects, actions, feelings, thoughts, and so on.

impromptu speech A spoken report to an audience given with little or no preparation.

in medias res The technique of placing the audience *in medias res*, Latin for *in the midst of things* (e.g., opening a story in the middle of the action and then supplying background information through a device such as **flashback**).

incident report A type of **informal report** that gives an account of one event.

informal report A detailed oral or written account, usually short (e.g., **progress reports**, **incident reports**).

informational text A written work with the primary purpose of informing or explaining (e.g., how-to article, **research essay**).

in-process reading The part of the reading process involving actually reading the text *and* making notes, rereading unfamiliar words, and so on.

instant messaging Immediate communication using a computer program (e.g., ICQ, which stands for *I seek you*) that lets users know when specified other users are on-line, pages these other users, and enables them to interact via the **Internet** (e.g., send messages, play games).

Internet A global network of computers (the Net) to which computers can connect to exchange electronic information.

intonation Modulation (variation and adjustment in **tone** and **pitch**) in spoken language.

inverted pyramid A news story pattern that presents the most important information earliest in the story, followed by less vital information; so named because it turns upside down the traditional pyramid style of starting with a foundation of background information and building to a conclusion or outcome.

irony A literary device involving contrast. Types are **dramatic, situational**, and **verbal irony**.

ISP An organization (Internet service provider) that enables access to the **Internet**, usually for money.

jargon Language used by a particular group that may be meaningless to those outside the group (e.g., "carbs" short for carbohydrates, as they might be referred to among athletes or nutritionists.

jest A playful, sometimes witty remark or brief **tale**.

jigsaw A group process in which every *home group* explores the same topic, individuals form new, *expert groups* (each to explore a subtopic), then home groups form again for experts to share their findings.

journal A personal (but not private) collection of notes, reflections, and so on.

jump-cut An abrupt change from one **scene** or shot or the removal of part of a shot in order to break its continuity; a film production technique.

KWL A reading strategy in which the reader notes what he or she **k**nows already about the subject, **w**ants to know, and anticipates **l**earning from the text.

lead The beginning of a news story, often the first sentence or two.

legend A type of **folk tale**; a popular story about, or based on, historical events or people (e.g., national heroes) but which may contain exaggerated elements.

letter of application A business letter requesting consideration for work and accompanying a **resumé**; also called a covering letter.

letter of inquiry A business letter making a request (e.g., for information).

letter of refusal A business letter giving a negative response to a previous request or **proposal** (e.g., a joint project between two companies).

letter to the editor A written response to a publication, typically to give praise, criticism, or clarification.

libel A *published* statement that is both false and damaging to a person's reputation.

limited omniscient narrator An all-seeing, all-knowing storyteller or **narrator** who is *outside* the **characters** but who tells the story from *one* character's perspective; one type of third-person narrator.

listserv A computer program that automatically distributes **e-mails** to all the names on a mailing list so that subscribers can post and read messages regarding the listserv's focus.

literary analysis A **critical response** to a **literary text** in the form of a **critical essay** or oral commentary; it includes a thorough interpretation of the work.

literary text A written work, often one that is artistic and original as in **fiction** (e.g., novel, poem, play).or **non-fiction** (e.g., essay, biography, autobiography) excellent in its execution.

logical fallacy A falsehood or misunderstanding based on flawed reasoning.

logo A business' visual **symbol** used as its special sign; it appears with the company name and address on business cards, letterhead, and advertising as a means of corporate identification.

long shot A photographic, filmed, or videotaped **image** made a long way from the subject (e.g., showing a person in full view).

lyric poem A subjective, emotional poem with musical roots (e.g., **rhythm** or **rhyme**). Forms include **odes** and **sonnets**.

mass media Media that reaches a very large audience.

masthead In a periodical publication, the listing of the publication's ownership, staff, contact information, possibly a motto, and so on.

media Means of communication, including **mass media**, such as newspapers, magazines, television, radio, films, video tape, and visual media. The singular is medium.

media literacy The ability to interpret and analyze media (e.g., how media texts are constructed, their **conventions**, implicit values).

medium A means of communication (e.g., newspapers); the means by which the content is conveyed or transmitted; the singular of **media**.

medium shot A photographic, filmed, or videotaped **image** made a middle distance away from the subject (e.g., showing a person's upper body).

melodrama A sentimental **drama** using overblown **characters** and **plot** primarily to appeal to emotions; like a **farce** but not humorous.

memoir Autobiographical writing—i.e., a person's story of his or her life.

memorandum A short document, often called a memo, used to communicate within an organization. Often these take **e-mail** form.

metaphor An implied comparison that does not use *like* or *as* (e.g., "your dress is a kite in the wind"), thus connecting two or more usually unlike things that have something in common (dress, kite).

metre The pattern of **rhythm** (stressed and unstressed syllables in poetry) as examined in **metrical feet.**

metrical feet The units of stressed and unstressed syllables; a way of examining **metre** and identifying the feet according to type and number (e.g., **iambic pentameter**).

minutes A written, official record of a meeting's content.

MLA style (name–page method) An approach (developed by the Modern Language Association) to documenting research sources with **parenthetical references**—e.g., (Abrams 34)—and a later list of **bibliographical information.**

mode In writing, a manner (e.g., **narrative**), kind (e.g., **comedy**), or way of writing that brings with it certain customs, usual ways of writing (e.g., precise use of detail in **descriptive writing**, the tragic flaw in **tragedy**); in statistics, the value that occurs most frequently in a set of data.

modem A device that enables a computer to transmit and receive information over telephone lines by converting information in analogue form to digital form and vice versa. The name comes from the words *mo*dulator and *dem*odulator.

moderator A person designated to oversee a **formal debate**, **chat room**, **newsgroup** or other forum to maintain order and see that any rules are adhered to.

monologue In **drama**, a speech spoken by one **character** (e.g., a **soliloquy**, an **aside**).

mood The prevailing feeling created in or by a work, also known as the atmosphere.

moral The lesson to be learned (e.g., from a **fable**).

motion A formal suggestion offered in a meeting.

moving image A **visual media** text that is not static (e.g., television commercial, film).

myth A story that involves supernatural beings or powers—that explains why things are as they are—i.e., some aspect of nature (e.g., how the world began, why the beaver's tail is as it is), or the human condition (e.g., romantic love, greed) and that is part of a culture's mythology (its system of stories passed down through generations).

narrative poem A poem that tells a story (e.g., **ballad**, **epic** poem).

narrative writing Writing that involves the telling of a story, often about an event.

narrator The storyteller in **narrative writing**; a function of the **point of view**. A narrator may use **first-person narration** or a more objective, third-person style such as **omniscient narration** or **limited omniscient narration.**

narrowcasting Targeting a small **demographic** group with, for example, a cable television program and accompanying advertisements; as opposed to *broadcasting*.

netiquette An informal code of conduct for use of the **Internet** (e.g., giving each **e-mail** a brief, informative subject description).

New Journalism A category of writing in which the writer's voice, point of view, and possible biases are apparent. Such writing combines aspects of non-fiction and fiction, and may include dramatized fictional events, conversations, and so on.

newsgroup A forum for discussion (and information about) a particular topic, with or without a **moderator**. Participants write notes to a central **Internet** site, which redistributes them.

non-fiction A general term for work in writing that is not **fiction**, thus reflecting fact (e.g., **essays, letters, reports, biographies**).

note making A learning strategy of independently recording facts, references, and ideas while reading or studying, then later annotating, summarizing, and so on.

note taking A learning strategy of listening to and recording facts and ideas received from others, then later identifying key words, questioning ideas, and so on.

octave A **stanza** of eight lines.

ode A **lyric poem**, typically long and formal, with a complex structure. It offers praise of a scene or to a person.

omniscient narrator An all-seeing, all-knowing storyteller or **narrator** who is *outside* the characters; one type of third-person narrator.

onomatopoeia A device in which a word imitates the sound it represents (e.g., the *buzz* of a bee).

open-ended question A question that requires more than a *yes* or *no* answer, so does not limit respondents' answers.

open-line show A radio or television show in which listeners can call in to participate in the show.

opinion piece A column written from (and presenting) the writer's particular perspective on a subject; like an **editorial**, but with a **byline**.

oral history Spoken **non-fiction** narratives collected and recorded, including details of the teller's experiences of specific events, people, and periods.

oxymoron A device that combines contradictory words for effect (e.g., the wisdom of fools).

pan Slowly move the camera horizontally on its base to capture a scene from right to left or vice versa.

panel interview A meeting in which two or more interviewers question one interviewee.

panoramic shot A photographic, filmed, or videotaped **image** with a wide view of the subject (e.g., as for landscapes or an establishing shot of a street).

paparazzi Photographers who follow celebrities to take photographs that **media** clients (e.g., **tabloids**) will buy.

parable A brief **folk tale** that teaches an *implied* **moral**, or lesson.

paradox An apparent contradiction or absurdity that is somehow true.

parallelism Similar constructions or treatments placed side by side, for effect (e.g., grammatical parallelism in "Early in the novel, the character Piers, did…. "In the fifth chapter, he did…. At the climax in the seventh chapter, he did….").

paraphrase A written or spoken explanation of someone else's words.

parenthetical reference A note *within* a work briefly giving credit to a source listed in full in a complementary **works cited** list or **bibliography**; also called an in-text note. Common styles for writing parenthetical references are **APA style** (name—date method) and **MLA style** (name—page method).

parliamentary debate A type of **formal debate** (held in Canada's House of Commons and other political bodies) involving a **motion**, discussion of a proposed **resolution** or order, and a vote.

parody A humorous, exaggerated imitation of a work, **style**, or person.

persona In **poetry**, novels, or other forms of literature, the **character** who "speaks to" the reader or imagined audience; also called the speaker in poetry.

personal essay An **essay** written from one individual's personal perspective and usually informal in **style**.

personal inventory A list or assessment of one's skills, achievements, aptitudes, goals, and so on.

personal journal A record of personal (but not private) thoughts, ideas, associations, and observations expressed in writing (but also sketches, clippings, etc.).

personal response A written or spoken reaction to a text involving one's feelings, thoughts, associations, and questions.

personification A technique in which inanimate objects or concepts are given human qualities, form, or actions.

persuasive writing Writing that attempts to convince the audience to adopt a certain **point of view** or to act in a certain way.

photo essay Photos arranged and presented to explore a concept, subject, and so on.

phrase collage A collection of written text and possibly other materials, arranged visually and artistically.

pitch The highness or lowness of a sound, determined by the sound waves' frequency.

plagiarism Using another's ideas or writings and attempting to pass them off as one's own.

planned speech A prepared spoken report, often delivered to its audience with the support of notes.

platform stage A raised, level surface used for **drama.**

plot The series of connected actions and events in a story, written or otherwise, often described as having a course of action and including rising action, **conflict, climax,** falling action, and a **resolution.**

poetry A **genre** in which words are arranged on separate lines for meaning, often with **images, rhythm, rhyme,** and other sound effects, and sometimes crafted into specialized forms (e.g., **sonnet**). The essence of poetry is conciseness, precision, and force.

point of view The perspective and **voice** from which information and impressions are conveyed— i.e., *physical* (e.g., from a tower, from within the grass) or *psychological* (e.g., from that of a police officer, from that of a robber)—which, in **fiction,** is determined by the choice of **narrator.**

pop-up A computer feature, such as a menu, that can be superimposed on the screen and then closed with ease. It is sometimes referred to as a *pulldown.*

portfolio A representative collection of material (e.g., career or writing portfolio).

post-reading The part of the reading process after reading the text, involving reflecting on it, responding personally and critically.

précis To precisely summarize a text in writing; also, the result, called a précis.

pre-reading The part of the reading process before actually reading the text, involving making predictions, exploring related knowledge, etc.

primary research First-hand or original investigation, based on the use of **primary sources.**

primary source A first-hand or original source of information and opinion (e.g., observation, discussion, interviews, questionnaires).

problem–solution chart A **graphic organizer** with two vertical columns, useful for identifying pairs of problems and solutions, or for listing problems and devising solutions.

pro–con chart A **graphic organizer** with two vertical columns, one in which to note arguments in favour of a particular action and the other for arguments against it.

profile A short **biography,** as often presented in the **media** or in anthologies.

progress report A type of **informal report** that tracks how a project is proceeding, including meeting interim deadlines, or any difficulties.

prologue An opening section of a **drama,** a kind o introduction.

prop An object appearing in the action of a **drama** and used to perform or enhance it. Props, or properties, include furniture, costumes, and so on.

propaganda Publication of information or ideas in such a way as to create a following for a particular practice or belief; the term has a **connotation** of dishonesty and manipulation.

proposal A long **report** that suggests, or puts forward, an idea for consideration.

proscenium stage A stage with an arch at the front that frames the **drama.**

prose The most common, everyday form of writter or spoken communication, without structured **metre.** Prose includes imaginative **narrative writing** (e.g., short stories and novels) as well as more **transactional writing** as in **reports** and **essays.**

protagonist The narrative's main **character,** the focus of our attention, often pitted against an **antagonist.**

proverb A brief saying in general use that expresses a general truth (e.g., "It is an ill wind that blows no good"). Some proverbs are the **morals** of **fables.**

pseudonym An assumed, false name, especially one used by an author.

pun A play on words using a word with two meanings, two words of similar meanings, or words that are similarly spelled or pronounced.

quatrain A **stanza** of four lines.

readers' theatre A dramatic reading of a written text focused on the oral interpretation.

reading circle A group of people that meets to discuss their own or others' writing.

real time Simultaneously or in the present (e.g., **chat rooms** use real-time communication).

rebuttal speech A concluding speech in a **cross-examination debate** that refutes the arguments presented by the other side.

refrain A phrase, a line, or lines repeated in a poem. In song lyrics, these are often called the **chorus.**

report A detailed written or oral account. Reports take many forms, such as **critical** or **analytical essays** (including **reviews**) or, in business, reports (including **proposals**) that often make recommendations.

research essay A **critical essay** requiring use of **primary** or **secondary sources**; typically long.

resolution In **fiction**, the **plot**'s end or conclusion (also called the **dénouement**); in a **formal debate**, the debate's topic, typically given in the form of a statement but sometimes as a question.

response journal A record of reactions to a visual or written text.

resumé A written summary of one's qualifications for work, plus contact information (name, address, phone number).

review An evaluation of another work (e.g., stage play, movie, novel) in **essay** or **report** form or a review of a product (e.g., a consumer **report**).

rhetorical question A question asked for effect and to promote thought and reflection, not to elicit an answer.

rhyme The sound effect of words that have, or end with, the same or similar sounds. **Poetry** that has a strong rhyming quality may be called rhyme.

rhyming couplet A pair of lines in a poem with rhyming ends to accentuate the unit of thought.

rhythm The sound effect of stressed (accented) and unstressed (unaccented) syllables; the pattern of rhythm is called the **metre.** It sets the beat and **tempo** of a poem.

romantic character A passionate, idealistic, individualistic, principled, or adventurous **character.**

round character A complex, three-dimensional **character.**

rule of thirds A principle for placing a visual **image**'s **focal point**(s): divide an image into thirds vertically and horizontally; the natural and most interesting places for focal points are where the dividing lines meet (rather than in the image's centre, or bull's eye).

sales letter A business letter trying to persuade a potential customer to buy a product or service.

satire A **form** that uses **irony**, ridicule, or sarcasm to expose human flaws.

scene A division within a dramatic work, usually within an **act**. Typically, a scene takes place in one specific time and place only.

script The written guide for (and record of) **drama**, including, for example, a cast of **characters**, **dialogue**, **stage directions**.

search engine A database and index search program that **Internet** users can use to sort through **Web sites** for their relevance. The search engine scans sites or site summaries for key words and ranks the outcome.

secondary research Investigation, or research, based on opinion gathered by someone else.

secondary source Resource of information or opinion gathered by someone else (e.g., newspaper or magazine articles, **essays**, books written on the subject, **Web sites**).

sestet A **stanza** of six lines.

setting The where and when, place and time, of a narrative piece.

shoot A film or still photography session, typically preceded by the creation of a **storyboard** or **shooting script**.

shooting script The detailed, final written text of material to be filmed or videotaped (e.g., a TV program), sometimes with **scenes** appearing out of sequence (grouped in the order most convenient for shooting); used to direct the actual production of the work and including dialogue, camera angles, and so on.

sidebar A short article, often boxed, appearing beside another article, typically to supplement or give background for the larger, main article.

simile A definitely stated comparison that uses *like* or *as* (e.g., "your dress is like a kite in the wind").

sitcom A situation comedy, a serialized television show that humorously presents a group of **characters** and their lives.

situational irony A type of **irony** contrasting what actually happens with what was expected to happen (e.g., a late-arriving boyfriend is met with unexpected, forgiving laughter).

slander An *oral* statement that is both false and damaging to someone's reputation.

slogan The key word or phrase in an advertisement crafted to attract attention or quickly convey an idea.

soap opera A serialized television show following the lives of a group of **characters**, typically televised in the daytime and named for their original soap-maker sponsors; like a **sitcom** but not humorous.

soft news News that is of less immediate interest to an audience than **hard news**. Soft news (e.g., lifestyle, entertainment) often focuses on personalities and sometimes gives background support for hard news.

solicited letter of application A **letter of application** to accompany a **resumé** in response to an advertisement or a direct request by the employer.

soliloquy A **monologue**, often long, in which the lone **character** expresses his or her thoughts and feelings.

sonnet A **lyric poem** with fourteen lines, sometimes written in **iambic pentameter**. The major types of sonnet are the *Italian* (*Petrarchan*) and the *English* (*Shakespearean*).

sound bite A short excerpt of an interview or recorded speech, chosen for its effectiveness in broadcast **media**.

speech balloon A shape in a **cartoon** or **comic strip** with a **character**'s speech written inside, connected to a character by a tail.

split-run Relating to publications sold in two or more markets in which most or all the editorial content (i.e., non-advertising content) is common to all versions, but the advertising differs in each.

SQ3R A reading technique of *s*urveying the work, asking oneself *q*uestions, *r*eading the work, *r*eciting key sections, and *r*eviewing the work to answer any assignment questions, summarize, and so on.

stage directions In **scripts**, performance requirements or suggestions (e.g., to say a line angrily, to enter from stage right).

stanza A grouping of lines in a poem, separated by a blank space on the printed page.

stereotype A type of **flat character**, one-dimensional, lacking complexity, and often reflecting some **bias**.

still image A **visual media** text that is static (e.g., a painting or a **cartoon**).

stock character A type of **flat character**, one who the audience will immediately recognize and who serves a familiar function.

storyboard A sequence of rough illustrations (sometimes with writing) used to outline or plan, for example, a TV commercial, video production, or film.

straw vote An unofficial ballot to test opinion; also called a straw poll.

style An individual's manner of expression. In writing, style is the result of the choices the writer makes as to **diction**, sentence structure, and figurative language.

subject journal A record of school notes (thoughts, reflections, ideas, questions) related to one or more school subjects; also called a learning log.

suspense Increasing tension in a narrative caused by uncertainty and excitement about the conclusion, created mainly by the **conflict**.

symbol Something that represents or stands for something else (e.g., a dove for peace, a maple leaf for Canada). Symbolism is many symbols collectively.

symbolic language Language, including **figurative language** (**metaphor**, **personification**, etc.), that is representative, metaphorical, not literal, thus including **symbols** and creating a work's **imagery**.

synesthesia A device of mixing senses and sensations so that one might, for example, smell a sight (e.g., smell the sunrise); from the Greek *perceiving together*.

syndicated columnist A writer who writes a **column** that is sold to various publications to appear simultaneously.

synopsis A brief outline, summary, or general account (e.g., a synopsis of a **plot**).

syntax The arrangement of words to form phrases and sentences.

tableau A *frozen* moment in a **drama**; the performers freeze in position, motionless and soundless. The plural is tableaux.

tabloid A publication focused on celebrities and sensational news.

tabloid journalism Publications (**tabloids**) or television programs focused on celebrities and sensational news; the practices used to create these.

tall tale An entertaining **folk tale** that is highly improbable and extravagant, through the use of **hyperbole**, for example.

target audience The chosen or intended readers, viewers, or listeners (e.g., of an advertisement); usually a distinct **demographic** group.

targeted resumé A **functional resumé** aimed at one specific desired job.

television drama A narrative televised in a serialized format and featuring performers.

tempo The rate or speed (e.g., of the spoken word, of music, of any activity).

temporal reference points Guideposts to show the audience when an action takes place (e.g., use of the phrase *before nightfall*).

theme The central insight or idea of a work (especially **fiction**) stated indirectly or directly.

thesis The main idea of a work of **non-fiction** writing.

thesis statement The **thesis** given explicitly in a sentence.

thought balloon A shape in a **cartoon** or **comic strip** with a **character**'s thoughts written inside. It is often connected to a character by a series of small circles.

thought web A **graphic organizer** to record ideas and information, and to note connections or categories among them using lines, circles, and squares.

thrust stage An open, peninsula-like stage surrounded by the audience.

thumbnail sketch A small, concise drawing, often used for planning.

time line A **graphic organizer** consisting of a line marked with dates and annotated with events (e.g., events in Canadian history, achievements in one's life).

tone In writing, the writer's attitude to the subject or audience as conveyed through **diction** and **style**, and in spoken communication, the attitude or feeling suggested by the diction, style, and delivery.

topic sentence The main idea of a paragraph, stated explicitly.

trade magazine A publication for those within a specific industry.

tragedy A **drama** focusing on the downfall of the **protagonist** (due to a flaw in character or a mistake) and ending unhappily. Traditionally the protagonist was of high social status (e.g., a god, a queen) but is often now an ordinary person.

tragic hero The heroic **protagonist** of a **tragedy**.

tragicomedy A **drama** that combines aspects of **tragedy** and **comedy**.

transactional writing Written work that is primarily functional (performing a certain task) and that often follows a specific format and **style** (e.g., a **resumé**).

transitional words Words to connect sections of a text (e.g., *because*, *thus*, *therefore*) and to help orient the audience to chronology, structure, and other elements of writing.

trickster tale A **folk tale** involving a character that plays pranks or practical jokes, sometimes by taking various forms (e.g., tales of Nanabush).

typeface A particular style or appearance of characters, including letters and numerals, for printing (e.g., Helvetica); sometimes referred to as a font.

unity A quality of oneness, in which the parts *hang together*—i.e., each part of a work is interdependent and no part is irrelevant.

unsolicited letter of application A **letter of application** to accompany a **resumé** that has not been requested by the employer.

urban legend A tale about contemporary people or occurrences that are unusual or exceptional.

URL The Uniform (or Universal) Resource Locator, an address of a site on the **Internet** that any user worldwide can use to locate the site.

usage The customary, established, or common manner of using words, phrases, and expression in a language (not necessarily reflected yet in dictionaries, as with computer terminology) *or* the particular manner of using a word, phrase, or expression (e.g., a writer's use of a word that indicates which dictionary definition or which preposition is appropriate).

Venn diagram A **graphic organizer** using two or more overlapping circles to compare and contrast subjects.

venue The location at which an event takes place or a delivery environment for an oral presentation (e.g., the size of room, the computer equipment available).

verbal irony A type of **irony** that contrasts what is said and what is meant (e.g., a character who gives a compliment grudgingly is told, "That's big of you").

visual media Media in which the communication is entirely or primarily through pictures and other images to be seen (e.g., **still images** such as photographs, **moving images** such as videos).

visualization technique A method often used to calm, focus, or motivate by forming a mental picture of something.

voice Broadly, the personality of the speaker or the author (**persona**) coming through in a work, created through the combination of **diction**, **point of view**, and **tone**. Narrowly defined, voice can be described as *active* (e.g., I made a mistake) or *passive* (e.g., Mistakes were made).

voice-over Narration (e.g., in film) in which the speaker is not seen.

volume The loudness or power of a sound.

W5H Referring to *who, what, where, when, why,* and *how;* questions that can be used to evaluate a work's answers or to research and communicate one's own answers.

walkabout A filmed or videotaped stroll with a person, used to show a person in his or her **context**.

Web page A single document within a **Web site**.

Web site A group of interrelated (**hyperlink**ed) **Web pages** owned and maintained on the **World Wide Web** by one organization or individual.

Webcast An audiovisual program like a telecast (television broadcast) but distributed on the **World Wide Web**.

witness In a **cross-examination debate**, each debater's opponent who is subjected to questions from the opposing side.

works cited A central list of **bibliographical information** for all sources cited (e.g., given in **parenthetical notes**).

World Wide Web A network of linked (**hyperlink**ed) documents (including visual **images**, text, etc.), stored on computers around the world, and accessible by the **Internet** and specialized software.

writing portfolio A portfolio of one's writing (e.g., various forms, purposes).

zoom in Moving a special (zoom) lens smoothly toward the subject (e.g., zooming in from a **medium shot** to a **close-up**).

Index

Credits

Every reasonable effort has been made to find copyright holders of the material in this anthology. The publisher would be pleased to have any errors brought to its attention.

Literary Credits

p. 2 Reprinted with permission of the publisher. Copyright © 1997 John Wiley & Sons Canada Ltd. All rights reserved; **p. 3** Quote from <www.ns.sympatico.ca/ Features/Road/safdie.html>, Dec 1995; **p. 3** Quote from <www.ns.sympatico.ca/Features/Road/bondar.html, Dec 1995>; **p. 11** With permission of Pendragon Ink; **p. 19** From *The Wars.* Copyright © 1977 by Timothy Findley. Reprinted by permission of Penguin Books Canada Limited; **p. 22** From *Selected Poems of Gabriela Mistral* translated by Doris Dana. Copyright 1961, 1964, 1970, 1971 by Doris Dana. Reprinted by permission of Joan Daves Agency, Baltimore: Johns Hopkins Press, 1971; **p. 27** From *Where I Come From: New and Selected Poems*, Toronto and Chicago: Guernica Editions, 1994, 1997. Reprinted with the kind permission of Maria Mazziotti Gillan and Guernica Editions; **p. 29** Courtesy *Equinox/Canadian Geographic*; **p. 31** James Cherry, reprinted with permission of *Maclean's* magazine; **p. 48** "Letter: Missive from a Prison Bed," by Ken Saro-Wiwa, *The Guardian*, May 18, 1995; **p. 51** Reprinted with the permission of Scribner, a Division of Simon & Schuster, from *The Skyline Trail* by Mary Carolyn Davies. Copyright © 1924 by The Bobbs-Merrill Company, renewed 1952 by Mary Carolyn Davies; **p. 52** Kay Smith (Author); **p. 58** From *Anne Frank's Tales from a Secret Annex* by Anne Frank, copyright © 1949, 1960 by Otto Frank. Copyright © 1982 by Anne Frank-Funds, Basel. English translation copyright © 1983 by Doubleday. Used by permission of Doubleday, a division of Random House; **p. 70** Reprinted by permission of Stoddart Publishing Co. Ltd.; **p. 76** "Ulysses" by Alfred Lord Tennyson, from *Verses for You Book Three*, by J.G. Brown, Longmans, Green and Co. Ltd., second edition, 1966; **p. 80** From *Woman in the Woods*, Mosaic Press, 1985; **p. 84** *Edmonton Sun*; **p. 98** Excerpt from *The Fellowship of the Ring* by J.R.R. Tolkien, London: HarperCollins, 1999; **p. 99** Excerpt from *The Two Towers* by J.R.R. Tolkien, London: George Allen and Unwin, 1966. HarperCollins UK; **p. 100** From *The Tolkien Relation* by William Ready, Vancouver: Copp Clark, 1968; p. 100 Excerpt from *The Two Towers* by J.R.R. Tolkien, London: George Allen and Unwin, 1966. HarperCollins UK; **p. 104** From *Writing Down the Bones* by Natalie Goldberg, © 1986 by Natalie Goldberg. Reprinted by arrangement with Shambhala Publications, Inc., Boston, <www.shambhala.com>; **p. 107** Robert Dawe; **p. 114** "Sharks" from *Modern Biology* by Albert Towle, copyright © 1989 by Holt, Rinehart and Winston, reprinted by permission of the publisher; **p. 115** Reprinted with the permission of Scribner, A Division of Simon & Schuster, from *The Old Man and the Sea* by

Ernest Hemingway. Copyright 1952 by Ernest Hemingway. Copyright renewed © 1980 by Mary Hemingway; **p. 116** From *Collected Stories*, published by JM Dent. Reprinted by permission of David Higham Associates Ltd.; **p. 120** From *A Pine Cone: A Toy Sheep*, published in Evergreen Review, Vol. 6, No 22 1962; **p. 122** From *Maclean's*, July 1, 2000, Vol 113 No 27, p. 38; **p. 125** From *An Autobiography: The Story of My Experiments with Truth*, by Mahatma Gandhi, Beacon Press: 1957, Navajivan Trust; **p. 129** "Prometheus Brings Fire to Man" by Barbara Drake from *Myths, Fables, and Folktales* by Albert R. Kitzhaber and Stoddard Malarkey, copyright © 1974 by Holt, Rinehart and Winston, reprinted by permission of the publisher; **p. 132** From *The Book of King Arthur and His Noble Knights*, by Mary Macleod, Wells Gardner Darton & Co. Ltd.; **p. 139** Hermann Hesse, *Der Wolf*. Gesammelte Werke. Werkausgabe in 12 Bänden. © Suhrkamp Verlag Frankfurt am Main 1970; **p. 146** Excerpt from "A Worn Path" in *A Curtain of Green and Other Stories*, copyright 1941 and renewed in 1969 by Eudora Welty, reprinted by permission of Harcourt, Inc; **p. 147** "Royal Beatings" originally appeared in *The New Yorker*, March 1977 and in book form in *Who Do You Think You Are* by The Macmillan Company of Canada Limited, 1978. First published in the United States under the title *The Beggar Maid* by Alfred A. Knopf, Inc. New York, 1979. All of the above reprinted by permission of the Virginia Barber Literary Agency, Inc. All rights reserved; **p. 148** From *Their Eyes Were Watching God* by Zora Neale Hurston, HarperCollins Publishers Inc., New York: 1990, © 1937 by Zora Neale Hurston, renewed 1965 by John C. Hurston and Joel Hurston. ISBN 0-06-093141-8, pp. 10 and 11.; **p. 149** From *A Fine Balance* by Rohinton Mistry, used by permission, McClelland & Stewart, Ltd. *The Canadian Publishers*; **p. 151** Copyright © 2000 Guy Vanderhaeghe. Reprinted by permission of Livingston Cooke, Inc.; **p. 152** From *Stephen Crane: Prose and Poetry*, text from the *University of Virginia Edition of The Works of Stephen Crane*, edited by Fredson Bowers, volumes I, III, V, VI, VII, VIII, IX, and X, published by the University of Virginia. Reprinted with the permission of the University Press of Virginia; **p. 153** Excerpt from "The Wednesday Flower Man," by Dianne Warren, in *The Wednesday Flower Man*, published by Coteau Books. Used by permission of the Publisher; **p. 157 top** From *Salvage King, Ya!* Published by Anvil Press, 1997 **p. 157 bottom** Alfred A Knopf, a Division of Random House Inc.; **p. 158** From *The Oxford Book of Gothic Tales*, Edited by Chris Baldick, Oxford University Press, 1992; **p. 159** From "The Expatriate" from *The Penguin Book of Short Stories*, edited by Wayne Grady, p. 529; **p. 162** "Overland to the Islands" by Denise Levertov, from *Collected Earlier Poems 1940–1960*, copyright © 1968, 1979 by Denise Levertov. Reprinted by permission of New Directions Publishing Corp.; **p. 164 top** From *The Life and Opinions of T.E. Hulme*, by A.R. Jones, 1960. Victor